The Deceived Husband

The Deceived Husband

A Kleinian Approach to the Literature of Infidelity

ALISON SINCLAIR

CLARENDON PRESS · OXFORD

This book has been printed digitally and produced in a standard specification in order to ensure its continuing availability

OXFORD
UNIVERSITY PRESS

Great Clarendon Street, Oxford OX2 6DP

Oxford University Press is a department of the University of Oxford. It furthers the University's objective of excellence in research, scholarship, and education by publishing worldwide in

Oxford New York

Auckland Cape Town Dar es Salaam Hong Kong Karachi Kuala Lumpur Madrid Melbourne Mexico City Nairobi New Delhi Shanghai Taipei Toronto

With offices in

Argentina Austria Brazil Chile Czech Republic France Greece Guatemala Hungary Italy Japan South Korea Poland Portugal Singapore Switzerland Thailand Turkey Ukraine Vietnam

Oxford is a registered trade mark of Oxford University Press in the UK and in certain other countries

Published in the United States by Oxford University Press Inc., New York

Reprinted 2011

ISBN 978-0-19-815190-6

Printed and bound in Great Britain by CPI Antony Rowe, Chippenham and Eastbourne

Cover illustration: *Evening* (from *The Four Times of the Day*) by William Hogarth. By permission of the Syndics of Cambridge University Library.

Cuckolds go to heaven.

(*Anon.*)

Acknowledgements

I am greatly in debt to a large number of people who have helped me in diverse ways in the writing of this book. For detailed discussions and reading of sections of the book at an early stage I am grateful to Jane Tillier, Jo Labanyi, Gill Paschkes-Bell, and Mark Millington, who was an invaluable sounding-board for initial ideas, and to Ellen Noonan, Jean Thompson, Gerald Wooster, and Elizabeth Gleed for the part they played in my understanding of Klein and object relations. Different sections of the book have brought me into contact with others: I am indebted in particular to Fred Parker, for his help on *Othello*, and to Felicia Gordon for many fascinating discussions on the novel of adultery. It would be hard to list all those who have provided ideas and references for the book, but they include Melveena McKendrick, Paul Lewis Smith, Mike Smith, Patrick Miles, Ted Buttrey, Richard Stemp, Stewart Sinclair, and Naomi Segal. To the University Library in Cambridge I am indebted in ways both formal and informal: for permission to reproduce the engraving on the dust-jacket, for the unfailing helpfulness of the staff, particularly Anne Darvall of the Reading Room and the staff of the West Room, and—not to be underestimated—for providing the tea-room, which, as a site for the exchange of information, ideas, and references, particularly in a project which has taken me a long way from my original field, has proved to be invaluable. Jinny Crum-Jones of the Computing Service has been the source of ever cheerful and professional service. Last but not least, I would like to thank my family, particularly Stewart, for all the tolerance shown during the long, and at times uncertain, gestation of what follows.

Contents

1. The Deceived Husband: A Theoretical Introduction 1

2. Cuckoldry, Honour, and Adultery: The Language of Infidelity 30

3. The Cuckold 50
   - The Cuckold and His Reader 50
   - *The Canterbury Tales* 65
   - *The Decameron* 80

4. Men of Honour 97
   - The Context 97
   - Wife-Murder Drama in Spain 120
   - *Othello*: The Obverse of Honour 161

5. The Adulteress's Husband 173
   - Models of Deception: Charles Bovary, Trevelyan, Instetten 175
   - Triangles of Transition: *La Regenta* 199
   - Denial and Splitting: *Dombey and Son* and *The Kreutzer Sonata* 217
   - Family Containment in *Anna Karenin* 234

6. Men of Distinction 253

7. Conclusion: Love and Death 277

BIBLIOGRAPHY 282

INDEX 293

I

The Deceived Husband: A Theoretical Introduction

It's he that has no wife who is no cuckold

What a man's gotta do

THE FIRST quotation comes from Chaucer; the second, taken from modern popular speech, is the title of a recent book on norms of masculinity.[1] What the present book tries to explore, among other things, is the relationship between the two statements, as they apply to husbands in the first instance, but also as they apply to the notion in general of being a man.

The time-span encompassed by this book is similar to that between the two quotations, that is, from the Middle Ages to the twentieth century. While both quotations come from the English-speaking world, however, the literary examples in this text come from a variety of European countries, principally England, Italy, Spain, France, Germany, and Russia. The quotations are linked in that they express expectations about men, the first about the fate of man as husband, the second about the (unspecified) things a man must do if he is to be a man. They express in brief form the much more extensive expectations about the nature of men as husbands and as deceived husbands that will be revealed by the literary examples to be discussed. What is fascinating about the portrayals of these husbands in their suffering of marital infidelity is the degree to which, despite the enormous variety of social and historical contexts in which they occur, or, to be more precise, in which the literary representations of deceived husbands occur, there are common characteristics to be observed in them, characteristics which suggest a generality of pattern, formation, and explanation.

I am concerned both with variety of example and with generality of formation and understanding—perhaps more with the

[1] Antony Easthope, *What a Man's Gotta Do* (London, 1986).

latter than the former, in that I am interested in the way in which, at least in literature, there are models of behaviour according to which these husbands act, models outwardly determined by the social norms of the circumstances in which these men are found, but inwardly determined by fundamental psychological mechanisms for dealing with threat, anxiety, and fear. There is a tremendous richness of variety, and for each of the general statements that it is possible to make, there are particularized exceptions to be made. One of the factors acting to produce both variety and generality is the degree to which the changing faces presented by different countries, with variations in economic, political, and social conditions, will have had their effect on the style of presentation in literature of those men we might variously call neglected, deceived, or betrayed.

What I have not tried to do is to conduct a comprehensive survey, across Europe and across the last six or seven centuries, of the portrayal of the husband whose wife has been unfaithful to him. I have opted for a procedure of targeting two main types of portrayal of the husband—the cuckold and the man of honour—then discussing the composition of each model, and examining a number of texts in which it can be seen as operating. The husband of the adulteress, as depicted in novels of the nineteenth century, is then discussed in terms of the two models, while texts that provide apparent exceptions to the models are discussed in the final chapter. The initial texts discussed are intended to be illustrative and paradigmatic, and to show the models in their clearest formation, thus revealing the foundations of the portrayal of this marginated character of the adulterous triangle, the husband.[2] Texts discussed at a later stage show up variations and vacillations, and the complexity of the models.

The principal theoretical framework which has informed my exploration of this topic is object-relations theory, the school of psychoanalysis deriving from the work of Melanie Klein and developed by Winnicott, Fairbairn, Guntrip, Bion, and others. As its name, 'object relations', partially suggests, this is an approach

[2] In taking some of the most clear-cut or extreme examples of the models to suggest general patterns of representation, I am applying a procedure somewhat analogous to that of Robert Stoller, who in his *Presentations of Gender* (London and New Haven, Conn., 1985) uses extremes of gender presentation and disorder to arrive at a more general theory of gender construction.

to human psychology which stresses the importance of relations with others in the formation and development of the individual. There is, inevitably, a general indebtedness to Freud in this theory (as there is, again inevitably, in this book), particularly in some of the fundamental ideas about the structure of the psyche and its functioning. One of the cornerstones of Freud's work was the idea that our neurotic symptoms are the result of the ego erecting defences against anxiety. Those defences, in the case of the neurotic, either prove inadequate to cut out the anxiety, or are liable themselves to form a problem. In his later work, Freud came to see the ego as a potentially harassed but central part of the self, which mediated between rebellious, chaotic, and unacceptable impulses from the child-like and basic id, and the over-controlling, over-authoritative voice of the super-ego.[3] Object-relations theory, in considering the development of the individual (in relation to others) also contains the fundamental idea of the ego's having to construct defences against anxiety, but lays stress on a stage of development prior to language, well before the Oedipal stage which arrested the attention of Freud, and on which most of his clinical attention was focused.[4]

Klein considered that formative emotional dramas occur long before the Oedipal stage, and, on the basis of her work with infants, she postulated that in the earliest period of infancy (that is, before even the age of 6 months) the child experiences a range

[3] See S. Freud, 'Anxiety and Instinctual Life' and 'The Dissection of the Psychical Personality' in *New Introductory Lectures on Psychoanalysis* (1933), in *The Standard Edition of the Complete Psychological Works of Sigmund Freud*, ed. S. E. Strachey (24 vols.; London, 1981), xxii. 81–111, and 57–80, esp. 77: 'We are warned by a proverb against serving two masters at the same time. The poor ego has things even worse: it serves three severe masters and does what it can to bring their claims and demands into harmony with one another. These claims are always divergent and often seem incompatible. No wonder that the ego so often fails in its task. Its three tyrannical masters are the external world, the super-ego and the id. When we follow the ego's efforts to satisfy them simultaneously—or rather, to obey them simultaneously—we cannot feel any regret at having personified this ego and having set it up as a separate organism. It feels hemmed in on three sides, threatened by three kinds of danger, to which, if it is hard pressed, it reacts by generating anxiety.'

[4] For a discussion of the role of anxiety in Klein, and its greater importance when compared with its role in Freud, see Elizabeth T. de Bianchedi, Liadia Scalozub de Boschan, Lia P. de Cortiñas, and Elsa G. de Piccolo, 'Theories on Anxiety in Freud and Melanie Klein: Their Metapsychological Status', *International Journal of Psychoanalysis*, 69 (1988), 359–67.

of emotions and sensations in response to which he or she engages in a series of reactions which, while they move progressively forwards as the child gains in age and understanding, will be repeated and reverted to in adult life, in different but comparable ways, in the context of the relation of the individual to the outside world.[5]

The first relevance, then, of an object-relations approach to the topic of this book, is that it deals with extremely early, and hence primitive and intense, feelings and reactions which will form the basis of later structures. It also helps to clarify other findings, particularly some of Freud's, which otherwise remain enigmas. Why, for example, should there be such importance attached, in the question of gender formation, to the role of the father, and particularly to his authority and negative law, when one of the most salient features of patriarchal society is that children are mainly cared for by women, and not by the more or less absent fathers? Furthermore, without positing womb-envy as such, object-relations theory provides a convincing alternative to Freud's pervasive notion of penis-envy. Naomi Segal has wittily and lucidly outlined the puzzling gap between Freudian theory and the reality observable by young children. The theory lays much emphasis on the little girl's disappointment at not being the possessor of a penis, it being assumed that a penis is desirable, and normal. What is discarded is the possibility, as Segal points out, that the penis might be thought of by the girl as 'an unnatural or shocking appendage, even if also a good toy'.[6] The importance of the mother, meanwhile, is revealed by that physical fact which both little boys and little girls will be able to observe, namely that babies actually issue from the mother (the connection between the

[5] While the Oedipus complex was thought to start at 3 or 4 years of age, Klein's observations led her to believe that it began much earlier. See Melanie Klein, 'Early Stages of the Oedipus Conflict' (1928) and 'The Oedipus Complex in the Light of Early Anxieties' (1945), in ead., *Love, Guilt and Reparation and Other Works 1921–1942* (London, 1988) (with introd. by Hanna Segal), 186–98 and 370–419; see also Hanna Segal, *Introduction to the Work of Melanie Klein* (London, 1964; new, enlarged edn. 1986), 2, 9, 103. The stage of development considered crucial by Klein ends at 6 months, whereas Lacan's mirror-stage is located between 6 and 18 months. See Lacan, *Écrits* (Paris, 1966, repr. London, 1977), 264, and Malcolm Bowie, 'Jacques Lacan', in J. Sturrock (ed.), *Structuralism and Since* (Oxford, 1979), 116–53, (122).

[6] Naomi Segal, *The Unintended Reader: Feminism and 'Manon Lescaut'* (Cambridge, 1986), 253.

father and the production of a baby remaining a mystery for some time to come). Elsewhere, Segal highlights Freud's extreme intellectualism, and its limitations, referring to his veneration of man's logical powers (exemplified both in *The Interpretation of Dreams* and in the major case-studies). He thus alludes to 'the advance in intellectuality', meaning that the individual is able 'to deduce paternity instead of observing maternity'.[7] That patriarchy is indeed introduced as a necessity in the face of uncertainty is spelled out nicely by Jane Gallop: 'The legal assignation of a Father's Name to a child is meant to call a halt to uncertainty about the identity of the father. If the mother's femininity (both her sexuality and her untrustworthiness) were affirmed, the Name-of-the-Father would always be in doubt, always be subject to the question of the mother's morality. Thus the Name-of-the-Father must be arbitrarily and absolutely imposed, thereby instituting the reign of patriarchal law.'[8]

Simply to decide to use the theories of Klein and those that followed her because she privileged the role of the mother, or, more accurately, observed the privileged role of the mother in the formation of the individual, rather than privileging the secondary and later authority and power of the father, would be to make a purely political point, and one not relevant to the discussion. Klein's work, and the theories derived from it, have been chosen as a basis here because they are convincing and illuminating, and because they are especially relevant to the present topic. In relation to the usefulness and standing of Klein's work now, there are three significant points to be made. First, her conviction that there was severe underestimation of what happens in the perceptions and reactions of the newly-born child has been corroborated by clinical observation of neonates in recent years. Second, the theories she derived from her clinical work with children—theories about splitting, projection, projective identification, the role of envy—are now recognized as prime psychological tools for understanding what goes on between individuals, starting with that first encounter with the same sex or the other sex in the initial child–parent relationship. Third, Klein's work forms the basis of theories of group psychology as pioneered by Wilfred Bion.

[7] Ead., *Narcissus and Echo* (Manchester, 1988), 207.

[8] Jane Gallop, *Feminism and Psychoanalysis: The Daughter's Seduction* (London and Basingstoke, 1982), 39.

Klein's own work provides us with a way of understanding on an individual level how a husband reacts to his wife's infidelity or feared infidelity; the development of that work, by Bion and others, into group theory helps explain on a collective level how the threats associated with the feminine are translated into certain social reactions and structures.[9] It is this collective aspect of the theory which provides a way of understanding the nature of the different types of literary portrayal of the deceived husband—in other words, a way of understanding why patriarchal society should, in its literature, throw up so many examples of men who appear not to embody patriarchal power.

Klein's view of the world of the small infant is not a comfortable one. It focuses on a period that comes well before the stage at which Freud envisaged the ego as constructing its defences against anxiety. Klein posits that the small infant exists in an environment which is, by turns, totally satisfying and comforting and totally terrifying. His[10] world consists primarily of his relationship with his mother, not yet in the early weeks perceived as a whole person, but merely as the source of good and bad feelings. The response of the infant to what is good is uncomplicated, produces no difficult reactions. But faced with what he experiences as bad (as when basic needs are not met) the child's response is of distress, anger, fear. Those feelings, however, are themselves too terrifying and distressing to be contained within him, so he projects them out, and comes to the belief that the part of his external world which is causing him distress is also the sole possessor of all the badness in the situation. That is, feeling himself threatened from without and within, he operates a split which ensures that he divests himself of the bad feeling within himself (hunger, pain, rage . . .), and these bad feelings, projected out of his self, now remain on the outside. This momentarily improves his situation (the badness has been sent outside him), but not for long, since the badness projected to the outside world is added to the badness which originally provoked the distressed reactions in him, and the situation becomes more terrifying than it was before. A vicious spiralling development ensues, and the

[9] See Wilfred Bion, *Experiences in Groups* (London, 1961).

[10] Klein's theory, of course, covers both boy and girl infants: I have deliberately retained 'he' and 'him' for the infant, however, since the concern of this discussion is above all with men and their early formation.

attempts to split off from it become ever more desperate and emphatic. Klein labelled the state in which this splitting takes place the 'paranoid-schizoid position'.

The splitting in this very early phase is severe. At a later stage of development, the infant learns to tolerate the fact that not all experience deriving from the outside world is good, though some of it may be, and learns to relate to that world in its diverse reality. He learns that the mother who comforts and feeds him is in fact the same mother whose absence or withholding of good things causes him such distress and anger. At this stage, the infant learns to relate to the mother as a whole person, accepting both her qualities and her defects, and realizing that he too has a part in the relationship with her. He develops a capacity for guilt and concern, and a recognition that he is as capable of being the source of anger and distress as she is.[11] This second position, which Klein named the 'depressive position', is complex, and represents a definite advance on the paranoid-schizoid position. For in the depressive position there is a new level of relating to the outside world (in the form of another person); there is an awareness of the other as vulnerable and at the same time a capacity within the self to tolerate pain and discomfort. Klein believed that this stage brought the capacity of concern for others, coupled with the ability to experience gratitude (and in the mature self, the ability to be prompted to actions and attitudes of reparation). The depressive position is a stage at which there is no longer need to have recourse to the processes of splitting and projection. Thus it is a state in which the external world is no longer experienced, and reinforced, as persecutory. It is also a position in which there is a capacity to live in the reality of things, rather than in a world of phantasy.[12]

The emotional quality Klein manages to evoke most clearly in her work on the relationship of the small infant with its mother is the sheer intensity of feeling that is experienced. Through her we are able to glimpse not only the state of bliss and security that may be enjoyed by the infant, but also its opposite, something which Klein communicates with notable power. Herself a child

[11] See Hanna Segal, *Introduction to the Work of Melanie Klein*, 24–33, 54–66, 67–81, for a full discussion of the two positions.

[12] The unusual spelling was adopted by Klein to denote the transferential and unreliable nature of this experience of the world.

whose relationship with her mother was difficult and painful, and whose relationship with her own daughter is notorious for the intense and negative feelings it produced, Klein was well-placed to highlight the sheer unbounded terror and anger of the infant in the face of its first negative experiences with a mother it can only suppose to be all-powerful. Thus while Freud was able to give a sense of the anxiety of the developing ego, as a course was negotiated from child to adult, and on the path of which secure gender-identity might be acquired, Klein tells us of the infant's terror at its mother's seeming omnipotence, and charts its reaction to that terror through her concept of the paranoid-schizoid position.[13]

Although the transition between these two positions—the paranoid-schizoid and the depressive—was held to be something which was effected in early infancy, it was never thought by Klein to be a conclusive move, and she considered that infants, and the adults they came eventually to be, moved backwards and forwards between the two positions. She realized, through clinical work with the disturbed, that the processes of splitting and projection described above continue to happen in varying degrees in adult life, in the face of threat and distress.[14] As a modern 'translation' of how the paranoid-schizoid position might work for an adult, we might consider an example from Antony Easthope, who outlines how a masculine fear of homosexuality might be turned outwards into homophobia. He details four stages: (1) a stage of homosexual desire, of the feeling of 'I love him', which leads to an attempt to ward this feeling off in (2), in the form of 'I do not love him—I hate him'; this feeling of hatred is then projected out in (3)

[13] Later, Winnicott and Bowlby established the positive elements of the relationship with the mother. For further developments, see Colin James on Bion, 'Bion's "Containing" and Winnicott's "Holding" in the Context of the Group Matrix', *International Journal of Group Psychotherapy*, 34 (2) (Apr. 1984), 201–13. Here he shows the interplay of positive and negative aspects of the child's relation with the mother in its emotional and intellectual development, which hinges on the capacity to tolerate frustration. See also James, 'W. R. Bion's Contribution to the Field of Psychotherapy: An Appreciation', in L. Wolberg and M. Aronson (eds.), *Group and Family Therapy* (New York, 1981), 28–37 (28–33).

[14] See Melanie Klein, 'Notes on Some Schizoid Mechanisms' (1946), in ead., *Envy and Gratitude and Other Works 1946–1963* (with introd. by Hanna Segal) (London, 1988), 1–24 (5–16). Discussion of the complications that can arise if splitting is imperfect, as in the case of envy, may be found in 'A Study of Envy and Gratitude' (1957), ibid. 176–235 (190–94).

as 'He hates me, which justifies me in hating him', and is then, in (4), turned into a generalizing statement of further defence and self-justification, 'I hate him, because he persecutes me'.[15] The depressive position would entail the acceptance of the feelings of (1), however uncomfortable they might seem, or whatever their feared consequences might be.

Two distinctions are often made between Freudian and Kleinian theory. First there is the fact that Klein believed the ego to be there in some form from the start, and thus able to contend with the experiences noted above (the success or otherwise of the outcome being to some degree an arbitrary fact of birth). Secondly, in the Kleinian notion that at a very early age (between 3 and 6 months) the infant is able to move to the depressive position there is embedded an idea of the essential moral potential of man. These are technicalities and emphases which do not concern me here, but which do emerge in any detailed comparison of those psychoanalytical approaches.[16]

The distinction between Kleinian and Freudian theory which does matter here, however, is that concerning the Oedipus complex. Klein accepted the existence of the complex, though, as noted above, believed it to emerge at a stage much earlier than that designated by Freud. Besides suggesting an earlier date for the emergence of the Oedipus complex, Klein gave a greater valuation to the pre-Oedipal period itself. The crucial nature of the Oedipus complex was not denied, but it was depicted now against a backcloth of other central experiences which preceded the formation and awareness of gender difference that characterize the complex. Thus in Klein's account, certain factors which in the Freudian interpretation of development appear as simply given, are revealed as having their roots in the experience of the pre-Oedipal phase. In other words, one sees that the awareness of the importance of the father (in the Oedipus complex) comes at a point later than the

[15] Easthope, *What a Man's Gotta Do*, 106–7.

[16] Some of the clearest discussion of the differences is in Michael Rustin, 'Kleinian Psychoanalysis and the Theory of Culture', in F. Barker *et al.* (eds.), *The Politics of Theory* (Proceedings of the Essex Conference on the Sociology of Literature, July 1982) (Univ. of Essex, 1983), 57–70. This is followed by a rebuttal, in the same volume, by Graham Seymour, 'A Reply to Michael Rustin: Kleinian Psychoanalysis and the Theory of Culture', 71–8. See also Juliet Mitchell and Jacqueline Rose, *Feminine Sexuality* (London, 1982), 3–5, 19–21, 25–6, for a contrastive discussion.

awareness of the importance of the mother (which will take place in the pre-Oedipal period). And for some, there is a direct correlation between the two. The strength of the figure who in the Oedipal phase embodies and is emblematic of the power of patriarchy is in fact a necessary strength. Nothing less would be able to combat and provide a counterbalance to the complete and terrifying power of the mother, already experienced by the infant. Instead of looking at the age at which the castration complex arises and when the child, through the process of that complex, is seen as a being who begins to be informed about the power structure of the patriarchal society, Klein thus examined the more primitive processes at work in the first experiences of the infant. In doing so, she shifted the focus from the father to the mother. Within Freudian understanding the father, or the awareness of the father, intervenes in a decisive way in development, and particularly in gender acquisition, moving the infant on towards possession of a mature gender-identity. Through the action of this developmental catalyst, thought to proceed from awareness of the father (the boy fearing that he will be castrated by the father for love of the mother, the girl fearing that she has been castrated already), the meaning of the first relationship, that held with the mother, is relegated to a secondary place. This relegation itself is a feature of the patriarchal society that produced Freudian theory.[17] It was Klein who, building on, and in reaction to, the work of Freud, reinstated the mother. This reinstatement not only has implications for the relative importance of both parents for the child, but also opens the way for a different view of gender-formation, in that its inception is located at an earlier stage.

Before considering these later developments in the theory of gender-formation, which take account of the mother, we need first to review the idea of gender-formation which emerges from Freud. His theory of the Oedipus complex, if considered in detail, goes a long way to explaining observable gender-differences, and even gender imbalance in the power structure of a patriarchal society. Indeed, Freud's concept of gender-formation is eminently more persuasive in the case of the boy than in the case of the girl—a

[17] For full discussion of the degree to which thought on patriarchy and associated issues has itself been influenced by the patriarchal context in which it was produced, see Rosalind Coward, *Patriarchal Precedents: Sexuality and Social Relations* (London, 1983).

symptom of the degree to which Freud was a product of his times.[18] According to Freud, the Oedipal crisis comes for the boy when he perceives that his mother, with whom he has a close, intimate, intense relation, also has an adult, sexual relation, not with himself, but with his father. The father is thus perceived as a rival for the mother's affections. The resolution of the complex for the boy comes about through fear of the father—who is not only larger than he is, but also possessed of a potency the child does not yet have. Additionally, he realizes that the father, with his size and strength, is capable of rendering him impotent, by castrating him. It is this fear, this threat, which resolves the Oedipus problem for the boy, and makes him desist from seeing his attachment to his mother as a mature sexual relationship which can have a future. We might note that embedded in this crisis there is an experience of betrayal (by the mother) which is coupled firmly with an apprehension of possible castration (which would come about if the boy should make a protest by holding on to the mother). For the girl, what was believed to happen was inferred from the above. It is an inescapable fact that the pattern of development of the girl's sexual relationships will be significantly different from that of the boy, since her first relationship is, as his was, with the mother. In her case, however, the same pattern of development cannot be followed, since the mother is not of the sex to which she will be attracted in mature heterosexual relationships. Freud introduced a sense of symmetry into his account of the development of the two by proposing the primacy of penis-possession for both boy and girl: the boy desires his mother, and is prevented from engaging in an incestuous relationship by the fear of castration; the girl, meanwhile, is close to her mother, but discovers that this object of her love lacks a penis, and thus turns to the father in disappointment, but also in acceptance of the fact that she is like her mother, and unlike her father.[19]

An alternative and more recent view of gender establishment is that advanced by Stoller, but its conclusions, although reached via

[18] For a detailed discussion of Freud's ideas on sexuality and gender-formation, particularly as they concern the girl, including the degree to which Freud writes as a thinker of his time, see Juliet Mitchell, *Psychoanalysis and Feminism* (Harmondsworth, 1974), 5–119. In her account, Freud's privileging of the function of patriarchy in gender-formation is a sign of his realism rather than of the degree to which he is culturally bound. See e.g. the comments on Karen Horney, 128.

[19] Ibid. 98.

a different route, provide the same sense of imbalance between the sexes. The central difference is in Stoller's privileging of the mother's role in gender acquisition in a manner consistent with Klein's highlighting of the mother's importance. Stoller, focusing on the first relation between any child and its mother, argues that there is a stage earlier in gender development than that proposed in the view of Freud which I have just outlined, according to which the sexual development of the boy is off to a proper start by being based on a heterosexual relationship from birth. He proposes a 'core gender theory' and argues that in this earlier stage in the development of gender identity, the boy does not relate to the mother heterosexually but is merged with her. This even earlier experience of relating to the mother, without having a sense of her as of a different sex, gives the child a 'primeval and thus profound part of character structure' and lays the groundwork for an infant's sense of femininity. This sets the girl firmly on the path she has to follow, but makes life difficult for the boy. What is then left for the boy to do is to perform a major task of separation, which makes his gaining of his sexual identity more conflict-ridden than is the case for the girl. The boy has to struggle to attain his sexual identity. The precariousness of what is attained then gives rise to his more assertive defence of his masculinity and, arguably, to his championing of masculinity, his belief that masculinity is strongest and best. As Stoller summarizes it: 'this newer view of gender identity holds that femininity in females is not just penis envy or denial or resigned acceptance of castration; a woman is not just a failed man. Masculinity in males is not simply a natural state that needs only to be defended if it is to grow healthily; rather it is an achievement'.[20] What is left behind for the boy in the wake of this struggle to establish masculinity is a fear of returning to the early symbiosis with the mother, and the 'proto-femininity' this entails. Thus masculinity comes to be a determined, and perhaps even desperate, urge not to be associated with

[20] Stoller, *Presentations of Gender*, 18. Stoller adds: 'For much of masculinity . . . consists of struggling not to be seen by oneself or others as having feminine attributes, physical or psychological.' The term 'masculine' needs to be used guardedly. As Evelyn Fox Keller argues in *Reflections on Gender and Science* (New Haven, Conn., and London, 1985), 77–8, the position of 'objective' masculine dominance will not necessarily coincide with that of maximum potent masculine sexuality.

femininity—hence the assertiveness and force with which it is maintained. Stoller underlines the apprehension beneath masculinity: 'One must maintain one's distance from women or be irreparably infected with femininity.'[21]

Despite the differences in emphasis between Klein, Freud, and Stoller, one factor is constant, whether implied or explicit: the linking of the first relationship of the infant and the mother with experience that is non-intellectual, bound to the body, the senses, and the feelings. And for the boy, it is crucial that this is an experience with the other sex.

Both sexes need to separate eventually from the mother, in each case at some cost. While the cost to the girl may well be an incomplete separation, so that she never forms her own independent identity[22] (thus handicapping her in the patriarchal power conflict), the cost to the boy may be that in struggling to free himself from the relationship he rejects all the things he associates with femininity (such as sensuality and the emotions), and in order to reject feminine gender, he also rejects feminine sexuality and any possible association with it.

The object-relations view of the Oedipal crisis, particularly from Winnicott onwards, places more emphasis on the transition of the child from an intense dyadic relationship to the realization that it must tolerate the existence of intense relationships existing between the object of its affections and another person. That is, the crucial step to be made at this stage is that of coping with the realization that there may be pairings in which he feels involved because he is attached to one or both of the individuals, but from which he is in some senses excluded.

[21] Stoller, *Presentations of Gender*, 18.

[22] See Luise Eichenbaum and Susie Orbach, *Understanding Women* (Harmondsworth, 1985), 36–67. A more positive view of this non-differentiation is given by Joel Fineman, in 'Fratricide and Cuckoldry: Shakespeare's Doubles', in Murray M. Schwarz and Coppélia Kahn (eds.), *Representing Shakespeare* (Baltimore and London, 1980; repr. in paperback 1982), 70–109 (103): 'At first the infant is its *umwelt*, but soon enough the infant must negotiate the duality inherent in that unity . . . the infant must first be and then not be the mother in order to discover its own individuation . . . this obliges us to reverse the poles of Freud's triangulating theory of gender generation. For if the male's first sense of self is implicated in femininity, his masculinity is then conditional upon establishing a self distanced from its first sense of self. Women on the other hand, because their gender is founded on a bedrock identification with maternality, have a kind of immediate gender reference to which they can refer their sense of self.'

At the heart of the theory of how the two sexes develop there is a subtext suggesting why it is that the two sexes are different, and why the rights of boys and men seem to win out over those of women in public statement. The degree to which the theory itself privileges authority as a concept is remarkable for the lacunae in its expression. That is, the assertion of the authority of the father is not to be accompanied by adequate explanation of that authority. The imbalance this produces is replicated in imbalances within the elaboration of Freud's theory, as in Ernest Jones's paper of 1929 on jealousy.[23]

None the less, the theory of the Oedipus complex does provide a focus which goes some way to explaining the questions alluded to above. It shows that the development of the child is different in crucial ways for each sex, and without actually stating it, suggests why it is that there could be in boys a much fiercer sense of possession, which is then arguably translated into their relations in adult life, particularly into their sexual partnerships.

Here the factor which is of prime importance is the nature of the first relationship of the child with an adult: for a girl this is a same-sex experience, for a boy it is a different-sex experience. Since for both the first experience (with all the heightened emotional colour that was revealed by Klein) is intense and intimate, with fierce reactions of love and hate, the consequences of that relationship for later ones are destined to be different for the two sexes (if in later life they move into heterosexual rather than homosexual relationships). Thus the ground is laid for the boy to have a fierce sense of relation and possession towards objects of the opposite sex, since this replicates the first experience; and thus also the girl lacks this initial intense emotional patterning for her future heterosexual relationship. For the boy, however, the sense of possession is also bound to a sense of handicap, relating to the

[23] Here Jones asserts at the outset that jealousy is more frequently experienced by women than men, but then discusses at length jealousy as experienced by the man, adding in his penultimate paragraph that 'there is little to add about the woman's problems because they are essentially of the same order'. Having argued that women are more prone to jealousy than men, it appears that he is unwilling or unable to focus on that jealousy. This seems to be a fine example of splitting, projection, and denial. The feelings so intolerable to man are lodged in woman, asserted as being more common and violent there, but their possession by women is summarily dismissed. See E. Jones, 'Jealousy' (1929), in id., *Papers on Psychoanalysis* (5th edn.; London, 1948), 325–40.

Oedipus complex. For him, sexual betrayal and sexual jealousy will go back to that original Oedipal situation, and there is thus an immediate association between the experience of betrayal and the fear of castration, since it is the fear of castration which, according to Freud, resolves the Oedipus complex for the boy.

We can apply these associations from early life, between gender-acquisition and betrayal, to what happens with the deceived husband. The husband who is cuckolded will have been encouraged by the patriarchal lines of the society in which he lives to believe, like the boy, that he has full rights over the woman he is married to. He may have, until the moment of cuckolding, believed his rights to be beyond challenge (though fabliaux and honour plays contain a multitude of examples of husbands who are overly jealous, thus expressing some deep-seated fears about the security of their rights of possession). The experience of sexual betrayal, when it is expressed as cuckoldry, is one in which the husband is seen, publicly, to be ridiculed. In the fact that he has 'lost' his wife, he is presumed to have 'lost' his potency: it is not enough to protect his claim against marauders. Thus according to Oedipal theory we have the boy who first fears that he will be made to lose his future potency through being vengefully castrated by his father in retaliation for his attachment to the mother and who is then made, by the sheer power of that threat, to feel effectively less potent anyway, as is the cuckold by the demonstration of the apparent superior powers of the lover.

Acts of betrayal in maturity will arguably thus carry powerful resonances of the original discomfort experienced in the Oedipal triangle. But at the same time, we need to keep in mind the sense of original possession the man will have felt of the sexual object, which in turn accounts for the fierceness of his reaction (then generalized at the level of society and its cultural expressions) when he is either betrayed or perceives another man to be betrayed. This sense of possession, when added to the effort Stoller notes he will have to exert in order to separate himself from his mother and establish his masculinity, will produce a style of masculinity which is fierce and assertive, and will lay the foundations for some types of reaction produced by deceived husbands. Translated into literature, these reactions will be codified into distancing (with mockery at failure), assertiveness (the imposition of the patriarchal-expressive honour-code), and, when they fit neither pattern, will lead to the confusions and more subtle emotional distress of the husbands of adulteresses.

It is not only the implications of Kleinian theory for gender-formation which have a bearing on the subject of this book, nor is my interest solely in the implications for individuals of such theory. I believe that the theory also provides us with a prime tool for understanding the differentiation between the various modes of portraying the deceived husband. In other words, the examples within literature relate, on a collective level, to the way that anxieties about identity and gender are experienced on an individual level. In later chapters we shall see how the paranoid-schizoid and the depressive position relate to the polarization between the two main models of the deceived husband, that is, the man of honour and the cuckold respectively, and that examination of the model of the adulteress's husband throws up a new concept of the depressive position which suggests limitation in the degree to which literature of cuckoldry exemplifies that position.

In the context of the deceived husband, the unwelcome experience which has to be dealt with is that of his wife's infidelity, which, as I have suggested, will have connotations of his early experience with the mother and her betrayal. The experience is also, and arguably more centrally, one of anxiety about the man's masculine identity and potency. On the collective level, literature dealing with woman's infidelity carries a powerful subtext that unconsciously undermines patriarchy—a subtext of the failure of masculinity.

The epigraphs at the head of this chapter allude both to the difficulties involved simply in being a man ('what a man's gotta do') and to the threat marriage is popularly held to bring to a man's masculinity. If literary examples of the cuckold in works later than those of Chaucer have posed the problem voiced in the second of the epigraphs in a slightly different form, they have none the less continued to pose it. What is striking, however, is that although literature is heavily populated with deceived husbands, relatively little attention has been paid to them. Thus they are made to suffer the double neglect, first of their spouses, and then of the critics. My aim in this book is to try to restore some equilibrium to the situation by focusing on these husbands, neglected third parties in adulterous triangles.

There is a paradox embedded in the interest which Western

European patriarchal society shows in the portrayal of these husbands who fail to meet the norms of manhood implicit in a patriarchal system. Literature abounds with examples of the husband who comes off worst in marriage (from the point of view of suffering the infidelity of a spouse), yet it is not clear that these men are intended to evince either our sympathy or our admiration: they emerge within a patriarchal system which seeks to proclaim the primacy of the man, yet they are embodiments of failure, which at worst will be laughed at, and at best merely evoke sympathy. Frequently they are ridiculed, and even where, as in the honour plays, they are made the protagonist, their implied tragic heroism may be undermined by the extreme, even exaggerated nature of their reactions. In the novel, their role may be diminished, so that they appear as shadowy figures, threatening others with the sanction of authority but unable to wield effective power over either their spouse or their fate. One might well ask what patriarchy thinks it is doing if it produces all these examples of its own failure. Is it merely seeking to instil fear in others by ridiculing those whose wives are found to be unfaithful, or might it, despite itself, in some sort of gargantuan Freudian slip, be revealing underlying truths about its own nature?

I did not set out on this study with a collection of preconceptions about the nature or possible forms of the deceived husband. Originally my interest was in what seemed to be a curious alignment of genres in literature: an emphasis on deceived husbands in drama or works of literature intended for presentation to a living public (songs or tales to be delivered within the oral tradition); on the other hand, an emphasis on deceiving wives, or adulteresses, in the novel. In the first case, it seemed that the object of attention, the husband, was held up for public ridicule, while in the second, the guilt of the wife rather than her silliness was emphasized. The 'man of honour' provided an apparent exception to the first case, in that he is not overtly held up for ridicule, although, as will be seen in Chapter 4, he often falls short of being an object of admiration. I concluded that a simple genre-division along gender-lines (husbands in 'public' literature, wives in 'private' literature) was, however, rather crude, and more appropriate might be a division according to the expected response of the reader—the deceived husband producing shock, laughter, or admiration, expressed in public, and therefore expressive of the more straightforward norms of patriarchy (whether positive or negative), and the deceiving wife, presented with sympathy, subverting the same norms for a reader to share in privacy.

The generic explanation applies most clearly to the emphasis on husbands in some genres and on wives in others. More refinement of the explanation is needed, however. The fact that drama as a genre contains husbands ridiculed (cuckolded) and husbands to be admired (men of honour) points to subdivisions. With reference to the Middle Ages, for example, a colleague remarked pithily on another such subdivision, 'But of course the authority of the husband varies generically', meaning that he tends to come off well (at least be presented positively, with strength, dignity, and authority) in the romance, whereas in the fabliau he is clearly a figure of fun. Another hypothesis was that the mode of portrayal of the deceived husband varied chronologically: the cuckold is essentially a medieval way of presenting this figure, whereas the outraged man of honour is typical of the sixteenth and seventeenth centuries. However, such a division does not explain why, in Spain in the seventeenth century, the focus is on the man of honour, while in the theatre of Molière, in a sense just next door, but perhaps significantly separated by the Pyrenees and several hundred miles, the husband is a simple *cocu*, or at least runs the danger of being one. Nor does it explain why one of the great novels of adultery, *La Princesse de Clèves*, should also be a product of seventeenth-century France. (These two examples are perhaps united in their material reticence: cuckoldry, in a form of literary titillation, is threatened more often than it is achieved in the French theatre of this period, while *La Princesse de Clèves* demonstrates with admirable clarity that the material establishment of adultery is, in emotional terms, rather beside the point.) With these exceptions made, however, there does seem to be a general move from cuckold to man of honour to adulteress across the centuries. One of the features of this shift is a transition between the sexes, in that interest quite decidedly moves from the deceived husband to the deceiving wife: the man who was centre-stage but ridiculed, or held up as a figure of awe or horror, is pushed to one side as we finally focus on the comparably terrible fate of his wife.

There is an underlying question here, namely is it possible to be both man and husband, or does the fact of becoming the latter endanger one's status as the former? Alternatively, the case could be put that it is not clear that a man is just that, a man, unless he takes on the role of husband also. There is every chance that he may prove his virility by having mistresses, and it could even be that there are children born of unions that testify to his fertility as well as to his potency. Without the monogamous state of marriage, however, and the safeguards against infidelity that are traditionally attached to it, there will be queries about how successfully a man may have proved himself to be a man. Whereas a woman can with ease visibly prove herself to be a woman by having a child, proofs of manhood are much less visible, much less clearly witnessed.

The difficulty is that, as Chaucer points out, as soon as a man establishes the situation—marriage—in which it becomes possible to have proof of manhood, he opens himself to the danger of that union proving fragile. Given the degree to which a wife's infidelity is thought to endanger the husband's identity and status, it is perhaps no surprise that legislation has traditionally been so weighted against the female halves of marital unions, or that the infidelity of wives, in Western European culture at least, has been an object of greater interest and disapproval than has the infidelity of husbands. Hence the large number of works of literature which treat of the infidelity of wives as an issue. (The infidelity of husbands occurs, with great frequency, in works of literature, but is simply not a cause for concern in the way that the infidelity of wives is.) What is curious, however, is the degree to which husbands, who stand to lose most in terms of reputation when an adulterous relationship is established between their wife and another man, risk being ridiculed or dismissed in the literary works that highlight their fate.

In my discussion of the factors that lie beneath society's concern with the infidelity of woman, and which have a bearing on the literary representations of the deceived husband, the majority of the explanations I shall examine come from the psychoanalytic field. As such, they form an argument which envisages certain elements to be essential, always present, in our development, regardless of historical, social, or geographical variation. There are, undoubtedly, arguments that can be drawn from fields such as history and anthropology which appear to explain the phenomena with which I am concerned. It would, moreover, be imprudent to underestimate the influence that particular socio-historic conditions have on the nature of gender relations and our perception of such relations. But explanations based on historical or anthropological evidence, while they may corroborate the impression given by literature that there is an overwhelming degree to which societies over the centuries and across the continents have been concerned with the fate of the deceived husband, do not provide an adequate explanation for it inasmuch as they do not give priority to the issues presented by our sexuality—that is, a part of us which is essentially ours.

It may be suggested, as already indicated in this chapter, that the concern for the deceived husband derives from a concern about inheritance. Fuel for this argument will be provided (although only partially) by the etymology of cuckoldry, which we shall examine in the following chapter. It is, moreover, the case that we can observe examples in legislation which express concern about inheritance, and hence, we may deduce, about the fidelity of wives. There may be disagreement about whether the law develops in order to reflect the changing opinion and needs of the society in which it operates, or whether it is brought in so that it will be in some way influential or prescriptive, but there can be little dispute about the fact that there is a close relationship between a body of law and the society that it is intended to serve and contain. We none the less need to be cautious in simply seeing law as the reflection of a society, just as we need to be cautious about seeing literature as providing another such reflection, and we should pay heed to a point made by Bloch on this question. He indicates that the prescriptions of the law may not reflect what actually happened but may simply have made it possible for certain things to happen or not, according to need. He argues that we can only glimpse, or mentally construct, the 'normal' for ourselves, by noting what provisions are made for transgressions against the norm, so that 'family history tends to become most explicit only when the standard prescriptions of permissible conduct are transgressed as in cases of prohibited marriages, disputed inheritances, bigamy, incest, and divorce'.[24]

If we consider historical evidence in the area of adultery, the

[24] R. Howard Bloch, *Etymologies and Genealogies: A Literary Anthropology of the French Middle Ages* (Chicago and London, 1983), 65. Bloch's comments are made with respect to 12th-cent. France, but hold good as a shrewd generalization.

conclusions to be drawn are far from clear. In the law of classical Athens, for example, there is an implied contradiction. That law required the wife, but not the husband, to be faithful after marriage—a requirement that appears to support inheritance theory. The provision in regard to adultery does not, however, do so. It was considered that in adultery the essential crime committed was one of seduction, and, if anything, the emphasis was on the corruption of a woman, rather than on an error on her part which could lead to a misdirected inheritance. Women in the society of classical Athens were considered to come in the same category as children, being dependants. Their seduction, therefore, could almost be construed as tantamount to child abuse, or at the least as interference with another man's possession, rather than as an action that would undermine the economic and social stability of a family.[25] Similarly the inheritance explanation appears inadequate to account for the legislation brought into Roman imperial law by Augustus in the first century BC in the *Lex Julia de Adulteriis*. Under this, adultery was removed from the private sphere to the public, but, more significantly, while the law declared that it was illegal for husbands to execute their wives in the private sphere, it was still permissible for fathers to kill their daughters if the latter were caught committing adultery in the family home.[26] Again, if we sample the history of the twelfth century, the evidence is partial, inconclusive, and contradictory. On the one hand, we observe the shift, noted by Bloch, from a 'horizontally structured' family to a 'vertical' one, beginning around the start of the eleventh century and apparently provoked by concern about the fragmentation of land: allowing all children, male and female, to inherit meant that any one family's land became split into ever smaller portions and thus became more difficult to manage.[27] The narrowing of the family to its vertical pattern was gradually linked to the primacy of the rights of primogeniture, again a factor which would place an emphasis on the fidelity of women, since more and more would hang on

[25] Douglas M. MacDowell, *The Law in Classical Athens* (London, 1978), 84–96, 124–5.
[26] P. Corbett, *The Roman Law of Marriage* (Oxford, 1930), 127. For further detail see R. Howard Bloch, *Medieval French Literature and Law* (Berkeley, Calif., 1977), 54–5.
[27] Bloch, *Etymologies and Genealogies*, 67. A similar fragmentation was to cause land-tenure problems in north-west Spain in the modern period.

ensuring that the children who would inherit were indeed the legitimate ones, since these would be the only ones entitled to do so. As Bloch summarizes it, 'the question of marriage is, ultimately, indissociable from that of land, of inheritance, and, in particular, of cognatic succession'.[28] Contrasting with this evidence, which appears to reflect a restrictiveness in matters of inheritance that would be consonant with extreme concern over the fidelity of wives, we have the pragmatism of English custom, also of the twelfth century, by which a child born within wedlock would not be considered illegitimate unless the husband had been away from home or had been prevented from having access to his wife for a period of at least two years.[29]

Anthropology may seem to come somewhat closer than history to providing an explanation for the importance attached to a wife's infidelity, but it too has limitations. As a discipline, anthropology recognizes the importance of symbols and boundaries, but has a tendency to concentrate on these as confined social phenomena, rather than as manifestations which may have their origin in the early stages of gender formation. This is so even when, as in the case of Goody, statements are made which come close to the area of generalization psychoanalytic theory allows us to enter. Thus, commenting on European law on adultery, Goody observes that in general 'marriage confers relatively exclusive rights on a man over the sexual services of a woman. It is most unusual to find that the woman acquires similar rights over the male, even in matrilinear societies'.[30] He does not, however, pursue the argument on to a more generalized level relating to sexuality. Again, we could consider the observations made about the symbolic attributions relating to gender and place in various societies, where further layers of explanation are not probed. In Bourdieu's comments on the Berber culture, for example, we learn that the house is forbidden to men during the day, when it is the women's domain. A whole range of emotional connotations is attached to the man who breaks this custom: 'The man who

[28] Ibid. 194.

[29] Chris Given-Wilson and Alice Curteis, *The Royal Bastards of Medieval England* (London, 1984), 45.

[30] Jack Goody, 'A Comparative Approach to Incest and Adultery', *Comparative Studies in Kinship* (London, 1969), 24.

stays too long in the house during the day is either suspect or ridiculous: he is "the man of the home", as one says of the importunate man who stays among the women and who "broods at home like a hen in the henhouse". A man who has respect for himself should let himself be seen, should continuously place himself under the gaze of others and face them ("gabel"). He is a man amongst men ("argas yer irgazen"). Hence the importance accorded to the games of honour which are a kind of dramatic action, performed in front of others who are knowing spectators, familiar with the text and all the stage business and capable of appreciating the slightest variations.' The house, Bourdieu observes, is not simply a social place inhabited by women while men go off and pursue other occupations during the day. This is demonstrated by its connection with what is fundamentally female, and with the night and water: it is the dark, nocturnal part of life.[31] Bourdieu's work, and that of other anthropologists, provides ample evidence of anxieties related to sexuality and gender definition in a variety of cultures, but there is a reluctance to explain them other than in terms of detail and custom.

While time and place undoubtedly leave their mark on the detail of gender differentiation, I would argue that there are certain essentials of sexual development common to us regardless of cultural limitation, and which transcend cultural limits. These are anxieties played out in the containing yet reflective phantasies of literature, and which can only derive their final explanation from theory based on primary experience, that is, psychoanalytic theory.

Why then should there be in literature this implied failure (and at times, textually speaking, relative absence) of husbands who are, or are thought to be, or suspect that they might be, the victims of their wives' infidelity, and who are accordingly dismissed, mocked, or ridiculed by the characters who surround them, and by the reader who is faced with their plight? My interest is to see what is meant by the presentation of their failure or absence, to explore the significance of their status (whether they

[31] P. Bourdieu, 'The Berber House' (1971), in Mary Douglas (ed.), *Rules and Meanings* (Harmondsworth, 1973), 103–4. This example is corroborated in the Spanish context by F. Sánchez Pérez, *La Liturgia del espacio* (Madrid, 1990) chs. 4 and 5, and by the studies examined at length in Ch. 4 of this book.

are simply the sexual failures they are presented as being, or whether their failure represents more complex and distressing issues), and at some level to direct to them the attention and concern denied them by their context and by those who read of their fate. I shall consider them in three groups: cuckolds, most characteristically present in medieval literature, but found later in other works, and being those men who are deceived and unable to take action about their fate (if indeed they reach awareness of it); men of honour, who can and do take action, but with a tendency to anticipation and exaggeration, and who are given their most extensive treatment in the Spanish theatre of the Golden Age; lastly, husbands who are but shadowy figures in novels of adultery, and yet whose reaction to infidelity may at times be delicately and poignantly sketched, when they are not being cast by themselves or others into one or other of the two preceding models for the type of the deceived husband.

Our attitudes to failure reveal as much, if not more, as our attitudes to success, both about the structure of our society and about the component parts of the individuals within it. Values and beliefs are often expressed in positive terms, but not exclusively so, and negative expression, avoided areas of discussion, and the presentation of failures will tell us as much about those values as any more formal prescriptive statements. In the examples of men who are failures in a patriarchal society, however, and in the style of their portrayal, in their failure or their absence, there may be profound meaning.

A curious feature of our patriarchal society is the lack of sympathy given to the fate of men in certain contexts, particularly in areas of failure. Feminist rereadings of works of literature have alerted us to the lack of understanding about the position of women in such works, about the extent to which masculine norms and assumptions concerning the personality and behaviour of women are those most frequently woven into texts, and about the degree to which such masculine-oriented texts fail to address or suggest the unspoken experience of women. It might seem, therefore, that it is inappropriate to offer yet another consideration of the representation of men in literature: the view could be taken that they have had at least their fair share already, if not more. So it may be with some male characters. We have accepted the focus of the *Bildungsroman* as being that of the development of a man in society, and in most circumstances the implication is that this is the development of a successful man.[32]

Readings of literature, and works of literature themselves, have a tendency to concentrate on the successful—a term which I would argue can also contain the idea of the 'successful failure'—that is, the character whose tragic failure is portrayed in a way that makes him hold our attention.

But the notion of the failure is arguably as important as the notion of the success story. This will hold whether the person who is deemed to be the failure is held up for public ridicule, as is the cuckold, or their failure is not obvious, as in the case of the man of honour, or their failure can be equated with the degree of their absence from the work of literature (ranging from the way in which cuckolds are passed over, even in the works which treat of their plight, to the disregard of husbands as effective creatures or literary characters in the nineteenth century).

These different styles of failure are related to different assumptions. If we look at characters who fail, it is because we can and do locate tendencies and characteristics in them—thus the clear-cut figure of the cuckold carries a spectrum of fears about ageing, loss of potency, loss of status. The man of honour seems at first glance to be as clear-cut as the cuckold but in a different way: that is, he comes over as effective, executive, able to deal even with the situation of dishonour. Yet if we regard him as one whose concern for form, family norms, and social respect are overriding, then the question of his self-sufficiency is raised: is he able to retain a self-image undamaged by the suspicions cast upon his wife, or is he so dependent for a sense of esteem on the opinion of the world that an attack on the integrity of his spouse, or some other member of his family, is an attack upon himself? The characteristics of husbands in novels of adultery are less clear in their meaning, but relate most closely to the pattern of the cuckold. In their expression of human and social inadequacy and the ensuing dulled yet real anguish they feel, they express, as did the cuckold earlier, a range of fears—this time relating not so much to the absolutes of death and loss of sexual power as to questions of performance and social and material adequacy. They are perhaps the saddest

[32] See ch. 1 of Carla L. Peterson, *The Determined Reader: Gender and Culture in the Novel from Napoleon to Victoria* (New Jersey, 1986), for discussion of expectations about protagonists in the nineteenth-century novel.

figures of all, and their sadness derives from what they, as neglected but real and functional literary characters, tell us about the nature of the time that has produced them. It is a time which, at least as viewed through novels, measures worth in terms of social, sexual, and economic performance, rather than on a scale of passion, but, being a mobile age, is also locked into relativism and equivocation.[33] It is this realization about the values that dominate characters of nineteenth-century novels that give them their peculiar dull pain; there is no primary or sharp sense of anguish deriving from the relations of particular binary or triangular relationships.

There is no lack of 'successful failures' in literature—if this is how we construe tragic heroes such as Othello or Macbeth—but in so far as they are tragic heroes their failure is not complete. Sympathy for men in their failure or their state of being overthrown, except in the case of tragedy, is a feature remarkably lacking in our culture: where there is real failure we ignore it or laugh at it. For characters to elicit sympathy in their failure it would appear that two things need to happen. They must retain some shreds of their dignity, if not of their grandeur, since their fallen, failed state is insufficient in itself to engage our warmth towards them. Secondly, our sympathy entails our recognition of their state as something potentially common to all of us: 'There but for the grace of God go I' impedes both laughter and dismissal.

My main focus will be on failures who are clearly failures, but part of their meaning can be deduced from a different sort of absence from literature, namely that of strong masculine figures who are also benevolent, positive. This lacuna in our culture has been highlighted by Brewer, who interprets it by viewing the 'family drama' as contained in the Oedipus myth. He relates this absence on the one hand to the primitive fears evoked by mother-figures (the most powerful of the feminine figures) and on the other to the awe inspired in us by a realization of the inevitability that youth will, in the fullness of time, overthrow age.[34]

[33] See Tony Tanner, *Adultery in the Novel* (Baltimore, 1979), esp. 3–24, 79–86, and S. Kierkegaard, *Two Ages: The Age of Revolution and the Present Age: A Literary Review* (1846), ed. and trans. Howard V. Hong and Edna H. Hong (Princeton, NJ, 1978), 63–80.

[34] See Derek Brewer, *Symbolic Stories* (Woodbridge, 1980), esp. 9–12, and Erich Fromm, who in *The Forgotten Language: An Introduction to the*

This absence of positive and strong masculine figures in our literature, given that it is the product of a patriarchal society, is remarkable. It takes two forms: first the absence of strong yet benign father-figures, and second the recurrent portrayal of weak masculine figures, particularly fathers and husbands.

The first form may be considered attributable to the fact that a patriarchal society will have an investment in fathers as a source of power, and that this power has a tendency to take the form of domination of others, rather than enablement for the growth and survival of others through the provision of a firm and reliable context. Patriarchy has come to be defined, in the terms of feminist criticism, in the former sense of domination, though theoretically the latter sense, of enablement, should be possible. Some of the causes of the urge to power in men are outlined in Chapter 2, in the discussion of the fear of women and the nature of gender-determination in the development of infants. The second form, the portrayal of failures, shows our culture at its most daring, most accommodating, most willing to accept and comprehend, even though the form of that comprehension is disguised by the outer trappings of mockery and belittling. In presenting failures it acknowledges, however cursorily, its own weak points, and in this achieves some of the strength of the depressive position.

The general relation of Kleinian theory to my subject is then the following: it helps us to understand the phenomenon in patriarchal literature of the man who is the counter-exemplum of patriarchal culture—the man deemed to have failed in relation to a woman, and hence a failure in the eyes of other men. Where literature produces a betrayed husband in all the potential horror of his state, that is, so grossly a failure that he is to be mocked and scorned, then that literature is stating a worst-case possibility, and by that very act of statement is tolerating it as a possibility. There is at some level an acceptance of the cuckold's occurrence and the

Understanding of Dreams, Fairy Tales and Myths (London, 1952), 174, comments on the Oedipus plays, and argues that *Oedipus Rex* needs to be read in conjunction with *Oedipus at Colonnus* and *Antigone*: 'the myth can be understood as a symbol not of the incestuous love between mother and son but of the rebellion of the son against the authority of the father in the patriarchal family . . . the marriage of Oedipus and Jocasta is only a secondary element, only one of the symbols of the victory of the son, who takes his father's place and with it all his privileges'.

fact that he might not be alone in his fate. He is not so shocking that he cannot be contemplated. The literary representation of the cuckold, being the product of a society which can bear to accept that it contains examples that run counter to its values, can be seen as an example of what we could term depressive-position literature. In so far as works of literature with husbands presented clearly as cuckolds tend to be comic, however, we can see at work the containing function of humour, which provides a safety-valve for otherwise intolerable fears, but also permits the society that produces it to state the source of the fear, and thus to work towards the tolerance of its own points of weakness.

Where, alternatively, we encounter works of literature that fail to accept the implications of the fate of the betrayed husband, they fall within the parameters of the paranoid-schizoid position. Here we can include, for example: early Norse sagas, where for sexual failure or irregularity even to be hinted at is a heinous crime; or epic literature, where any values other than masculine ones cannot be contemplated; or honour dramas, where, in a type of reaction-formation against sexual humiliation, husbands are (apparently) shown as honourable, decisive, and potent (and demonstrate that they are all of these things by murdering wives and lovers). The paradigm of the man of honour is built upon a mechanism of splitting and projection, with all the social and personal fragility that this entails.

The model of the deceived husband as he is portrayed in novels of adultery presents, as suggested earlier, a more complex view of the husband's situation. The husband is seen moving between the position of the cuckold and that of the man of honour in a way which allows us to perceive fleetingly a vulnerable being who is contained by neither of the representational models. In novels of adultery such as *Dombey and Son* and *Anna Karenin* there is an exploration of the question of man's relation to emotion, as opposed to his reaction to infidelity. What we see of the deceived husband in the novel allows us to see that his portrayal as cuckold in fact constitutes only a partial evidencing of the depressive position. Literature of cuckoldry, with its reliance on the distancing of comedy, provides only a first type of the accommodation of the threatening nature of experience. That very distancing tempers the real degree of accommodation possible. The novel of adultery, by contrast, in its closer and more painful depiction of the pain and grief of the deceived husband, comes nearer to the depressive position. It is significant that only the novel of adultery explores the wider issues of family, children, and life after adultery. As such we might regard it as a genre of maturity, in contrast with the more limited explorations of the impact of infidelity as shown in literature depicting the cuckold or the man of honour. It is risky to venture a view that suggests historical progression in either culture or literature, but this 'developed' state of the novel of adultery, in contrast with a number of earlier paradigms, is consonant with the observation in clinical practice that a true depressive position is one of acceptance reached only after the mid-life crisis, where the inevitability of death and the limitations it imposes are fully realized.[35]

Although a strict adherence to Kleinian chronology might suggest that it is most appropriate to begin with the man of honour as paradigmatic of the paranoid-schizoid position, I have opted to take the cuckold first, as representing a merely apparent depressive position, a true depressive position being more closely approached in the novel of adultery. The sequence adopted does not in fact run against the grain of Kleinian theory, since the two positions can be observed throughout life. The order adopted allows the discussion to progress in chronological sequence of the works discussed, which may or may not be significant. As I have indicated, it is tempting—but risky—to advance the notion that there is in fact a progression in the attitudes of Western Europe to the painful experience of the deceived husband. To take this idea beyond the level of risky speculation would, however, require a different book.

[35] See Elliott Jaques, 'Death and the Mid-Life Crisis', *International Journal of Psychoanalysis*, 46 (1965), 502–14.

2

Cuckoldry, Honour, and Adultery: The Language of Infidelity

The concept of sexual infidelity is both widespread and ancient. It requires, as a precondition, the concept of sexual fidelity, and further that it have as its context a society in which there is the institution of marriage, or some similar long-term heterosexual and exclusive relationship, and in which the expectation is that there shall be conjugal fidelity, at least on the part of the wife. These conditions are fulfilled by European society throughout the period for which we have written literary evidence. Other times, other places may have thrown up different social and matrimonial patterns, but the overwhelming preponderance in Europe of patriarchal and patrilineal societies is striking.

In the previous chapter I argued for the recognition of fundamental psychological pressures and issues as forming the bedrock, or at least the revealing subtext, of the literature of woman's infidelity. I stress that it is woman's infidelity that is at issue, not because I wish to continue that historical vein of gendered partiality that we can see in early psychoanalytical writers, but simply because—if we take the evidence of literature—man's infidelity has caused little explicit public or literary concern. The absence of concern with man's infidelity, I would argue, is not a sign of its unimportance, but may rather be indicative of a public, literary avoidance of a social issue, and is barely surprising in a patriarchal society where the majority of works in traditional literary canons have been written by men.

Our attitudes to life's events are conveyed—or, to put it more forcefully, are simultaneously enshrined and promoted—by the words we use to denote them. Hence the language relating to infidelity reiterates patriarchal concern with the infidelity of wives rather than with that of husbands. This emerges with particular clarity in the vocabulary used for sexual infidelity and those men who are thought to be its victims. There is a striking absence of vocabulary to refer to the women whose husbands are unfaithful to them, and this betrays the lack of attention paid to the women as individuals whose status and personal well-being are undoubtedly affected by such infidelity.

At first sight, some of the language relating to the cuckold appears to give weight to the socio-historical argument that matters of inheritance are the reason why the fault of wives appears to cause interest and concern, whereas the sexual fault of husbands that leads them from the marriage bed is taken so much for granted that it is not equally regarded as a fault. As we shall see, however, the etymology of words relating to infidelity only lends partial support to the inheritance argument, and other anxieties about potency and masculinity are clearly evident.

The reasoning about the importance of inheritance runs as follows: if a man is to pass on his property to his children, then he needs to know that they are indeed his children. A wife who errs will interfere with the efficient transfer of property to a man's children, whereas a man who goes to seek his sexual pleasures outside marriage, and happens to father illegitimate children, will interfere with the passing-on of his property to those children he has by his wife only if he tries to divert some or all of it towards the children fathered by him illegitimately.

It is important to remember, however, that although etymology may support this reasoning, when we see men presented as the victims of women's infidelity in literature, the transfer of property to legitimate offspring hardly appears centre-stage, and is usually not even given a mention. What *is* prominent is the constellation of patriarchal values connected with the actual preoccupation of the handing-on of property by a man to his children, in that what affects such a handing-on is seen to be an area of concern: the man's interests are at stake, as well as his reputation. This emphasis on the one hand affirms the urgency of focus on the sexual misdemeanours of the wife, and on the other hand, renders concentration on the sexual misdemeanours of the husband—at least in so far as they cause emotional distress to his wife—of little interest, or even otiose.

In the literary treatment of the deceived husband, as we shall see in later chapters, what comes to the fore is the personal, the social, and the connections between the two. The social is understood in terms of reputation and standing, rather than in terms of patriarchal society's requirements for vigilance over matters of inheritance, and thus also for vigilance over sexual fidelity. The personal is of importance in so far as the individual has lost some measure of reputation and standing: others (the lover and the wife) have not considered either him, or the family of which he is the centre, to be of sufficient significance to merit fidelity. The concern which may have had its base in matters of land and property is thus converted into a concern with the individual figure. Although in earlier times he was regarded as subservient to his family or dynasty rather than important to himself, the individual nevertheless emerges in literature as a man struggling with the constraints placed upon him by his social role and standing, and as someone to whom loss of reputation is of personal importance. In the portrayal of matrimonial upsets in literature, the wronged husband is cast as a figure of fun in cuckoldry, as a figure of potential tragedy when shown as a man of honour; in the major novels of adultery he is a man, sad and wounded, moving between the dignified and the pathetic.

The etymology of the terms we use to allude to the cuckold and his state is both illuminating and confusing, and in the words used in different languages for this state we see a difference of emphasis. In broad terms, we see in countries of Northern Europe (including France and Provence) an underlying or original concern with property, in that most terms relate to the cuckoo. With the dramatic exception of Norse literature, the concern in the North seems to take account of what the infidelity does to the husband's material status in the world, and is rather more detached from the area of pure sexual jealousy. In Spain and Italy, by contrast, there is concern with the loss of masculinity which is suggested to the onlooker by a man's having been made into a cuckold. One might therefore say that in Southern Europe, despite the concern with honour and the family, which we shall examine later, the overt interest is in what cuckoldry does to a man as man, and as a sexual being who has failed to keep his mate.

According to the *Oxford English Dictionary*, 'cuckold' as a derisive term for the husband of an unfaithful wife was first used in English (in the form 'cuckeweld') in 1250, in the anonymous poem 'The Owl and the Nightingale'. The Middle English word 'cuckeweld' or 'coke wold' is an adaptation of an Old French word, which appears in 1463 as 'cucualt', a spelling which points to an earlier form of 'cucuald'. The cuckoo is known for two rather contradictory traits. It can be seen as clever, in that it manages to lay its eggs in the nest of another bird, thus ensuring that its kind is propagated without having to engage in the tedious activity of feeding and caring for its own young. But we might also remember that we use the term 'cuckoo' colloquially, and that here it does not primarily refer to someone who is astute or wily, but implies someone rather soft in the head, a little stupid, one who stands out as being not of the common run. These allusions presumably derive not from the ridiculous figure cut by the cuckoo in a nest of smaller birds, but from the parent bird who continues to feed the intruder. The stupidity of the cuckoo was related, in English medieval literature, to its limited range of utterance ('The cook how syngen can but a lay' in Lydgate, 'The Churl and the Bird'). Not only does this show up the cuckoo as impoverished in expressiveness when compared with other birds, but indicates its rather boring nature (a criticism that can often be levelled at the cuckold).[1] It is the second trait, implying mockery and condescension, that links the cuckoo with the cuckold. The link between cuckoo and cuckold is there in Old French, where 'cucu' for 'cuckoo' appears also in the fifteenth, sixteenth, and seventeenth centuries as 'cocu'. In addition, the term 'coucou' was also used in the sixteenth and seventeenth centuries with the meanings of both 'cuckoo' and 'cuckold'. It is only in Modern French that the distinction between bird and man has been retained with clarity. In German the terms 'Gauch' and 'Kuckuck', and in Provençal the word 'coudieu', were used in the same way as the terms for cuckoo/cuckold were in Old French. Both 'Gauch' and 'Kuckuck' are used in the first instance as 'cuckoo', but 'Gauch' is also used for 'fool', 'booby', 'simpleton', 'ninny', presumably as developments of the archaic meaning of 'deceived husband' or cuckold. When we look at the meaning of 'Kuckuck' other than the ornithological one, we can detect perhaps some exasperation with all the state of the cuckold, since in familiar contexts 'Kuckuck' is used for the devil, in expressions such as 'Go to the devil!'[2]

In looking at these origins of the word 'cuckold' we notice a peculiarity: the cuckold is the fool in the sexual story, but the bird

[1] I am indebted to Dorothy McCarthy for this information.

[2] *Harraps Standard German and English Dictionary*, ed. Trevor Jones (London, 1977).

that gets another to care for its young is nobody's fool. Indeed, when we look at the etymology of 'cuckold' we find that there seems to be a lack of clarity about who does what to whom in this story of the sexual triangle. The fact that in Nature's story the bird appears to be the clever one is actually contained in the etymological roots. Not only do the terms used in French, German, and Provençal have a double meaning, in that they are used for both cuckoo and cuckold; those in German and Provençal are applied to both offended and offending parties, that is, not just to the wronged husband but also to the lover of the wife who has sent him into a state of 'cuckoldry'. In these cases, the passing of time, and the development of language, means that the husband appears to have got left with the term—holding the baby, as it were. We may regard this double and contradictory usage either as an example of confusion (the disruption of a marriage has confused everyone about boundaries and identities) or as an unconscious recognition that the fate of the cuckold is freely available to all, and that no man is immune to it. Thus the language of cuckoldry, as much as the literary realizations of the cuckold, bears out its depressive-position recognition and acceptance of the threats to man's status and sexual identity.

In English, where 'cuckold' has never been the name of the bird, we do not find it applied to the adulterer, although we do find a variety of terms for the state of the cuckold, which is variously described as 'cuckoldry', 'cuckoldom', and 'cuckoldage'. In English, then, we see a clarity which is shared with the countries of the Southern Mediterranean about what has happened, and in the multiple terms for being in the state of a cuckold, we can also see our society's intense concern with the state, presumably because it is a state men would rather not find themselves in, since it is clear that they and no others, such as the lovers, are the cuckolds. Incidentally, the corresponding lack of terms to describe specifically the state of a woman whose husband is unfaithful to her (just as there is no feminine equivalent either for 'misogyny', other than the phrase 'hatred of men') could be seen as the natural product of a patriarchal society, or even of a misogynistic one, and certainly of a society which does not even permit the masculine province of language, or public language, to be used for purposes it would rather ignore.

When we look at later uses of the word 'cuckold' we find that it has acquired firmly pejorative connotations referring to the diminished potency and masculinity of the deceived husband. A cuckold passes from being a man whose wife is unfaithful to him to one who is less than a man, and considered by others as diminished and ridiculous because of his state and his tolerance of it (which appears to make him as much a cuckold as the original infidelity itself). Cuckolds in Boccaccio are ridiculed, held up as examples of those who are so weak that they get what they deserve. Chaucer, despite his heightened compassion for those who are deceived and a prey to their sexual weaknesses, also reiterates the message that the unfortunate state is one that is earned. His attitude to that state is of robust recognition of disaster and its causes.

By the time we reach the age of Dr Johnson and his dictionary (1755), the definitions offered for 'cuckold' are unequivocal in their emphasis on the shamefulness of the condition, and high in their moral tone. The cuckold is defined in passive terms. He is 'one that is married to an adultress; one whose wife is false to his bed'. In this curious reversal of social and linguistic norms, we find that the man is defined in terms of the woman to whom he is married, rather than the opposite. He is not what he is of his own accord: he is passive, and he is what he is because something has happened to him, and this thing defines him as a cuckold. He continues to be one (rather than a husband who avenges his honour), since, as we shall find, one of the prime features of a cuckold is that he is unable to take action in defence of his damaged honour once the damage has occurred. In so far as it confirms him as weak, this *ex post facto* incapacity is at least as important as the original 'weakness' which is presumed to have given rise to the infidelity. Had the cuckold's wife been happy, and sexually satisfied in the marriage, there would have been, barring rape or, conceivably, seduction, no infidelity.

Seen through Dr Johnson's eyes, these sexual misdemeanours of spouses are not merely sent to try us: it is clear that they are deserved, and mark the cuckold as of a lower rank of humanity. Three definitions of the verb 'to cuckold' emphasize Johnson's moral, even priggish, approach to the subject. To 'cuckold' another man is 'to corrupt a man's wife' (marking woman out as the weaker vessel, and the way through to the diminishing of a man's honour). The second definition emphasizes the loss of status implied in having a chattel who is unfaithful: 'to bring upon a man the *reproach* of having an adulterous wife'. The third is the one which carries echoes of a concern with property, but without the preoccupation about offspring. It is 'to rob a man of his wife's fidelity', giving us to understand that a man owns his wife's fidelity along with so many other things. The momentary compassion conveyed by the image of a man robbed is removed by Dr Johnson's poor opinion of the state of cuckold when he gives his definition of the adjective 'cuckoldly'. Here we see how the cuckold is, by his state, considered to have lost most manly, or rather, gentlemanly, merits. Thus the adjective 'cuckoldly' which appears in Shakespeare's *Merry Wives of Windsor* (1598) is 'having the qualities of a cuckold; poor; mean; cowardly; sneaking'. The escalation of Johnson's terms give us a clear signal as to why anyone would prefer to avoid the state of cuckold. It is no mere breach of marital fidelity, but a total reduction in the respectability and self-worth of the man thus deceived.

The etymology of 'cuckold' points to a cause for concern with the state which initially comes from a sense of family, of property, and from the need to pass on inheritance. It also carries, less explicitly, a notion that what concerns a *man* is property, and that being a man includes the sense of possession of other things, or rights over other things. There is also the sense, in the image of the cuckoo, that a man should not expend his energy needlessly in providing sustenance for young that are fathered by others—which is what he risks doing if his wife has been unfaithful and then brings the 'products' home, to be cared for in the original matrimonial setting. In the image of the cuckoo, of the alien bird in the nest, we see one of the prime features of cuckoldry, a phenomenon which, according to Tanner, does not, unlike adultery, threaten the institution of marriage, because it is thought of as separate from it.[3] The nest is not broken up because of the intruder. This is a point we shall have cause to return to later, in considering how far cuckoldry, as a cultural expression of sexual infidelity in marriage, may be regarded as characteristic of a stable and socially organized society, and adultery as characteristic, or indicative of the uncertainties of, the societies that produce it.

Cuckoldry, then, does not signal the end of the marriage, but

[3] Tanner, *Adultery in the Novel*, 17.

rather that the role of the man in the marriage is not what it was. Although the word 'cuckold' has at its origins an awareness of the alien offspring that may be introduced into the matrimonial home, the emphasis in the labelling is not on the status of those offspring, but rather on the man, the father, who allows this position to occur, who tolerates it, and is prepared to provide for what is not his. Johnson's ever more scathing terms to describe the cuckold denote scorn for the man who is in this situation, and point us to what may be a useful distinction in working out what being termed a 'cuckold' means for the man concerned and for others.

Theoretically, the husband could be regarded as the cuckold as soon as the act of infidelity occurs, but the way the cuckold is treated in literature suggests that it is not the actual status of the cuckold that matters but the fact that a man is known to be one, or supposed to be one, by society. In works of literature where infidelity is presented in terms of cuckoldry, two features are common. There is absolutely no doubt at all in the mind of the rest of the society in the work of literature that the infidelity has occurred (or even, as is frequent, that it is about to) and there is no doubt on the matter in the mind of the reader (even though the act of infidelity itself is rarely, if ever, narrated at length, just as the act that brings adultery into being in novels is usually kept discreetly off the page). The second feature is that the husband is different from the rest of society in that he appears to be the last to know of his changed state—this lack of awareness being most characteristic of the cuckolded husband in Boccaccio, Chaucer, and the *commedia dell'arte*.

The husband's lack of awareness about his state of cuckoldom is but the tip of the iceberg of the other feature of his state as seen by, amongst many others, Dr Johnson, and reflected in the idea that the husband will provide for the offspring of another man. In the first place, he will do so because he is simply unaware of what has happened, and will continue to provide for the aliens in his domestic nest just because he has no notion that they are not his. But secondly, as we see from Dr Johnson's definitions, and in the words used for cuckolds in other languages, he is a man who will not seek to redress the marital wrong which has been done to him by his wife, because he is incapable of doing so. The willingness of the cuckold husband to care for children is more explicit in novels of adultery, where the husband's domesticity may betoken, not a lack of awareness, but the ability to depart from a view of marriage which considers only the erring wife.

The cuckold's lack of awareness about his state, and his unwillingness or inability to do anything about it once he *is* made aware, are clearly reflected in the terms for 'cuckold' used in the Southern Mediterranean, notably Spain and Italy, countries where, curiously enough, honour codes are prominent in the regulation of sexual conduct.

In Spanish the unfortunate victim of a wife's infidelity, as soon as it is perceived by others, is variously referred to as a 'cabrito', 'cabrón', 'comblezado', 'cornudo', 'cuclillo', 'gurrumino', 'novillo paciente', 'predestinado', 'sufrido', and 'marido complaciente'. In these terms there are two emphases: first, that the husband is weak, and unable or unwilling to take any action in response to his wife's infidelity, and secondly, that his state is clear to the rest of society, because of the horns of cuckoldry he wears. The 'gurrumino' is defined first as a husband who is too accommodating towards his wife's infidelities (and the plural used here is perhaps significant in emphasizing the gravity of the repeated situation), but secondly as 'raquítico', that is, as suffering from rickets.[4] When a wife is unfaithful, one of the popular terms for indicating the event is 'poner el gorro', to place the cap on someone. The cap in question is the sort of hat worn by babies in nappies, with clear implications about the standing of the husband who has been deceived. The other, more general, meaning of 'poner el gorro' is to force another person into a ridiculous position by placing them in an embarrassing situation, and the commonest example given is of a couple who make love while in the presence of a third party, a meaning which has graphic implications as far as the state of the cuckold is concerned. 'Predestinado' again denotes weakness, or passivity, since the husband's state is one against which he could have no recourse, and the 'sufrido' is one who tolerates his state when he finds himself in it.

Of the other terms in Spanish, 'cabrito', 'cabrón', and 'novillo paciente' refer to horned animals. Here there is irony embedded

[4] These, and other terms from Spanish are as defined in María Moliner, *Diccionario del uso del español* (Madrid, 1966).

in the epithets, because of the normal 'macho' characteristics ascribed to those animals; at the same time there is a reference to the horns the cuckold was believed to sprout on his forehead when the marital deception occurred. The 'novillo' is a young bull or cow, or, in some countries—for example Chile and Mexico—a bullock (a castrated bull). Thus there is the combination of the idea of the young, even immature, male, and the reference to the fact that he has been castrated, or is likely to be castrated in the near future. As he is 'paciente', we are given to understand that he awaits his fate (the fate indicated by 'predestinado') with patience, and no protest. The irony of all this, perhaps an irony always reiterated in the context of farming, where it is the strongest of animals that will require castration in order to make it possible to handle them, is that the image of the castrated male used for the deceived husband alludes to the castration of the animal that is known for its strength, and potency, namely the bull, whose horns combine a clear show of aggression with a phallic symbol of the most obvious kind. 'Cabrón' and 'cabrito' both refer to a male goat, traditional symbol of lust, and thus also of potency. When we refer in English to someone as 'an old goat', it is with the idea not only that they have a higher level than average of sexual desire, but that they are not without the wherewithal to satisfy that desire. The two suffixes, 'ón' and 'ito' introduce mockery into the term, the former indicating that this is a big goat, the latter that it is rather small. Thus in the first case the 'goat' (the husband) is ridiculed for being big and strong yet still not able to hold on to his wife's fidelity; and in the second the 'goat' is too small and was evidently unable to hold on to his wife's fidelity in the first place. In María Moliner's definition it is stressed that the 'cabrón' in particular, a common and vulgar term, is used not just for a deceived husband, but for one who does not protest at his state.

Italian shows a similar concern with the cuckold as a weak and deceived man, forced into a state of passivity, and whose horns are a visible ironic comment on his condition. The cuckold is referred to in Italian as a 'cornuto' (horned one) or 'becco' (buck, he-goat, billygoat), and in terms for the verb 'to cuckold' we again find an emphasis on horns; 'fare le corne a' and 'far becco' (to put the horns on someone, or to make a man a he-goat). The 'becco' is sometimes referred to more precisely as a 'becco contento', a term which, curiously enough, the *Cambridge Italian Dictionary* finds it necessary to translate by reference to French, as a 'mari complaisant' or a 'husband in a ménage à trois'.[5] It does seem that apart from the term 'cuckold', English has very few expressions for this husband who complies with his condition.

Both the goat and the bull, of course, are noted for their horns, and for the aggression they are prepared to mete out with them. It is tempting to suppose that here we have the origin of the idea that the cuckold sprouts horns as the sign of his deceived state, made evident to society. But this is not a simple matter. Why should animals renowned for their strength, virility, and lustiness come to be connected with a man who appears to have lost precisely those attributes? A first supposition is that here we may have a symbolic inversion. The horns of the animals connected with the cuckold are clearly phallic symbols, even to the least Freudian among us. This partial but suggestive focus on the parts of the beasts which are their tools and expressions of male aggression could be a case of simple irony, in which scorn is poured on a powerful horned or even 'horny' creature which has now been outmanœuvred from its position of domination on the sexual scene. Our attention may also be being directed to the state of these animals in a civilized society, in which they have been domesticated and tamed. Just as marriage and cuckoldry are part of a stable society, so too, at least in Europe, is the image of the domesticated animal, so that all that strength and vitality is now contained in farmyard pens. In this situation, the horns of the animal are a present and direct ironic comment on what they have lost in the assertion of their strength, individuality, and sexual desire (since they will be called on to 'serve' female animals at the wish of the farmer). This connection with the sad state of the domesticated animal is alluded to by Cirlot, who points out that some of the unfavourable interpretations of horn-symbolism are due to association with the ancient symbol of the ox, which represents castration, sacrifice, and persistent toil.[6] Significantly, perhaps, the horns of animals in the wild do not appear to be involved in the process of symbolic inversion: there is a longstanding belief that powdered rhinoceros horn is an aphrodisiac,

[5] *Cambridge Italian Dictionary*, gen. ed. Barbara Reynolds (Cambridge, 1962).

[6] J. E. Cirlot, *A Dictionary of Symbols*, trans. from Spanish by Jack Sage (2nd edn.; London, 1962), 248.

whereas there is no such belief in relation to powdered bull's or goat's horn.

The association between horns and domestication—which involves either castration or a limitation of the animal's ability to prove and exercise its sexual potency—goes beyond hoofed animals. The *OED* offers a disturbing origin for the cuckold's horns in traditions concerning the cock. The connection of the cock with the cuckold appears to derive from the practice formerly prevalent in Europe of castrating a cock and then planting its spurs on the root of the comb which had been excised. The spurs would then grow and become horns, thus announcing publicly the now reduced state of the cock.[7]

There are yet more theories about the derivation of this association of horns and cuckoldry. Natalie Zemon Davis relays what seems to be a simple verbal transposition, between 'conard' (fool) and 'cornard' (horned one, cuckold) in sixteenth-century France.[8] A persuasive and attractively neat anthropological theory, which unfortunately suffers from being geographically restricted, is advanced by Stanley Brandes in his account of metaphors of masculinity in Andalusia. In Monteros, there is a binary opposition by which men are associated with sheep and God, while women are associated with goats and the Devil. In the process of becoming a cuckold, it is clear from local expressions used that it is the wife rather than the lover who bestows the horns on the husband, and the horns (of the goat) are placed on the head of the husband, transforming him symbolically into a woman, feminizing him and robbing him of his masculinity. Suffering the consequences of his wife's uncontrolled sexuality, he becomes 'forever branded with this female symbol'.[9]

Further puzzles, however, derive not just from the particularity

[7] A reference to a practice of this type occurs in *La Regenta* by Leopoldo Alas, discussed in Ch. 5, in the description of Frígilis: 'A man who in his orgy of absurdities had reached the extreme of grafting English cockerels onto Spanish cockerels—she had seen them herself! Poor creatures, with their combs cut open and on them, held in place with pieces of rag, stumps of raw, bleeding flesh—how nauseating!' (*La Regenta* (1884–5), trans. John Rutherford (Harmondsworth, 1984), ch. 10, 209. All references will be to this edition.

[8] Natalie Zemon Davis, *Les Cultures du peuple* (originally *Society and Culture in Early Modern France* (1965)), trans. into French by M.-N. Bourguet (Paris, 1979), 161.

[9] Stanley Brandes, *Metaphors of Masculinity: Sex and Status in Andalusian Folklore* (Philadelphia, 1980), 77–8, 90–91.

of origins of the association, but also from the fact that the references to horns and sexual infidelity are not exclusively masculine. One rather strained connection of references, also offered by the *OED*, is in the idea of the horns of the moon, the pointed extremities of the moon which appear when it is in its first and last quarters. The most traditional associations of the moon, of course, are with woman, her changeability and her sexuality, all areas of perceived danger for man, and at the heart of much of the lore and concern with cuckoldry, in which if the man is weak and defeated, woman is wily and inconstant. More precisely, the horns may refer to Mercury or Venus in similar phases, and since mythology tells us that Venus was given in marriage to Jupiter's ugly and deformed son Vulcan, and subsequently went on to be unfaithful to him with Mars, Mercury, Bacchus, and Neptune, we can see that there are clear, if rather indirect, allusions to marital discomfort.[10]

Much more puzzling than the above is the fact that in Japan it is the women who wear the horns of cuckoldry. In this case, the wives' horns are horns of sexual jealousy, roused to an unbearable pitch, because of their husbands' many and frequent infidelities. Japanese women, in traditional Japanese society, have no recourse against the infidelities of their husbands. They are strictly closeted in their domestic dwellings, and the only outlet they have for reaction to their spouses' infidelity is an emotional one that takes its form in horns. It is anticipated that Japanese women will form these dreaded horns of jealousy and for this reason the traditional bridal head-dress is an enormous one, designed to cover from the public gaze (or perhaps the husband's gaze) the horror of the horns of jealousy that the woman may sprout in later time.[11]

As far as honour is concerned, the vocabulary used is simpler, less variable in its form, although the underlying systems (outlined in Chapter 4) are extremely complex, with a tendency towards binary forms and polarities. The understanding of 'honour' in the *OED* relates essentially to status, and highlights the hierarchical tendencies and touchiness about position that can arise in honour-code societies. A first meaning of the word is that of high respect,

[10] J. Lemprière, *Classical Dictionary of Proper Names Mentioned in Ancient Authors Writ Large* (1788; 3rd edn.; London, 1984).

[11] I am indebted to Dr Mitsuru Kamachi and Dr Carmen Blacker of Clare Hall, Cambridge, for this information.

esteem, or reverence, as accorded to exalted worth or rank. But more than this, and crucially so, the word 'honour' designates 'deferential admiration or approbation', which indicates pointedly the degree to which one's sense of standing in regard to others is raised by the possession of honour and lowered by its loss. Although the English terms do not declare 'honour' to be an attribute solely possessed by men, the subsidiary meaning of 'honour' (for a woman) is clearly distinct, since it is 'chastity, purity', or the 'reputation for this virtue'.

In the majority of discussions of the meaning of 'honour', three main areas can be distinguished: the idea of innate worthiness (which may then be given public reward); the idea of public reputation (which in any logical system derives, or is believed to derive, ultimately, from the first type of honour); and the idea of a separate type of honour for a woman, which is associated with shame. Barber, in his survey of the meanings of 'honour' in Renaissance England, distinguishes between honour which is linked to high rank, title, or noble birth, honour as it is concerned in the regulation of the behaviour of the gentry, and honour understood as relating to the chastity of woman. Within Barber's second category—honour concerned with the regulation of the behaviour of the gentry—there is a subdivision between a sense of external regulation (we do what is honourable because it is expected by our honourable peers) and a sense of internal regulation (we do what is honourable because of the honourableness in our character).[12] There is clearly a widespread (if perhaps naïve) belief, not that virtue is its own reward, but that there is a good match between innate honourableness and the reputation one has for it—hence the statement of Aristotle that 'honour is the prize of virtue and is paid to none but the good'.[13]

Although the idea of an inherent type of honour is relatively widespread, it is none the less much more elusive than the idea of honour as something dependent on the opinion of others. The second meaning of honour predominates in linguistic and social usage, so that the notion of inherent honour is relatively absent

[12] Charles Barber, *The Theme of Honour's Tongue: A Study of Social Attitudes in the English Drama from Shakespeare to Dryden* (Gothenburg Studies in English, 58; Gothenburg, 1985), 12–14.

[13] Quoted by F. R. Bryson, *The Point of Honor in Sixteenth-century Italy: An Aspect of the Life of the Gentleman* (New York, 1935), 2.

from literature. In its place we find honour as a quality that exists in the minds of others, and that is subject to pressures, hearsay, and a bad press. By the time we reach the Spanish theatre of the Golden Age, for example, the internal sense of honour seems to have been sent so far below the surface that it is possible to propose, as Robert Pring-Mill does, when speaking of the theatre of Lope de Vega, that honour could be understood as 'the demands made on the individual by the conventions of the society of which he is a member'.[14] In E. M. Wilson's article on family honour in Shakespeare and his predecessors and contemporaries, the understanding of honour again seems overwhelmingly concerned with externals. Thus, in the lecture on honour given by the duke to his son in *El Caballero bobo* by Guillén de Castro, honour is reputation: 'the man is honoured whom others think honourable'.[15]

While English has only one term for honour, Spanish has two: 'honor' and 'honra'. Although there is, as one would expect, a theoretical distinction between 'honor' as relating to internal honour, and 'honra' as relating to the external,[16] and although 'honra' clearly relates to what one can gain in the way of honour either by being honoured, or by inheriting honour by blood, 'honor' is also frequently used to indicate this external and visible meaning of the word.

There are further divisions in the way that honour may be alluded to, the most common being along the lines of sex. In many cultures, honour is a matter for men, an attribute that can be possessed only by men. There is a general asymmetry in the major honour-cultures: men gain honour, but women can only lose it (their honour then being understood in terms of 'shame'). This asymmetry seems to apply throughout Europe. In sixteenth-century Germany honour for men was an economic and social term which seems to have derived its sexual import from this social meaning; honour in this context was established through the guilds, those who were not members of the guilds being unable to possess honour. For woman, by contrast, honour was personal,

[14] R. D. F. Pring-Mill, introduction to *Lope de Vega (Five Plays)*, trans. Jill Booty (New York, 1961), p. ix.

[15] E. M. Wilson, 'Family Honour in the Plays of Shakespeare's Predecessors and Contemporaries', in id., *Essays and Studies* (London, 1953), 19–40 (19).

[16] Américo Castro, *De la edad conflictiva* (2nd edn.; Madrid, 1961), 66–78.

mainly dependent on her sexual behaviour.[17] This arrangement, by which honour for the woman related to her sexual chastity, is found commonly elsewhere in Europe, and is indicated in the various meanings for honour given earlier.

A particular feature of the gender division in honour was to be found in Spain, where it was possible to inherit honour from the father, but only 'shame' from the mother. That is, honour entailed the idea of racial purity; and racial impurity entering the line through a female member was felt to be especially pervasive, creating a stain on lineage. Class, like blood, was handed down through the father. Thus if a man were noble, his son would be noble, even if the mother were a villein, whereas the son of a villein father would necessarily be a villein also.[18]

In some other cultures, the types of honour relating to men and to women are designated by distinct terms. The Bedouins have the concepts of 'sharaf' and ''ird', the latter being the honour a man has that can be damaged by a woman. In the case of the Bedouins, offence deriving from a woman's behaviour is thought to affect her blood relations more directly than her husband—a convention which underlines the patriarchal and patrilineal tendencies of that society.[19] The Kabyle, meanwhile, also in North Africa, make a distinction between the right hand and the left hand, so that one type of honour, 'h'urma', is related to the left hand and the intimate feminine world, while another, 'nif', is related to the right hand, and public life.[20] Thus at a linguistic level there is recognition of the separation between worlds, an explicit codification of the divisions between the sexes, a separation which, it would appear from systems of honour to which it is attached, is imposed as a protection, just as in the paranoid-schizoid position there is a need to separate from what is thought to be dangerous and threatening.

In the nomenclature of both cuckoldry and honour there is a

[17] Lyndal Roper, 'Will and Honor: Sex, Words and Power in Augsburg Criminal Trials', *Radical History Review*, 43 (1989), 45–71 (58).

[18] Julio Caro Baroja, 'Honour and Shame: A Historical Account of Several Conflicts', trans. from Spanish R. Johnson, in J. G. Peristiany (ed.), *Honour and Shame: The Values of Mediterranean Society* (London, 1965), 81–137 (101–2).

[19] Abou A. M. Zeid, 'Honour and Shame Among the Bedouins of Egypt', in Peristiany (ed.), *Honour and Shame*, 245–59 (256–7).

[20] Pierre Bourdieu, 'The Sentiment of Honour in Kabyle Society', trans. Philip Sherrard, in Peristiany (ed.), *Honour and Shame*, 193–241 (219–21).

sense of separation, of boundaries, of internals and externals. The cuckold is one who is perceived as such, who may have in the family nest children that are not his (and are perceived as such), whose wife is not united to him since she sets up in an alternative dyad with her lover (or series of lovers). Where honour is the focus in the treatment of marital infidelity, emphasis is again placed on the external world, since honour is what others may or may not accord to us on the basis of their knowledge about us, and their knowledge can come only from externals (which may be as unreliable as hearsay, but still constitute an external view).

Situations involving cuckoldry or honour each entail, in their different ways, a process of distancing—cuckoldry to permit what is ultimately the healing power of laughter and mockery, honour because only distancing will permit us to tolerate the horror of what happens when the honour code is followed through. In neither case can we be involved in an empathic relationship with the protagonists. In both cases, however, we need to subscribe to certain basic principles of judgement about proper behaviour in order to appreciate literary works that invite us either to laugh at deceived husbands or to condone or accept the bloody action of husbands who apply the rigours of the honour code. In order to conceive of sexual infidelity as cuckoldry, we have to place ourselves outside the nest, as it were, and observe the fact that one person is made a cuckoo of by two others. In that situation, we are generally invited to laugh. If we fail to do so, then arguably the phenomenon which we are experiencing would not, in our case, be defined as cuckoldry, although it *would* be for others who remained detached in their witness and experience of it. It is for this reason that it is difficult to conceive of Othello as a cuckold, or a potential one; although we are given that impression of his state at the start—witness the exaggeration of his reaction to his wife's carelessness with her laundry—our feelings towards him are rapidly redirected, so that we have a much greater involvement and empathy, and therefore can no longer laugh at him.

When we speak of adultery, the etymology indicates that there is not this situation of separation in relation to those who view it. The *OED* definition of 'to adulter' is 'to debauch, to corrupt', with a concomitant figurative meaning of 'debase'. The word is thought to come from the combination of the Latin 'ad' and 'alter', that is, to add another element. Such an addition inevitably affects the 'purity' of the original substance, and thus it is thought that corruption takes place. In using the term 'adultery', then, we refer to a voluntary or wilful mixing of elements whereby some original element ceases to exist in its pure, or unadulterated, form. The image, therefore, is not of something broken, of some rupture of relations, or even of the breaking of a contract; the image suggests rather that the thing which contained those relations, or was bounded by that contract, is now affected by the introduction of a new element, and as a consequence can never be the same again. In works depicting cuckoldry, the marriages continue as before. There is no renunciation, nor even a sense that there has been something lost or made impure, although writers such as Chaucer may give us hints of a more complex state of mind in the participants of the drama of cuckoldry. In adultery, however, the state of marriage comes under threat of adulteration, and with it of essential extinction, the moment that the first adulterous thought enters the head of the person who will finally break the marriage vow.

The word 'adulterer' introduces an element of criminality. Whereas words associated with the cuckold carried, as we have seen, meanings of weakness and despicability, and were loaded with scorn and contempt, the use of 'adulterer' brings a new moral edge. Thus the examples in the *OED* include: from 1585 (Pilkington), 'And called him proud, advoterer, a thief and heretic'; from 1611 (Heb. 13: 5), 'Whoremongers and adulterers'; and from 1653 (Baxter), 'Hereticks, Advouterers, Church-robbers'. If we are to judge by the company that the adulterer keeps in these texts, we see that what is at issue is no longer simple human status, or reputation for honour, but blasphemy and crime. And for the first time, there is reference to the provision in the Ten Commandments which censures the act of adultery, whereas in the vocabulary associated with cuckoldry and honour there is no such recourse to moral and religious sanctions, merely to social ones, however elevated (as in the case of honour) they may seek to be.

In works of adultery, as in works of cuckoldry, there is a virtually exclusive concentration on the infidelity of wives. Part and parcel of this is the wife's anguish and guilt, or at least uncertainty of mind. The only novel in which there is a notable exception to this, in that we witness above all the guilt of the man who is husband in one relation and lover in another, is *The Fourth Night Watch* (*Den Fjerde Nattevakt*) by Falkberget.[21] But aside from the shift in gender interest constituted by the novel concentrating upon the wife, the etymology of 'adultery' itself reveals that institutions not individuals are what is to constitute the focus of concern. So although the great novels of adultery bear the names of individuals (albeit in a form that denotes their position in society by marriage) the individuals are subordinate to the activity in which they engage and the structures they disrupt. In such novels, it is essentially an institution which is adulterated (or so the etymology of the term 'adultery' informs us), not any single person; and although we have more detailed and more compassionate insight into the emotions of the wife who is caught in the drama of adultery, it is significant that neither she nor the husband to whom she is unfaithful receives recognition in the word which alludes to the state their marriage has reached through her action and/or desire. In saying that what is adulterated is the marriage, or the marriage-bed, we are including in our allusion a sense of the reduction of the position or worth of the individuals involved. In the initial establishment of the contract the woman at least has been reduced to the status of object, but at the same time the contract in its breaking, or threatened breaking, diminishes the husband, in so far as he relies on legal provisions rather than strength, attractiveness, or potency to maintain the marriage boundaries for him and his wife. This destruction of the individual is shown with particular power in the case of Karenin and his wife, and is presented both for ridicule and as an object of pathos in Dickens's *Dombey and Son* and Trollope's *He Knew He Was Right*.

We do, of course, have the terms which refer to individuals: adulterer and adulteress. What we should notice here, however, is that in so far as they are agents, they operate with regard to the institution of marriage, not to the individual husband who might be wronged by their action. Furthermore, what is stressed, as Tanner points out, is the activity, not the identity of those concerned.[22]

[21] Johan Falkberget, *Den Fjerde Nattevakt* (The Fourth Night Watch), trans. Ronald G. Popperwell (Madison, Wis., and London, 1968).

[22] *Adultery in the Novel*, 12.

The language of adultery gives some weight, at least in the more northern terms of reference to the cuckold, to historical explanations for interest in the figure of the deceived husband. But we can also see that there is a strong interest in the sexuality of the husband, in his success or otherwise as a man, and in the idea that there is some shame attached to his condition. While there is a body of opinion which tends to belief in the idea of a gender-construction based on circumstance, a large proportion of the language does seem to emphasize elements of our lives which are less likely to be susceptible to historical change, namely our sexuality, our fears, and our reactions in the face of elements of life which will not change: the original infant-and-parent dyad, the experience of the first Oedipal triangle, the fears and threats presented by our relation with the outside world, the ultimate experience of death. We can return to that original triangle and observe that here are the roots for man's rage at his experience of infidelity. The route towards identity takes the infant through the throes of emotional experience articulated by Klein. Having then come to a sense of identity, he simultaneously comes to the sense of possession (of the mother), only to find that this possession is contested. His brief perception of himself as having power over the world is thus rapidly terminated. It is because the moment of his betrayal by woman revives this difficult early experience, with the traumas of the paranoid-schizoid position resolved in the depressive position, only to be revived in the complexities of the triangular Oedipal form, that it is returned to with such insistence in literature. The representation of the deceived husband is the transferential return to the sensations of original betrayal, evoking some of the force of the original response, and because that early experience is rarely one that we fully resolve, it remains a central focus in the literature with which, in the tradition of Winnicott, we continue to play.

3
The Cuckold

THE CUCKOLD AND HIS READER

AN OLD man takes a young wife, is thoroughly in love with her, and apprehensive that she might make him a cuckold. His young lodger rapidly comes to the conclusion, with the wife, that they must take the first opportunity they can of making love, and a plot is elaborated to allow this. The old man is persuaded that a second Flood is coming; as a precaution they are all to be suspended from the roof in large tubs. This will allow the lovers their chance to be alone. A subsidiary thread presents another would-be lover, who, like the husband, is outwitted and submitted to gross insult. The second lover is thus equated in fate with the husband.

In considering this tale of a cuckold (Chaucer's *Miller's Tale*) and others in the light of Kleinian analysis, there is a major distinction to be made. Within the character of the cuckold himself, we can observe an extremely primitive level of development, characterized by splitting, denial, reaction formation, envy. As often as not, the cuckold is one who can barely tolerate the taking-in of information—that is, he is in an infantile state that appears to be even prior to the paranoid-schizoid position, in which there is at least the defensive splitting of the self to cope with information, welcome and unwelcome, from the outside world.

This primitive state of the cuckold as a character, however, contrasts sharply with what we can construe as the meaning of his portrayal in literature, and it is this meaning that I shall explore first, before turning to examples of cuckolds in Chaucer and Boccaccio.

The meaning of the cuckold entails a paradox. The cuckold in works of literature is characterized by his denial of what goes on, and his inability to cope. The reader, on the other hand, exposed to this image of denial and ineptitude, is forced to absorb it, and to come to terms with it. It is in this second part of the process that the Kleinian concept of the depressive position is involved, in that the portrayal of the cuckold enables patriarchal society, which might find examples of masculine failure unsettling, to perceive such examples and come to terms with them.

The word 'reader', in English at least, is not gender-specific. There is, however, a clear difference between the situation of a female reader or spectator who is confronted with an example of masculine failure, and that of the male reader or spectator. In the former, the reaction will be of detached observation, in so far as the female reader cannot imagine the fate of the cuckold to be her own. In the latter, the reaction will inevitably entail the perception or awareness that the fate of failure might be shared.

In tracing the ways in which the perception of the infidelity of wives in literature—whether in works of cuckoldry, literature of honour, or novels of adultery—can be related to Klein's observations about the reaction of the infant to the external world, I have in mind principally the reaction of the male reader. In particular, in my discussion of cuckoldry (and later novels of adultery) as an area of literature which might be related to the depressive position, the reader I have in mind is primarily a male reader who is obliged to accommodate images most directly relating to himself. A concept to which I shall periodically return is that of smut, but with the awareness that for the male reader faced with examples of deceived husbands in literature the concept of smut will be undermined. 'Smut' denotes the situation in which a man tells a joke to another man at the expense of a woman, this being a defensive move against the fears provoked by the woman. By engaging in male–male bonding, the two men exclude the woman, relegate her to a different social sphere, render her less threatening.[1] The bonding need not take place within the work, but can operate between character (or narrator) and reader. Appeals to a male reader's feeling of solidarity with a patriarchal text are particularly strong (on the surface) in literature of honour, where the supposed masculine reception of the tale of woman's infidelity is one where the woman is condemned and where the man's reputation is all-important.

Male–male appeals for identification and solidarity are not totally absent from novels of adultery, where texts with a strong element of the man-of-honour model will move, if briefly, into an

[1] Naomi Segal, *The Unintended Reader*, pp. xi–xii.

invitation to collusion with the masculine offended position. Thus *The Kreutzer Sonata* is narrated by the husband to a masculine listener within the text, and the only view of the erring wife is through the eyes of that necessarily biased witness.

How does the concept of smut, however, relate to cuckoldry? We could argue that the bonding and excluding function of smut is undermined, in that the image presented is that of a man discomfited, producing (possibly) amusement in the woman reader, but a possible vestigial discomfort of identification in the male reader. There remains the possibility that the male reader has the option of collusive mocking, achieved by bonding with other male characters, or by an implied bonding with a masculine narrative culture, if (as we shall see in examples from Boccaccio) woman becomes marginated in the fiction and is firmly relegated to the position of object. When such bonding is not available, the male reader is faced with the image of masculine failure, and in this he is engaged in a move towards the depressive position. The female reader, meanwhile, is not faced with this, and indeed may receive images of female independence and the pursuit of pleasure, apparently validated by the literary text. If there is a depressive accommodation to be made by the female reader, at least in the image of the cuckold, it will be in the degree to which he is emblematic of human frailty and transience, and of our common fate of ageing, failure, and ultimately death. The alternative depressive position for the woman reader, that of perceiving that the world is sadly not so topsy-turvy as the cuckold tale might indicate, is one which is there, as it were, as a shadow-interpretation, but not substantially enough to explore here.

A further constraint to be borne in mind in considering the literature of cuckoldry as related to the depressive position is the degree to which the image of failure is made safe and contained, and thus may not expose the reader (whether male or female) fully to its possible implications. I have mentioned that Tanner's view is that cuckoldry, unlike adultery, does not disturb or affect the institution of marriage.[2] His reasoning is that cuckoldry is conceived of as being separate from that institution, which does not come under threat from those who engage in wayward activity. While agreeing with Tanner that cuckoldry is seen as contained

[2] Tanner, *Adultery in the Novel*, 17.

and therefore safe, I would argue that it is not totally so, and that what happens is that a tension results because risky information (that men may fail) is presented, but has its impact defused because of the humorous presentation.

In the depressive position the unwelcome is not only tolerated, but seen as part of a totality of experience. That very act of giving recognition to what is intolerable shows that it is capable of being tolerated. The depressive position is thus a mark of maturity, and, as it is successively reached on a variety of occasions, comes to be not only a sign in itself of stability and strength, but also a position conducive to further strengthening.

In the plays and stories in which cuckolds figure, there is never the impression that the society which contains this aberration from the agreed norm of sexual fidelity is threatened by it. This obtains whether we consider the texts from Chaucer and Boccaccio examined later in this chapter, or the figures of the *commedia dell'arte*, or the figures of classical mime from which the *commedia dell'arte* characters, including the old man/cuckold are derived.[3] In the presentation of the cuckold, the rules of patriarchal behaviour are apparently broken, but the audience can, and does, laugh. And this seems to suggest that the society in which this is the cultural 'celebration' of infidelity is a robust one which can look at the worst cases of the breaking of its rules, or that the way in which that breaking of rules is presented is such that it becomes safe to engage in the risky venture of celebrating infidelity. The structure of cuckoldry literature makes it possible for the society to be confident about the essential survival and strength of its social norms, and thus it can afford to laugh when those norms are broken.

The way in which cuckoldry is presented is such as to accentuate the daring nature of the enterprise, rather than the safety of the manner in which the presentation takes place. Hence the robustness and vigour of the literature. In the work of Boccaccio, for example, the view which emerges is that infidelity is actually

[3] On the connections between mime and the *commedia dell'arte*, see Allardyce Nicoll, *Masks, Mimes and Miracles* (London, 1931), and Maurice Sand, *The History of the Harlequinade* (London, 1915). For a discussion about the way in which the Italian *commedia dell'arte* tradition is carried through into France, see Philip A. Wadsworth, *Molière and the Italian Theatrical Tradition* (York, SC, 1977).

one of those norms which comes along as part and parcel of marriage. It is shown to be the thing which happens, and must be expected to happen, when there is an unreasonable reliance on the conventional boundaries of marriage alone to provide the sexual containment of those involved in it, and a neglect of what may be the personal and human qualities needed to keep a marriage alive and intact.

On the surface, then, cuckoldry is not about a threat to marriage, or to anything else, and its expression of the ability to contemplate and accommodate failure, and to joke, constitutes a collective experience of the depressive position. Such an assertion of course raises the question of what it is that we need to accommodate, that is, of what the uncomfortable elements are which need to be contained. In discussing this, I shall suggest that there is a text and a subtext: a text which speaks of uncomfortable features of sexuality, and a subtext which speaks of other aspects of life, unavoidable and yet no more easy to tolerate. In this, I shall be following in part the lead given by Melveena McKendrick in her reconsideration of the roots of concern about honour in the Spanish Golden Age,[4] where she has argued convincingly that concern about honour is the transference of an expression of concern about racial purity, and hence about safety within Spanish society of the sixteenth and seventeenth centuries. A similar but more extensive transference of concern could be argued for the cuckold story. Its long lineage suggests that its concerns go beyond historically specific issues, and also that those concerns may not be restricted to the fidelity of a sexual partner, or to the possibility that matrimonial property will be passed on to illegitimate offspring. In particular, these are concerns about loss of potency, and the threats posed to all of us by the processes connected with ageing, which will inevitably culminate in death. In the contexts in which cuckoldry occurs, there are safe boundaries around the social aspects of most situations. This means an enabling container is provided for the apprehension of knowledge about infidelity (a risk we may not run), but also about death (a reality we are obliged to face).

The concept of the container itself, and its role in the depressive

[4] Melveena McKendrick, 'Honour/Vengeance in the Spanish *Comedia*: A Case of Mimetic Transference?', *Modern Language Review*, 79 (1984), 313–35.

position, requires some explanation, particularly in this application to the question of the role of particular models or concepts of literature. In a characteristically lucid essay,[5] Mary Douglas traces the type of understanding which has been given to the activity of joking, an activity which anthropologists have found fascinating, if not always easy of comprehension. In her discussion she delineates the essential differences between Bergson and Freud on the question of laughter, while highlighting the fact that they have common ground in their perception of the importance of control. For Bergson, she points out, humour derives from our perception of something mechanical in association with something living, and he has an investment in showing the superiority of intuition to logic, of life to mechanism—thus bringing moral judgement into his analysis, an analysis in which he perceives the joke as a chastisement. Freud, by contrast, concentrates his attention on the economy of a joke, and the linking of disparate ideas. The two see the joke as a release from control, whether social or personal. In a nicely contrastive example, Douglas spells out the difference between the two, notwithstanding their apparent similarity on the question of control: 'for Bergson the man who slips on a banana peel would be funny because he has lost his bodily control and so becomes a helpless automaton: for Freud this man would be funny because his stiff body has for two seconds moved with the swiftness of a gazelle, as if a new form of life had been hidden there'.[6]

Douglas argues that the point about a joke, whether a one-liner or extended traditional farce, is that it relies on the very thing that it subverts. That is, it expresses the potential for instability (an enlivening, exciting gesture), but its expression is only possible in a situation where there is some stability. In this respect, it is analogous to the creative role of play in the dyad formed by the infant and mother, in that, according to Winnicott's model, the mother creates the safe context for the child to play and explore. Furthermore, the presence of a safe container for the child's explorations means that there is a defusion of the potential riskiness of exploration or play (for which, in the context of society, we can substitute the saying or playing of a joke) which

[5] Mary Douglas, 'Jokes', in ead., *Implicit Meanings: Essays in Anthropology* (London and Boston, 1975), 90–114.

[6] Ibid. 95.

actually enables that process of exploration.[7] Douglas shows the fine balance between subversion and the maintenance of order which are involved in a joke. For her a joke will always have two elements, in a special relationship of subversion which is simultaneous with control: 'the juxtaposition of a control against that which is controlled, this juxtaposition being such that the latter triumphs'. What it does not do is to present a real threat to existing order; it merely 'affords opportunity for realising that an accepted pattern has no necessity'.[8] The consonance between Douglas's explanation and the mechanisms of the depressive position is evident through Winnicott's elaboration of that position, within which the mother (for whom we could read 'literature') provides a container of security in which new and potentially disruptive experience may be tolerated.

In applying to the question of cuckoldry as portrayed in patriarchal society the idea of a joke as both a subversion of stability and yet an activity which will allow that stability to remain, we can see a number of transgressions being permitted, at least in the literary imagination. As pointed out earlier, in the image of the man who has failed sexually (in that another has been successful in supplanting him), the cuckold provides the counter-example to the successful man who would otherwise embody the norms and ideals of the patriarchal society. The cuckold represents a fissure in the presentation of hegemonic masculinity in the patriarchal society that produces him, and allows the possibility of failure to be glimpsed. In so far as this occurs, and the occurrence is presented as an occasion for laughter, the cuckold and his fate are envisaged and accepted as possibilities. Although they are mocked, using the distancing that permits laughter, they are not excluded or relegated to silence and shadow, like guilty secrets. Within a depressive-position model, their presence or possibility is recognized and accepted.

The cuckold is, as it were, part of a joking statement to the effect that it is only apparently the case that society is organized

[7] See James, 'Bion's "Containing" and Winnicott's "Holding"' for the function of the mother as a containing matrix, in the sense of S. H. Foulkes: 'The matrix is the common shared ground that ultimately determines the meaning and significance of all events and upon which all communications and interpretations, verbal and nonverbal, rest' (p. 23).

[8] Douglas, 'Jokes', 96.

this way. In so far as his appearance has joking status, it provides a statement of protest against the social controls of the patriarchal society, and simultaneously provides a statement of all those things the society most fears. Yet the cuckold is part of his society, and for 'joker' we could read 'jester'. He serves the members of his society, the readers, who, by seeing him, are able to lay a ghost, or view the skeleton in their private cupboard.

The presentation of the cuckold in literature crosses two boundaries. It crosses the boundary between the public and the private, and this entails the crossing of a second boundary, between men and women. As we shall see in Chapter 4, public life in patriarchal society belongs emphatically to men, private life (often linked to what is 'sinister' or associated with the left hand) being the domain of women. Sexual life belongs in the private domain, that is, for the man, it takes place in the uncharted territory belonging to the other sex. When failure occurs, and there is a betrayal of the man which is then made public, and his example is made the butt of public ridicule, what has happened is that the shocking failure which has occurred in the private field is suddenly, ridiculously, presented to the eyes of others. Thus we have the combined spectacle of the man losing in sexual gamesmanship, the field of his defeat being the field of the woman who is the vanquisher, and the presentation of his failure to the censuring eyes of the public of his time.[9]

As we shall see in the chapter on honour, behind the relegation of woman to the private sphere there is a fear of her sensuality, and thus the desire to contain her, to render her safe, unthreatening. But as will also emerge from the discussion of honour, the establishment of very rigid demarcations between different social spheres is an activity productive of fragility rather than strength. The public enactment in literature of the sad tale of the cuckold brings that private, potentially rejected area into public view, and, although it does so in the form of joking and mockery, thereby performs an act of acceptance of what theoretically would be a resounding failure in a patriarchal society. This contemplation

[9] The symmetry may not be as absolute as the situations examined in Ch. 4. An alternative is posited by Hegel's view of society in which the man is involved in both public and family life, while woman's sphere remains family alone. See Genevieve Lloyd, *The Man of Reason: 'Male' and 'Female' in Western Philosophy* (London, 1984), 80.

and acceptance of shortcoming, and of the fact that life is not composed solely of the masculine, but of the masculine in relation with the feminine (which entails risk, dishonour, and loss of status), is an acceptance characteristic of the depressive position.

We must remember, however, that the cuckold story also conveys a message which is in accord with patriarchal norms, namely that since women are a source of life and unruliness, they are creatures to be controlled. They need to be kept safely in a position of subservience, or rather, men for their own safety need to keep them in this position. Men who fail to keep them subservient should be held up to public ridicule, because in a sense their carelessness represents a public danger. This dual perception of woman is analogous to the perception of the child who, in the depressive position, is able to perceive the mother as a single person who may be good or bad, or, more significantly, both, whereas in the paranoid-schizoid position such a bringing-together of attributes is not possible.

To understand the containing function of cuckold figures in literature, we can draw an analogy with the functions in society of carnivals and festivals of misrule, where the non-acceptable is made acceptable because it occurs in situations that are limited. In cultural expressions such as popular literature, the field of activity and expression are public, and such literature is therefore able to hold public, communal concerns, and offer them for public consumption. It therefore fulfils social functions in a more explicit way than will be the case with cultured, or non-popular literature. In it we can see how individual concerns and fears about sexuality can be converted into public ones, and the interest a society apparently takes in the sexual misfortunes of individual couples can be a way of expressing fears that are held commonly by the community. When some perception of the situation that produces the fears is ritualized, the fears are contained, because they are expressed.

The appearance of the cuckold as a cultural phenomenon is a sign of the strength of the society which is able to use him as symbol. At the same time he is the medium for a learning process, in which symbols allow us to mediate and harness experience.[10]

[10] On the Kleinian concept of symbol formation see H. Segal, 'Notes on Symbol Formation', *International Journal of Psychoanalysis*, 38 (1957), 391–7, republ. in *The Work of Hanna Segal* (New York, 1981), 49–64.

Within this symbolic function he is, of course, part of a much larger statement about the things which are not permissible in our society, and is linked to other manifestations of the world-upside-down motif characteristic of popular literature and celebrated in carnivals and festivals of misrule.[11] The cuckold thus joins the fool, the clown, the master beaten by the valet, and the man beaten and dominated by his wife (who is presumably capable also of deceiving him).

Why do we have carnivals and other festivals of misrule? They have not yet disappeared (I write this on Shrove Tuesday, when pancakes will be made in England, and Mardi Gras celebrated in fine style in more southern areas of Europe). I pose this question because it is evident that these carnivals are not simply celebratory, in the way that Christmas celebrations coinciding with the passing of the darkest period of winter are a celebration of the renewal of life, after a period of waning and death. In carnivals and celebrations of misrule as they were in earlier centuries, there is something much more emphatic, dramatic, and tinged with the violent; they are an assertion and demonstration of a power which runs counter to the orderly society.

In studies of carnival-related phenomena two main views about the function of producing images of folly or topsy-turvydom emerge, beyond the simple belief that misrule celebrations and the cultural phenomena connected with them are either just the repetition of old magical customs, the meaning of which is long lost, or are put on in order to allow the lower echelons of the populace to ape their superiors.[12] Both are consistent with Kleinian

[11] A survey of popular expressions of the World Upside Down which gives indication of the trans-European nature of this as a topos is given by Helen Grant, 'El Mundo al revés', in Dorothy M. Atkinson and Anthony H. Clarke (eds.), *Hispanic Studies in Honour of Joseph Manson* (Oxford, 1972), 119–37; ead., 'The World Upside-Down', in R. O. Jones (ed.), *Studies in Spanish Literature of the Golden Age Presented to Edward M. Wilson* (London, 1973), 102–35; ead., 'Images et gravures du monde à l'envers dans leurs relations avec la pensée et la littérature espagnoles', in Jean Lafond and Augustín Redondo (eds.), *L'Image du monde renversé et ses représentations littéraires et para-littéraires de la fin du XVIe siècle au milieu du XVIIe. Colloque international, Tours, 17–19 novembre 1977* (Paris, 1979). Ian Donaldson, *The World Upside Down* (Oxford, 1970) shows the continuity of the world upside down in English comedy. Discussion of more modern manifestations of the topos are in Giuseppe Cocchiara, *Il Mondo alla rovescia* (Turin, 1963), and Stephen M. Hart, 'Some Examples of the *Topos* of the World Upside-Down in Modern Hispanic Literature and Art', *Revista Canadiense de Estudios Hispánicos*, 12 (3) (Spring 1988), 459–72.

[12] Natalie Zemon Davis, *Les Cultures du peuple*, 165.

theory. One view is that these celebrations act as a safety-valve, thus ensuring that society retains its essential stability. It was neatly expressed by Claude de Rubys, a French lawyer of the sixteenth century: 'Il est quelque fois expedient de tolerer que le peuple face le fol et se resiouisse, de peur que en luy tenant trop grand rigueur, on ne le mette en desespoir.'[13] Underlying this idea is the conviction that if some place is made in society which will ease that society's rigours by allowing some sort of counterflow, then the basic structure of the society will be upheld. That is, a non-splitting, non-denying activity takes place, as opposed to a reaction of fear and belief that the self is threatened, which would cause the individual (or the culture) to project out unwelcome information, or deny it (provoking the counter-productive effect of rendering it more frightening, as evidenced in honour literature). A related, but slightly different view is that of Roger Caillois, who holds that in societies which may not be totally stable the apparent disorder of misrule festivals represents some factor of order.[14]

A second view is that such celebrations and festivals are a point of growth, of expression of the unexpressed, which may have consequences for the society in which they occur. This view relates to the way in which the depressive position, in its acceptance of what is not known or is difficult to tolerate, is a position of greater maturity than a state of splitting and denial or splitting and projection, and itself will lead to greater stability and growth. This second view of the purpose or function of celebrations of misrule is characterized by Bakhtin in his book on Rabelais, in which he argues that the carnival is an essential source of liberation, destruction, and renewal.[15] There is, both here and in Natalie Zemon Davis's examination of the possible function of

[13] Quoted ibid. 159.

[14] Roger Caillois, *Les Jeux et les hommes* (1958), trans. Meyer Barash as *Man, Play, and Games* (London, 1962), 89: 'The festival—the destruction of wealth accumulated over a long period, disorder transformed into order, all norms inverted by the contagious presence of masks—is climaxed by shared vertigo. It seems to be the ultimate basis for a society not too stable in other respects. It reinforces a fragile coherence, dull and not too significant, which would be difficult to maintain without this periodic explosion which draws together and integrates persons absorbed at all other times in domestic preoccupations and exclusively private concerns.'

[15] Mikhail Bakhtin, *Rabelais and his World* (1965), trans. Helen Iswolsky (Cambridge (Mass.) and London, 1968), esp. 11–24, 91–2, 256.

carnival and misrule celebration, an underlying idea that these manifestations of things gone wrong, of misrule, and of the world of topsy-turvy, show us the underside of, and the alternative to, what is static and unchanging, and thus give the society in which they occur a sense of the possibility of change, at the least, or, in extreme cases, a potential incitement to change. Thus Davis argues, for example, that in images of female disorder which occur in festivals of misrule there is actually some sense of a struggle for change.[16] I would argue, following on from Davis, that the images of female disorder are related to the image of the cuckold as a symbol of male disorder, both because he is not in the 'proper order' of masculinity himself (having lost his wife to another) and also because he is the result, or the victim, of a woman being 'out of order' in that her role in a patriarchal society is to be faithful and subservient to her man. Curiously enough, the other result of a woman being 'out of order', the birth of an illegitimate child, does not always reflect adversely on the child—at least in literature. There is even a tendency for bastards to be regarded as superior in strength and value to legitimate children. See the example of Edmund in *King Lear*, and the level of regard in the popular term 'love-child' to denote the illegitimate offspring. What we have expressed here, perhaps, is respect for the transgressing potential of those who produced the child, combined with greater esteem for romantic love (over marriages of convenience), and conceivably also the practical sense that the mongrel is often sturdier than the thoroughbred.

In seeking to understand the function of celebrations of misrule, I find myself close to the view proposed by Davis, but without the emphasis that she places on the power these festivals have to provoke real disruption and change in the societies in which they occur. There is indeed a recognition of real and threatening power, but I would see it as recognition of the power that lies within the system, rather than a power identified as capable of changing it (with the underlying hope that it might actually do so). Whether we look at the way in which literature portrays the infidelity of women, and the husbands deceived by them, or whether we look at the celebrations of festivals of misrule, we find that the societies where such celebrations occur possess or express

[16] N. Z. Davis, *Les Cultures du peuple*, 218.

two opposites: the norms and values of the societies, and forces that such norms and values are designed to contain. What characteristically occurs in the literature of cuckoldry is a containment within a comic structure, and this contrasts with the very real sense of disruption and disorder that emerges from adultery novels. This latter genre thus represents yet more fully a depressive position in relation to the deceived husband, in that the degree of grief and disruption that is permitted is greater.

There are different ways of viewing this function of the portrayal of opposites. Earlier I alluded to the possibility that our portrayal of cuckolds constitutes a laying of ghosts, a facing of things which we would rather not see. But the reason why we none the less appear to find it necessary to see these things is, in my view, that we recognize that these opposites, undesirable though they may appear to be, are actually a part of our existence. By looking at them, we are facing the worst that could apparently happen to us, and, by seeing the reverse of all those norms which we have set up for society, are arguably gaining strength from that position of worst-case knowledge acquired. Freud indicated the cost in energy and effectiveness which such denial and repression of urges entailed, and how they formed an obstacle to growth.[17] The primacy of our need to include the rejected and repressed was formulated in much more positive terms by Jung, in his idea of individuation.[18] We can also see it in the concept of the depressive position, in which strength is drawn from the ability to face the totality of experience, including those things we might wish to repress or deny. The age-old celebrations of disorder, misrule, and topsy-turvy opposites can be seen as an instinctive recognition of the deleterious effects of repression.

In her survey of festivals of misrule, Davis highlights how they are used both to censure and to punish various aberrations of behaviour in society, and at the same time to give recognition to the urges and forces which bring those aberrations about. The Abbots of Misrule, for example, in twelfth-century France, had jurisdiction over a number of activities to do with marriage.

[17] Anxiety and Instinctual Life', 87, 91–5.

[18] On individuation, and for a distinction between the attitude of Freud and Jung to the unconscious, see Alison Sinclair, 'Avant-garde Theatre and the Return to Dionysos', in Peter Collier and Judy Davies (eds.), *Modernism and the European Unconscious* (Cambridge, 1990), 246–64 (249–50).

Groups of young men acting under the rule of the Abbot caused disturbances when norms concerning marriage were not observed. This might be, for example, when wives were found not to be pregnant within a year of marriage, or when husbands were dominated by their wives, or when there was adultery. The first two examples may help us to understand the underlying preoccupations about the third. The failure to make a wife pregnant and the failure to dominate a wife could both be seen as failures in potency and virility. The first of these two forms of failure is embarrassingly evident in its material absence, undercutting in unavoidable fashion the belief held in the society of the time that the husband was not only the legal head of the household, but in a real, and arguably more important, sense, the more powerful of the two sexes in the partnership of marriage. It was expected that his power would extend to the fathering of children.[19]

Another area we can explore in order to gain understanding of the function of the cuckold in our culture as a manifestation of the depressive position is the tradition of the outsider or transgressor. Most societies have their outsiders: mavericks, outlaws, scapegoats, and marginally more integrated figures such as fools, clowns, and shamans, who are included within societies but transgress the majority of the norms of their environment. As this distinction makes clear, all these outsiders are not the same: the former are cast out or marginalized by their society, the latter either opt for margination or remain just inside the boundaries of the society. In this second case, there seems to be a sort of institutionalized permission for the outsider to remain just within the confines of the structure on the margins of which he stands. Some of the latter, like the fools (in Shakespeare and elsewhere), speak unwelcome truths from their privileged position of less than full responsibility. Others, such as clowns and shamans, act out for the society diverse transgressions of norms. Their transgression has a double function. It both affirms the norms (something has

[19] It is, of course, the case that the failure of a wife to become pregnant could be considered to be her fault, and not that of her husband. But here we are concerned not with the state of medical knowledge at the time of the customs of the Abbots of Misrule, but rather with primitive belief about the respective attributes and powers of the sexes. It is possible that there was public concern about the barrenness of the woman rather than the lack of potency of the man, but given the other 'abnormalities' mocked by the Abbots, the latter seems the much more likely target, and the more painful one in a society decidedly patriarchal.

to be there in order for the transgression to occur) and suggests that such norms are not absolute. In this inclusion, or co-existence of opposites, there is the 'both . . . and' aspect of the depressive position, in which both good and bad, both order and chaos, are perceived as real and operative, neither of them to be dismissed.

The cuckold is neither fool nor clown, in the sense of the man who deliberately stands aside from society and comments on it. He lacks the transgressive moral authority of those characters brave enough to act in a way that runs counter to the norms of their society and who, in their courageous disregard of the context, are revered for their capacity for transgression. The cuckold can lay claim to none of this. He commits no transgression, other than in those cases where his cuckoldry is consequent upon an age-inappropriate marriage. But his occurrence, his existence, though it may be only in literature, is a type of transgression, against the norms and expectations of the patriarchal society. Although he is not the transgressor (he did not commit the act of infidelity), he can be perceived as the one who first transgressed, in that he was the weak link in a system, such a weak link that the transgression was able to occur.

Part of the function of both fool and clown is to show us extremes of behaviour and reaction which we know to be contained within the bounds of our personalities and our society, but which we do not opt to express or put into action. Thus as cultural phenomena they carry, on behalf of others, a range of possibilities that the others do not dare to express but none the less have a need to own, at least in the context of the total society. In societies where shamans exist, these special transgressors of norms are held to have particular power, derived from their willingness and ability to transgress.[20]

But the most important aspect of these outsiders is that they are, by definition, a part of their society, in so far as they are defined by the ways in which they are aberrant from its norms. By being made part of the system, and institutionalized—whether as clown, fool, shaman or trickster—they are the living proof that their society is not in fact confined to its own explicit norms, nor perhaps to its own rationality.

Although the cuckold cannot be equated with one of these

[20] See e.g. Laura Makarius, 'Ritual Clowns and Symbolical Behaviour', *Diogenes*, 69 (1) (1970), 44–73.

wilful transgressors, the action of society in including him in its literature is analogous to the recognition or institutionalization of shamans and fools. In portraying him, society achieves strengthening through self-awareness, and thus a containment of its own fears. It is enabled to face its own totality. This totality contains reverses, infidelities, failures, and, at the very heart, a weakness and fragility which is for the moment ascribed to men, but can be understood as the fragility and transient nature of the human race. Thus portrayed, cuckoldry can ultimately be understood as having the power to confront us with our own transience.

By being distanced from the cuckold, yet still able to recognize his fate as potentially ours, we are able to view those features of his situation which might connect, rather painfully, with our own—including fears of the consequences of ageing, and fears in other areas (for example, the fear of the power of women) which ageing provokes and intensifies. The depressive position exemplified in the literary portrayal of cuckoldry operates, then, on these two levels: the reader is faced with an image of simple sexual betrayal (to which we may or may not be exposed in adult life, but which will perforce have occurred at the infant stage of development), and of the process of ageing and death, to which we are all subject. The following discussion of major cuckold figures, drawn from Chaucer and Boccaccio, will explore how the process of accommodation characteristic of the depressive position takes place in the reader, while at the level of the cuckold character himself we are faced with the most primitive and infantile splitting, denial, and phantasy. Our exposure to the primary disaster of infidelity which has overtaken the protagonists makes us aware of elements in the action—in particular, lack of potency and youth—which have rendered the cuckolds' marriages inappropriate, but which also have a wider significance. We may escape cuckoldry, but we cannot escape ageing. Faced with the fictional inevitability of the one, we encounter the real inevitability of the other, tamed and made more acceptable through the medium of laughter.

THE CANTERBURY TALES

Both Boccaccio and Chaucer draw, in differing degrees, on the tradition of the fabliaux, in which duping, deceit, and sexual misadventures figure prominently,[21] but both place their stories in a frame which itself gives meaning to the short, earthy narratives. In Per Nykrog's analysis of the fabliaux he classes 106 of the 147 themes as erotic, and indicates a triangular relationship in 63 out of 160 stories. That the triangle figures prominently is not all: the outcome has a tendency to favour lovers rather than husbands. Thus of 36 triangles analysed by Nykrog, 24 had an outcome favourable to the lover, and in 12 the husband was happy (which has implications for his status and level of awareness in the tale, in that he is habitually portrayed as stupidly rather than deservedly happy). Although the description of a fabliau as a tale in which wives outwit husbands does not apply globally to all the stories concerned, the impression that it is such is none the less easy to gain. This is shown by a definition given in the *Disciplina clericalis*, where a fabliau is defined simply as 'un conte à triangle dans lequel la femme se tire d'un embarras par une ruse'.[22]

The figure of the cuckold, important if not central in the fabliaux, appears as a prominent motif in Boccaccio's *Decameron* (1350) and Chaucer's *Canterbury Tales* (1387–). The first is a carefully structured series of tales supposedly told by a group of young high-born people who have fled the city of Florence because of the threat of the Black Death. The second, never completed, is a collection of tales by an assorted group of travellers making their way to Canterbury on a spring pilgrimage. Both can be understood as responses to the constraints of life and death, but whereas in Chaucer the response takes place on the level of individual stories, in Boccaccio it is also firmly expressed in the overall structure of the work.

There are two lengthy accounts of the fate of the cuckold in *The Canterbury Tales*. In addition, various narrators in the work add their own comments and reactions to the institution of marriage and its hazards, and these influence the way we respond to the content of individual tales. The settings of *The Canterbury Tales* are varied, the characters who act as narrators coming from across the whole class spectrum.[23] This results not only in a variety of

21 For Chaucer's awareness of the fabliaux see D. S. Brewer, 'The Fabliaux', in Beryl Rowland (ed.), *Companion to Chaucer Studies* (London, 1968), 247–67; Charles Muscatine, *Chaucer and the French Tradition* (Berkeley, Calif., 1957, 6th impr. 1969).

22 Per Nykrog, *Les Fabliaux* (Copenhagen, 1957, repr. Geneva, 1973), 55–62.

23 See Jill Mann, *Chaucer and Medieval Estates Satire: The Literature of Social Classes and the General Prologue of the Canterbury Tales* (Cambridge, 1973).

content and approach in the narrative, but also—and much more entertainingly—in a complex dynamic of personal and contextual reactions by the characters to one another's tales. (The intensity derived from class and status is not so prominent among the more united social group of the storytellers in *The Decameron*.)

'The Miller's Tale' is the first of the major cuckoldry narratives in *The Canterbury Tales*. Tales of cuckoldry have a habit of paying little attention to the one who is the cuckold: he is important functionally (what is the point of the tale of infidelity if there is not a character in relation to whom the infidelity occurs?), but he is lacking in importance both to the lovers and to the spectators/audience. This lack of attention reinforces his weakness as character, but is arguably also a way of softening the message of the cuckold to the reader, who is not overly exposed to him. So with the husband of 'The Miller's Tale'. He is introduced in three brief lines:

> Whilom ther was dwellynge at Oxenford
> A riche gnof, that gestes heeld to bord,
> And of his craft he was a carpenter.[24]

and is then forgotten, or set aside, while the attractions of the lover are set out at length. The husband thus enters, in real terms, after the lover, with the disadvantage of less attention from the poet. Furthermore, when he does appear in greater detail, he is exposed in all his vulnerability. He has had the simplicity to deny his age by falling in love with, and taking to wife a girl who is only 18. In this respect we can see him engaged in denial of the realities. His split, however, does entail some apprehension of what might occur, that is, that he might lose her, and he engages in some of the insecurities of the man of honour. Not only is he in love; he is already jealous and apprehensive:

> Jalous he was, and heeld hire narwe in cage,
> For she was wylde and yong, and he was old
> And demed hymself been lik a cokewold. (68)

His gullibility is picked on by his narrator. He is reprimanded (and thus lodged in a position of inferiority) by the Miller, who comments that he should have known better than to pick a young

[24] Geoffrey Chaucer, *The Canterbury Tales* (1387–), *The Riverside Chaucer*, ed. Larry D. Benson (Oxford, 1987), 68. Subsequent page references are to this edition and are given in the text.

wife, and must now put up with the consequences. Thus from the outset it is emphasized that the cuckold has set himself up for what is coming to him by doing something inappropriate to his age (however common the marriages of old men to young women might have been in reality, and whatever the 'sensible' reasons of law, inheritance, and economics might have been for such age-disparate matches).

Chaucer's handling of the husband in the early sections of the text is designed to emphasize his weakness, his status as one who can be dismissed. He is a protagonist who has no right, it would appear, to be one. The dynamics of the text and the atheatrical handling of the 'entry' into the poem, signal the advent of a husband destined to be overlooked and disappointed, one who cannot hope to hold the attention of the reader (let alone that of his wife). This neatly emphasizes his status as a figure to be dismissed, but also softens his impact on the reader, who is enticed into the far more acceptable phantasies provoked by the plotting of the lovers to have their affair. Scarcely has the husband been rebuked by the narrator for his inappropriate action (he should have known better than to marry a young wife) than he is passed over yet again, for the detailed and enticing description of his young wife, Alisoun. She is delicate, a wench, skittish, coquettish, a 'peach' (83), deftly characterized by Muscatine as a 'small-town heroine', with her plucked brows and rather daring dress.[25]

The husband (for whom, let it be noted, we still have no name) is further pre-empted and passed over for the image of the second (would-be) lover, Absolon, the parish clerk, also prey to Alisoun's charms, and not lacking in charms himself. As with the first lover, Nicholas, we are given a detailed account of his attractions, his talents, and his desire for the young wife of the carpenter. Indeed, the reader at this stage is moved either to substitute Nicholas as some sort of husband into a mental triangle in which he helps his 'wife' to outwit a lover, or to regard Absolon, in the role of spurned lover which he now adopts, as a parallel to the original husband, as the outer, rejected corner of the triangle of infidelity.[26]

[25] Muscatine, *Chaucer and the French Tradition*, 229.

[26] Compare this with the observation of a triangle in Spain by J. Pitt-Rivers, related in 'Honour and Social Status', in Peristiany (ed.), *Honour and Shame* 62–3, commenting on the upper-class attitude to cuckoldry in Spain: 'A man's

Absolon does effectively here take the place of the husband as the one to be tricked, fooled, and jilted by the carefree couple of Nicholas and Alisoun (and thus forms a shadow cuckold-figure). What we actually see in the course of this tale is the direct discomfiture and spurning of Absolon; there is little concentration upon the cuckolding of Alisoun's husband. Thus the unfortunate husband is trebly passed over—by his wife for one lover, by his wife and lover over another would-be lover, and by the reader, who is hard put to it to retain a sense of this man whose emotions and needs are barely outlined, and certainly not presented as worthy of consideration. An alternative view of the role of Absolon in the plot is that his submission to the grosser indignity of those outwitted by Nicholas and Alisoun detracts from the discomfiture of the husband, and thus the husband's discomfiture is mitigated. Absolon, this substitute husband, also has some of the essential qualities of the cuckold, notably lack of awareness. There is an air of contentment, of complacency, an anticipation of consumption in him that initially fit with the character of the unaware husband rather than with the lover who is to act as predator. Even when his nature as predator is revealed, there is a luxuriance of phantasy:

> To looke on hire hym thoughte a myrie lyf,
> She was so propre and sweet and likerous.
> I daw wel seyn, if she hadde been a mous,
> And he a cat, he wolde hire hente anone. (70)

This contrasts with the directness of Nicholas, who has already upstaged him and whose speech and actions clearly belong to the real world, not a phantasy-world:

> And prively he caughte hire by the queynte,
> And seyde, 'Ywis, but if ich have my wille,
> For deerne love of thee, lemman, I spille.'

sexual honour is attained not only through the purity of his womenfolk but through his commitment to any other woman in whom he has invested his pride. The infidelity of his mistress leaves him a cuckold also. Thus on one occasion a lady of the upper classes whom gossip had credited with a clandestine lover over a number of years transferred her favours to a fresh admirer. Shortly afterwards her abandoned lover was seen lunching with her husband and the comment was made: "There go the two cuckolds!" The abandoned lover was equated with the infelicitous husband.'

> And heeld hire hard by the haunchebones,
> And seyde, 'Lemman, love me al atones,
> Or I wol dyen, also God me save!' (69)

(an impatience to be echoed by Damian in 'The Merchant's Tale'). The device thought up by Nicholas the lover to deceive John the husband echoes the latter's isolation, and relegates him to infancy through the practical arrangements. Nicholas has told of a flood to come, and to save themselves from the flood, the three are to be suspended from the eaves of the roof in large tubs or kneading-troughs, the plot of the lovers being to leave John to sleep soundly in his tub all night while they descend to the bedroom. John is thus relegated to a place away from the action, and left swinging in his tub, rather like a baby in its cradle being left to sleep by parents eager to be about other business. The image immediately conjured up is of a medieval cradle placed at the foot of the parental bed and equipped with a cord to allow the parents to rock it from a comfortable distance. A suggestion of the husband's infantility and limited development is contained in that image of the cradle: the original Oedipal situation is sketched out, and his eager assumption of his role in it is laid open for all to see.

The husband's name is not revealed until after he has been deceived, thus creating an equation between the fact of being a husband and that of being a cuckold: he is allowed no identifying reality by name until he has fulfilled his destiny of cuckold. This ignominy is counterbalanced by an alternative association, since he is linked by his profession of carpenter to Joseph, first of cuckolds and much passed-over (at least in respect of his feelings) in the story of the Holy Family. We are thus told that he is of no importance, and yet of supreme symbolic importance; a man not worthy of regard, and yet associated with a man, who, through the Bible story, has become the patron saint of fathers.

John the husband disappears from view, into his tub, into his infantile position. His naïvety, his gullibility are truly amazing, and are such as to suggest that what he feels bears a relation to the fascination so frequently felt by husbands for lovers in adulterous triangles in the novel. However, the reader is yet again diverted from contemplation of the frailty of the husband, and is drawn into the more accessible thrills of Nicholas's ingenious plot to gain leisurely access to Alisoun, and then into the intertwining of this plot with the efforts of the love-lorn and ever more pathetic Absolon. The latter takes John's place in the plot, and thus tempers for the reader the impact of the cuckold's disgrace, rendering it easier to contemplate. The sexual slighting of Absolon is unabashedly coarse and concrete. But while we are so absorbed in the tangible and uncomfortable distress of Absolon, we are liable, or rather we are able, in company with the other characters in the tale, to overlook the man who is in fact cuckolded: the presentation of him as 'silly', impotent, without rights, is so effective that we do not even allow him the diminished status he properly has in the domestic drama.

In so far as we dismiss the cuckold, or are encouraged to dismiss him, we deny this real evidence of failure. We are simultaneously apprised of the reasons for which he is to be ridiculed—his denial of his old age, and his lack of awareness of what goes on around him—and we are permitted, by that process of ridicule, to contemplate his fate. Two features counterbalance our act either of dismissal or ridicule. John is not unlikeable, and his fate not entirely separate from our own. In this playing-out of the story of failed masculinity we are apprised very firmly of the failure, but allowed to escape it through the process of comedy; meanwhile a substratum of sympathy and identification maintains in us a capacity, associated with the depressive position, of recognizing that we too may be betrayed, if not by wives, then certainly by death. John is a man prey to fear, but he shares the reader's fate in so far as it is a fear of death rather than of sexual betrayal. His first thought on the feigned indisposition of Nicholas is indeed of death (what if Nicholas should die?) and the fear he expresses underlines the possible function of the cuckold as the container for displaced fears not just in regard to potency, but also in regard to the ultimate loss of potency in death. The whole ploy invented by Nicholas, though turning on the fear of death, is distanced for us in that it is, of course, only the 'silly' husband who fears death by the flood. The flood itself is only a ploy by Nicholas, but in its symbolism it touches on all that is to be feared in woman; her sexuality, her life, and the urges that are liable to overtake and 'drown' us given half a chance.

'The Merchant's Tale' opens with a declaration of the inappropriateness of the husband, signalling him as unfit for wedlock, since he is over 60 (the age declared by Andreas Capellanus to be a bar for men as lovers[27]). He is unfit, but suddenly (and inappropriately), denying his age, or in reaction-formation to it, he is overcome by his urge to wed. January feels that he may well have missed out, though this does not apply to physical pleasure (of which he has apparently had plenty), only to marriage. Ageing, he seeks the 'pleasure' that otherwise he may miss. As in the case of John, the more ridiculous the husband appears, as a man given to infantile denial, the greater his accessibility to the reader, since his representation is tempered in its impact by the comforting mediation of comic distance. The pleasure of marriage itself is uncertain, at least to the onlooker, and there is more than a little idealization in January's vision of his union, which he (in an act of hypocrisy or self-deception?) envisages as spiritual bliss. The match does, however, contain that particular pleasure offered by the young woman to the old man—the illicit pleasure of getting a tender young morsel when you are an experienced eater of many years. (In this, as frequently in the literature of both cuckoldry and honour, there is a tacit appeal to the male reader, who is likely to be titillated and engaged in collusive phantasy, rather than to a female reader, whose construing of January's marriage plans may be quite other.) The Merchant as narrator comments, presumably with tongue in cheek (given the tale he is to unfold), that this is well done:

> To take a wyf it is a glorious thyng,
> And namely whan a man is oold and hoor; (154)

The Merchant narrator, with his sardonic commentary (based no doubt on his own bitter experience of a marriage of two months), thus places the reader at a distance from the cuckold-to-be. At the same time, given that his statement is a general one, he faces us with the unpalatable reality that we might, like January, also be exposed to the sneers of the young when in our old age. It is also the Merchant narrator, not the husband, who brings in the idea of inheritance, and perhaps here we have Chaucer's insight into what really motivates us in our reaction to the waning of our sexuality: it is the passing of time, and the sense of our ageing,

[27] Andreas Capellanus, *The Art of Courtly Love*, trans. J. J. Parry (New York, 1969), 32: 'Age is a bar, because after the sixtieth year a man and the fiftieth in a woman, although one may have intercourse his passion cannot develop into love.'

as opposed to what is publicly believed and affirmed in social structures (concern with family and the passing-on of wealth). It is so clearly stated here that we might even speculate that it is concern with ageing and not sexual misdemeanour that is at the root of patriarchal belief about the unacceptability of cuckoldry, and that provides the impulse for preoccupations about inheritance so often adduced as the reason for the belief. That is, our concern with family and our name, and a desire that they should ensure our continuation, are our answer to what is unanswerable in our existence: the fact that we age and die. Faced with death, we deny it, or seek a way around it.

Jill Mann highlights the emphatic way in which Chaucer's own attitude emerges from his treatment of narrative voices. In relation to *Troilus and Criseyde* she indicates the significance of his avowal of his own gender. He 'comes out', one might say, increasing rather decreasing the power of his statement. As Mann convincingly argues, 'he acknowledges his own masculinity, rather than dissolving it in the impersonal authority of the invisible author, and deflects the moral of his story on to the sex of which he can speak with personal authority'.[28]

The Merchant also rehearses the idealized arguments for marriage that may be present in his character's head. The status of the married man is presented as stable, and contrasts with the brittle one of the bachelor. As Mann comments, there is more than a little tension, in the Merchant's speech, between innocence and experience, and this colours the intention and meaning of what he says.[29] There is thus an irony between this and the 'man's view' of marriage (that of the naïve January) as contained within the tale. The goal of permanence and stability underlying January's decision signals not sexual appetite but concern about age. Though the concern is appropriate and realistic, January is none the less naïve in the form of his expectations. This married state to which he aspires is to be crowned by an obedient wife (the service-oriented view of the spouse is enough to tempt any woman to rebel). The counter-argument from Theophrastus, with its warning that any husband is likely to be cuckolded, is stated but

[28] Jill Mann, *Geoffrey Chaucer* (London, 1991), 19.

[29] Ibid. 58–64, has a detailed and subtle discussion of the varying masculine attitudes conveyed between author, narrator, and content of this tale.

dismissed. Sobering information is thus presented for us to take in, but in the reassuring early stages of the depressive position, does not remain for long enough to disturb us, and we are again diverted, with the eulogy of marriage. Retrospectively we are told that the eulogy of marriage, and the justification of the wedded state in terms of the service and comfort a man can expect to derive from it, comes from January, not the Merchant, who, given his bitter introductory remarks about his own marriage of two months, may be savouring the irony of his character's gullibility. The reassuring narrative frame is thus itself finally undercut, and the reader is obliged not just to face January's disaster but to absorb the uncertainty of the containing experience itself. The double exposure thus forces the reader to an inclusion and admission of what is uncomfortable at a variety of levels, the safety of splitting and denial being only briefly essayed, in the comic outer trappings of the husband-protagonist.

This double reading continues, ever more pronounced, when we read further about marriage as seen by the husband, and a view emerges which proclaims his gullibility and self-centredness. The reasons he gives to his friends for marrying constitute a painful exposure of naïvety or wilful self-deception. He seeks a young wife in particular not so much for her attractions (which are presumably greater, except to those who prefer older women) as for her malleability, and because an attractive wife is less likely to provoke him to adultery. This emphasis on the liveliness of his own sexual reactions (phantasy mixed with denial) is combined with a quick, and in the circumstances contradictory, canter through St Paul's reluctant arguments in favour of the married state (a reassuring diversion). He is displayed as a man rendered vulnerable by his extreme and untimely desire to enter marriage, his justifications for taking a young (and presumably sexually desirable) mate all being linked to his self-importance and vanity.

This phantasy-land of January, combined with the topos of the old man, speaks of his emotional and irrational investment in this act, and, in so far as we are prepared to recognize his state as eventually our own, invites us to feel some sympathy towards him. He is weak, but also vulnerable to phantasy, and this vulnerability, of which we can also have a part, is our link with him as readers. The cuckold is not totally distanced from us, even by the measured story-telling of Chaucer. But Chaucer keeps his example of failure safe for the reader by moving the narrative between prompts to identification and prompts to distance and ridicule, the latter conveyed, for example, in January's foolish calculations as to whether married bliss might rob him of his right to eternal bliss.

What happens when we are given the account of January's self-conscious and clumsy fumblings on his wedding night and later is similarly a complex affair in terms of the reader's relationship with the text. Initially, the reader is invited to replace regard for the husband with concern for, and interest in, the longings of May and her youthful suitor, Damian. That is, we are moved towards a standpoint of censure on any relations which are not age-appropriate. This denial of the realities of age is arguably comparable with the denial of age which has taken place in January himself, and as we briefly deny him, we move away from the mature depressive approach which obliges us to retain a view of life that contains both youth and age. The detail with which Chaucer shows his aged husband preparing for the exertions of the wedding night seems designed to repel those who assign the right to sexual pleasures to the young alone, and to prolong that state of denial in both characters and reader. Yet it is possible to read this section from a different point of view: that of compassion which also takes in our recognition of our own ageing to come. This, however, we can only achieve by adopting an attitude of distance from the main players of the moment, the youthful lovers, or at least sufficient distance to hold both them and the husband in view.

Another way in which Chaucer (as Boccaccio) introduces the security of the depressive position is to locate the reader firmly outside the narrative by engaging in the recognition of play with the generic possibilities of the narrative. In so far as the reader is thus drawn into the process of art, he is kept safe from the truths of a reality that might be his. We are led from the simple, primitive reactions of either identification or denial to a level of interaction with the text that allows us to perceive complexity without the need for either of these—that is, the depressive position. This is a model generally applicable to the texts under discussion, but particularly pertinent to the idea of intertextual play. While the artist engages in it, and the reader recognizes it for what it is, safety at a distance is achieved, even though moments within the play may strike uncomfortable chords. In Chaucer, the mode of play is with the fabliaux,[30] a mode from which he is departing, by the amount of detail he gives. Fabliaux pay scant attention to the detailed emotional state of the man who is to be relegated, by virtue of the plot, to the role of the cuckold; however, they do include all such practical detail as may be necessary to the appreciation of the plot.[31] The level of detail given us in Chaucer allows us the aesthetic view of intertextuality, in that its provision departs from practice in the model of the fabliaux. It also pushes us towards the less tolerable edges of the depressive position, as it denies us the escape into literary phantasy. As the text draws on, with details of bristly chins, aphrodisiacs, and anticipatory panic, the invitation to denial and rejection in the reader is strong. As blindness falls on January, so he is eclipsed from the main action. Set on one side first by immediate evocation of scorn, disgust, and ridicule, and then by our discomfort at seeing what we may become, he is finally distanced by the narrator as he becomes an evident non-participator, even a non-starter in the stakes of sexual love, and we as readers are released from the difficulties of the depressive position. Denial is uppermost in the lysis of the tale, which unfolds with the intervention of the gods. Pluto decides to restore January's sight to him at the very moment of his wife's infidelity, and the narrative threatens briefly to depart from the norm of the cuckold who is what he is with greater force and ridicule (or poignancy, depending on your point of view), because of his ignorance.[32] But the stereotypical gullible husband of the fabliaux is finally reaffirmed by May's rapid speech-work, in which she persuades her old spouse of the most unlikely visual misperceptions.

The naming of characters is a further safe way in which the story is enabled to carry a message of ageing and death. 'January', the chill, sterile month of mid-winter, is coupled with 'May', the

[30] See Brewer, 'The Fabliaux'; Muscatine, *Chaucer and the French Tradition*; Thomas D. Cooke, *The Old French and Chaucerian Fabliaux: A Study of their Comic Climax* (Columbia, SC, and London, 1978).

[31] Muscatine, *Chaucer and the French Tradition*, 60.

[32] See Mann, *Geoffrey Chaucer*, 64–7, for discussion of Pluto's view and the response by Proserpina in which Pluto reveals the anti-feminism of the rapist, but Proserpina henpecks him, demonstrating—as indeed the tale as a whole does—that 'shrewishness is both the inevitable response to male aggression and its proper punishment'.

month of full spring. Thus age is coupled with youth. But there are further layers of meaning. January normally signifies for us the depths of the winter, the dead heart of the old year, which must be superseded by the vitality of the new one. The name derives from the god Janus of Roman mythology, the two-faced god of beginnings or transitions, and alludes to the process concomitant upon any ending: with the death of the old comes the birth of the new. What is new, however, is not a rejuvenated form of the old; new life comes to supersede the old. January, in Chaucer's version, is old, hoary, on the way out, and pathetic in his attempts to participate in the activities of youth, assisted by a young and potentially vigorous partner. Like Janus, January is positioned at the transition, but is not the one who himself moves forward.

May, meanwhile, is linked with both death and women, in an association which points to the dangers of the latter. Thus the products of May were thought to have slender chances of survival. May kittens, for example, were thought unlucky in English superstition, and were drowned. Like May-born babies, they were thought to be weak and unlikely to grow into strong, mouse-catching cats.[33] In the French folkloric context we also find the tradition or warning that the husband who marries in May will be kept in harness by his bride for the rest of his life.[34] The month of May was also associated with the Virgin Mary, and hence was a special month for women. Thus the time was linked with a woman whose sexuality is denied by Catholic doctrine but who, as we saw in the Miller's tale, made Joseph into a holy cuckold by her acquiescence to divine will.

One may ask whether the general implications of Chaucer's treatment of old age and its associated problems in these two tales are as great as I am suggesting, namely whether his portrayal of the declining powers of men (specifically) does allude to the common fate of the two sexes, and their shared destiny of increasing age and declining potency. The alternative would seem to be that he is indeed showing a more particular concern with men

[33] E. Radford and M. A. Radford, *Encyclopedia of Superstitions* (1948), ed. and rev. Christina Hole (1961, 3rd impr. London, 1969), 229.

[34] For further detailed references on traditions associated with May, see Natalie Zemon Davis, 'The Reasons of Misrule: Youth Groups and Charivaris in 16th-century France', *Past and Present*, 50 (Feb. 1971), 41–75 (45). This is an earlier but more complete version of ch. 4 of *Les Cultures du peuple*.

and their potency, and the power and effect women may have on it. The Wife of Bath's robust attitude to men, for example, goes at least as far as the events of the two tales I have discussed in raising doubts about the power and dignity of men in relation to their womenfolk. Men do not come out of *The Canterbury Tales* with flying colours. Brewer, for example, has commented on the lack of dominating father-figures in Chaucer, and Spearing has added that what is missing is something more subtle still—not just fathers, but fathers who are wise and benevolent, in the way that a patriarchal age might have expected.[35]

The concern of Brewer and Spearing about the attributes portrayed in the sexes in Chaucer, or, more specifically, with the attributes lacking in the portrayal of men in *The Canterbury Tales*, contributes to the impression that the work presents particular lines of sexual balance and division, and expresses particular views about the role and nature of men and women. Viewed in this light, the tales are indeed short on strong fathers or husbands, or strong and benevolent old men, and they are also peopled with (meek Griselda excepted) robust, rebellious, and vivacious women, not all of them morally attractive, but most of them possessed of a definite level of animal vitality. We might conclude that Chaucer thus bravely portrays the threat to man that is posed by women. The sharpness of the threat is bracing, but does not entail splitting and denial: rather the portrayal of that threat is included in a complex and sobering whole.

If we respread, as it were, the figures and attributes on the canvas, the potential complexities of reading the message of that sobering whole emerge. At every turn, the appeal to compassion presented by the portrayal of age is balanced by the appeal to excitement contained in the portrayal of youth. There is slowness, failing potency in January, and there is the speed and urgency of Damian. One is measured against the other, at least in the first instance. January seems the older and the weaker for being contrasted with his youthful rival. If we connect at any level with the defeated husbands and fathers, we are indeed confronted with our own future failing power. More than this, *The Canterbury*

[35] D. S. Brewer, *Chaucer and his World* (London, 1978), 43, and Anthony C. Spearing, 'Chaucerian Authority and Inheritance', Piero Boitani and Anna Torti (eds.), *Literature in 14th-century England* (The J. A. W. Bennett Memorial Lectures; Perugia, 1981–2) (Cambridge, 1983), 185.

Tales also contains general and unpalatable reminders of old age. As the Reeve reiterates in his prologue, 'for thogh oure myght be goon, |Our wyl desireth folie evere in oon.|For what we may nat doon, than wol we speke;|Yet in oure asshen olde is fyr yreke' (77). Age is inevitable, but it neither brings wisdom nor diminishes desire.

Sharp contrasts, as between January and Damian, emphasize the bitterness of these truths to be lived with. But other, lateral comparisons may be drawn. Janet Boothman, for example, contrasting John and January (and finding January the more consistently lustful, John finally the more aware) argues that, if they are taken together, they convey a view about societal order, as though they were moral object-lessons.[36] A different point to be made from the same contrast is that John shows a marginally better accommodation to his fate, and in so far as there is a generality about that fate (the generality of ageing and decline), he shows an advance on January in that he moves slightly closer towards a depressive accommodation to reality.

A further point regarding depressive accommodation emerges from the tales, and from their polarized contrasts. As mentioned above, if we connect with the defeated husbands and fathers, we are confronting our own decline. But the opposite pole is also contained in the tales—the pole of life and vigour. The overthrow of old men, and all they stand for, is not simply due to their failing powers: it implies the triumph of youth. This fact may be applied to the fate of man, or rather Man. The cuckold represents our inevitable dwindling and stupidity, but he is also part of a vital pattern in which new life comes, repeatedly, to supplant the old. This is the ultimate 'seasonal message' which is contained in the paradoxical figures of January and May. For it to emerge we have to read the text on a general level, in which life is perceived as self-renewing, rather than on a particular one, where individuals necessarily age and reach death—the ultimate betrayal, perhaps, for which all others might be regarded as preparation.

The depressive position is characterized by the ability to receive

[36] Janet Boothman, '"Who hath no wyf, he is no cokewold": A Study of John and January in Chaucer's Miller's and Merchant's Tales', *Thoth*, 4 (1963), 3–14: 'Both men with their inappropriate marriages violate an existing societal order, and their unsanctimoniously sensual motives evidence an almost utter disregard for the virtue of, if not sexual chastity, at least sexual propriety and moderation' (p. 12).

and incorporate difference and conflict. It is a position of balance, humour, and wry and sober acceptance. Chaucer demonstrates this in the texture of the tales discussed, while not making his cuckolds themselves over-complex.

THE DECAMERON

On reading Boccaccio's *Decameron*, one is struck by the images of resourcefulness, vitality, and humour that crowd the tales. If there are those that are duped, there are those who are clever enough to dupe them. The tales are full of tricks, deceits, strategies. In the context of our discussion of the cuckold, one of the interests of the *Decameron* is that ingenuity and stupidity are distributed without discrimination between the sexes, and rewards characteristically go to those who earn them by their sense, foresight, and good use of their natural gifts, whichever their sex. Thus some men are shown as cuckolds, but others escape that fate; women are able to get their way, sexually or otherwise, some of the time, and so are men; revenge is possible for both men and women for sexual and other slights, though not in all circumstances. In the portrayal of situations in which some win and some lose (their money, their spouse, their reputation), due respect is paid to those who are both intelligent and able to find appropriate action, whether on their own initiative or in reaction to the trickery or misbehaviour of others.

Boccaccio moves us yet more decisively into the urbane and civilized practice of art. In this, the clearly delineated artistic and sculptured container provided by the narrative frame of the *Decameron* allows more extremes of experience to be incorporated. The text thus moves between the outer limits of simple sexual betrayal within the stories and the ultimate betrayal of life by the plague that establishes and dominates the narrative frame. The way in which it exemplifies the depressive position derives as much from the dynamic between the stories, and between the stories and the frame, as from the dynamic within the stories themselves.

What emerges most strongly from the *Decameron* is a sense of a natural order, which lays down its own contract and rules, and which may or may not fit with the order, contract, and rules of a patriarchal society, which lodges power with men and subordinates women. Neither contract—natural or patriarchal—is given final predominance in the work, though some sense of the intentions of the author about balance can be derived from elements related to the context and the overall structure.

Given the formality of the *Decameron*, we might be led to believe that a formalized treatment of the cuckold would emerge. The strength of the containing frame, however, permits considerable variation. The collection conveys the general precept that a man who becomes a cuckold deserves his fate, because he has, in his behaviour in marriage, done something inappropriate to nature. From this it follows that not all men are destined to be cuckolds (this runs counter to the advice offered to Chaucer's January that 'It's he that has no wife who is no cuckold', with its implication that whoever does have one will be a cuckold), and that, of those who technically become cuckolds, in that their wives are unfaithful to them, not all remain in that state, and in this way perhaps do not qualify for the epithet. This is because the concept of the cuckold, I think, necessarily includes not only the fact that the man allows it to happen to him, or so behaves that it is likely to happen to him, but also that he is inadequately equipped to deal with the situation once it has arisen.

There is a mixture in this formula of what is there by right, and what is earned. The stories of the *Decameron* suggest that there is a natural right to, or at least a natural expectation of, sexual pleasure for both sexes, and that just as husbands can expect to get it from their wives, so wives should also be considered as creatures who can expect to get it from their husbands (though other rights for women, such as that of withholding their consent to sexual intercourse, or marriage, do not seem to be promoted). Thus in the natural order, if husbands enter a sexual contract without being fully able to honour its requirements (i.e. provide those things of which wives will have natural expectations), then they cannot expect the fidelity which they may—given the order of patriarchal society—consider their right. There is some sort of *quid pro quo* in this: I will give you fidelity if you will give me satisfaction, or rather, if you satisfy me, you will have earned the right to fidelity. Now the idea of a bargain in which the wife offers fidelity for the price of satisfaction is at odds with the patriarchal view of the wife as a mere possession, a subordinate creature.

Possessions, by their very nature, cannot have rights. Thus, underlying the explicit patriarchal code of the society is a natural subcode which accords sexual rights to women, or at least recognizes women's expectations in this regard. When that subcode is infringed, a cuckold is produced, and he gets no sympathy.

Thus, implicit in the idea that a man might become a cuckold because he has failed to satisfy his wife sexually (and this is the burden of many of the tales of the *Decameron*) is a negation of the patriarchal concept of marriage, by which man is automatically the dominant partner and woman his subordinate. Therefore, cuckoldry, when it occurs, is not necessarily the factor which upsets the power relationship within the couple, but is itself caused by an imbalance further back in the relationship, whereby the man did not earn his rights to the fidelity marriage might seem to grant him.

We are thus faced with a challenge to the patriarchal structure—which asserts the husband's dominance—at the point where that structure needs to be justified. Rights—to property, to good name, to the fidelity of another—may officially be conceded by a structure, but, it is suggested by Boccaccio, they also have to be earned—continuously.

The claims that are being made in the challenging of a patriarchal structure of marriage which guarantees the supremacy of the husband are those of the flesh, of vitality, and sometimes (though in Boccaccio only consequentially) of youth. The implication is that the patriarchal structure needs to be as strong as it is in order to hold strong impulses and powers of vitality in check. Behind this there is a respect for the power that is subordinated, and a recognition of its force—reactions that are exemplified, in the safety-valve mechanisms of popular celebrations such as Carnival, outlined earlier. If the structure set up by society to be strong and containing becomes empty or unjustified, then it no longer serves its purpose, and it needs to be reminded of that purpose by contraventions to its code.

The *Decameron* focuses on a type of here-and-now challenge to patriarchal marriage-guarantees. That is, although some husbands have their marital rights infringed because they are elderly and have, in a sense, entered a flesh-and-blood contract they lack the flesh and blood to honour more than perfunctorily, there is a more general awareness of the failings of those who do not earn their marital rights and pleasures, and yet would appear technically able to do so. In other words, they are engaged in an age-appropriate activity (unlike Chaucer's two deceived husbands, John and January), but they lack other features required to make them appropriate mates.

I shall first deal with two examples of husbands in the *Decameron* which show that husbands whose wives are unfaithful, whether wittingly or unwittingly, do not have to emerge from stories as cuckolds, in that they have the human resources to deal with the ruptured situation. In the second story of the third day, King Agilulf discovers that his groom has managed to make love to his wife without the lady realizing she has committed an infidelity, since the groom has been coming to her by night, and in the dark, as the king does. (One is tempted, in the face of literary examples such as this, either to speculate about the stunning lack of perceptual sensitivity shown, or to wonder at the degree to which the invention of gas and electric light might have altered the content of narratives earlier than those of the last two centuries.) The king ingeniously discovers the identity of the lover, and shears a lock of his hair off to mark him. The groom, awake and appropriately fearful (since he realizes how clever the king is and that he is not a man to be trifled with), may have lost his hair but does not lose his head. He cuts the hair of all the other men sleeping with him in the dormitory, so avoiding recognition in the morning.

The king's wisdom is commented on by Pampinea, the narrator of the tale. He is wise enough to realize his wife has no blame, so that it is inappropriate to involve her in repercussions which, he anticipates, might sow 'the seeds of a desire on her part, to repeat the experience'.[37] Even in this detail, we could consider the king as operating according to a natural rather than a patriarchal structure or contract, in that he considers that his wife's ignorance or innocence cancels out the marital offence. This runs counter to the pattern of honour structures, where *de facto* infidelity is held to obtain despite such suppositions of innocence, and where mere suspicion of guilt is sufficient to allow the husband to consider that an infringement of rights has occurred. The king has insight

[37] Giovanni Boccaccio, *The Decameron* (Il Decameron) (1350), trans. G. H. McWilliam (Harmondsworth, 1972). References to the *Decameron* will be to this edition, and given in the text, roman figures being used for the day, first arabic figure for the number of the story, and second arabic figure for the page number.

enough to realize that in making a public fuss he would make himself ridiculous, and, when he is thwarted in his attempt to reveal the identity of the other, he has the resilience and open-mindedness to react in a way that concedes due recognition to the lover (he acknowledges that, though low-born, he 'clearly has all his wits about him' [III. 2. 244]). Thus he finds his solution: he utters a word of public warning understandable only to the guilty man, and this has the desired effect of preventing him from trying to sleep with the queen again.

In this story, where trick is balanced by countertrick, cuckoldry is seen as an affair between men. Although unusual respect is paid to the queen, in that her innocence protects her from any repercussions that would affect her personally, there is none the less some slight on her person within the narrative: in addition to being portrayed as unable to tell another man from her husband (even though he does take the precaution of having a long soak in a hot bath before visiting her), she never gets to know what has happened.[38] The only hint that woman might be an unrecognized source of threat to man is in the gentle admonition of Agilulf's queen when the king visits her after she has already been visited by the groom. In her comments on his energy, in her surprise that he has returned for more, and in her gentle 'Do be careful now', there is a hint of man's sexual limitations, of factors he may need to consider if he values his health and well-being. Although emphasis is laid on the king's concern for the queen's public honour, no attention is paid to the invasion of her private person: the fact that she found it pleasurable is deemed sufficient justification, presumably. Though the king is technically a cuckold, he does not behave like one, and thus arguably loses the qualification, since he is not a *mari complaisant*.

Due credit is given, then, to those who can conduct themselves with insight and intelligence, who can assess situations and devise responses that meet their needs and do not unnecessarily damage

[38] For the elaboration of the concept of affairs between men, see Eve Kosofsky Sedgwick, *Between Men* (Columbia, SC, 1985) and Coppélia Kahn, *Man's Estate: Masculine Identity in Shakespeare* (Berkeley, Calif., 1981). For a modern version of this story, see Robertson Davies, *The Lyre of Orpheus* (Harmondsworth, 1989), 244, where, in a replay of Arthurian deception, Maria is seduced in the dark by a man whom she fails to recognize as not being her husband. In this case, however, the lover's declared intent is to deceive (and arguably to ridicule) the wife rather than the husband.

honour. Agilulf comes out of his story well because he manages his difficult position with exceptional skill, and shows himself on a par with husbands of the calibre of Arthur and Marc.[39]

Ingenuity is likewise employed in VIII. 8, and again, to some degree, at the expense of the women involved. Here an ultimately compassionate resolution is achieved (contrasting with VIII. 7, where a lady causes her lover to stay freezing outside all night, only to be left out herself, symbolically stranded on the phallic symbol of a tower, in the heat of the mid-day sun). In VIII. 8, Zeppa and Spinelloccio, close friends, run the risk of their friendship (an affair of men) being disrupted when Spinelloccio becomes the lover of his friend's wife. Zeppa's response is to arrange to seduce Spinelloccio's wife, or rather simply to make love to her (since seduction hardly seems an accurate label for his approach). This he does when her husband is hidden in a chest in the room: indeed, so fine is his sense of revenge that he makes love to her on the chest itself. The original guilty pair are thus made to feel acute embarrassment, and the affair results in a general sharing of spouses between the two couples.

The appeal to the (masculine) reader is a double one, stemming on the one hand from Zeppa's knowledge of his rival literally beneath him, and, on the other, from the enforced auditory voyeurism in which the rival is obliged to engage. The double masculine reaction—of titillation and triumphant pleasure in Zeppa and of imagined but not articulated horror in the rival in the chest—evokes in the reader both the hope that he may be triumphant and the fear that he may be triumphed over and humiliated. At the same time, the female reader is marginated, both by sexual distance from what is going on (there can be no complicity or empathy with either victor or victim) and by a story in which wives have been marginated. Zeppa meets his loss of honour in a practical and effective way, but it is one which shows honour as being a matter which concerns only him. The tale thus stresses two aspects frequently to be found in stories of cuckolds, and indeed in other portrayals of the infidelity of wives: the marital transgression is seen as an affair to be resolved between the two husbands alone. In a characteristic disregard for any

39 For a full consideration of Marc, and the moral development that his reaction implies, see R. Howard Bloch, 'Tristan, the Myth of the State and the Language of the Self', *Yale French Studies*, 51 (1974), 61–81.

accidental victims of reactions to loss of honour, there is no notion of Spinelloccio's wife being avenged for any loss or disrespect she might be thought to have suffered; the story is seen as a question of possessions, and the usurpation of possessions. Zeppa's approach to his friend's wife fits entirely within this framework:

> I loved Spinelloccio as a brother, and I still do, but yesterday I discovered, without his knowing it, that my trust in him had come to this, that he makes love just as freely to my wife as he does to you. Now, because I love him, the only revenge I propose to take is one that exactly matches the offence. He has possessed my wife, and I intend to possess you.

He adds as a warning (presumably lest the lady think she have any room to object):

> If you refuse to co-operate, I shall certainly catch him out sooner or later, and since I have no intention of allowing his offence to go unpunished, I shall deal with him in such a way as to make both of your lives a perpetual misery. (VIII. 8. 648)

Zeppa is here defending himself from the epithet of cuckold as much by his treatment of his friend's wife as by his treatment of his friend in seducing her. The macho disregard for the wife's feelings is a defensive measure against his apparent fate of cuckold, that is, as a man placed in his ignominious position by two agents: the wife and the lover. The latter we may regard as the active agent, the wife as the treacherous accomplice. This is the likely evaluation of the situation in a patriarchal society, although we might bear in mind an example from Andalusia which declares firmly that wives, not lovers, are those who make a man a cuckold.[40] Anne Parten has taken exception to Coppélia Kahn's emphasis on cuckoldry's being an affair between men, but this example appears to bear Kahn out (though in no way does it prevent us from looking at the role of the women involved).[41] In so far as the colluding wife can be seen as the traitress in the cuckold plot, we can see the husband's position undermined and demoted to that of cuckold by the person who, according to the understanding of marriage, was his subordinate (that is, his wife).

[40] Brandes, *Metaphors of Masculinity*, 90.

[41] Anne Carroll Parten, 'Cuckoldry in Shakespeare' (Ph.D. thesis, Yale, 1983), 15.

It is indeed the power the wife retains, in a concept of unequal marriage, which allows her to lessen the standing of the man who has been placed in a dominant position over her. As Parten points out, the effect of the double standard which allows husbands to be unfaithful with impunity is to render the husband unable to take revenge on his erring wife by submitting her to the same fate. This is because the double standard declares that it is of no consequence to his wife if he is unfaithful to her. She does not have the same type of honour as he does, that is, one which can be offended by the spouse's actions. What he can perhaps do, as suggested by the account of Zeppa's revenge, is generally to take revenge on women by being intransigent with the sex, as he is with Spinelloccio's wife. At the same time he is treating his friend's wife as a piece of property to replace the conjugal property (his own wife's chastity) which has been taken from him.

If, however, Zeppa treats women as simple property, other tales in the *Decameron* suggest that women are people with needs or expectations (as under the natural contract), and that if these are not met, then men will be judged accordingly, and be found to be cuckolds. That is, the disregard of women's claims to attention and consideration, at the heart of this story and that of King Agilulf, does not obtain when the natural contract is breached.

Cuckolds proper in the *Decameron* are censured because their behaviour, or simply their mode of being in relation to women (rather than primarily to men), does not earn them minimum respect. Husbands who fall below the mark of respectable, sensible, and vital men are treated without compassion for the results of folly or stupidity, or simply for their lack of physical resources.

Thus Messer Ricciardo di Chinzica's wife, who has found herself sexually deprived during her marriage because of the number of holy days her husband declares must be observed by abstinence (a nice refuge for one who needs to economize his sexual powers), upbraids him not just for his neglect, but for his lack of awareness about her needs. It is implied that any sensible being might be aware of such things to some degree:

You showed very little sign of knowing *me*, when I was living with you, because if, either then or now, you were as wise as you wish to pretend, you should certainly have had the gumption to realize that a fresh and vigorous young woman like myself needs something more than food or clothes, even if modesty forbids her to say so.

She adds the proper conclusion: 'If you were more interested in studying the law than in keeping a wife, you should never have married in the first place' (II. 10. 225).

Some nice twists are added to the situation of the husband who is confronted with his inadequacies. In VII. 5 a husband is taken in by his wife's story covering up her infidelity with a priest. She sees him as thickheaded and stupid, but scolds him for his stupidity in being blinded by jealousy so that he believed (rightly as it happens) that the priest was her lover. She tells him to stop watching her so closely and appeals to his sense of propriety and dignity: he is behaving like a cuckold—and she threatens to make him one:

Isn't it time that you took yourself in hand, started behaving like a man again, and stopped allowing yourself to be made such a fool of by someone who knows you as well as I do? Leave off keeping such a strict watch over me, because I swear to God that if I were to set my heart on making you a cuckold, I should have my fling and you'd be none the wiser. (VII. 5. 549)

As a result of this reproach, the husband comes to look on his wife as 'a model of intelligence and virtue', with the unfortunate consequence that 'just as he had worn the mantle of the jealous husband when it was unnecessary, he cast it off completely now that his need for it was paramount'. (VII. 5. 550)

The central point of this particular story is contained in the reason for the action leading to the denouement outlined above. This is not a story of a woman who simply fancies a lover, but rather one of a woman who is driven to action by the tensions and limitations of living with an over-jealous husband. He is so zealous for the honour of his wife that he will allow her no normal social contacts: 'It wasn't just a question of her not being able to attend a party or a wedding, or go to church, or step outside her door for a single moment: he wouldn't even allow her to stand at the window or cast so much as a solitary glance outside the house' (VII. 5. 543). It is stressed that the behaviour of this particular husband is unreasonable: the wife's existence is a misery, and this is compounded by the fact that 'she had done nothing to deserve it'. In this detail is esconced again a hint of what might be involved in the natural contract. A husband secure in himself would not need to take the drastic measures employed by the one in this tale: in many ways he is the forerunner of the paranoid husbands depicted in the honour drama of the Spanish Golden Age, whose life is burdened by the need to keep any whisper of suspicion about their family honour at bay. In his fearfulness and over-protective attitude towards his honour he is already showing that breach of the natural contract which destines him to be a cuckold: he is a man not sure of his position, not naturally confident that he is an equal partner in a well-balanced sexual relationship (that would be implied by the natural contract), and thus fearful of losing whatever ground is, according to the letter rather than the spirit of the patriarchal code, granted to him in protecting his rights over his wife.

Consistent with the idea expressed above—that those who default from the natural code can expect to do badly within the context of the patriarchal code—is the possibility that one may contravene the patriarchal code deliberately, and do well out of it, if the action is in accord with the natural one. Thus, for example, in II. 10, with Paganino, the pirate chief who abducts the wife of Ricciardo di Chinzica: it takes him little time to establish himself as a natural 'husband' for the wife who has been so sorely neglected by her husband.

A much more daring example of how the breaking of the patriarchal contract can prove to be advantageous for the transgressor is given in the story of Masetto of Lamporrecchio in III. 1, where Masetto, by becoming gardener to a convent, manages to become the lover of the whole female convent community, thus 'cuckolding' Christ—conceivably the ultimate transgression. He does well, fathers a number of children, and eventually retires. The ending of the story points to the lesson to be learned about using one's ingenuity and willingness to break rules:

> Thus it was that Masetto, now an elderly and prosperous father who was spared the bother of feeding his children and the expense of their upbringing, returned to the place from which he had set out with an axe on his shoulder, having had the sense to employ his youth to good advantage. And this, he maintained, was the way that Christ treated anybody who placed a pair of horns upon his crown. (III. 1. 241)

The message here is not only that the one who breaks the patriarchal code (with the husband embodied in the person of Christ) is likely to do well for himself—and this is presumably why lovers habitually come off better in these stories than husbands do—but also that the code-breaker in general is likely to be seen as a repository of enviable strength in a society, as is the case with shamans.

I have been emphasizing the extent to which Boccaccio shows the fate of the cuckold as not necessarily linked to age, but rather to the ability or otherwise of either men or women to fulfil the natural code, and enjoy the rights and privileges it guarantees, as opposed to the sometimes empty promises of the patriarchal code, which may guarantee neither satisfaction to either party (particularly the wife) nor security from jealousy for the husband. In contrast with the examples we saw in Chaucer, there seems from the above sample to be less concentration on the linking of the cuckold with age, that is, there is less of a sense that time will inevitably bring limitations to us all, including our ability to stake our claim over others in sexual unions. Instead there is a robust and dramatic exposure of the possible ways that life can turn out, according to whether or not men and women have the guts, willpower, and initiative to say what they want, and to grab for it.

In v. 10 it is argued that age affects men and women differently, but it is not clear just how the chips fall. One might argue, in objective terms, that men may well retain their potency and ability to father children well into old age—going with not much difficulty beyond the sixty-year age-bar set on lovers by Andreas Capellanus. But it is also the case that when their potency fails, there is no mistaking it. By contrast, though women reach the end of their child-bearing years in middle age, they have no feat to perform comparable to that of the man involved in making love. Additionally, as pointed out in v. 10, the short-term sexual capacity of women easily outstrips that of men: 'a woman's always ready for a man, but not vice-versa. What's more, one woman could exhaust many men, whereas many men can't exhaust one woman' (v. 10. 472). The bawd who proclaims this message also recognizes, however, that society has a tendency to put away or neglect its women once they have reached old age, so she enjoins women to make the most of things while time permits, so that, as she says, 'when you're an old woman your heart will have no cause for complaint against your flesh' (v. 10. 472).

If age is not entirely absent from Boccaccio, neither is compassion, that is, if it is deserved. In the case of Puccio, compassion is not accorded, because he has no claim on our admiration. Puccio in III. 4 is a man who becomes a tertiary with the Franciscans, having reached 'a certain age', and thus withdraws from most or all of his marital obligations. The implication is that he uses age as an excuse for not maintaining the full role of a married man, a decision understandably unwelcome to his wife, who is aged 28 or 30, and clearly not of a mind to retreat to a life of sexual abstinence. The story inevitably relates how his retreat from sexual life in no way guarantees his freedom from becoming a cuckold, and indeed guarantees that he will become one. Again, in II. 10, which relates the case of Ricciardo di Chinzica, there is a combination of age with stupidity. The age of the husband is only implied—by the mention that his wife is young and beautiful (suggesting some level of mismatch), and perhaps also (as is the case of John and January in the *Canterbury Tales*) by the fact that he is wealthy (II. 10. 221), and it may be assumed that for most people it takes time to accumulate wealth. But as we have already seen in the case of Ricciardo, age is far from being the prime factor in his downfall. Much more influential is what we sense as the misdirected attention of the man. Although he seems to be almost 'past it' sexually (if we believe the dismissive comments about his need to take restoratives after the wedding night (II. 10. 221)), this may be less damning than the fact that he fails to use the brains he has applied in the exercise of his profession to assist him in the human situation he has so carefully (like Chaucer's elderly bachelors) arranged himself into.

Age is presented in a much more extreme degree in I. 10, the tale of Master Alberto, aged 70. He is not a husband, so cannot in fact be a cuckold, but the example he presents of extreme age (rather than moderate old age coupled with ineptitude, reluctance, or stupidity, or any combination of such attributes) is not one which proclaims that those who reach old age can expect to be mocked for their failing powers. Rather, if they are clear with themselves and others about their limitations, including that of falling prey to the passions of youth, then they may be worthy of respect.

Initially the story seems set to display such a moral: Alberto falls in love with a widow, and we glimpse youth and the prime of life as being ages not just of enjoyment, but also of danger:

> He was mightily attracted by the lady, and, no differently than if he had been in the prime of his youth, he felt those flames so keenly in his mature old breast, that he never seemed able to sleep at night, unless in the course of the day he had seen the fair lady's fine and delectable features. (I. 10. 108–9)

In depicting Alberto's passion—that of the young—the narrator (Pampinea), is less slighting than the women characters of her story: while the latter make fun of Alberto, she comments on their lack of perception: 'the good ladies seemed to suppose that the delightful sensations of love could take root and thrive in no other place than the frivolous hearts of the young' (I. 10. 109). But Alberto, though old, 'proves' himself, in a way comparable with that of the husbands who have the ingenuity to remove themselves from the situation of helpless cuckold. His proving is not by any show of strength, but rather by demonstrating that he has the attributes proper to his years—insight, honesty, and a witty logic. He makes claims for the consideration due to the old, and his argument rests on a concept of earned or justified rights: 'For albeit old men are naturally deficient in the powers required for lovemaking, they do not necessarily lack a ready will, or a just appreciation of what should be loved' (I. 10. 109), and the fact that he has an accurate insight into his own state, yet retains his wit, earns him the respect of the ladies who mocked him.

The story of Alberto is significant and exceptional in its expression of an unexpected warmth and compassion for a man at the mercy of the vagaries of emotion (rather than a man who is simply foolish or over-anxious). But it is also significant in two other respects: it is the last one told before Dioneo claims his right always to be the last story-teller (and to depart from the chosen topic of the day if he so chooses), and it occurs early on in the work, namely at the close of the first day's stories.

These two factors are pointers to some of the overall ways in which the *Decameron* can be viewed, and its meaning understood. It is an extremely tightly structured work, set carefully within a frame of narrative recounting how a group of young men and women flee the perils of the plague, take themselves to the country, and amuse themselves by telling stories. The background to the work, then, is one of chaos, death, the disintegration of a structured society. It affects the population adversely, not only by giving them mortal disease, but also by infecting them morally, so that even simple compassion for the sick is lost. As the Introduction states, with the dry and dispassionate understatement that is so frequently the container for emotionally charged material, 'almost without exception, they took a single and very inhuman precaution, namely to avoid or run away from the sick and their belongings' (I. Intro. 52). There is an almost total breakdown of the normal containing structures of the society, and much emerges that is contrary to normal order. Even some of the structures and customs that are set up to replace those that are broken down are 'quite contrary to established tradition'. Of particular interest, given what has been said above about women and their role in society, the threats they pose, the expectations made of them, and their 'natural' rights, is what is noted about the change in their activity in the face of the plague. Previously, women had been associated with death, with accompanying those dying, and with dealing with the dead body afterwards. This is a traditional linking of women with the major rites of passage of human life: just as they usher it in, it is thought appropriate that they should usher it out. Now, in the face of imminent death, the women change their role:

> For not only did people die without having many women about them, but a great number departed this life without anyone at all to witness their going. Few indeed were those to whom the lamentations and bitter tears of their relatives were accorded; on the contrary, more often than not bereavement was the signal for laughter and witticisms and general jollification—the art of which the women, having for the most part suppressed their feminine concern for the salvation of the souls of the dead, had learned to perfection. (I. Intro. 55)

The external world is turned topsy-turvy by death, and there is also a sense of topsy-turvy in the internal narrative world of the stories. Yet, as we have seen, the disorder of the patriarchal code, with its rights, limitations, and obligations, is the result of the establishment of a more proper order in the natural code. This topsy-turvy of the narrative world, in which nothing is accorded in response to theoretical rights, and all must be earned, by personal worth, action, or attitude, is one in which vitality and response to desire (the hallmark of vitality) are made paramount. In this way, it provides the natural counterbalance to the world dominated by death that is the world of the frame, and the real external context behind the composition of the stories.

As such, the overall message of the narrative of the stories might seem a little robust, astringent in its portrayal of how those who are quick of both mind and body are likely to reap the rewards of life. But this is a superficial view. Two factors provide a pointer to a softening of that astringency. One is the function of Dioneo, and the other the positioning of the story of Alberto, the compassionate exception to the treatment of the foibles of old age.[42]

Dioneo is linked throughout the *Decameron* to sensuality. In book I, he changes the course of the stories, and makes his first story, I. 4, unashamedly sexual in its interest, after the clever but less blunt stories that precede it. Then, after the conclusion of I. 10—which is the story of Alberto—Filomena, the newly elected queen, proposes that a further order be given to the activities of the group. The group has already agreed that they should take turns day by day to preside over the story-telling (hence the election of Filomena as queen), and she adds to this the suggestion that a fixed theme be announced for the stories of the day. In this way yet more structuring is added to the activities of this group which is fleeing the chaos of the plague-ridden city. Yet just at this point, where we get a sense of increasingly strong bulwarks being erected by the group against the disorder of the external world, and ones which will ensure the greater order of the world of leisure and recreation they have escaped to, Dioneo claims the right to impose his own disorder by not adhering to the convention that all the stories must conform to the given topic of the day. It should be noted that he claims this right in an extremely orderly and courteous fashion: 'I would ask you to grant me a special privilege, which I wish to have conferred upon me for as long as our company shall last, namely, that whenever I feel so inclined, I

[42] Commentary on the frame and the overall meaning of the *Decameron* may be found in the following: Thomas Greene, 'Forms of Accommodation in the *Decameron*', *Italica*, 45 (1968), 297–313; Joy Hambuechen Potter, *Five Frames for the Decameron: Communication and Social Systems in the Cornice* (Princeton, NJ, 1982); Joan M. Ferrante, 'The Frame Characters in the *Decameron*: A Progression of Virtues', *Romance Philology*, 19 (1965), 212–26; Giuseppe Mazzotta, *The World at Play in Boccaccio's 'Decameron'* (Princeton, NJ, 1986).

may be exempted from this law obliging us to conform to the subject agreed, and tell whatever story I please' (I. Conc. 112). Furthermore, he affirms both his courtesy and story-telling ability by declaring that he is willing always to be last to speak.

This request of Dioneo places him unequivocally in the position of rule-breaker, and thus of pivotal importance as one who will show where the limits are by breaking them. This accords him an exceptional and shaman-like status in the group, and makes it more likely that we will pay attention both to his stories, and to the line of sensuality that he represents. In this way, the affirmation of the natural code, based on sensuality and natural desire, which we have seen is made so prominent in the content of the stories, is reinforced at a structural level by the function of Dioneo.

The story that precedes this request is itself of the utmost significance, not only in its assertion of the value and importance of the natural code, but also in the compassion it unexpectedly concedes to the possible functioning of this code. Being the tale of Alberto, the elderly man who falls hopelessly and romantically in love, yet who has no pretentiousness, it serves to remind us that the law of the senses is not necessarily a harsh one, except for those who deserve it to be so. Thus, whatever the rough-and-ready justice that is meted out to characters in later stories by Dioneo, there is a corrective note of compassion sounded at the start. This power to include the exceptions, deviations, and vagaries of human behaviour is not only part of the sheer vitality of cuckoldry literature, but also what marks it out as more flexible and vigorous than the literature of honour.

Finally, however, the role of Dioneo as a shaman-like figure leads us to raise doubts about the validity of the parallel between the portrayal of the cuckold and the depressive position. Throughout this chapter, and in the Introduction, I have argued that this comic representation of man's infidelity is a way of bringing into society's view of itself a recognition of those elements which are contrary to its value-system, and that this act of bringing those contrary elements into consciousness and representation is not just the simple safety-valve that the carnival model might suggest, but is akin to the accommodation of the intolerable that is characteristic of the maturity of the depressive position. What emerges above all from the *Decameron* is, however, that this accommodation takes place in a situation of control, just as, for example, in carnival or in popular foolery which incorporates opposites, there is a very firm sense of structure, and of ritual enactment. Shamans, fools, carnivals, and set-piece jokes (which include the portrayal of the cuckold) are thus a highly stylized, controlled, and therefore unspontaneous mode of the representation within patriarchal society of those elements which run counter to it. This element of control I alluded to earlier in the discussion of jokes. A joke is a possible subversion because it takes place in an orderly situation, and where there is no real possibility that the situation about which the joke is made is susceptible of real change. The sheer degree of safety which is ensured in the ritualized form of comedy that we find in cuckoldry literature is one of the factors which make it possible for it to occur, just as the safety of the sexual motif of the cuckold makes it possible for us to contemplate the threat of ageing and death. What we shall need to consider eventually is whether there can be some more authentic form of the depressive position which is related to the portrayal of the husband who is the victim of sexual infidelity, and whether the responses it elicits are perceptibly different from those provoked by the safe and humorous portrayal of the cuckold.

4
Men of Honour

THE CONTEXT

MARITAL INFIDELITY can, as is shown by the tales of Boccaccio and Chaucer, take a variety of forms, but essentially reduces to a simple model, that of the triangle. While in theory this triangle may consist either of the husband, the wife, and the wife's lover, or of the husband, the wife, and the husband's mistress, the second variety has caused relatively little concern in our literature and culture. Traditionally, as already pointed out, offence can only be given to the husband by the unfaithful wife, and although Christianity, for example, has argued for equality of offence and responsibility in this area (while continuing to be strongly patriarchal in its own institutional structure), the susceptibilities of a wife to her husband's unfaithfulness have largely gone unrecognized.

The only level at which there is, as it were, an argument on behalf of the wife, is within the portrayal of her infidelity. In the case of the cuckold, the wife's case is constructed on the base of a recognition of her as someone with expectations and desires that are not being met within marriage, and showing her therefore as justified in seeking solace elsewhere. The cuckold, meanwhile, is portrayed as someone who has forfeited his rights to fidelity.

The resulting impression is one of a topsy-turvy world which manages to incorporate a vision of the woman as a real and active being, while focusing on both the inadequacy and the discomfiture of the man. There is no doubt, in the cuckold story, that something happens (or the desire for it to happen is there) and that the husband cannot, or will not, take action. It is a story in which the efficiency of the wife is counterbalanced by the inefficiency of the husband.[1]

[1] The combination is thus unlike that commented on by Renoir in relation to the epic and the romance. See Alain Renoir, 'The Inept Lover and the Reluctant Mistress: Remarks on Sexual Inefficiency in Medieval Literature', in Edward Vasta and Zacharias P. Thundy (eds.), *Chaucerian Problems and Perspectives: Essays Presented to Paul E. Beichner* (London, 1979), 180–206.

In literary forms where the husband is presented as a man of honour, the original triangle is essentially the same, with three exceptions. The lover is frequently illusory, or, if real, may well be uncongenial or unwanted (thus not providing in the antagonist of the plot a male figure who will be preferable to the protagonist),[2] and so is the love affair. The husband is aware, active, and ultimately decisive. And the wife, though apparently a major cause for concern, is effectively put to one side, in that her expectations and wishes within any 'natural' code are passed over.

In Chapter 3 we saw how the world in which the cuckolds of Boccaccio and Chaucer appear is one of rough justice, where the natural law of vitality (expressed in sexuality) is given precedence over man-made law which protects the status and position of the husband (and his heirs) in the patriarchal structure. In this world, either husbands or wives may triumph, according to whether or not they use their wits and observe the fundamental conventions of the natural code by which certain human activities, such as marriage, are deemed age-appropriate only for the young. If they transgress, by entering marriage without the vitality or the inclinations to fulfil the requirements of the natural law, then they stand to 'lose their rights'—that is, they stand to lose their partner or their mate to another, and with them their good name.

In the atmosphere of mirth that surrounds the cuckold, little or no attention is paid to his standing. If anything, his tendency to think too much of his status may count against him. In his cuckoldom he loses what pretensions to standing he might have had. He is a passive, almost negative, factor in the matrimonial triangle. He has not been considered in the establishment of the adulterous relationship, and his destiny, indeed his identity of cuckold, is that he will continue to be the person not considered. This being the case, there can be no concern in the literature for either his feelings or his status.

The cuckold becomes what his situation of betrayed husband makes him. This is his new identity: to be the cast-off, the man who has lost power. There is no sense of identity other than that of cuckold.

A different, and complementary, view of the wronged husband

[2] For exceptions to this, see David Larson, *The Honor Plays of Lope de Vega* (Cambridge, Mass., 1977), 24 and 28.

is presented by the concept of the man of honour. The clearest example of the literary treatment of the man of honour is to be found within Spanish Golden Age drama, but the base from which he springs is broader, and reveals concerns of an importance equal to those which we have seen underlie the attention paid to the cuckold.

To distinguish in general terms between the two, let us highlight the respective attributes of the cuckold and the man of honour, taking as paradigms for this the characterization of the cuckold as he has emerged from Chaucer and Boccaccio and the man of honour as he is generally conceived in the drama of the Golden Age in Spain, in the sixteenth and seventeenth centuries.

First, the cuckold is a man unaware, incapable of grasping a situation and its meaning, and subsequently incapable of grasping the implications of what develops. He is a man not deprived of power (or a wife), but shown as unfit to be the possessor of power (or a wife) in the first place.

The man of honour is, by contrast, hyper-aware. Where the cuckold seems to live self-absorbed in his own concept of the world (and may, as January is, be given the attribute of blindness, to emphasize the degree of self-absorption), the man of honour is the model or epitome of vigilance. But it is a vigilance which reaches the level of paranoia. This vigilant man always has his gaze and attention directed towards the outside, and most particularly towards the perception that those on the outside may have of his external presentation—a presentation constantly under threat of appearing less perfect, less complete, than he would wish it to be.

Second, the cuckold is not a man of action. He may make a gesture at confronting his wife with her infidelity, as January does, but she, like so many of Boccaccio's wives (for example, in *Decameron* VII. 1, 2, 3, and 4) is adept at spinning a yarn that will convince her gullible spouse that he was wrong to make the accusation in the first place.

The man of honour, by contrast, is virtually defined by his action—not only his willingness to undertake it, but his ingenuity and efficaciousness as he does so. His honour having been slighted by his wife (or the action of another with his wife), he makes speedy and effective retaliation.

In doing so, the man of honour operates entirely within the

patriarchal code, which is what provides both the strength and the fragility of his position, though his action may fall foul of the civil code, and may require final sanction from a figure of authority such as the king.

In the case of each type, there is a question of identity at stake. Both are shown to possess their identity in relation to others. The husband who is cuckold is automatically removed from centre-stage and placed firmly in an ancillary role: he is the block to a successful and enjoyable sexual union. His identity has depended upon his status as a husband who could assert his patriarchal rights in marriage, and this identity disappears with his failure to do so. The man of honour retains his social identity intact only so long as all facets of it (including the honour and honourable behaviour of both wife and dependants) remain beyond reproach. His identity is dependent on his retention of a superior position within the patriarchal structure.

Finally, there is what, for want of a better term, we might call a distinction in the temporal orientation of the two models of husband. With the cuckold, there is a sense of past, of dismissal, of pre-empting. The cuckold is pushed off-stage, first in the marriage, then in the literature that tells of his fate. He becomes an event of the past, and his nature, his definition as cuckold, is such that there is no perception of a future—or at least of one where things might be different. Where a future is glimpsed in literature of cuckoldry, it is generally one which includes the continuation of the cuckolded state. By contrast, literature concerning men of honour has a focus towards the future. If honour has been damaged or endangered in the past, then it must be re-established for the future, not only for the survival of the wronged husband in his society, but also for the future of his name and that of his lineage. The man of honour takes bloody revenge to restore both his honour and the family name.

The transition from cuckold to man of honour appears to represent a shift in attitude and presentation that denotes a complete sea-change, from the ridiculing of the slighted husband to the affirmation of his power and authority. I would emphasize here the fact that there is an apparent shift only, since it is debatable in the end whether the man of honour's position as delineated in literature is fundamentally distinct from that of the cuckold in the matter of his identity, his security, and the degree to which we may or may not feel admiration for him.

But to understand the functioning and meaning of the man of honour in literature, we need first to grasp the principles of the context that forms him and provides him with his course of action.

Honour systems as a way of regulating, symbolizing, and understanding relationships are particularly characteristic, in Europe, of the countries bordering the Mediterranean, but also find their counterparts in more northern parts of Europe.[3] The period in which this concept seems most prominent in literature is the sixteenth and seventeenth centuries, and thus marks a chronological move forward from the literature of cuckoldry considered in the previous chapter.

The relationships governed by honour systems are of various types. In the context of this study, and the understanding that many may have of 'honour', it may seem that, while there may be general norms about 'honourable' (in the sense of ethical or upright) behaviour, the prime function of an honour code is to define the roles and relationships of the sexes. Thus a man is, typically, liable to consider himself 'dishonoured' by his wife's infidelity. That is, he is dishonoured by an infringement of the boundaries and power-structure of the matrimonial relationship as understood within the honour code.

To see an honour system in this way is too narrow, however, and will make it hard to grasp the distinction between principles affecting the view held of cuckolds and that held of men of honour.

The understanding of an honour system comes best, I think, from the realization that the primary relationship which appears to be involved for those living within an honour system is with peers, with the outside world, and with other families. In this primary relationship, where few, if any, concessions are granted, worth is something which has to be proved. At the same time, worth is open to diminution if there is a failure in the secondary relationships within the private life which could bring the reproach of 'dishonourable'.

[3] The best collection of studies on this topic is Peristiany (ed.), *Honour and Shame*. For work on the understanding of the honour system in other countries, especially as revealed in literature, see: Wilson, 'Family Honour in the Plays of Shakespeare's Predecessors and Contemporaries'; George Fenwick Jones, *Honor in German Literature* (Chapel Hill, 1959); Charles Barber, *The Theme of Honor's Tongue*.

When there is a 'challenge' to honour, it is always understood to come from the outside. The situation which stimulates the challenge may come from the individual's private life, but the only real dishonour consists in that fact coming to light publicly.

The distinction made by Pitt-Rivers in his discussion of honour in the Mediterranean[4] (and which is adopted broadly as a concept by other contributors on the same subject) is between honour and shame. This coincides, though not exactly, with the distinction I have been making between the primary relationship for a man in an honour-based society, which rests on his relationship with his peers, and the secondary relationship, with his subordinates (including wives and children), which is capable of having a destructive influence on the quality of the primary relationship.

Honour which is linked to shame is distinct from honour which can be gained positively. Even in the Mediterranean, where there is an emphasis on the honour/shame system (involving a hyper-awareness of the possibility of honour-loss), there is none the less the idea that honour can be won, through virtuous conduct, through display of strength or bravery (within the society or alongside peers), and is a level of status and prestige which situates an individual socially and determines his right to precedence.

It will be noticed that the terms used to define this type of honour which may be gained indicate with little room for equivocation that it is a quality which pertains to men. Men are able to gain honour. This, in a patriarchal society, where the emphasis will be on the status of men in their power relationships to one another as much as to their women, is hardly surprising, but no less worthy of emphasis here. The positive aspect of honour, then, is within an activity of men: the source for the gaining of honour is bravery in battle, or prowess in public life. Since, as we shall see later, public life is what belongs to men, honour cannot be other than the thing which men (rather than women) gain.

Honour which is linked to shame is honour which stands to be lost—that is, it is by definition a quality the possession and retention of which are highly uncertain. And although the honour to be gained is historically present in the honour systems of Mediterranean societies, and is an element, for example, of honour as it appears in our major epics and romances, it comes to

[4] Pitt-Rivers, 'Honour and Social Status'.

be superseded, as far as fundamental social activity is concerned, by honour to be lost, the honour linked to shame.

An honour system contains a paradox. It asserts the importance of an individual *per se*—each one must look to and defend his or her honour—and yet it bases that importance on two sorts of dependence: dependence on the peer group or superiors to accord the title of 'honour', or to hold the view that amounts to giving someone 'reputation' or 'good name', and dependence on those intimately connected with the individual not to cause a breach in the reputation gained and held, usually precariously, in relation to the outside world. It is impossible to have the concept of 'reputation' or 'good name' without the concept of the source from which they derive. Although that source could be considered to be the action, activity, or conduct which cause 'reputation' or 'good name' to be accorded to an individual, there has to be the body of people which will form the subject of the verb 'to accord'. That is, reputation cannot be gained through an action unless there is a context in which that reputation is established, and it can only be established by agreement, by recognition, or by acclaim. Unless reputation is given by a body of people, it cannot be held to exist.

Thus the system which gives paramount importance to the individual also decrees the extreme dependence of that individual upon the context from which he derives his importance and his value. This may seem like a truism, but needs to be emphasized in order to understand, not the explicit reasons and feelings that are entailed in living within an honour code, but rather the implicit circumstances and consequential feelings that are also entailed, and which operate in just as powerful a way as what goes on at the explicit level.

Pitt-Rivers, outlining the meaning of honour in a society which also gives importance to the concept of shame, shows how easily the idea of 'acquired honour' can be lost sight of, the fragile honour-to-be-lost being the quality that chiefly remains: 'As the basis of repute, honour and shame are synonymous, since shamelessness is dishonourable.'[5] Since he then goes on to point out that honour is the thing or quality linked to men, and shame the thing which is linked to women, we can see how life falls out between

[5] Ibid. 42.

the sexes in an honour-based society: men not only stand to gain honour but need to retain it, whereas women—in so far as they are liable to lose their 'shame'—are those who endanger their honour and that of their menfolk, while appearing not to have the facility of gaining it.[6] There is thus a sharp distinction between the qualities attributed to the two sexes, but the distinction is sufficient neither to protect one sex from having its quality damaged when the other is dishonoured, nor to endow the sex which has 'shame' with anything more than that.

At the heart of this situation of distinction in the nature of the honour considered appropriate to each sex is a sense of power, and two things come into play here. First, there is the 'original' sense of honour—'honour gained' by the man for actions showing particular bravery or other worth. Thus he has shown his 'power' over others. But, as a 'strong man', he is also considered to have power and authority over his womenfolk and his children.

For the woman, honour as shame is linked to her sexuality, and in a swift denial of woman's sexual freedom, it is considered, within an honour system, that she is 'dishonoured', that is, she loses her shame, as soon as there is any 'tainting of her sexual purity', whereas with a man this simply does not apply.[7] This readiness to see 'sexual tainting' in a woman is part of the acute ambivalence about the role of the woman, who is seen as the uncontrollable source and repository of sexual feeling, and for that reason is forbidden, as far as it is possible, to have anything to do with such feeling. With sexual tainting as a possibility lodged in the woman only, the man can lose his honour, in sexual matters, only through the agency of a woman over whom he is considered to have power. (Instances where a man may lose honour other than in sexual matters do, of course, exist, but will be related to the action of the man himself, as in the case of a man who fails to meet a challenge offered, or a man guilty of untruth.)

This parcelling-out of qualities, attributes, and responsibilities between the sexes does, of course, have its relationship with some of the preoccupations underlying the mockery of the cuckold.

[6] For discussion of how women, in order to assert their rights to honour, take on man-like, or 'varonil' qualities, see Melveena McKendrick, *Woman and Society in the Spanish Drama of the Golden Age: A Study of the 'Mujer Varonil'* (Cambridge, 1974).

[7] Pitt-Rivers, 'Honour and Social Status'.

There are preoccupations to do with lineage, but also to do with the power of sensuality, and the control it may have over a man (in the form of his excitement and response), and his concern at his inability to control it in a woman.

The etymology of 'cuckold', as shown in Chapter 2, points us towards an explanation for the concern to retain the fidelity of woman as deriving from a desire, felt on the part of the man, to pass on his property to children he could be certain of being his own. When we move to an honour system, we find two approaches to inheritance, as far as honour and related qualities are concerned. Again, as with the cuckold, what matters mainly is what a man inherits, and in patriarchal society honour which is based on name and family honour, in the sense of honour gained, is passed down the patrilineal line.[8] But dishonour can come from anywhere, whether from women or slights regarding women, and the smallest quantity is sufficient to taint the whole inheritance of a family name of honour.

There are two issues here. First, that if the man is to pass his good name down to his children, then for them to receive it properly, he needs to be certain that they are indeed his children, and thus also that his wife is faithful to him. Second, that there is the concept that a 'not totally good' name might be passed down to future generations, because of some slight slip or sexual misdemeanour in the past of a female antecedent.

Caro Baroja makes this particularly clear in his discussion of the way in which in Spain in the sixteenth century only a direct line of male noble antecedents was necessary to prove possession of a noble title, whereas to prove purity of blood (found necessary by many at a time when Jews were persecuted socially and economically by being debarred from a whole series of official and influential posts), it was necessary to prove that one had a complete set of pure-blooded parents and grandparents. One

[8] Pitt-Rivers outlines the interface between status and birth in Spain, where a woman can in fact pass on the family name: 'Status derived from birth is not uniquely a male attribute. A woman is granted the status of her husband, but she does not thereby forfeit that which she received by birth. Legally she retains her maiden name, merely adding her husband's name to it, and she passes it on to her children as their second surname. Moreover, unlike English titles, Spanish titles pass through the female line in default of a male heir in the same degree of kinship. The result is that they freqently pass through women, changing from one patriline to another' (Ibid. 68).

impure grandmother was sufficient for the grandchild to be deemed of impure blood. In cases where simple proof of nobility, as opposed to purity of blood, was at stake, however, grandmothers of lower class could be admitted to without fear that they would weaken the claim to noble title.[9] Again, this distinction points up the extra security and solidity of 'honour gained', which is given to, and passes down through, the man, as opposed to the 'honour to be retained' or 'shame', which is the part of the woman and any defect in which can be passed on. Thus the inheritance from a man can be positive; the inheritance from a woman, at least within an honour/shame system, can at best only be not negative. And hence the fact that an even worse insult than one referring to the conduct of a man's wife is that of casting doubt upon the purity of his mother.[10]

Pitt-Rivers points out both how there is an intended balance in an honour system such as he describes, by which the system distributes roles and responsibilities. It 'obliges a man to defend his honour and that of his family, a woman to conserve her purity'.[11] None the less, there is every danger that the division of attributes and responsibilities may effectively become a split, in that there is exaggeration of the qualities considered inherent to either side, and imbalance occurs. As Pitt-Rivers outlines it, 'Yet the concepts of honour and shame also extend to the point where they are no longer synonymous, and at this point they lose their ethical value. Shame, no longer equivalent to honour, no longer equivalent to shame, becomes *an exclusively male attribute as the concern for precedence and the willingness to offend another man*' [emphasis mine]. A further consequence is a delineation of modes of being for each sex. When this is the result of the exaggerated split, possession of the attributes of one sex by the other comes to be seen as 'dishonouring': 'for a man, to show timidity or blush is likely to make him an object of ridicule, while a woman who takes to physical violence or attempts to usurp the male prerogative of authority, or, very much more so, sexual freedom, forfeits her shame'.[12]

In the honour system as it exists in the works of European

9 Caro Baroja, 'Honour and Shame', 102.
10 Pitt-Rivers, 'Honour and Social Status', 52.
11 Ibid.
12 Ibid.

literature with which we are concerned, there is a belief that usurpation of the right to sexual freedom by the woman offends most strongly against the husband's honour, and thus that a woman's infidelity constitutes a matrimonial offence. A heightened view of how this is conceived of as an act by a woman which damages a man's good name (and thus removes the argument from the simply practical field of whether a man can consider his children as legitimately his own) can be gleaned from the honour system of the Bedouins of Egypt, where, as noted in Chapter 2, the language used for honour indicates a clear gender-differentiation. The system here resembles that outlined by Pitt-Rivers—that is, one by which the man's honour can be gained and increased, and the woman's honour can only be lost. For the Bedouins, 'sharaf' and ''ird' are the respective terms denoting man's and woman's honour. Thus ''ird' is the portion of honour a man has which may be adversely affected by a woman. Curiously, however, when offences against ''ird' occur, retaliation is taken not by the husband, but by close male blood-relatives, as those most directly offended by the woman's behaviour.

This custom singles out for us the quality of honour which has been placed in the woman by her parental family for safe-keeping, and emphasizes the way in which her infidelity is viewed as an offence against the family of which she is a daughter, rather than an offence against the family in which she is a wife. The husband cannot, in any case, fully regain his lost ''ird', but does not need to—he has not been offended in a significant way: 'The husband of the adulterous woman cannot impose any punishment on her, apart from divorcing her and recovering the bridewealth. Her shameful conduct does not affect the *'ird* of his lineage in the least. Thus if he kills her for adultery he will be subject to retaliation or the payment of bloodwealth to her kinsmen. Marriage does not sever the bonds which link a woman with her own agnatic group.'[13]

We can already see how extreme the honour code can be in its separation of roles between the sexes. There is a basis for understanding why this should be in the concern to ensure the boundaries of the patriarchal society so that it is possible for a man to know that his children are his own. Other features of the

[13] Zeid, 'Honour and Shame Among the Bedouins of Egypt', 256–7.

honour code, however, suggest that there are more fundamental reasons for the divisions made, reasons linked to the dynamics of emotional development.

The résumé I have given so far of honour has largely drawn on recent anthropological work in the Mediterranean. This work combines direct observation of social and sexual mores with, particularly in the case of Caro Baroja in his comments on Spain, some awareness of historical factors which have affected the growth and evolution of the honour/shame system. A different but complementary perception of the meaning of honour/shame systems can, however, be gained from using another area of psychoanalytic theory. This is not at odds with the approach of scholars such as Caro Baroja, which provides the factual flesh to clothe the bones of theory, and, in its turn, theory suggests some of the less obvious forces that may be at play, in seeing phenomena not just as historical occurrences, but also as psycho-social manifestations.

Klein's theory on the paranoid-schizoid position provides a set of concepts relevant to an understanding of the cultures and literature of honour. As outlined in Chapter 1, the paranoid-schizoid position is the earliest, most primitive emotional state, and as such the most intense. In this position, unwelcome experience is projected out into others, is disowned, but then feared when it is perceived as residing in others. Particularly relevant to the link between the paranoid-schizoid position and honour systems is the context in which the former originally occurs, which allows us both to appreciate the primitive level of reaction involved and to estimate the immense level of fear and threat that leads to, and results from, the reaction of splitting. It tells of extremities of reaction that are fleshed out in the workings of an honour/shame system.

In Chapter 3, in the discussion of the meaning of carnival, charivari, and the sudden domination by women which is produced in the celebrations of the Abbots of Misrule, I advanced the idea that these were ways of 'including in' what men in a patriarchal society might see as the worst-case possibility. When a society is confronted with the events and situations it (or its menfolk) would least like to imagine, and when it contains what is most feared in a celebration and a ritual, the capacity of such events and situations to inspire terror lessens, since they become known aspects of society that can be contemplated, rather than being things so terrible and fearful that they cannot be tolerated. The celebration and acceptance implied in the topsy-turvy world, the world not run according to the principles of the originating society, is an activity analogous to the recognition and containment which are features of the depressive position, since it is in this position that what is feared is examined, given room, and related to. It cannot remain at the level of a terrifying bogey that is alien and that persecutes.

In that it constitutes acceptance and elaboration of worst-case events in the matrimonial sphere, the portrayal of cuckoldry is part of an attitude of humour, realism, and ultimately strength, since what is feared is not cast out but included in the world view of the society that returns time and again to it as a motif. The safety afforded by the comic framework furthermore permits a confrontation with death as an inescapable fact of life, made the more tolerable by its being accommodated in an appreciation of the essential dynamics of life.

By contrast, cultural systems based on honour, and the literature they produce, are more closely allied to the paranoid-schizoid position, as we can see from examining the degree of splitting, projection, and polarization that occur within an honour-based construction of the relation of man to woman, and of each of these to their family and peers. This splitting is both represented within the literature of honour and has its effect on the spectator. In terms of the response of the spectator, the splitting within honour literature arguably has an analogous effect to the impact made on us when in life situations we experience splitting taking place in others.

Honour literature in Europe has the interesting characteristic of being chronologically clustered in the sixteenth and seventeenth centuries, a fact which makes it seem licit to ask whether, given this apparent extensive concern with matters of honour, there might have been external circumstances which became particularly threatening, and which may account in part for this concentration.

One approach to this is to consider the reverse case, that is: what are the circumstances which make it possible for the depressive position to be attained? As mentioned in discussion of the cuckold, for the infant to learn to relate, and to accept that a terror need not be so terrifying that he has to project it vigorously from himself, there has to be a containing and accepting environment that will receive his fears, and return them to him in a less terrifying form.[14] On the face of it there seems no reason why the fourteenth century, which produced both Chaucer and Boccaccio, and which suffered the terrible scourge of the Black Death, should be less terrifying than the period of honour plays in Spain, of Molière in France, and of Shakespeare and Restoration comedy in England. But if we consider the 'message' contained in those medieval texts about natural laws, the acceptance of ageing and death, and the reasonableness of expecting vitality and potency in the sexual relationship of marriage, then we might speculate that the context which produced such literature was one of acceptance—albeit enforced—of natural disasters and natural limitations. Here, of course, we find ourselves involved in a circular argument. The literature which produces evidence of the depressive position is also being used as evidence to say how it is that the depressive position is possible. What other types of evidence could be adduced? An answer emerges with greater sharpness from considering those features of life which come to be threatening in honour literature.

In a society, a principal source of anxiety for any individual is the security of that individual's status within the society. The same applies, with no less force, indeed arguably with more, to particular groups or classes in a society. What causes such anxiety? A simple, indeed simplistic, first answer to that question is that it is a sense of threat. If we ask the question in the context of why one might think of the period that produced Chaucer and Boccaccio as depressive, and hence relatively stable, and by contrast, the sixteenth and seventeenth centuries as a period in which there appears to be evidence in literature about anxious concern with social identity, with legitimation, and with social structures, we might first be led to indicate the advent of Protestantism in Europe as a fundamentally unsettling occurrence that provoked religious and intellectual anxiety. Thus, judging from the fabliaux and literature following in that mode, we might observe that it seems possible to joke about the vagaries of the Catholic Church and its priests in medieval literature, because

[14] This development of Klein's theory is the foundation of the work of Donald Winnicott on the relationship between mother and child. See also James, 'Bion's "Containing" and Winnicott's "Holding"'.

there is no severe threat to its existence or its power. There is, however, a difference between experiencing anxiety about where one stands in the universe, or *vis-à-vis* the godhead, and experiencing anxiety about where one stands in society, since for the latter there can be tangible and practical manifestations of threat which both provoke and intensify anxiety. The greater the degree of uncertainty in the social context of institutions (in relation to civic rights, status, employment, economic well-being), the greater will be the anxieties in those areas. Thus the acute persecutory form of anxieties to do with standing and identity are particularly prevalent in Spain, where social anxieties became more pressing in the Golden Age because of religious/social questions centred on purity of blood,[15] and are also evident in literary examples such as *Othello* which reflect such anxiety. In periods of social change, there are accompanying manifestations of social retrenchment, and a tendency, in the face of the new and the mobile, to redefine and declare more legitimate the claims of the old order—an order of which 'honour' is frequently a part. This retrenchment may—as in the case of the honour plays of Spain—be picked up and reiterated (so as to form part of the declaration of the pre-existing culture) in the literature of societies undergoing a wave of social change.

I have outlined the difference between cuckoldry and a concern with honour as being the difference between a modified depressive position and a paranoid-schizoid position. Another way in which cuckoldry can be understood as different from concern with honour is that to the awareness expressed by the former of the pressures deriving from the nature of life itself (with death, ageing, and lack of potency as prime factors) is added awareness of the local pressures of religion and social standing. What comes to be all-important is not the relationship of man (and woman) with

[15] See Caro Baroja, 'Honour and Shame'; Castro, *De la edad conflictiva* (2nd edn.; Madrid, 1961); and McKendrick, 'Honour/Vengeance in the Spanish *Comedia*', esp. 318–20 and 324–30. A more general discussion of the degree to which social development in Spain provided the context for an increased emphasis on lineage in the period is provided by Michael R. Weisser, *The Peasants of the Montes: The Roots of Rural Rebellion in Spain* (Chicago and London, 1976). For a detailed discussion of the social background of anxiety to honour, and its relation to the increasing complexities of economic, social, and political life in the development of the modern state in France in the sixteenth century, see Kristen B. Neuschel, *Word of Honor: Interpreting Noble Culture in Sixteenth-Century France* (Ithaca, NY, and London, 1989).

life, but the relationship of man with man. The latter is a competitive situation in a way the former cannot be (we cannot compete against death), which accounts for the man's hyperawareness as he stands *vis-à-vis* his peers. It is also one in which individual relationships continually seen as a measure of worth and standing come to blot out any perception of the wholeness of life, including its ending.

Earlier I suggested that the treatment of the cuckold gives a sense of past, with the dismissal of the main figure from centre-stage, whereas honour literature is orientated towards the future. What we have seen about the wholeness of the context for cuckold literature, as opposed to the splitting and partiality of honour literature, enables us to see where a sense of the present fits in the orientation of the two types. In cuckoldry, the inadequate protagonist is dismissed from centre-stage to give way to the claims of vitality of the present. The man who cannot keep his wife by giving her enjoyment gives way to the man who *can* keep her—the lover. In the honour situation, there is a rejection of this vital present, and habitually there is an ending in death, all because of the future-orientated concern for honour and the family name. What is lacking is an ability to cope with the implications of dishonouring in the present. Honour literature is thus not only based on a split, but also produces a temporal and experiential void. Having denied sensuality, interaction, and connection between the sexes, by creating rigid divisions, it then goes as far as it can to restating denial by imposing annihilation as the solution to slighted honour. Thus the challenge of living with the emotions provoked by the dishonour is avoided.

The analogy with the context in which these two positions occur within the individual hinges upon memory. In the paranoid-schizoid position, the infant is suspended in a terrifying present, with eternity as its sense of time. Thus if there is deprivation, it is the more painful, since the infant has as yet no sense of time passing, only of a chasm into which it is plunged. There is not the comforting adjunct of memory to enable the infant to realize that time passes, that distress does not last for ever, that there will come again a time of comfort and well-being. The depressive position, being a characteristic of the slightly older infant, entails the infant's tolerance of his discomforts, because by this stage he is beginning to gain some sense of the realities surrounding him. The past, in a sense, has a meaning of stability and continuity (though it may contain both good and bad experience). The infant in the paranoid-schizoid position, however, can take no comfort from such realization, and is faced only with future horror.

The split in honour cultures, viewed as related to the paranoid-schizoid position, can be seen, then, as a reaction to the threat posed by fellow men, and by the endangering of social standing they may be able to bring about. The actual sense of threat is enormous, and there is little or no feeling that a wrong will ultimately be righted. To an even greater degree than in cuckoldry, problems of honour appear, on the surface at least, to be an affair between men,[16] the difference being that while in cuckoldry the power a man exerts over a woman may be sufficient to give him status, in honour literature such power is a necessary but not a sufficient condition: it is the bottom line. In honour literature the ability to keep or conquer women is essential (how can honour be retained untarnished otherwise?), and some would consider it as of prime importance, but it is added to, and at times veiled by, considerations of quality connected with general strength, prestige, integrity, or the like, that is, qualities to do with competition between men.

The relationship between man and woman in an honour system tells us something about the nature and strength of man's anxiety which leads him to adopt such a rigorous code. I spoke earlier of the primary set of relationships in an honour culture being those with other men. (It is hard to speak of the honour relationships for a woman in this context, since she and her worth are always taken to have second place in relation to the man.) It may be more accurate to say that it is these relationships which come to the fore in the honour culture, but they are none the less tightly bound to the attitude to women held by men in such a culture. Unless we consider what meaning there is in the mode of relations between men and women, the competitive, defensive nature of the relations between men in honour/shame cultures will elude us, since their behaviour is part of a reaction to anxiety in the face of the threat posed by women.

To understand this further we can look at some Mediterranean honour/shame cultures other than that of Spain, since some of

[16] See Kahn, *Man's Estate*, 19 and 150.

them highlight dramatically and explicitly the splits and projections at the root of an honour/shame system, and show how these refer not just to the relations with peers of the same sex, but also to relations between the sexes.

We saw in Chapter 2, and earlier in this chapter, how the Bedouins use different terms for honour to be gained as a man ('sharaf') and the honour which can be lost by the misconduct of a woman (''ird'). In Chapter 1 we also saw how this is expressed in terms of the public and the private by the Kabyle of the Atlas mountains, who use different terms to designate what is sacred in different parts of life, in ways which are aligned according to gender. Thus they distinguish between 'h'aram' (taboo), where 'h'urma' is the type of honour felt, and which is the sacred of the left hand, associated with private, intimate life, and the feminine world, and 'nif', the sacred of the right hand, associated with public, social life. The left hand contains the life of senses and feeling, the right hand the relations of man to man in public life. The two are inextricably linked, as are the types of honour pertaining to men and to women in the system outlined by Pitt-Rivers: 'It is respect for the sacred of the right hand, for, that is to say, the honour of the agnatic family, which impels one to avenge the offence done to the sacred of the left hand, to the weaker party, through which the group is vulnerable.'[17]

This example shows us the extreme care taken in Kabyle society to keep male and female worlds separate, so much so that their functioning in a moral system is itself subject to clear division and demarcation of responsibilities, and a clear level of linguistic distinction. Despite its sharper delineation, the Kabyle differentiation of types of honour is in its essentials little different from the concept of honour in Spain, where this same division of the honour considered to pertain to men and women respectively exists but is not distinguished so clearly on a linguistic level. This division of responsibilities and attributes is often continued into 'territory', where different domains are considered to pertain properly to either men or women. This is so in the example from Berber culture given in Chapter 1, where the man who stays at home in the day is ridiculed and thought suspect, opening himself by his action to enfeebling influence;[18] or in Greek village life,

[17] Bourdieu, 'The Sentiment of Honour in Kabyle Society', 219–21.
[18] Bourdieu, 'The Berber House', 9.

where the absence of a woman from her house is seen itself as a type of spiritual infidelity.[19] The association between a woman and shame, and the consequent connection between the house and public shaming, is also clearly exemplified in the custom of 'house-scorning' in late sixteenth- and early seventeenth-century Rome.[20]

Although the example of Spain alerts us to the need to be aware of local historical, social, or political factors which may have a bearing on honour literature, the question may nevertheless be posed of whether such systems may have more deeply rooted, less transient features which have their source not in historical change but in attitudes to gender, which may alter less rapidly and less perceptibly. The attitudes to gender underlying the divisions made between male and female domains and responsibilities within societies where an honour/shame system operates (and which we could see as an exaggerated form of the patriarchal model) are therefore of particular interest here.

In Chapter 1, in the discussion of gender-acquisition theories, I considered the way in which such theories might account both for the boy's sense of possession and for the likely nature of man's experience of jealousy, given his experience of gender acquisition. How can we now see these theories of gender acquisition in relation to the existence of honour/ shame cultures? First there is a general point to be made, which is that they go some way to explaining the prevalence in a whole range of cultures of social arrangements which prescribe quite separate lives and roles for men and women. There also seems enough evidence to indicate that the reason for division is not simply that power may be exercised by men over women. Division and subordination allow this to take place, but why does it have to happen?

If we follow Klein, then we see that division is caused by the need to separate from a source of fear, or feared power. There is no need to subjugate anything that is not feared. In the process, denigration of the subjugated group frequently takes place—

[19] Juliet du Boulay, *Portrait of a Greek Mountain Village* (Oxford, 1974), 133.

[20] See Elizabeth S. Cohen, 'Honor and Gender in the Streets of Early Modern Rome', *Journal of Interdisciplinary History*, 22 (4) (Spring 1992), 597–625. The article provides an excellent discussion of historical examples of the anthropological view of honour societies discussed in this chapter and contains full bibliography indicating further examples of this type. See also Sánchez Pérez, *La Liturgia del espacio*, on the consequences of the association between the woman and the house.

whether it be in the scorn of women's sexual functions, promoted by envy,[21] or in the conviction within an honour/shame system that the vulnerable part of a man's honour is where it reposes within the shame of the woman.

A general explanation for division between the sexes does not, however, account for the extremes we find in honour/shame systems. An answer may be found in the interaction of general and particular fears.

The work of Stoller and Keller presents a view of man in which the latter is represented as rejecting all the attributes of the mother in order to establish and assert both his separateness and his masculinity. In his separation and rejection we can see two layers: he rejects the mother, because of her feminine qualities, from which he needs to dissociate himself, and he rejects what we could call the feminine, nurturing environment, linked as it is to the life of the feelings, and physical sensation. Once rejected, it is kept in place, in society, by a relationship of dominance of men over women.

What there is a danger of, and this is borne out in the extremes of honour/shame cultures, is that the baby of sensuality is washed out along with the bathwater of dissociation from feminine gender. All that is associated with woman is rejected, and this partly through a positive urge towards masculine gender acquisition, and partly through a fear that the acquisition may not happen unless drastic and decisive action is taken. Thus the separation, and the maintenance of separateness which ensues, speaks of the continuing underlying fear that no leeway may be given in what may well be experienced by the man as a life-and-death struggle for his identity as masculine being. Thus also the prevalence in honour/shame cultures of a belief that a woman needs to be under the tutelage of a man, passing from the power of the father to the power of the husband.

The reason for this care that the woman should be under the authority of a male figure is shown in the level of anxiety dis-

[21] See Karen Horney, 'The Flight from Womanhood', in Jean Baker Miller (ed.), *Psychoanalysis of Women* (Harmondsworth, 1974), 10–20, and Chris Knight, 'Lévi-Strauss and the Dragon: *Mythologiques* Reconsidered in the Light of an Australian Aboriginal Myth', *Man* (NS) 18 (1) (Mar. 1983), 21–50, for re-examination of some rites which can be understood as the alienation of women's potency, simultaneous with denigration of women's functions.

played when a woman is not under male tutelage. One of the most striking and curious manifestations of this is the suspicion shown towards widows, sharply ostracized, for example, in Greek village life. Campbell tells us of the Sarakatsani's rejection of sensuality which is articulated in the requirement that woman in her sexual 'shame' must be virtually devoid of sexuality. A woman must have an 'instinctive revulsion from sexual activity, an attempt in dress, movement and attitude, to disguise the fact that she possesses the physical attributes of her sex. Maidens must be virgins, and even married women must remain virginal in thought and expression'.[22] What we have here is an attitude of intense denial of sensuality, so that even the sensuality which has been denied in man and lodged in the woman has also to be denied or controlled. As outlined by du Boulay, the attitude of the Greek villager (of which Campbell's Sarakatsani are an example) is 'so dominated by the concept of woman as weak and sensual that any possibility of a personal relationship with them which is not physical, or which is not strictly controlled by ideal roles, is completely excluded'.[23] The understanding in Greek village life of sexuality and the sexes is both split and yet understanding. This split between the sexes expresses the need that women in society be the repository of sexual shame. At the same time, within this society it is believed that a woman unprotected by the control of a man (which would be the case of a widow) is liable to engage freely in sexual activity, because it is natural. Thus, since 'sex is considered to be something that every normal person wants, and that it is natural for them to have', the unattached girl or woman will naturally want to have it, once away from the 'sanctions of society'. Since, however, woman is the repository of shame for the society, her sexual freedom, while admitted as natural, constitutes a danger for that society.[24]

The mechanism at work in this splitting (modified and softened in the Greek example by some level of acceptance of the naturalness and inevitability of sexuality) is one which we could see as a mixture, or rather a compound, of the processes to do with gender

[22] J. K. Campbell, *Honour, Family and Patronage: A Study of Institutions and Moral Values in a Greek Mountain Community* (Oxford, 1964), 270.

[23] Du Boulay, *Portait of a Greek Mountain Village*, 118.

[24] Ibid. 112–13.

acquisition, and with the infant's splitting and projection in the face of experiences which are felt to be terrifying. It works on a continuing basis, since its roots are in a paranoid split which, if it is fierce enough, will never move towards the more accepting and accommodating depressive position. Thus the split between the sexes is not a once-and-for-all cleaving, in which threatening forces are placed safely outside the self of the man. It will be added to from two sources. Each time there is a re-encounter, in the persons of the women met in later life, with the qualities originally rejected in the mother, there will be a need to dissociate. And each time there is a response from within the man which echoes the maternal environment from which he has separated, there will be a tendency to split again, and project out into women that tendency in himself which was threatening. Once projected out it becomes the more threatening, and has to be kept separate by even fiercer splitting and separation.

What I have just outlined is a tendency which may well be there at a general level—and may explain the divisions, power-structure, and denigration or undervaluing of feminine attributes—in a patriarchal society. But it does not of itself explain why some societies produce more acute and drastic splits than others.

The explanation for the more extreme types of separation may be found in local, circumstantial factors. This at least seems to be the case, as mentioned earlier, of the honour culture in Spain in the sixteenth and seventeenth centuries. There, a mechanism for splitting (though not on gender lines) was institutionalized at a national level, in the form of the Inquisition. In addition, local historical concerns about the purity of blood had solid practical consequences, in the debarring of those not of proven 'pure' Christian blood (despite the questionable viability of such a concept) from influential and status-linked positions in society.[25]

In this context, one of the best-known modern discussions of the characteristics of Golden Age drama is pertinent. Unamuno, in *En torno al casticismo*, speaks of the polarization of qualities within Calderonian drama. What is of particular significance, however, is that he comments on the absence of sensuality also,

[25] See Caro Baroja, 'Honour and Shame', and McKendrick, 'Honour/Vengeance in the Spanish *Comedia*'.

and on the remarkable absence of love as a factor which moves and informs the characters.[26] From this emerges a frame, a scheme in which the prime considerations are man's name, honour, and prestige, placed under threat by what he sees as the weak point in his system—woman—which is arguably the most disturbing and frightening part of his world.

Viewed in this way, the man of honour has as a starting-point an uneasy relationship with women. Yet the relationship cannot be avoided if his lineage is not to die out. Caught between the need to remain separate from woman and the need to connect with her (because only she can ensure that continuation of his lineage which is the practical and visible extension of his identity), he reacts by binding that relationship as tightly as he can with rules which will ensure both the continuation of his line and also his freedom from threat by femininity. The act of marriage thus represents a danger for man, since it places him in such close proximity to woman. Not only does it expose him to possible loss of honour through his wife; it also brings him closer to the sensuality of the feminine that men in honour cultures reject, deny, and project into women.

Honour systems, then, can be construed as systems based on fear of the feminine, in which the dominating ethos is masculine in so far as it is dominated, apparently, by men, but tending more towards the asexual, since the sensual side of sexuality has been jettisoned into the feminine territory in life. Honour systems are based on fear, and this is consistent with their fragile, almost brittle quality, which renders the literature associated with them both tense and puzzling. Added to this, the unconscious denial of threat of women is frequently converted to an articulation of a sense that threat to the man will come from other men, since it is by men that the man of honour will be judged. Although he will, on the face of it, be judged according to whether he has been 'dishonoured' by some technical slip (or suspicion of it), this judgement will, at a more primitive level, operate on the question of how far he has succeeded in protecting himself from the threat posed by women. That is, there is concern about transgressions of the norms of honour (has a wife or daughter been unfaithful?) but

[26] Unamuno, *En torno al casticismo*, *Obras completas*, ed. M. García Blanco (9 vols.; Madrid, 1966), i. 818–22.

there is also concern that this failing in the man shows that he is insecure in his own relationship with femininity.

The following section will explore how a number of honour dramas can be seen as carrying not only a text of honour, and marital propriety, but also a subtext of anxiety about possession of masculinity. This aspect will be examined primarily in relation to paranoid-schizoid behaviour within the characters, a behaviour which will have an effect on the spectator analogous to the effect on others of the behaviour of those who engage in intense splitting-mechanisms, and thus establish disturbing counter-transferential waves.[27]

WIFE-MURDER DRAMA IN SPAIN

A man is led to believe that his wife is unfaithful when he learns that a ring he has given her has been seen by the king on the hand of another man. The husband lays a trap for his wife, and, having told her that he is going out on a hunting-trip, returns to his house to catch his wife and his niece entertaining their respective suitors. No actual adultery has been committed, but it is abundantly clear that this is what was intended. The husband and his slave kill not only all the principals in the drama, but also servants, domestic animals, and pets. The king, when told of the events, praises the husband for the vengeance taken, and gives him another woman in marriage. (*The Knights Commander of Córdoba* [Los Comendadores de Córdoba], Lope de Vega, 1596)

A man who has just married by proxy is relieved of further military duty so that he can go to his wife. On her journey to meet her new husband, the wife is approached by a former suitor, whom she had believed dead. The former suitor, somewhat unreasonably, reproaches her for marrying. Despite the wife's extremely correct attitude to her former lover, the latter continues in his attentions. This arouses the suspicions of the husband, who

[27] The term 'counter-transference' is used here, as elsewhere, in the sense developed within Kleinian theory. That is, it does not simply designate the feeling evoked in the analyst or therapist in relation to the transferential feeling of the patient, but rather is an emotional source for understanding the symbolic and mute communications of the patient, whether by empathy or by an understanding of the processes of projection or projective identification. See R. D. Hinshelwood, *A Dictionary of Kleinian Thought* (London, 1991), 255–62.

is additionally alerted to awareness of the fragility of honour by the plight of a close friend whose honour has recently been slighted. He arranges for the lover to die in a sailing-accident, and for the wife to die when the house she is in is burned down. By arranging such 'natural' deaths, he aims to keep the shame of his dishonour a secret. (*Secret Revenge for a Secret Fault* [A secreto agravio, secreta venganza], Calderón de la Barca, 1635)

A man marries, somewhat late in life, so that he may have a legitimate heir. After marriage he continues with his earlier habits of debauchery, and neglects his wife, a younger woman, who falls in love with his illegitimate son. The husband is informed of this adulterous love by an anonymous letter. He has his wife bound and gagged and covered with a cloth, then tells his son that this is someone who has betrayed him. He requires his son to kill this 'traitor', as an act of filial obedience. When the son complies, the husband calls the household to witness what has happened. The son has killed the wife, he says, prompted by the news that he was to be ousted by a legitimate heir. He orders the son to be killed for this outrage. (*Punishment without Revenge* [El Castigo sin venganza], Lope de Vega, 1635)

A woman who is married comes into contact, accidentally, with a former lover. Despite her own care to maintain correct behaviour, the lover pursues her, and the husband, himself involved in a dubious earlier dealing with another woman (which caused her to seek help from the king), becomes prey to jealousy. He gives his wife two hours' notice of her coming death, and arranges for her to have a blood-letting which is to be fatal. The man who is made the instrument of the killing, horrified at what he has been obliged to do, tells the king. The version of events given to the king by the husband is that his wife has died by accident. The king, while realizing an act of vengeance has occurred, takes no punitive action, and disposes that the husband should now marry the woman whose honour he had originally damaged. (*The Physician of his Honour* [El Médico de su honra], Calderón de la Barca, 1635)[28]

[28] The editions used for these plays are: *Los Comendadores de Córdoba* (The Knights Commander of Córdoba), edn. of Real Academia Española in *Biblioteca de Autores Españoles*, xxiv (Madrid, 1968); *El Castigo sin venganza* (Punishment without Revenge), edn. of C. A. Jones (Oxford, 1966); *A secreto agravio, secreta venganza* (Secret Revenge for a Secret Fault) and *El Médico de su honra* (The

These are brief accounts of four well-known honour plays that focus on marriage, infidelity, dishonour, and death. It is made eminently clear that there needs to be little transgression of marital boundaries for husbands to take retaliatory action. Indeed, only in the first example from Lope is the wife blatantly unfaithful with no provocation, and while the second example from Lope is unequivocal about guilt, ample explanation, if not justification, is provided for the wife's infidelity in the neglect by her husband.

We can see from the above that infidelity, or the merest suspicion of it, brings retribution which needs to be swift and effective. Such action is needed in order to avoid the slur on honour that would result from tolerance of extra-marital affairs, or even of the slightest extra-marital interest. The emphasis is always on the simple slight of honour, rather than the understood challenge to power and authority which is, of course, also implied by the wife's act of infidelity. Secrecy is paramount. In the interest of honour, the act of vengeance, as we have seen, may be so rigged as to appear an accident, and judicious monarchs, faced with the evidence of a husband's vengeance, will agree to the concealment of the true action in the interests of preserving the husband's honour. Furthermore, as can be seen from the denouement of the plays, the act of vengeance is regarded in a variety of ways as the restoration of the proper order of things, and is either uncontested, condoned, or even praised and vindicated by the monarch, public source of honour and authority. Women emerge from the plays as transgressors and/or objects to be used in honour transactions (as in the post-vengeance marriages in two of the examples).

The synopses of plots with which we began suggest that the paradigm of the man of honour, his motivation, his mode of action, and the outcome of that action, is relatively straightforward. What we must remember, however, is that it accords with the external view, or external reality of the honour story, the text as opposed to the subtext. In this, honour is gained by valour and good social standing, is then lost or endangered by the imprudent or even wilfully errant behaviour of a wife, and then

Physician of his Honour) in Calderón de la Barca, *Obras completas*, ed. A. Valbuena Briones (3 vols.; Madrid, 1966, repr. 1969), i. *El Médico de su honra* is translated by Gwynne Edwards in *Calderón Plays: One* (London, 1991), where the title is *The Surgeon of Honour*. References are to this edition.

cleansed or reclaimed by the process of shedding that wife's blood. The paradigm which is not revealed by these external details is that of the powerful and private emotional agenda underlying the honour code, and which forms the subtext of the plays. In looking in more detail at our four examples, then, I would like to distinguish between text and subtext, between sequence of events and the manner, the way of being, of those characters involved in the events. The complexity of the text–subtext dynamic and the conflict between them produce disturbing and confusing effects on the spectator, a simple label for this being that honour plays are thus 'moving'.

Drama is a public event, a staging of a phantasy perhaps, but one for public consumption. Even though some theatre audiences were segregated by sex, there is a sense in which, as in language, the feminine is held to be subsumed in the masculine, so that the public text is addressed to a group of spectators who, although mixed, are considered as masculine in reactions expected or invited.

The reaction produced by being in the presence of someone engaged in splitting and projection is extremely intense and disturbing. In the case of schizophrenics, for example, the subliminal communication via the projected feelings which can be picked up and experienced in the counter-transference is often the only way of receiving information from the schizophrenic, who characteristically engages in displacement and avoidance of feeling.[29]

The reaction of an audience to projected feeling is clearly somewhat distinct, since the spectator is a bystander. Yet in the sense that we frequently feel that the theatre addresses us directly, there is the possibility that we, as spectators, will experience projected feeling (or, more precisely, the actor's articulation of projected feeling) in the disturbing way in which we might be affected by the person who resorts to intense splitting.

A further phenomenon to take into account is that if feeling is not articulated in the text, but relegated to a subtext of denial, this will not mean that it is without effect on the audience. On the

[29] For discussion of the complex and indirect communications of the schizophrenic see Harold Searles, 'Schizophrenic Communication' (1961), in id., *Collected Papers on Schizophrenia and Related Subjects* (1965, repr. London, 1986), 381–428.

contrary, denied feeling is often felt most strongly in the counter-transference, to which the audience's situation is analogous. Denied feeling is thus picked up by the spectator, and conflict between this feeling and the articulated feeling of the text will then take place within the spectator.

The fact that the audience consists of both men and women will produce complications because of the differing processes of identification involved, and because of the patriarchal structure in which both audience and text are situated. My principal concern here is with the masculine spectator as indeed the intended public spectator who will be expected finally to endorse the outcome of the honour drama. The drama of honour as witnessed by women spectators will not involve the same level of identification with masculine protagonists engaged in fierce splitting, although there will no doubt be identification with female characters who receive projected emotions within the plays.

The difficulty in locating a suitable paradigm which expresses both text and subtext should indeed be the factor which alerts us to the complexities of the honour code and to the impossible pressures which surround the man of honour, pressures which act principally on his external, social self, and crush the private, emotional self. These pressures bring about a further feature of the honour story, which is the apparent detachment of the man of honour—a man who is generally seen as undertaking his final act of vengeance as a matter of propriety, of justice, and not as an act of jealous passion. As a mode of behaviour, we have seen how the 'honourable' response to marital infidelity is, as required by the honour code, swift, effective, and, so that honour is not publicly besmirched, necessarily secret. Yet this very swiftness and (literal) power of execution, combined with what is felt to be the proper motivation (a concern with honour, with the social and public self that will be judged by others) constitutes a contradiction. To act swiftly and properly, the man of honour needs to be separated from his emotional entanglements and to be unattached to the spouse he is about to murder—otherwise his action becomes a simple act of passion, and not the action of a man impelled by a sense of what is right. That is, his act requires, if it is to be the true act of a man of honour, that he be not attached. In other words, he should, ideally, act as either honour or justice demands, rather than as his natural feelings as a jealous husband prompt him to behave. Yet in so far as he is able to act as this instrument of the code of honour, he is proportionally at risk of losing his humanity, his capacity to be attached to another, and, by extension, his capacity to arouse and engage the feelings of the audience who view him. It is questionable whether simple admiration of the power to act, as exemplified in the man of honour, is going to be sufficient to arouse and hold the emotional response of those who witness his actions. Since, however, the spectator will witness both act and denial of feeling, the theatrical tension will in fact result from unarticulated conflict between the absorption of the text and that of the subtext.

One could therefore argue that, for an honour play to be truly paradigmatic of the action of a man of honour, it needs to take the form of a mystery play, or an *auto sacramental*, in which dogma, in humanly accessible form, is enacted, and given recognizable human flesh: that is, it would simply display to the audience necessary if difficult truths about human and social existence. This detached display would be emotionally distinct from a form of drama which contained both conflict and suspense, and uncertainty of resolution. Such a form of play would, however, be undramatic, lacking in the capacity to arouse: it would simply be an enactment of accepted behaviour, with the complications of difficult and varying circumstances which would make the final outcome hard to see in its full detail, but none the less ineluctable in its essential form.

Contrasting with what we might expect of a true paradigm of the honour play, the examples to be found in the Spanish theatre of the Golden Age, while having a surface text which appears to conform with the ineluctability of final outcome, in fact carry strong subtexts which both allow for their emotional and literary enlivening, and point to the levels of anxiety, paranoia, and human fragility which underlie the outward appearance of strength and incontestability of the man of honour.

The gap between surface text and subtext, and the tendency for different ages to concentrate on the primacy of either one or the other according to their own socio-historical assumptions and investments, gives rise to a striking diversity in the type of critical judgements made in relation to these plays. The major shift which has occurred in the recent critical evaluation of honour plays has been from a position where it was believed that the surface text was the prime factor, and hence that honour plays were a simple exemplification of a set of beliefs held by the society in which they were written, and to which their authors necessarily and fully subscribed, towards a position where more attention is paid to the subtext, and to the possible hollowness or suspect nature of the surface text. This shift means that critics have been enabled to work towards a reading of the honour plays as extremely problematic works which deal with complicated, not to say unresolvable, issues. In particular, recent critical work on honour plays has now raised the possibility of the offended husband being presented as ridiculous, or as being far from admirable. That is, we now have readings, focusing on the subtext, which question the essential rightness of the man of honour. Through this, honour plays may now be seen to a large degree as plays in which the man of honour fails, or cannot know how to succeed, in living up to the mythical expectations of his role. What results, in the rereading of these texts, is that they can be viewed, not necessarily as a critique of the honour code itself, but rather as an examination of the difficulties in living up to its impossible precepts, given that men are merely human, and as susceptible to passion and weakness as the women whose actions are so frequently presented as their undoing.

In the preceding section, I discussed the concept, the abstract idea of the man of honour, and surveyed both the psychological mechanisms involved and some of the socio-historical factors which in the case of the Mediterranean, and most particularly in the case of Spain, have led to the formation of a code of behaviour which is volatile and inflammable at the same time as it is rigid, categorizing, and demarcating. Now, by looking at a number of examples of honour plays written in Golden Age Spain, I would like to examine the way in which the anxieties and mechanisms of projection underlying the concept of the man of honour are not only clearly delineated in the plays, but also serve a useful function in enabling us to come to terms with the plays as works of literature with which we can engage emotionally as well as intellectually.

But before this, a certain amount of ground needs to be cleared to avoid the begging of some obvious questions. Why, first of all, concentrate on Spain, and its examples of honour literature? Has Spain no examples of cuckolds? Has Spain nothing in its literature of the Golden Age but examples of men of honour?

To the second and third of these questions, the answer is, unsurprisingly, 'yes, it does': both in Cervantes' short stories and plays and in the theatre preceding Lope we can find models of the cuckold that are closely related to cuckolds elsewhere in Europe. Cervantes shows an awareness of the robust fabliau tradition, and a capacity both for bawdy burlesque (as shown in the comical interlude *The Jealous Old Man* [El Viejo celoso]) and for a compassionate portrayal of the cuckold (as in the related short story *The Jealous Extremaduran* [El Celoso extremeño] discussed in Chapter 6). The picaresque novel of the sixteenth century, where it touches on matters sexual, can be as scabrous and disrespectful as anything found in medieval literature, the cuckolding of the *Lazarillo de Tormes* being a prime example of the type.

But to return to the first question—why concentrate on Spain? Other countries have concepts of honour, and, curiously, present concentrations of concern with honour at the same period as this question is of acute import in Spain. But whether in Germany, England, France, or Italy, the intense preoccupation with honour and, in particular, with the threat to honour posed by the sexual misdemeanours of a wife, seems not to be present to the degree and with the intensity that we encounter in Spain.[30] The theatre of Molière, for example, sketches out a series of situations in which there is the threat that a husband may be made cuckold, but the emphasis is on the ridiculous figure the man presents in social terms, rather than on any deeply felt shock at the possibility that he might be dishonoured by his wife's actions. For Molière, the major threat presented by potential cuckoldry is to the often fragile social status and desire for upward social mobility of his predominantly bourgeois characters.[31] In other countries, concern is as much with general reputation, with slurs on the man's public and known character as a gentleman, as with conjugal threats to

[30] See Fredson Bowers, *Elizabethan Revenge Tragedy, 1587–1642* (Princeton, NJ, 1940), esp. 279–81; George Fenwick Jones, *Honor in German Literature*; Bryson, *The Point of Honour, in Sixteenth-century Italy*.

[31] J. F. Gaines, *Social Structures in Molière's Theater* (Columbus, Oh., 1984), 141–2, points out e.g. that in *L'École des femmes* (1662) Arnolphe's aim is to rise socially. He sets out to marry a woman of lower social standing, so that she does not threaten his status. This leaves him just with the threat of his wife making him a cuckold, 'thus shattering his precarious respect and proving his lack of honour or worthiness. Since Arnolphe defines his own honor not in positive terms but according to the dishonor, lowliness and misfortune of those who surround him, one incidence of cuckoldry will be enough to destroy his chimerical ambitions of power and prestige as a noble'.

honour. Even in Italy, which, along with Greece is arguably the closest to Spain in the attitude shown towards the honour of men, there is a measure of tone and capacity for debate on the subject of honour which contrasts sharply with what is articulated in Spanish honour plays. In Italy, for example, women, children, Jews, and other marginated groups were excluded from the possession of honour, and a woman could only dishonour the husband under whose control she was deemed to fall (rather than herself).[32] It appears, furthermore, that opinion in Italy was finely balanced on the relative gravity of words or acts, and even in the case of words, made fine distinctions on the force of different types of verbal insult. Landi held that insult by word was worse than insult by act, since the former offended the soul and the latter the body, and thus the soul, being deemed the master of the body, could receive greater insult. This we could read as a microcosmic reflection of the belief within the honour code that it is man, the wielder of power, who is also the party in marriage who stands to be most dishonoured.[33] There was also quite finely balanced opinion on whether it was worse to be called a cuckold or a traitor[34] (which we could view as the debate on the relative importance of the private or the public man), and, compared with Spain, the Italian attitude to adultery, in contrast to the wife-murder sanctioned by Spanish law, showed a much more legalistic approach, since such matters might be dealt with by courts.[35]

The Spanish honour code, of course, incorporates general sensitivity to slurs on honour, and men of honour are as likely as their other European counterparts to react fiercely to suggestion that their honour, their honesty, and their general social reputation might be thought wanting. However, in the theatre at least, honour is primarily bound to, or associated with, matters sexual or conjugal, and within this sphere produces the most intense reaction. And within the theatre, we can see how attitudes in Spain stand in sharp contradistinction to those elsewhere in Europe.

In an early and excellent article comparing Spanish honour-

32 Bryson, *The Point of Honour*, 24, 26.

33 Ibid. 39.

34 Ibid. 41–2.

35 Ibid. 76. The dispositions in Spanish law are given in McKendrick, *Woman and Society in the Spanish Drama of the Golden Age*, 15–17.

literature with works by some late Elizabethan and early Jacobean dramatists in England, E. M. Wilson outlined similarities between the honour plays of the two countries, but also indicated some striking differences in their attitudes to honour. One of the chief areas where English practice diverged from Spanish (at least as reflected in their respective dramas) was on the connection between honour and revenge. In English plays, for example, Wilson observes that the revenger seldom escapes undamaged.[36] Wilson's most striking point, however, is on the non-correlation between the guilt of wives and their fate as victims of murder. Where there was wife-murder in English plays, it tended to be committed on an innocent wife, and led ultimately to the death of the avenger. In those cases in English plays where the wife was in fact guilty, what Wilson acutely, and in passing, notes as the prevailing literary (as opposed to real or historical) solution was for the husband to kill the lover and then shut his wife up somewhere.[37] If wives died, it was more likely to be by their own hand, motivated by remorse, rather than by the hand of their husband.[38]

Standing in contrast both with Italian casuistry about the relative gravity of offences and with the English reaction to wifely infidelity, which falls short of murder, is the Spanish example. Here wives, guilty or not guilty (and more frequently the latter than the former), are killed by husbands who profess to be motivated by honour not jealousy, and whose actions appear to be upheld by the social environment.[39]

Wilson's study already marks out the Spanish theatre as different from other, more northerly and, one is tempted to suggest, more phlegmatic traditions. That Spanish drama is in a class almost on its own is suggested both by the relative lack of com-

[36] Wilson, 'Honour in the Plays of Shakespeare's Predecessors and Contemporaries', 24.

[37] Ibid. 27. See also McKendrick, 'Honour/Vengeance in the Spanish *Comedia*', on the gap between the literary and social realities of wife-murder in Spain.

[38] Wilson, 'Honour in the Plays of Shakespeare's Predecessors and Contemporaries', 30–1. For more detail, see the discussion of Thomas Heywood in Ch. 6.

[39] See Larson, *The Honor Plays of Lope de Vega*, 180, n. 27: 'It would seem . . . that in no other country—except perhaps Italy in the sixteenth century, where, if we accept the suggestion of Burckhardt, the phenomenon reflects Spanish influence—has the honor of the male been so closely identified with the chastity of the women of his family.' The reference is to *The Civilization of the Renaissance in Italy: An Essay* (London, 1960), 272.

parative theatre-studies encompassing it and by the diversity of opinion it has provoked within the Hispanic field itself.

In an article of 1965, C. A. Jones asked why it should be that Spanish plays about honour are so little understood and appreciated, at least outside Spain.[40] I think that one can focus on the reaction of puzzlement in the face of these plays as one that has meaning. That is, the diversity of reactions that the plays evoke suggests not just that the texts may be puzzling in themselves (an effect partly produced, I would suggest, by the gap mentioned earlier between surface text and subtext), but also that they act as a sort of emotional or intellectual litmus-paper which tells us as much about the plays as the critics. This confusion arises because the plays are as divisive as the nature of the honour code itself, and the splitting and projection which is at the heart of the system of honour is thus carried over into the reaction provoked by literature which is based upon it. Thus readers are caused to be ranged on different sides in their interpretation, rather than being able to agree upon a common, if complex, dramatic ground.

Notable attempts have been made to move away from such critical polarization—witness A. K. G. Paterson's close reading of texts for their imagery and dramatic qualities.[41] Despite such excellent exceptions, there is elsewhere in the corpus of critical literature on honour drama a tendency to try to decide whether honour-play protagonists are worthy or unworthy, good or evil, frail or strong. The difficulty of arriving at an adjudication points us to the probability that, unless we read the plays as simple expositions of the posing and solving of honour problems to an audience that both adheres to and accepts the honour code, by authors who are themselves fully paid-up card-carrying members of a society that believes in the code, then what we are presented with in the plays is itself fragile, uncertain, susceptible of a number of interpretations.

[40] C. A. Jones, 'Spanish Honour as Historical Phenomenon, Convention and Artistic Motive', *Hispanic Review*, 33 (1965), 32–9 (38).

[41] A. K. G. Paterson, 'The Alchemical Marriage in Calderón's *El Médico de su honra*', *Romanistisches Jahrbuch*, 30 (1979), 263–82; and id., 'Calderón's *A secreto agravio, secreta venganza*: A Theatre of the Passions', *Modern Language Review*, 79 (1984), 589–608. See n. 1 of the second of these articles for a review of those critics who have succeeded in treating these plays in their dramatic complexity.

Just as it would be inaccurate to suggest that Spanish literature of the Golden Age is monolithic in aspect (the shadow of the cuckold is there in the background of the public image of the man of honour) and monolithic in its portrayal of concern with honour, so also with the theatre of honour itself.[42] The four examples cited at the start of this section demonstrate the diversity of that drama. But, whether we consider Golden Age literature in all its forms or just in the particular form of dramas of honour, the following question arises: do we simply have a diversity among the plays, or is it possible to trace a development, in the course of which the delineation of the man of honour alters, and moves from the more intransigent husband of *The Knights Commander of Córdoba* to more subtle forms of the model? Alternatively, is the theatre of Calderón simply different from that of Lope de Vega (born nearly forty years earlier), or could it in some way represent a development, a move along a trajectory in the portrayal of personal and social anxieties and tensions? And, if it did represent a development, would the examples of cuckolds from Cervantes cited above fit into what could be claimed to be a trajectory from cuckold to man of honour? The examples of cuckolds from Cervantes (1613–15) antedate major honour plays by Calderón by a good twenty years, so might we here be seeing a general motion away from the ribald and towards the respectable, away from the accommodating and towards the shocked and the fearful?

Just as it is tempting to postulate that the model of the man of honour is posterior chronologically to that of the cuckold, and comes to be articulated in its full clarity later than the cuckold in European cultural development, so it is also tempting to focus microcosmically on the man-of-honour model itself, and to see it growing, and intensifying, during the period in Spain when it was most prominent in literature.

Early plays by Lope, for example, do not fit the extremes of the man-of-honour story as exemplified in the two cases cited. David Larson has traced a development in the theatre of Lope de Vega which suggests that the early work contains a much more lenient

[42] Husbands in honour plays, even in Spain, are not a single breed, nor do they all react to infidelity in the same manner. On this, see, e.g., Peter Podol, 'Non-conventional Treatment of the Honour Theme in the Theater of the Golden Age', *Revista de Estudios Hispánicos*, 7 (1973), 449–63.

and accommodating attitude to honour than is displayed later. With reference to those of Lope's plays written before 1600, Larson highlights features which resonate markedly with the cuckold model. He sees, first, a tendency to view the fate of the protagonist (the man who is dishonoured) as one for which the protagonist himself is, in the last analysis, responsible. This judgement we might recast, bearing in mind the cuckold as that earlier protagonist presented as one who had earned his come-uppance. Second, and consequently, Larson sees the actions of the 'offenders' as at least in part excusable—just as, in the cuckold story, the part of the wife and lover is there for the audience to support, rather than being encouraged to be on the side of the ineffectual husband who is outwitted. Third, the works do not allow the 'offenders' to be punished excessively. Rather the tendency is for them to be allowed to be rehabilitated socially. This does not, of course, fully reflect their habitual fate in the cuckold story, which is to escape scot-free, but is distant at least from the extremes of vengeance and punishment found in later honour plays. This implies an attitude which can at least tolerate the thought of marital transgression, and one might even suggest that these earlier plays, along with the cuckold story, have some level of pragmatism about them.

Larson's view on these early plays, however, is not that the accommodation shown therein reflects some realistic, pragmatic, and reconciling attitude to life and its vagaries. Rather, he argues, it is life as viewed through the wishful fantasy of a young man—in this case the young Lope. It is life as this young 'and rather immature' writer (in the eyes of Larson) would have it at this stage. It is life as in the topsy-turvy form of the cuckold story: 'the man who is the protagonist and nominal hero of the piece is blamed and ridiculed, and the man who is the antagonist and nominal anti-hero is vindicated and praised'.[43]

Having committed himself to this reading of the early plays and having dismissed their licence as pertaining to youthful (and presumably unrealistic) wishful thinking, Larson is then perhaps irrevocably committed, by his own logic, to seeing the 'middle period' plays, which do not have this degree of leniency towards dishonour, as being somehow more right-minded.

[43] Larson, *The Honor Plays of Lope de Vega*, 28.

A difficulty here is the assumption that we have a move from young man's folly to mature man's wisdom, from wishful thinking that would allow youthful desire to have its way, to 'mature' thinking that reveals a 'proper' reaction to sexual transgression and slights upon honour.

There are, however, other ways of reading the shifts in Lope's writing. Instead of viewing youth as the age which fancies and which has no sense of proper social structure, we could view it as a period where there is little to fear, at least in terms of personal vigour. By contrast, middle age brings bogeys of all varieties, and the creeping realization that both potency and life are limited. Hence, perhaps, the greater likelihood that this period might produce works which are more power-conscious than desire-conscious, more paranoid about threatened loss than conveying youthful expansion and the delight in stolen liberties.

Much more of a problem, however, is how we should read those works felt to fall within the category of 'serious' honour plays, and in particular the four examples we started with.

In *The Knights Commander of Córdoba*, as the synopsis shows, there is no doubt about the guilt of the wife, Beatriz. Indeed, if we follow in more detail the sequence of events, we can see the line of the plot as a mechanical presentation of factors and consequences. Despite the constraints of time naturally operating in the theatre, there is a surprising and shocking suddenness in the way the fickleness of Beatriz, and of her companion Ana (her husband's niece), springs into being as soon as the absence of the Veinticuatro, Beatriz's husband, presents the opportunity. One can almost hear the cogs of this plot clanking, as the opportunity to err is seized upon as soon as it arises, to be followed by the husband's suspicion, the laying of a trap to catch the wife, and the bloody retribution that follows on the discovery of guilty intention (if not quite of guilty action).

The play opens, with heavy intent, presenting the temptation first. In Act I, horses are offered, on behalf of the king, to two men, Don Jorge and Don Fernando, so that they may ride through the city. This recognition of their worth (with symbolic implications about their *masculine* worth) is undermined by their wariness that the horses may be too lively for them. Shortly afterwards, the overt masculine concern with masculinity is reiterated in a comment by Galindo, a lackey, about an insult he has received: 'Jew of the Veinticuatro, with more skirts than a bride, take this blow from me.' The insult plays on anxiety about both blood and masculinity. Later in the act, the honouring of Don Jorge and Don Fernando is followed by the public honour done by the king to the Veinticuatro who has rendered military service by bringing the city of Granada and the surrounding country to order. The king presents the Veinticuatro with a ring, which the latter accepts, speaking of it as an emblem of his bondage to the king. In this way, on the surface, we are given the view of both suitors and husband as men who are accorded public recognition of honour: they are held in esteem by the king, source of honour and authority, and he has given visible signs of their honouring.

That this exchange is followed at once by the sight of the Veinticuatro's wife and niece comparing notes on the various physical attractions of the young men they have seen jousting could be seen as the swift contrast of honourable men with flighty, would-be dishonourable women, only too ready to flirt with Jorge and Fernando when they meet. Again, the theatre's conventions naturally urge swiftness of action, but the move to flirtation here is at a speed which justifies any concern men may have about the fidelity of their wives.

Initially the 'eyeing up' of the men by the women is also significant. While it may seem to us an activity more usually associated with men, it has an explanation (or rather its exposition has an explanation) in the anthropological observations on the split of attributes between the sexes expressed in the honour code. Since within this framework sensuality is lodged with the woman, as are chaos and instability, it is appropriate not only that women should be portrayed as those who will disturb order, but also that they should be seen as taking a decidedly physical view of their relationships with men. The women themselves emphasize the gender-division within the society. It must be perceived to be absolute. As Beatriz, the Veinticuatro's wife remarks, men must be robust, 'Since it is not fitting that a man should have the semblance of a woman.' The very swiftness of the move to focus on the flightiness and 'unfeminine' behaviour of the women may be a representation of the splitting process of the honour code, or a splitting which is engaged in by the masculine author. The invitation to the supposed male spectator is arguably to collude in the condemnation of women. No public space is allowed for the reaction of the female spectator.

To rub in the contrast between faithless wife and devoted honourable husband, the scene of flirtation is followed by the return home of the Veinticuatro. He praises both his wife and the married state (is it possible that he does not distinguish between the two?), and of course his words will ring hollow for the audience, which has just witnessed the scene of the women's flirtations and which will see his wife's attentions to him as empty, even ironically excessive: 'Oh, what pleasure I receive! | Who would say that we are diminished by marriage? | Who was that ignorant person | who spoke ill of marriage? | Does happiness have any other form | than that which I have present?'

As a proof of his delight, the Veinticuatro, in a further musing on the delights of marriage at the start of Act II, presents his wife with the ring the king gave him. Almost immediately after this, he announces his departure for Toledo, having introduced his wife to the young men of the first scene—that is, he acts as the agent for the men who will dishonour his household, showing in this some of the lack of awareness of the cuckold. The men are, however, his cousins, and he is full of praises for them. It would appear he is either full of faith in his wife, or, as noted above, remarkably naïve—the latter being confirmed by his wife's next move; in the Veinticuatro's absence, Jorge announces that he too is to go to Toledo, and Beatriz gives him her husband's ring. At this point we could question whether the author himself has become involved in the unawareness of the cuckold, in elaborating this unlikely plot, or whether there is something more complex at work here. A general feature of the cuckold is his gullibility, and in showing this characteristic even in a man of honour, the author may be falling prey to a subsidiary desire to protect his male character from the ridicule of being the over-jealous husband, while failing to see that he is consequently likely to be associated with that other model, the unaware cuckold.

The ring, which has travelled so far and so fast for an emblem of love and respect given specifically by one person to another, is spotted in the next scene by the king, who sees the reward he had given the Veinticuatro on the hand of Jorge. Not unreasonably, he reproaches the Veinticuatro for this apparent lack of care with the precious gift. The Veinticuatro now has two issues to face: the reproach from the king and, implicitly, the problem of regaining his approbation; and, what seems to capture his attention much more acutely, the suspicion that his wife may not be as virtuous as he had believed. He sets off for home. On his return he is told by Rodrigo, his slave, of the dalliance of his wife and Ana with their respective young men. The information is superfluous, at least for the Veinticuatro, but adds to the general dynamic within the play in which men alert other men to the precariousness of their honour. What may be of some interest here is that the Veinticuatro is alerted by the two extremes of the social structure: by the king, source of all honour, and by a man whose social standing is low (and therefore may have no real claim to honour on his own behalf) and whose racial purity is more than a little questionable.

After a strained and hypocritical homecoming-scene, full of hidden meaning and suggestion for all parties on stage, and even more for the audience, the Veinticuatro announces that he is going out hunting. This unconvincing announcement is followed by Beatriz in her turn both implausibly and imprudently making plans to receive her lover. Again this is a point of possible division in spectator reaction—there is the tacit appeal to the male spectator that this is all-too-plausible, that this is just what one would expect of a woman, while the reaction that what is going on is implausible is allowed no public space, or rather is not articulated or commented upon. Thus the husband's action, which is both deceitful and lacking in verisimilitude, is followed by the wife's action, which is shown to be incautious and blatantly immoral, the impression of the latter being strengthened by the degree to which the wife is now quite outspoken in her plans to delight the senses and to sate physical desire. She prepares eagerly and impatiently to receive her lover in splendour: 'Ah, don Jorge! Quickly lay out four fine sheets. Take out the pastilles, the ones in the small desk, to regale the new master. What are you waiting for? Take the keys. Perfume this whole chamber.' Again, as we noted above in the style in which she and Ana eyed up the physical attributes of the young men, she is being type-cast by her male creator as the woman who is, virtually by her nature, sensual, immoral, or even amoral, concerned exclusively to secure physical gratification and having no spiritual or moral eye to the requirements of the honour code as it pertains to her husband.

The sudden return of the Veinticuatro breaks up the illicit

activity (made rather obvious by the state of undress of the two young men), and wholesale bloodshed of guilty parties and innocent bystanders (who have witnessed the dishonour, and therefore must also die) ensues.

Thus the detail of the action. But the question is, what are we to make of it? Do we regard it as the triumph of the man of honour, or his misfortune, or conceivably something else? And are we to judge the meaning of the play by the action alone, or to pay some attention to the manner of action, the manner of being of the characters, none of whom, going on the evidence of the sequence of events, seem to stand out for their morality, their intelligence, or their ingenuity?

Not surprisingly, critics have been divided about how to approach this play. It is only when they move below action to manner, from text to subtext, that it is possible to see the emotional dynamic of the honour story, as opposed to what is *meant to be* the emotional dynamic (one of admiration, moral uplifting, wonder at the fortitude and valour of the man of honour). The contrast is between the reception of denied or avoided emotion, and the communication of the defensive precepts of the honour code.

An example of a critic who views the Veinticuatro as a man of honour who is to be admired is David Larson. In order to do this, he focuses critical attention on the figure of the husband, and puts on one side the question of vengeance, and the relation of the husband with both wife and suitors. That is, the Veinticuatro is viewed within the context of an abstract situation of honour, rather than within the practical and human relations and interactions which are in fact the stuff of his life (and of everyone else's) and which is shown in the text. This focus on the abstract is one which is naturally provoked by the apparently unemotional nature of the honour code itself, which retreats into structures and demarcations, or pushes the non-abstract away from itself, as a mode of survival. In the face of threat, rigidity and a system of rules are to be adopted: such is the attitude of people, groups, societies who are threatened. Thus Larson, reacting as critic to this situation, adopts here the same retreat from reality as is theoretically the justification for the Veinticuatro's action in the play. He views the protagonist as a man to be admired, who 'having been cast into adversity, exerts will and strength together not simply to recover his former position, but actually to climb above it'.[44]

In psychodynamic terms, he identifies with the defensive masculine attitudes apparently embodied in the male protagonist. We could view his interpretation as one which in part derives from an identification with the process at the heart of the honour code: one of splitting and projection in which the emotional, the weak, and the intolerable are cast aside, so that the comforts of the abstract and ideal position can be retained. We can also view this interpretation of the Veinticuatro in the play as resting firmly on a defended and masculine view of the husband's place in the honour code. That is, if we see the masculine part of the honour code, and the attributes given to men more generally in society, as being concerned with externals and with action, then we can see how this reading of the Veinticuatro concentrates on externals and action. It gives credit for action which is appropriate to the code, yet passes over both the question of the Veinticuatro's responsibility for his own fate, and his questionable attitude both before and after the occurrence/discovery of his wife's infidelity.

That Larson is viewing the play according to externals is confirmed when he makes a comparison between the fate of the Veinticuatro and that of the Cid, arguing that in both cases the pattern of action is the same and consists of affront, loss, and the regaining of honour through valour. Again, there is no reference to the manner of being of the Veinticuatro, simply the reference to his role and status in a network of social relations which has come to reveal his dishonour, his lack of proper social place due to the less-than-faithful behaviour of his wife.

Larson's views, and others like them, have not, of course, gone unchallenged. But it is interesting to note how far, even in the activity of critical challenge, there is a lack of emphasis on the shortcomings and weaknesses of the Veinticuatro as man and husband. Alix Zuckerman-Ingber, for example, while commenting on how the Veinticuatro carries out his vengeance in a rage, and how the vengeance is an extreme and extravagant one (thus paying some critical attention to his manner of activity, rather than to the simple fact that the activity takes place), does show a degree of sympathy for a man caught in the 'injustice' of an

[44] Ibid. 42.

honour system in which 'a man's honor, linked to his wife's behavior, is often beyond his control'.[45] In her attention to his rage and violence, Zuckerman-Ingber comes close to his emotional state, as well as his manner, and this leads her, none the less, to a position of sympathy when confronted with this protagonist. That is, there is an identification with some of the emotional issues involved, but still a complete acceptance of the honour code as such, so that the man with his emotions is seen to be the victim of the system.

An alternative way we might adopt in trying to come to terms with this set of perceptions is to see that the system itself is formed ultimately as a defence against those very emotional extremes which are displayed by the Veinticuatro. In this light, we can see how the honour system itself has broken down. Only in a situation where the protagonist is able to act with cold detachment could we perhaps say that the honour system is functioning well. Here we have its breakdown. The catch-22 of seeing the play like this is to establish that the Veinticuatro does at least betray himself as human and emotional, whereas the 'perfect' mode of functioning within the honour system would be less than wholly human (a natural consequence of the process of splitting by which half the attributes of the human are discarded and projected elsewhere).

The most consistently critical attitude to the Veinticuatro is contained in an article by Melveena McKendrick.[46] She gives close attention to the words, manner, and actions of the man himself, rather than to the mythical expectations of the 'proper' man of honour. One of the first challenges made to conventional belief in this article is the questioning of the idea that the male characters will necessarily (because men of honour, who furthermore receive their public honour in the play) elicit our admiration.

The questioning of the value of the protagonist is based primarily on his manner (revealed as ridiculous, sycophantic towards figures of power, inappropriate in response, inadequate at all times) rather than to his expected functioning within the story of

[45] Alix Zuckerman-Ingber, *El Bien más alto: A Reconsideration of Lope de Vega's Honor Plays* (Univ. of Florida Monographs (Humanities), 56; Gainesville, Fla., 1984), 26–7.

[46] 'Celebration or Subversion: *Los Comendadores de Córdoba* Reconsidered', *Bulletin of Hispanic Studies*, 41 (1984), 352–60.

the man of honour. The reminder, a salutory one, given us by McKendrick is that 'the type of man an avenger is is surely important in our assessment of what he does'.[47]

Now, what the Veinticuatro is can be judged not only by the excess of what he does (that is, the manner and extent of the act of vengeance), but also, and primarily, according to McKendrick, by the excess of what he says, and the way he deals with other people. We may understand his excess (exemplified in his verbosity) and his sycophancy as traits resulting from anxiety. Nervousness and anxiety are notorious triggers for verbal diarrhoea, and this seems to be a trait of the Veinticuatro so extreme that it is noted by the king himself.

That it is noted and remarked on by the king, who momentarily stands back to comment on manner, enables the audience to move briefly towards an integrating depressive reaction to what is happening. That so few critics have noted this, however, suggests the degree to which our reaction is much more strongly directed by being involved as spectators in the dynamics of splitting which impede such an observation of excess. We can also view the way of being of the Veinticuatro as resulting from reaction-formation—the class of defence against anxiety which consists in a vehement and excessive production of acts and attitudes contrary to the real emotion felt.

The Veinticuatro's delight in marriage can be seen as one example of reaction-formation. In a society where sharp divisions exist between men and women, and where the fickleness of the latter will inevitably dishonour the former, marriage must, at the very least, seem like a risky step. Yet the Veinticuatro's reaction on returning home from war is to delight in marriage, and to dismiss the views of those who are critical of the state. In this attention to the possible dangers of marriage (although they are denied) we have a precursor of the feelings about marriage as a danger to masculinity and masculine functioning in society which are expressed in *Secret Revenge for a Secret Fault*.

To turn to the play itself, what are we to make of a protagonist whose reaction to his wife's infidelity, even if it is a rather blatant example, is so very extreme? His activity in killing the whole household, including servants, domestic animals (dogs, cats,

[47] McKendrick, 'Honour/Vengeance in the Spanish *Comedia*', 357.

monkeys, and a parrot) is excessive by any standards. The bare action alone indicates an extremity of response. The justification, if such it can be called, is that all witnesses to the dishonour must be killed, giving thus a novel turn to the belief that vengeance should ensure secrecy about damaged reputation.

The reasoning (and one is tempted to add, 'if such it is') behind the wholesale slaughter of the innocent as well as the not-so-innocent in this play is, within the context of the honour code, as follows: one's honour is not simply a matter of personal, intimate, and private worthiness ('honor'), but also, and more predominantly in effect, what others believe to be one's worthiness ('honra'). For a man, this latter form of honour stands to be lost by the action of his womenfolk. Should they dishonour him, the dishonouring consists not just in the infidelity itself, but also in knowledge or suspicion of that infidelity. Suspicion appears to be as important, or conceivably even more important than, fact in the process of a man becoming dishonoured. The 'qué dirán' in this case says all. The slaughter carried out by the Veinticuatro, then, can be seen not only as his attempt to undo present reality, that is, to kill those people and creatures considered to have witnessed the infidelity, but also as a preventative measure: the dead do not speak (except in the glaring horror of their slaughter).

The Knights Commander of Córdoba presents an extreme case, and raises acutely the question of what constitutes an appropriate response to it. One way of reading the honour plays is simply to take the requirements of honour as an unquestionable absolute. Frank Casa, in his article 'Honor and the Wife-Killers of Calderón', for example, argues that at some level we are unjustified in considering as extreme the touchiness about personal status which is contained in the honour code. He rightly indicates, for example, that most of us feel a degree of offence if our integrity or honesty is questioned publicly. Casa also argues that Golden Age husbands do not murder for reasons that are trivial: 'rather, they respond to an action which they and many other societies still today understand as the ultimate threat to their being: the seduction of their wives'.[48]

Casa, I think, makes a valuable point in reminding us that the

[48] Frank Casa, 'Honor and the Wife-Killers of Calderón', *Bulletin of the Comediantes*, 29 (1) (1977), 6–23.

actions of husbands in honour plays are not totally distinct from the actions of husbands in other contexts. Modern studies continue to show violence as a frequent reaction to the infidelity of a wife, a violence which will often have fatal results.[49] His comments, however, require some questioning, and examination of whether they might reiterate a masculine view of the situation that may be as socially constructed in its defensive nature as is the literary work that produces it.

What is it, then, that makes honour plays, and the actions and reactions within them, distinct? Two principal features need to be highlighted here. One is the emphasis laid on the action of husbands in honour plays being motivated not by jealousy or passion, but by belief in values, a hierarchy, the proper order of things. The other is that in reading such plays, we need to consider not only the degree to which we may or may not be sufficiently culturally attuned to the norms of their time,[50] but also the degree to which we need to understand those cultural assumptions which are determined or influenced by gender.

At first sight, *Secret Revenge for a Secret Fault* by Calderón de la Barca has a male protagonist who is much closer to the 'normal' in terms of emotions and behaviour than the extreme and apparently unstable Veinticuatro of *The Knights Commander of Córdoba*. As in the previous play, considerable attention is given at the outset to the status and standing of Don Lope, who has been serving as a soldier under the king. At the point at which the play opens, this activity, which ensures him his social respectability, is about to be exchanged for a domestic life, since Lope has just married, and will therefore be discharged from military duties for the time being. Again, with the speed which seems to be characteristic of honour plays, we see his wife, on her way to meet him for the first time. It is evident that for her part, the marriage has been entered into in a state of distress, since she had a former suitor, Don Luis, now believed dead. Action moves swiftly as she is met *en route* by Luis, now disguised as a jewel-merchant, and then by Don Lope, who develops reactions of jealous suspicion on

[49] See Pamela Smith, 'Perfect Murderers', *New Statesman*, 7 July 1989, 12–16: 'Every three days in Britain, a woman dies at the hands of her husband, cohabitee or lover, or a man with whom she's had such a relationship.'

[50] See McKendrick, 'Celebration or Subversion', 352–3, and the initial discussion of Casa, 'Honor and the Wife-Killers of Calderón', 6–10.

the basis, initially, of little or no evidence (although in the later action of the play, Luis's attentions to Leonor are sufficient, within the terms of the honour code, to arouse the suspicions of a husband).

As Lope's suspicions become sharper and sharper, exacerbated when he seeks permission from his wife to return to the war and finds her willing to grant it (her reasoning running contrary to that used both by the king and by Lope's friend Don Juan), there is the presentation to him of what he sees as an analogous object-lesson in what one should do about honour. His friend, Don Juan, appears abject and wretched because of an honour conflict which, though 'solved', appears to leave him still with the taint of being known to have been dishonoured, despite the immediate action he took to protect his honour.

Lope is clearly viewed as the centre of the play, the male protagonist who should be our principal concern. That is, the appeal is to the spectator as identifying with masculine defensiveness about honour. Although attention is given to the less-than-easy plight of Leonor, newly married and immediately the focus of attention not just from any suitor, but from the man she had truly loved before her marriage, and whom she would, no doubt, have waited to marry had she not been told he was presumed dead, there is really no sense on the level of articulated text of this being a drama which affects the wife, but rather one affecting the husband.

Despite the apparently legalistic and unbending requirements of the honour code, and the ultimate requirement expressed in the theoretical paradigm of the man of honour that he be able to act in relation to the demands of society and the preservation of his honourable status, honour plays in no way lose sight of the emotional turmoil in which this may initially involve the man. This, it could be argued, is in fact at the heart of their success as drama: without the emotional conflict expressed at some level, they would be little more than dry, inhuman, and intellectual pieces, object-lessons in 'proper' honourable behaviour. But it is also the characteristic of honour plays that emotional turmoil tends to be within characters rather than between them, and, more specifically, that turmoil is seen principally, though not exclusively, within the husband, since it is on him that the decision to act will rest. The wife may agonize, but she is not destined to be a prime agent in the action. Furthermore, the turmoil within male characters is mediated for the spectator by a masculine framework of honour that upholds the precepts of the honour code as absolute and necessary.

The nature of Don Lope's emotional turmoil has attracted a variety of analyses, and raises in a very particular way the question of whether it is licit to apply modern psychological theory to these texts of the seventeenth century, or whether one should remain within the intellectual theoretical structures of the time at which they were written. It is clear from the approach adopted in this book that I believe that it is indeed licit to apply such theory, but some points may need to be answered. One standpoint adopted on this, and which argues for dismissing approaches to such texts from modern theory, is that they may fail to take into account the theories obtaining at the time of composition, and therefore cannot take into account the intentions of the author.[51] This is clearly a valid point, but what of course the seventeenth-century author was doing was to represent the human manifestations of his time within the intellectual structures of his time. This will affect both nomenclature and emphasis, but cannot alter the fact that the subject under consideration is human behaviour, certain fundamental elements of which will remain constant, regardless of changes in the intellectual concepts and systems which are used to define and/or understand such behaviour. In relation to this particular play, an example of a particularly helpful use of contemporary intellectual systems is given by Alan Paterson, who combines a clear exposition of underlying intellectual and moral systems concerning the passions with a live appreciation of the presence and portrayal of those emotions in the play.[52] His reading does not exclude the possibility that Calderón either represents projected anxieties, or indeed engages in such projection within his plays. The evidence of the text is that we, as modern spectators or readers, are able to perceive such anxieties, whatever their source.

By contrast, if we look at Teresa Scott Soufas's discussion of melancholy in Calderón's wife-murderers, then some problems

[51] This is the view of Teresa Scott Soufas, expressed in relation to seventeenth-century authors, in 'Calderón's Melancholy Wife-Murderers', *Hispanic Review*, 52 (1984), 181–203 (182).

[52] Paterson, 'Calderón's *A secreto agravio, secreta venganza*'.

arise, since the term 'melancholy', when used by Calderón's contemporaries and predecessors, as she indeed points out, is one that covers a variety of states, and includes a range of emotional reaction and response within which today, in the light of modern psychological theory, we would now make certain major distinctions. Furthermore, these distinct aspects are also presented as distinctive responses in the affects of the characters (and are well outlined by Paterson), even though they may all come under the general heading of 'melancholy'. Scott Soufas argues, in connection with Don Lope, that what we see is the degenerative process of a character's transition to pathological melancholy, and that in the course of the play, he passes from a choleric temperament to a melancholic one. This is a conclusion which stands distinctly at odds with a more modern one which would see him as a man predisposed by his nature and by circumstances to a particularly defensive sort of action. Thus what Soufas sees as Lope acting within his 'proper' nature as a choleric, that is, being a soldier, within which the tragic events of his marriage are a melancholy-dominated episode, after which he returns to the role of the soldier which suits his essential temperament, an analysis based on splitting and projection produces a less buoyant view of his mental state and its development.

Following the understanding of the psychological mechanisms at the heart of the man of honour, we can see Don Lope as a man who, from the start, is unable to cope with the emotional exposure that marriage brings. But, more than this, given the splitting at the base of the honour code, and the intense separation between the activities considered appropriate to the two sexes, we can see that his life in military activity may be not so much, or not solely, his 'natural' choleric way of being, but rather a way of life possibly adopted because it offers an apparent clear definition of masculine identity, one not open to threat from contact with women.

We see little of what Lope is as a military man. As a married man, however, we see in him a number of features that raise questions not only about his nature in general, but also about his view of marriage, especially in relation to the military career he has had.

The marriage has been by proxy, *por poderes*, and this in itself is significant, since it suggests that Lope has adopted a way of keeping the feminine at bay even at the moment of contractual joining. At the opening of the play Lope and Leonor thus meet for the first time after they have become man and wife. Yet his attitude to his marriage, revealed in a brief scene with his manservant, is ecstatic. He declares that he wishes love might lend him wings so that he might fly burned and blind. The image itself warns of some of the dangers of love, but the most striking thing about what Lope is saying is that he appears to be wildly in love when he has not even seen his bride (he later tells her how much more beautiful he finds her, now he sets eyes on her, than he had imagined her to be). Even his manservant comments on what appears to be his unseemly haste to go and meet his bride: 'If today, when you are to wed, you complain of the very wind, what is there left for you to do, what is there left for when you lose your bride to death?' If we regard him as a man who has managed to fall in love, then the passion he expresses hints at a dangerous level of feeling. If he has not, which seems to be the case, since he has not seen Leonor, then his protestations about being inspired, fired by his love for his wife, are both artificial and exaggerated.

Why should Lope's portrayed or stated emotion at marriage take an exaggerated form? We are given no direct information, but certain details in the text present possibilities for understanding. One is that marriage is dangerous, that it may enfeeble the masculinity of those men who engage in it. The dangers of love itself are signalled in Lope's imagery of fire and blindness, referred to above. Although the type of love thought proper for marriage in Spain, as elsewhere in Europe, had, in times of courtly love, been expected to be of a type and quality different from the wild love of infatuation that gives rise to affairs of the heart, here it would seem possible, a dangerous possibility we might note, that wild love, *loco amor*, might occur within marriage. Certainly the way Lope initially refers to love suggests the excesses of passion and infatuation rather than the stability of the love on which marriages and societies were to be built. Even were we to put aside the possibility that Lope is engaging in this marriage-inappropriate passion, we could still look back at our anthropological model for the honour system, and see the dangers inherent in marriage, at least as far as the man was concerned. As mentioned earlier, marriage itself brings man close to woman, that very part of society whose particular capacity it is to deprive him of earned public honour by acts of feminine dishonour. And moving beneath the honour-defined dangers of marriage within the honour code, we reach the level of fear resulting from the contact with those parts of humanity—sensuality, changeability—from which men within the honour system are defended by the severe and rigorous splits of the honour code. In the face of these various dangers that marriage presents, we could then view Lope's delight at it (similar to the delight of the Veinticuatro in *The Knights Commander of Córdoba*) variously as being delight at access to an area of hitherto forbidden delights (unlikely as a reaction), or, more plausibly, as an engagement in a bout of reaction-formation by which Lope expresses delight about an experience that for him will involve risk, and be a source of fear.

The notion that marriage is problematic for men is voiced in a number of ways in the play. Leonor, for example, in giving Lope leave in Act II to return to his military activity (a permission that he is to interpret as suspicious, and a sign that she may wish to engage in extra-marital dalliance, offensive to his honour), says that she does so lest it be thought that marriage diminishes man. Marriage affords a change in the power structure between the sexes, because of the degree to which a husband and wife become involved in an interdependence in respect of honour. Although, as in any patriarchal society, the husband has power over the wife, within the marriage, Lope speaks of his subservience to his wife's will, in that he needs to respect it—something which would not have been required of him before marriage. It is because of this shift in the power relationship (which may be nothing more than a courtly nicety, but is none the less an allusion to a significant loss of power) that Lope actually seeks her permission to return to the war. It is because he is married that he does so, and thus a reversal of the accepted 'proper' roles of marriage is emphasized.

There is, moreover, a social reality which appears to proclaim that marriage diminishes men. It is clear that they gain honour and status by their activity in battle. But on marriage it is recognized that they have other obligations. Thus the king himself articulates the need for men who are married to attend to their domestic obligations, and even in the case of Lope he is of the view that this should take precedence over his military duties. The exchange of arms for love, or rather domesticity perhaps, is made clear by Lope's opening speech of Act I, in which he asks the king's permission to go to his bride, and the obligations consequent on his marriage are outlined by the king's opinion that he should remain at home even when, having seen his bride, he asks if he may return to the fighting. The effect of marriage on Lope's public and social identity is clearly a sore point, since the king asks him if he is not married, and Lope is at pains to argue that his married state does not prevent him from fulfilling his true identity ('to be the one that I am')—a defence which suggests that there is a need to protect his masculinity from being thought to be lessened by the acquisition of domestic ties.[53] Arguably only this degree of insecurity about marriage is the cause for Lope's immediate high level of suspicion provoked by the straightforward situation of seeing his new wife conversing with a jewel-merchant. For the spectator, the articulation of this problem area is another example of where an approximation towards a depressive-position awareness is obscured by the insistence within the text of the view held by the split and defensive male protagonist.

By contrast, the marriage as viewed by the bride is not a point of view that is privileged in the play, although it is noted. Here, in addition to the threats that marriage presumably brings for women (they are instantly subject to threat of death from their husband on the least suspicion of an infidelity, and it takes little for suspicion to be aroused), there is the fragility of the situation which is particular to Leonor's case. She has married as a desperate and rather precarious reaction to grief at the news that her lover, Luis, is dead. She argues, using the vocabulary of the honour code, that her marriage was a proof of feeling: 'Look how much I felt when I heard of his death, since I married under duress only to take revenge on myself.' That is, she declares that the fact of marrying is itself not a sign of infidelity but a clear indication of how badly she was affected by news of her lover's death. Her view reflects, however, the accepted social view of marriage as it affects woman—she marries under duress, or pressure—so that even her

[53] See W. McCrary, 'The Theatricality of Male Orientation in the *Comedia*', in Robert Fiore, Everett W. Hesse, John E. Keller, and José A. Madrigal (eds.), *Studies in Honor of William C. McCrary* (Lincoln, Nebr., 1986), 27–33 (29), who puts this yet more forcibly, and notes that the arrival on the scene of Luis as Leonor's lover presents Lope with a needed let-out: 'For all the mental anguish he occasions, Luis nevertheless is a colossal convenience to Lope, because now the protagonist can justify the excision of Leonor from his life.'

subversive view of it as a voluntary action of self-directed revenge is couched within the terms of the code which encloses her.

We have, then, information from early on about the dynamics of the marriage as viewed by the two principals, which bears out the anthropological theories about the nature of marriage in countries where an honour code is at the base of social organization. When we look at the trajectory of Lope's reactions to his newly entered state (and to the ensuing threats to his honour and his masculinity which are immediately presented), we can observe how swiftly he moves into splits, projections, and reversals.

In Act II, for example, he makes a clear split between feeling and reason, and between himself and his wife. The distinction he makes first and overtly is between his wife, a Castilian, and himself, a Portuguese. In his defence against the expression of emotion, however, he speaks as one who feels that his sense of honour is superior, and declares that if one gives voice to feelings, this robs them of their worth.

If Lope does indeed have unarticulated feelings, these will be conveyed with the habitual strength of denied emotion, and will be detected by the spectator in Lope's projection of feeling on to Leonor. More than this, Lope off-loads on to his wife all the weakness which is associated with the expression of feeling. His proclaimed view is that man's feeling is of the strong, silent type, but what he also achieves, for himself, is removal from the danger of direct emotional entanglement with his wife. His desire to be able to split is further revealed in Act II, when, already prey to doubts about the prudence of returning to the war and leaving his wife behind, he longs for the ability to split so as to counsel himself: 'Oh that one might wisely counsel oneself, if in the event there is any that does take counsel.' Significantly, he goes further than this, and wants to separate from feeling: 'Oh who could sanely make another half of the self, so that, disposed in different parts, the voice might give plaint without the breast knowing of it? That the breast might feel without the voice declaring it!' His wish is for a situation in which his voice could give vent to feelings without the heart being aware of it, or, alluding to the public existence of the man of honour, he longs for the power to feel without that feeling being articulated and made public. More crucial than all this, however, is his own reaction to his decision to return to the war. Here we need to bear in mind the association for him of the traits of masculinity with the activity of warfare. By being unable to engage in war, he feels his masculinity at risk, or diminished. His manner of presenting the problem to his wife is such as to engineer the response he requires, but he is then immediately suspicious about that response. He presents himself to her in downcast manner in Act II, Scene iv, sufficiently so to provoke her comment and questioning. He then reveals that he is brooding over the fact that he is not fighting for the king, Sebastian, in Africa. Clearly he feels marginalized, a loner: no other *caballeros* have remained in Portugal ('no one stays asleep when reputation clamours'). The form he gives to his complaint reveals the underlying concerns with both masculinity and honour: indeed, it almost seems as though the two are fused together. But he then shows himself, as it were, submissive to the married state (a sign perhaps of what he feels as his loss or diminution of his independent masculinity) by now declaring that he must receive his wife's permission to go. His concluding words constitute a rationalization. They imply an equilibrium that has been achieved in marriage, but this is severely undercut both by his preceding attitude of despondency, and by his subsequent attitude to her granting permission. This attempt at verbal denial of anxiety and conflict is so at odds with what has preceded that audience reaction will be left with the poles of opposition, and no real sense of reconciliation or acceptance of his position.

Not surprisingly, his wife responds to his emotional leaning on her, and gives him permission to go. Perceptively, she picks up his concern about his reputation (which seems to be what motivates him, rather than the simple desire to support the king's cause), and declares that she would not have it be said that cowardly women rob man of his bravery, when in fact they should be increasing it. Thus she articulates the required relationship between man and woman in the honour code, the doubt remaining, for Lope, and conceivably for the audience, about the level of her sincerity in saying this. He immediately has suspicions: the audience will still, for its part, have in mind the degree to which Leonor is, in marriage, operating in a situation of self-imposed restraint, and thus may only be paying lip-service to the required attitude of the wife of the honourable man.

It is, of course, the case that Lope has manœuvred his wife into this reaction, a fact he seems to forget when he is later suspicious about it, thinking that she just wanted to get him out of the way, so as to have freedom to see her lover. Thus in his recall, he reverses the influence, and remembers her not only as granting him permission but as persuading him to go when he was not actively trying to do so. ('What does it mean for Leonor to so lightly give me leave to go, to depart happily, and not only to give me leave, but to tell me and give me such persuasive argument, that even if I were not trying to go, I should be obliged to do so').[54] A similar but rather more serious reversal, this time about intentions, occurs in Act III, when Lope, having heard of 'a friend's case of honour' from Don Juan, attributes to his wife the desire of killing him, when it is he who has murder in mind (and will eventually accomplish it), and declares 'Who doubts but that what is happening between the two is the case that he was relating, and that he knew Leonor intends to kill me?'

We are given a measure for understanding Lope by the fact that the play contains another honour-story in the background. The presence of this second story gives us evidence that, however touchy Lope appears to be in his suspicions about his wife, he is not alone in his touchiness. The subsidiary honour-story concerns Juan, who in different circumstances has dealt with a challenge (or what he construes as a challenge) to his honour. In Juan's case, he has had a mistress, has been in competition with another man for her attentions, though has believed himself to be the preferred suitor. A remark in public, however, that suggests that the other one is the favoured suitor (or is believed to be the favoured one) is deemed by Juan to be a slight to his honour, and he kills the offender. Here a factor of interest is that this is not even the case of a husband, but, since there is no marriage bond to be violated, there is simply the more openly primitive response of the man who, for his sense of public standing, which is bound to his masculinity, has to be believed in public to be the preferred male. This detail suggests strongly that an emphasis which underlies the honour code, at least for men, is on their capacity as men (that capacity which is ridiculed in the cuckold story) rather than some less highly charged social capacity as husband. This emphasis found within an honour-code situation is consistent with the

[54] This type of reversal is characteristic of projection. See Searles, 'Schizophrenic Communication', 382–6.

Mediterranean focus on sexual capacity (or lack of it) in the vocabulary associated with cuckoldry (discussed in Chapter 2).[55]

Some critics, on reading this play, have seen Juan as the character who provides Lope with an example to be emulated: an example of 'good practice' for the man of honour when doubts, however slight, are cast upon his reputation.[56] What Juan does provide, however, as observed by Anne Cruz, is a safe relationship for Lope, that is, a relationship with another man,[57] the safe relationship that, within the lines of the honour code, cannot be possible with a woman to whom a man is attached by affection, marriage, or blood.

This interpretation argues for Juan's story as offering a safe depressive container for Lope's anxiety, but closer examination challenges such a view. This is because Juan's case highlights not only the vulnerability of man's reputation, but also the fickleness of woman, since the slight to his reputation could not have occurred had his mistress not had two suitors. What Juan shows in the extreme is that he feels wounded, slighted, damaged as an individual, but makes no reference to the emotional implications of his situation *vis-à-vis* his mistress: that is, a less defended man, one less intent on his own honour, his own reputation as a man with potency, might have been more open to the emotional hurt of the dyadic relationship, in which he would have to face the distress of his mistress's lack of faith or regard for him.

[55] For the way in which a man's honour might be deemed to depend on the fidelity of a mistress (as opposed to a wife), see also the example from Pitt-Rivers, 'Honour and Social Status', quoted in Ch. 3, n. 26.

[56] A particularly positive view of D. Juan (as one who is courageous rather than touchy) is offered by Anne J. Cruz, '*Homo ex machina*? Male Bonding in Calderón's *A secreto agravio, secreta venganza*', *Forum for Modern Language Studies*, 25 (2) (Apr. 1989), 151–66, though she does emphasize the sensitivity of male characters to their peers. Paterson, 'Calderón's *A secreto agravio, secreta venganza*', 603, gives a much more negative view of Juan as a role-model: 'It is important to realise that if Lope had decided in favour of self-advertising violence, then he would occupy the undistinguished, even ridiculous, role of Don Juan, its abject victim. Furthermore, quick-tempered assault would dismantle the problem of violence before properly examining it.' Casa, 'Honor and the Wife-Killers of Calderón', 18, likewise sees D. Juan as one whose example is to be eschewed, at the same time as he provides a prefiguration of D. Lope's fate.

[57] Cruz, '*Homo ex machina*?', 158, referring to Joseph Pleck: 'male bonding is not a vehicle for male–male emotional relationships, but rather is a substitute for them' (Joseph H. Pleck, *The Myth of Masculinity* (Cambridge, Mass., 1981)), 149–50.

Emotional vulnerability is also kept at bay in the portrayal of Don Lope. The only point at which an emotional bond is fully declared is at the end of Act III, when he carries his wife's corpse from the house he has had burned down, and says, with all the force of simple statement, 'This is my wife, whom I loved with so much tenderness of love.' To my view, his declaration of love for his wife (which could possibly be read as the expression of the love of the man of honour for his wife despite the fact that she has caused him dishonour and he has had to kill her) is arguably part of a face-saving move which comes with producing the version of events intended for public consumption, that is, the version that her death in the fire has been an accident.[58] A less sceptical reading of this speech affirms the tragedy for man that is represented by the honour code, a more traditional critical view.

Standing in contrast with the generally restrained and self-concerned attitude of Lope, and the honour-based touchiness of Juan, a much more openly emotional reaction to 'betrayal' by a woman comes from Luis, the disappointed lover. The text gives every evidence (not least from the lips of the two parties concerned) that the love affair of Luis and Leonor was an affair of the heart, not of social convenience. Leonor's desperation at the news of her lover's death is sufficient to drive her to another marriage as an act of vengeance upon herself; on Luis's side, there are the unreasonable but revealing (and perhaps understandable) protestations about Leonor's fickleness, his very unreasonableness revealing the level of emotion involved. This relationship is unhallowed by marriage (as was the case with Don Juan and his affair), and thus the emotional rather than the social and honour-linked aspects are brought to the fore. The emotional force is indeed so strong that it prompts Luis into an ill-advised and passionate pursuit of his mistress, despite full knowledge of the implications for both her honour and her physical safety (not to mention the honour of her husband and his own physical safety). Luis presents himself as the true partner in the relationship, giving no weight to the fact that Leonor had only married because she

[58] In this context, it is interesting to compare E. M. Wilson's reading of *Othello* as a play whose prime motivation is honour not jealousy. See '*Othello*, a Tragedy of Honour', *The Listener*, 5 June 1952, 926–7, collected in id., *Spanish and English Literature of the 16th and 17th Centuries: Studies in Discretion, Illusion and Mutability* (Cambridge, 1980), 201–19.

believed him dead. In his reproaches to Leonor in Act I, Luis voices all the general fears men may have about women: 'What can you say in answer to me, oh woman so easy, fickle, changeable, inconstant and vain, you woman, in short, you woman . . .'. Here is a case of true love, not social arrangement, yet the woman concerned has failed to keep faith—showing that she is, after all, a woman. He reproaches her for being easy, fickle, and vain, that is, all that one might expect of a woman, and suggests that there is nothing she can say that will give an acceptable response or will account for her change of heart and her forgetting him. Thus Luis too takes refuge in a stereotyped view of woman, one which is conceivably the more comforting to him. By classifying her as belonging to a group of people (women) declared by the nature of the honour code to be unreliable, he thus assures his own position (what he has suffered is the working of a general rule rather than a personal slight), and preserves himself from vulnerability. Luis thus corroborates the condemnation of Leonor (one which rests on the unreliability of women in general, a view shared with other male characters), and does so definitively. As outsider and transgressor he closes masculine ranks with the other male characters, leaving her as chief fault-bearer.

A further sign that Luis is the mouthpiece of the emotional side of man is that in the same act he declares, on finding Leonor married, that his only future is to die. This is the only course left to a man deceived in love ('the only remedy is that I should die, having seen Leonor married, since Leonor mocked my love and my hope'), and yet is impossible, since jealousy seems not to have been sufficient to kill him. Thus he stresses the impact of his emotions upon him. That he then goes on to court Leonor, and threaten her honour, rather than committing suicide, may, however, suggest that his is not the attitude of total despair that it might at first have seemed.

If we summarize and consider the dynamics of this play, it becomes evident not only that splits exist in the mind and attitudes of Lope, the protagonist, but that possible attitudes of men to the infidelity of women within the honour code are split between three men: Juan, who voices the touchy extremes of reaction against hints that his masculinity is less than entire; Lope, who plays out the way that marriage threatens man (in a combination of his social standing and masculinity); Luis, who voices the underlying general fear of man that woman will betray him. A consequence of the splitting of attributes is that, as mentioned above, the lover has no concern for the honour of the others involved, nor even, it would appear, for his own (since his references are all to the direct loss and consequent jealousy that results from Leonor's marriage). It is the disregard of the lover for honour that both enables him to take the risky actions that will endanger the honour of others in the play, and is simultaneously the indication that this is the character in whom feelings associated with attachment, love, and loss operate, rather than the sense of offence, and feelings of anxiety and paranoia, although, as noted, he too projects guilt on to Leonor. The role of the lover in embodying these aspects of the reaction of the man in honour plays is widespread, and necessarily so, since without such disregard, the destabilization caused by honour problems would never arise. Enrique, the king's son in Calderón's *The Physician of his Honour* performs a similar function, as does, in yet more blatant manner, the Captain in *The Mayor of Zalamea* (El Alcalde de Zalamea), also by Calderón.

Two further examples I would like to discuss briefly, one from Lope and one from Calderón, look respectively backwards and forwards to different models of husbands. *Punishment without Revenge* (1635) by Lope contains much in the subtext that is relevant to the cuckold story, while the text itself still voices a concern with honour; *The Physician of his Honour* (1635), meanwhile, by Calderón, articulates the idea of dishonour within a medical model, a construing of the behaviour of infidelity which will come to be much more pronounced in the major European novels of adultery of the nineteenth century.

As will be evident from the summary of the plot at the start of this chapter, *Punishment without Revenge* contains a strong line which links the threat of infidelity with awareness of the processes of ageing and degeneration. The Duke of Ferrara, its protagonist, is a questionable figure to have in the position of hero. Age of itself would not disqualify him, but his past history of debauchery (and continued extra-marital excesses after he has married late in life) means that it may be stretching the audience's empathy for him, and commitment to the principles of the honour code, if they are to take seriously the matter of his dishonouring. The duke's claim to the status of hero is further problematized by the fact that the dishonour results from the affair between Casandra (his young wife whom he neglects) and Federico (the illegitimate son he forces into the double role of avenger and victim).

Much of the play provides the audience with evidence about the duke's concern with his masculinity, and desire to prove it. Federico, his son, provides a clear physical proof of his potency, but since he is illegitimate, this is insufficient in social terms—if the duke is to be able to pass on his property (another sign of his power), then he must produce a legitimate heir. Added to these unsatisfactory aspects of the duke's position, there is the disapproval of his behaviour voiced in local opinion. Cintia, for example, comments, Act I, ll. 96–100, that his licentious behaviour has been notorious since his youth. There is, furthermore, frank disapproval of the fact that he has chosen not to marry 'so that he might live as he pleases' (I. l. 102). By implication these comments set marriage up as the honourable state which the duke has either failed to, or chosen not to, embrace.

An issue which comes into prominence here is one mentioned above, in relation to *Secret Revenge for a Secret Fault*, that is, that marriage diminishes man, or rather, that the social contract of marriage produces constraints which, if they are adhered to by men, indicate some lessening of their masculinity. It is a truism based on the physical realities of the act of coition that man is the penetrator, woman the penetrated. That very act of penetration, expression of the man's potency and masculinity, is then one that is simultaneously subverted, since he is contained and enclosed by the woman. By analogy, in the social act of marriage, by which—in a patriarchal society—man expresses his power over the woman he marries, he is bound or contained both socially and sexually (albeit not to the same extreme as is the experience of the woman).

Federico is the expression, or product, of the duke's uncontained masculine potency, and as such cannot serve to further the duke's consolidation of his social standing. Thus the provision of an heir within the law might be construed as a taming of the duke's potency, as is the act of marriage itself.

The Duke of Ferrara, in his debauchery, provides an interesting example of the Don Juan model of behaviour. Don Juan is a major literary creation whose behavioural values are unclear. His multiple seductions are an activity that we might regard either as the proof of his potency or as the proof that he entertains considerable levels of anxiety about that potency, an anxiety which is so great that there is an obsessive compulsion to repeat the action which proves it.[59] The obsessive repetition of an act (in this case seduction, or debauchery) speaks at one level of a lack of imagination, and at another, more anxiety-driven level, of a disturbance which has become somatized into a behavioural pattern. The marriage of the Duke of Ferrara to a young wife is in part the act of the destined cuckold, an act undertaken, paradoxically, to prove his non-cuckold quality, that is, his potency. The swift return to the pre-marriage habits of debauchery reaffirms, now in plural form, the unresolved anxieties about that potency. What is worse, we learn this from his disappointed and aggrieved wife, Casandra (II, ll. 1034–8). Interestingly, Casandra complains that he treats her as an *object*, as if she were not his wife but a chair, writing-desk, or portrait.

The cuckold story, as we saw in Chapter 3, draws much of its strength from the way it highlights the inexorability of our confrontation with ageing and death (occurrences which are inevitable in a way that the pain of sexual disappointment or infidelity are not). A crucial feature of the way this is communicated is that a young lover supersedes an older man, whether the husband or the father. The feature of age as a factor in the story of infidelity is embodied not only in the fabliaux, which provide the clearest of the cuckold examples, but also in the theatrical forms which provide in part the basis for the honour plays, namely the Italian tradition of the *commedia dell'arte*, and its source, classical Greek mime. In this tradition the character of the old man, the Pantaloon figure, frequently but not exclusively the father, has his authority flouted and is ousted from his position of power by a younger, stronger man.

In *Punishment without Revenge*, the primacy of age in the play is emphasized by the fact that it is the son who displaces the father

[59] A frequent association of Don Juan, besides that of blasphemy, is one of sterility and, ultimately, emptiness. Nice examples of the essential vacuity of the Don Juan figure will be produced in the nineteenth-century novel, from Rodolphe, who feels threatened by Emma Bovary's plans for elopement (but places an artificial tear on his farewell note) to Alvaro in *La Regenta*, who finds Ana, the object of his seductive activity, so exacting, when finally she becomes his mistress, that he is provoked to extremes of keep-fit to protect his constitution.

in the wife's bed, a wife who has been patently neglected by her spouse. This shows the reverse of the coin of the Oedipal threat. In the classic version of the Oedipal conflict, the son is deterred from his sexual designs on the mother by the authority of the father, a man who is more powerful than the son and who can present in real terms the threat of castration. Eventually, however, the process of ageing means that the son can and must overcome the father—although not generally in such direct sexual competition for the mother, or the father's wife, as is the case in this play.

A factor which particularly supports a reading in which ageing is crucial is the extreme sensitivity of the duke to the fact that it is his son who has betrayed him. This comes out forcefully in the monologue of Act III, where he reads the letter that proclaims his dishonour. The belief that the son presents a real threat is reiterated. His suspicion is that if his son is able to deprive him of honour, there is every risk he will deprive him of his life. While the threat to life is presented here as murder (which could be avoided) there is an underlying threat of being victim to the passing of time. The threat to honour within the social system is retranslated into the cruel reality of the life system, in which the son must eventually kill/supersede the father, through the latter's death.

The investment of the duke in maintaining the balance of power with his son is brought to a climax in Act III, where he exerts his paternal authority to the maximum in order to get his son to kill the person concealed beneath the cloth. That his need to exert authority is all is expressed in his desire for unquestioning obedience: 'When a father commands something of his son, be it just or unjust, is it a matter to be disputed?'

Presenting another aspect of the threat of death is the shadow of it that hangs over the passionate but despairing exchanges of Federico and Casandra at the close of Act II. Again we see an example of the polarization of content that occurs within these plays, in that here full emotional expression is given to the consideration of love threatened by death, whereas at the other pole, embodied in the Duke of Ferrara, there is suppression of feeling, a resort to an imposition of rules or authority, that is, the refusal to admit the emotions.

The Physician of his Honour (1635) by Calderón presents a

medical model for the problem of dishonour. That is, the state in which honour is possessed is a norm, a healthy model, the thing which must be thought natural, whereas the state of dishonour is one which is a disorder, a malady.

The designation of a state as being one of illness is, since illness is associated with weakness, a statement of power. Hence the relegation to their beds, to the mental hospital, or simply to the status of insane, of women over the ages.[60] Hence also the model presented in the nineteenth-century novel of the adulterous woman who, by her 'unwell' behaviour, will demonstrate the 'social derangement' of infidelity.

The illness at the heart of *The Physician of his Honour*, however, appears to be that of the husband. This we could regard as a daring suggestion, in that it contains the admission that the husband enjoys less-than-complete 'health' in his state of honour. At the same time, it is a defensive model, in that the plea of ill health is an admission or a claim that our dishonoured state is out of our hands, something which is sent to plague us rather than something for which we bear a direct moral responsibility. The state of 'physician' in this context is also a retreat from emotion, from chaos, from dishonour. Thus to make himself physician is, for Gutierre, a defence, and his need to defend against emotion made clear in his monologue of Act II, even though the task becomes well-nigh impossible as soon as he has articulated that emotion in language:

Until
I'm able to, I shall conceal
This pain, this hurt, this misery,
This ache, this anguish, agony,
This nightmare, fear, jealousy.
Did I say jealousy? Let me
Retrieve the word at once. But no!
For if it is a poison now
Conceived within but did not kill
Me when I uttered it aloud,
To swallow it again could bring
About my death. (58)

[60] Elaine Showalter, *The Female Malady* (London, 1987); Roy Porter, *A Social History of Madness* (1987, repr. London, 1989), ch. 6. For a wide-ranging and perceptive discussion of the metaphorical attributions of illness (TB and cancer) see Susan Sontag, *Illness as Metaphor* (1977, repr. Harmondsworth, 1983).

As Cruickshank points out in his introduction to this play, the metaphor of illness, and how it is to be understood, is not straightforward. Doctors are meant to cure their patients, yet Gutierre prescribes death for his wife; if Doña Mencía is 'ill', then she cannot be cured by being killed (although—and Cruickshank does not make this point—in so far as she causes 'disorder' in society, her removal effects a cure); if the patient, the ailing one, is honour itself, then it is honour that should be caused to be bled by Don Gutierre, not his wife; at the close of the play, Gutierre is unwell, as far as he is concerned, since the king has obliged him to marry a woman he had previously abandoned. The marriage then becomes cure, in the form of the restitution of honour to the woman, as claimed in the closing lines of the play, and this action in its turn restores Gutierre to the status of honourable man.[61]

A different construction put on the metaphor is that honour itself—or rather an excessive concern for it—is what constitutes the illness of all the characters.[62] Yet again, there is the alternative theory that Gutierre's illness is a state of mind where he (wrongly) places himself on a level with God.[63] A neat differentiation is that of Wardropper, who sees the role of Gutierre as prescribing death as a cure for the malady but not as a cure for the patient.[64]

Whatever the detail of the interpretation, the metaphor of illness and cure is there, an admission that all may not be well in the world, and yet also a recognition of the mortal nature of the affliction involved: loss of honour is not trivial, but sufficient to necessitate the very draining-away of life. Thus this play both looks forward to the nineteenth century, in which the model of illness is a way of explaining away or of failing to confront instances of infidelity, and yet simultaneously reaffirms that loss of honour is so serious that only the loss of life may wipe the slate clean. Unlike the nineteenth-century model, however, it is a medicine of surgery and death rather than of relegation to the social margins—as for Effi Briest—or of retreat to the role of

[61] D. W. Cruickshank, introduction to *El Médico de su honra* (Madrid, 1986), 23.

[62] Ibid. 24.

[63] Id., '"Pongo mi mano en sangre bañada a la puerta": Adultery in *El Médico de su honra*', in R. O. Jones (ed.), *Studies in Spanish Literature of the Golden Age presented to E. M. Wilson* (London, 1973), 45–62.

[64] B. W. Wardropper, 'Poetry and Drama in Calderón's *El Médico de su honra*', *Romanic Review*, 49 (1958), 3–11.

carer by the husband—as with Karenin, Charles Bovary, and Víctor Ozores.

OTHELLO: THE OBVERSE OF HONOUR

> IAGO: Utter my thoughts? Why, say they are vile and false:
> (*Othello*, III. iii. 140)

Othello is an honour play which shocks by the degree to which it reveals the underside of the honour code, by the way that it lays bare the repressions and splits on which the honour code, at least in Mediterranean terms, is based. The way in which *Othello* could be understood as an honour play, in the Spanish (or Mediterranean) sense, was delineated by E. M. Wilson, who outlined the reasons why the play should be considered as one concerned with honour rather than with jealousy.[65] Wilson makes it clear that within such a code not only is there a concern for public reputation, but also affronts to honour may occur through the actions of wives or sisters, requiring that violent action be taken to remove the dishonour so brought about. Other critics, meanwhile, have tended to concentrate on the concern for honour in *Othello* in terms of general public reputation, and have drawn back from seeing the killing of Desdemona as a normal occurrence within an honour-based situation.[66] Thus the discussion of Leavis which (perhaps predictably) does not take account of the role of the honour code and its requirements, and which views the play as a character study.[67] Thus also the emphasis even in studies which

[65] 'A Hispanist Looks at *Othello*', originally a talk for radio published in *The Listener*, 5 June 1952, 926–7, collected in Edward M. Wilson, *Spanish and English Literature of the Sixteenth and Seventeenth Centuries*, 201–19. As an antecedent to Wilson, see the thoughts of Coleridge in *Table-Talk*, 1822 and 1827, where Othello is perceived as acting from honour not jealousy (extracts published in *Coleridge's Criticism of Shakespeare*, sel. and ed. R. A. Foakes (London, 1989), 115–16).

[66] See e.g. Curtis Brown Watson, *Shakespeare and the Renaissance Concept of Honour* (Princeton, NJ, 1960), and Norman Council, *When Honour's at the Stake* (London, 1973), 114–33.

[67] F. R. Leavis, 'The Criticism of Shakespeare's Late Plays', in id., *The Common Pursuit* (London, 1958), 173–81. Similarly, G. Wilson Knight's impressive study, 'The Othello Music', in id., *The Wheel of Fire* (London, 1930), 107–31, deals with major features of the play such as passion, control, discrepancies, but without reference to the honour code of which they are, if only in part, a reflection.

do acknowledge the importance of honour in the play. Curtis Brown Watson, throughout his study of honour in Shakespeare, for example, gives precedence to the concept of honour as renown and reputation, and Norman Council, in an otherwise perceptive study of honour in *Othello*, argues that the second mode of honour that causes concern in the play, that is, the honour endangered by Desdemona's supposed actions, is a debased form of honour associated with Iago. As a result, he views Othello's 'tragic error' as consisting, not in his jealousy, but in his involvement with revenge, and argues that 'the moral reversal which will determine his action for the rest of the play, is his henceforward unwavering assumption that since, as he believes, Desdemona is adulterous, he must kill her', and that by succumbing to Iago's persuasion that Desdemona is guilty, Othello 'falls into Iago's world'.[68] There is in this a distinction made between 'good honour', which is all to do with public name and reputation (in this case achieved by Othello through his activity as a soldier), and a less worthy concern for honour, which is associated with Iago's suggestions. The distinction that in fact may need to be made is between the requirement of the honour code that an affront to honour caused by the dishonourable action or state of a wife be acted upon, and the belief, in the mind of the critic or the spectator, that, given the reprehensible nature of Iago, it would be fundamentally dishonourable to succumb to the unsavoury suggestions of such a man. Tragic fall there may be in the lack of judgement in becoming prey to Iago, but the activity with regard to Desdemona is something which, within an honour-code interpretation of the situation, can and will remain free-standing.

There is, of course, the point made in the preceding section that there is some difference in the Spanish and English traditions concerning dishonour by wives, at least as expressed in the theatre of the sixteenth century. It is none the less strange that in relation to a play set in the Mediterranean, with its protagonist firmly classified as a Moor, there should be a reluctance to take on board the bloodier aspects of the honour code (a reluctance, that is, on the part of the critics, rather than on the part of the protagonist). Even if we view the Mediterranean style of concern with honour as alien to the world viewing the play, if not to the Venetian

[68] Council, *When Honour's at the Stake*, 127.

backdrop for it, Othello's concern for public name is a prime factor for understanding his reactions. As an outsider, a Moor, he is a self-made man, without the guarantee of lineage that others possess, hence the added intensity of his defence of honour, and investment in looking after a reputation that has been hard won.

In the same way as we can see a revision of critical opinion about Spanish honour drama, there are shifts to be seen in relation to *Othello*. There is a tradition of English criticism which concentrates upon Othello's nobility and worthiness. Thus Bradley's attempts not only to acknowledge the possible shock wrought in some readers by Shakespeare's 'representing on the stage a violence or brutality the effect of which is unnecessarily painful and rather sensational than tragic', but also to salvage the admirable aspects of the man of honour in Othello. While arguing that Othello's tragedy lay in his nature (being open to jealousy and susceptible to deception), he lays emphasis on his ability to act, so that he was 'if once wrought to passion, likely to act with little reflection, with no delay, and in the most decisive manner possible'.[69] There is T. S. Eliot's insight into Othello's distancing of himself from event and feeling (in his last speech), bracingly referred to as 'cheering himself up', as an 'aesthetic' rather than a moral attitude, one in which the aim is self-deception, a type of *bovaryisme*.[70] More recently, discussion has opened up which concentrates upon the manipulation of Othello by Iago, and the degree to which the play concentrates on that relationship. Within such discussions, Desdemona becomes, as it were, incidental.[71]

As with some of the Spanish honour plays discussed, *Othello*

[69] A. C. Bradley, *Shakespearian Tragedy* (London, 1905), 183, 186.

[70] T. S. Eliot, 'Shakespeare and the Stoicism of Seneca', an address read before the Shakespeare Association, 18 Mar. 1927 (London, 1927), 8.

[71] See Michael Neill, 'Changing Places in *Othello*', *Shakespeare Survey*, 37 (1984), 115–31; Joel Kovel, '*Othello*', in Maynard Solomon (ed.), *Myth, Creativity, Psychoanalysis: Essays in Honor of Harry Slochower* (Detroit, 1978), 113–19; Edward A. Snow, 'Sexual Anxiety and the Male Order of Things in *Othello*', *English Literary Renaissance*, 10 (1980), 384–412; and Martin Wangh, '*Othello*: The Tragedy of Iago', *Psychoanalytical Quarterly*, 19 (1950), 202–12, which, as its title suggests, focuses attention on Iago's relation with Othello as the centre of the play, to the degree of shifting Othello himself away from his own central position. That so much jostling for pride of position goes on in critical discussion is itself some indication of the competitiveness, envy, and jealousy which are manifest in virtually every part of the play. (For a distinction between envy and jealousy, see Philip M. Spielman, 'Envy and Jealousy: An Attempt at Clarification', *Psychoanalytical Quarterly*, 40 (1971), 59–82.)

opens after a number of major transitions have taken place. For Neill, this provides the key to the play, which he describes as a 'tragedy of displacement'.[72] Iago has been displaced, or rather failed to get a placement, an honour, which has gone to Cassio. Othello himself is nominated to go and serve the cause of Venice by defending Cyprus. This decision has been made by the authorities before they hear that he has made another major transition, into marriage. The audience is already aware, not only of the transition, but of the extreme disruption that it has caused, well before Othello's arraignment before the Doges by Desdemona's father occurs.

The marriage between Othello and Desdemona, sudden and secret, is never really explained in the play, though much commented on within the text. It is never revealed why Othello did not approach Brabantio for Desdemona's hand. Thus suspicion is left in the air. Is it because of some notion of racial unacceptability? Othello appears to have overcome his blackness in Venetian eyes because of his activity as a soldier, and has won public honour, but it would appear that he has not won acceptability as a husband. To allow him to bear arms for Venice is one thing: to allow him to mix his blood with Venice might be rather different. That he may be unacceptable because of his colour is, however, something which is not made explicit: his 'blackness' is labelled as his fault in having stolen Brabantio's daughter. The secret and precipitate marriage will, of course, provide excellent fuel for the plot later, as Othello is tormented with the idea that a woman who could disobey (dishonour) her father may easily do the same to her husband. As a major event which is both dramatic and unexplained, and which unalterably affects the social standing of Desdemona, and places in question that of Othello, the marriage gains additional impact from the very fact that it remains unexplained.

A number of consequences derive from this. It brings into question the naturalness of Desdemona. She is a character who, at least in the first half of the play, stands out for her unencumbered and spontaneous demeanour and behaviour. But within her society her open manner is scarcely characterized by the restraint normally required of the sex within the honour code to bear

[72] Neill, 'Changing Places in *Othello*', 115.

'shame', and she has moved against society's expectations in that she has preferred Othello to other suitors. Her initial refusal of other suitors is cited as a sign of her earlier virtue (the honourable woman has no truck with sensuality), but a different message about her refusal can be inferred. Is it perhaps, after all, her most natural feature? Given that the other suitors are referred to even by Brabantio himself as 'The wealthy curled darlings of our nation' (I. ii. 69), their desirability as masculine sexual objects seems less than clear, and her preference for Othello over these pampered youths is perhaps really not so surprising.[73] The act of marriage raises a different question for Othello and faces him with the same problems as those experienced by Don Lope in *Secret Revenge for a Secret Fault*, that is, that there may be some incompatibility between the domestic role of husband and the life of the soldier. Since Othello has been formed, certainly in the eyes of the Venetians, and been made acceptable to them as a man of renown, to have a dent made in this by the step into marriage makes his situation instantly more precarious.

From the first moments, the plot of *Othello* is driven by Iago—so much so that the spectator is led to question the correct naming of the play. The idea that the play is essentially about the relationship between the two men and is not about a simple matter of marital jealousy has considerable force. This holds good whether we consider Othello to be the character who is the object obsessively thought about by Iago, or whether Iago is the means for revealing the inner depths of Othello.

If we take the first of these two, we could view Iago as being the more tolerable focus of the play, in that he apparently possesses all that is unsavoury in thought and fulfilled action, driven in a strange love–repulsion relationship with Othello. Iago is all innuendo, all cajoling, a not-so-hidden persuader. He is the confidant turned traitor, and thus the focus for the whole idea of treachery. Since it is treachery contained in a figure portrayed as loathsome, however, it is that much easier to tolerate, just as the obsessiveness, competitiveness, and disgust that Iago expresses and embodies are that much easier to tolerate. That is, if we focus

[73] References to *Othello* are from *William Shakespeare: The Complete Works*, ed. Stanley Wells (Oxford, 1986). The outsider status of Othello is emphasized by the original title of the play, *The Tragedy of Othello, the Moor of Venice*.

on Iago in the play, we make him the scapegoat, and he carries all the intolerable or unacceptable feelings and attributes. He relieves us of the obligation to contemplate any such feelings in ourselves.

Within the play, a different dynamic obtains. Iago thinks obsessively about Othello, and transfers on to him all that he, Iago, is apparently unable to tolerate. The question of whether he really considers Othello to have cuckolded him ('it is thought abroad, that twixt my sheets|He's done my office', I. iii. 379–80) or whether he is just going through the motions of thinking so, is left open. His emphasis in his egging-on of Rodrigo is on his own activity as 'sport'—an image used to express, perhaps, his own willed distancing from what may concern him rather intimately, just as men of honour have recourse to stating that they act, in taking vengeance on their wives, in accord with the dictates of honour. Yet Iago draws back on taking revenge directly himself, and places most emphasis first on the bond with Rodrigo ('let us be conjunctive in our revenge against him. If thou canst cuckold him, thou dost thyself a pleasure, me a sport', I. iii. 366–8), and, at the conclusion of the temptation scene, on the bond with Othello ('I am your own for ever', III. iii. 482). He is a bystander, one who wants to side with men, be the companion of men who act on his behalf. While it is possible to interpret this as an expression of Iago's homosexual desires, it would be insufficient to see it as only this: Iago seeks the support of other men, not for simple camaraderie, but to persuade or to oblige others to take direct action on women. While he is Othello's lieutenant, appointed as such in the broadest sense at the close of the temptation scene,[74] it is equally the case that Othello acts as Iago's lieutenant, in that he acts on his behalf. What occurs is an acted-out version of the male bonding in the recounting of 'smut'.[75]

Alternatively, Iago can be viewed as the container within the play for all the repressed feeling and thoughts of Othello. The speed with which Othello moves from noble, upright, and honourable husband to a man obsessed with violent jealous thoughts is one of the stranger transitions of the play. It is hard to believe that the figure we see in the first two acts can become the un-

[74] Neill astutely observes that this is a 'holding of place' in which Iago is 'second to Othello's jealous passion', that is, a sexual, not just a military lieutenant. Neill, 'Changing Places in *Othello*', 128–9.

[75] See Naomi Segal, *The Unintended Reader*, pp. xi–xii.

reasonable creature who first listens to the poison of Iago, and then acts upon it in so violent a manner. The play contains a level of expression of physical disgust in relation to sexuality which is unknown in any of the Spanish honour plays, and indeed surpasses anything contained in other works discussed in this book. One of the most plausible explanations for the sudden move into the mode of the jealous husband by Othello is that Iago's outlining of the physical details of Desdemona's supposed activity is merely tapping into what Othello fears in his unconscious self. This has been examined with insight by Edward Snow, who is alive to the level of denial and repression in Othello.[76] There is a further element to the dynamic of the relationship between Othello and Iago as seen by Snow, however. Corresponding to Othello's firm denial of knowledge (that is, everything which it is not tolerable for him to hold in the conscious mind) there is the void and neediness for support and companionship which is expressed throughout by Iago. The essential void of Iago is revealed by his concern over possession of others, of honours—as though they might fill him, although these things with which he would fill his void will only ever be substitutes, even Othello. But Iago also defends against his void by representing himself as a man with more than enough to give, demonstrated in his unsavoury outpourings, or, in an apparently more acceptable manner, by his desire to give himself, to present himself to others as an honest man. Othello and Iago consequently exist in a symbiotic relationship. The void of Iago, however, means that he and Othello are locked into a complementary relationship more complex than the one I have just suggested and which could be seen in terms of the Kleinian concept of projective identification.

According to the concept of projective identification, a person who finds a particular quality or personal facet difficult to tolerate in themselves disowns it, but only partially, and is drawn to the manifestation of that quality in others.[77] The consequence is not that they are then enamoured of that quality, but rather that they find it even more irritating, even more intolerable. They are drawn to it, but cannot cope with it. This mechanism of projective

[76] Snow, 'Sexual Anxiety'.

[77] See Klein, *Envy and Gratitude*, 68–9, 152–4, and Hanna Segal, *Introduction to the Work of Melanie Klein*, 27–8.

identification forms the explanation for tensions in relationships, and is frequently found in marital discord, since the situation of marriage permits the process of choosing, and, given the degree of irrationality and the unconscious inevitably involved, choices are made which if fortunate take the form of complementarity, and if unfortunate the form of projective identification which can be the source of conflict.

Following this analysis, Othello will unconsciously be drawn to Iago as embodying and expressing all that he has rejected (to the degree of blindly believing in the 'honesty' of Iago), while Iago in his turn can be seen as drawn to Othello because of the latter's very capacity for containment and denial of troubling thoughts about woman, sexuality, and the risk of betrayal.

This close relationship between the two leads to the ultimate closeness of their speech in the temptation scene (III. iii), and after Iago has tiresomely repeated back to Othello his own speech ('Indeed? . . . Honest? . . . Think?', III. iii. 103–9), Othello comments on it, unwittingly pointing to the possible truth of the matter: 'By heaven, thou echo'st me | As if there were some monster in thy thought, | Too hideous to be shown', III. iii. 110–12).

Is Othello's emotion in the play primarily of jealousy? This we might assume, given that the action consists of his giving in to the persuasion that his wife is unfaithful to him.[78] What can be questioned, however, is the nature of this jealousy. In Freud's essay of 1922, 'Some Neurotic Mechanisms in Jealousy, Paranoia and Homosexuality',[79] the idea that jealousy itself was a defence against homosexuality was refined, so that an additional concept emerged: that jealousy was a defence against aggressive masculine rivalry. How this works out in the case of *Othello* will have been evident to some degree in the discussion of the close relationship between Othello and Iago. If we think of jealousy in the context of the paranoid-schizoid and depressive positions we might in the first instance declare that it cannot occur, since the positions are pre-Oedipal, at least in origin, and jealousy is essentially related to

[78] It is also an assumption by many, if not the majority of critics, including those working from a psychoanalytic viewpoint. Thus Kovel, '*Othello*'; Wangh, '*Othello*: The Tragedy of Iago'.

[79] 'Some Neurotic Mechanisms in Jealousy, Paranoia and Homosexuality', *The Standard Edition of the Complete Psychological Works of Sigmund Freud*, ed. J. Strachey (24 vols.; London, 1981–6), xviii (1981), 223–32.

the Oedipal crisis. But even some of the early studies of jealousy show an awareness that the strong feeling aroused by seeing a loved one apparently in the possession of another relates back to insecurities and difficulties of much more infantile origin. The study of Jones, for example, as early as 1929, identifies the relationship between jealousy and an ambivalent attitude towards being loved, so that there is, as Jones puts it, 'a craving for it and a dread of it' (a phrase that links uncannily with those extremes of emotion which for Klein are present in the first months of life of the infant). That this is followed by the gloss 'it represents at once the highest security and the greatest danger' shows the way through to understanding the jealousy of Othello both in the context of the honour code, and in his own special position as a racially different outsider.[80] That is, jealousy is an emotion which may be called upon, as it were, so that other, less tolerable ones do not have to be felt. In the case of Othello, jealousy, dramatically described as it is, may simply be the cover, the substitute for feelings of longing or insecurity which cannot be tolerated.

As indicated at the start of the discussion on the man of honour, one of his characteristics is that he takes action. He *does* something. That activity not only provides his means of saving face publicly (even though it also proclaims his dishonour, unless he is one of the more devious and subtle exponents of the art of avenging one's honour); it means that he does not have to think about his hurt. From the evidence of Othello, it would seem that the experience of jealousy itself is bad enough, but it is worth concentrating on the degree to which he finds the actual uncertainty about jealousy itself intolerable, and has to cut a way through quickly to certainty of action. He has a hunger for the absolute, in terms of knowledge about whether Desdemona has really been unfaithful to him. Iago plays on this in his depiction of the happiness of the cuckold, compared with the state of the man Othello is to be pushed into: 'That cuckold lives in bliss,|Who, certain of his fate, loves not his wronger:|But O, what damned minutes tells he o'er|Who dotes, yet doubts, suspects, yet strongly

[80] Ernest Jones, 'Jealousy', 337. A variation on this appears in more recent considerations of jealousy. See Stanley J. Coen, 'Pathological Jealousy', *International Journal of Psychoanalysis*, 68 (1987), 99–108: 'Pathological jealousy [will be viewed as] a substitute for as well as a defence against the fantasied dangers of full loving intimacy with another single person, man or woman' (p. 99).

loves!' (III. iii. 171–4). It is to this that Othello will swiftly make rejoinder in a way that reveals his determination not to be in that intolerable limbo, with 'No, to be once in doubt,|Is once to be resolv'd' (III. iii. 183–4), although he seems to see this as an escape from jealousy, which he equates with uncertainty. He does not perceive that jealousy itself, labelled as such, is a defensive feeling taken over so that other, more fundamental, insecurities do not have to be tolerated.

In this manner we can see how Othello is distant from the depressive position, in that he cannot face the idea that one to whom love has been committed could betray, although the fact that Shakespeare allows him to be so articulate about his insecurity brings the spectator closer to a depressive appreciation of these dynamics of two- and three-person relationships.

Not only might we question whether what moves Othello is simple sexual jealousy (rather than being an emotion that is produced in substitution). So far I have implied at least that what might be at issue is the vulnerability involved for this man in pledging his love to a woman, and that it is betrayal in the dyadic relationship which troubles him, rather than having to oust a rival from the triadic relationship, or to face the scorn of other males. Again we could turn to Neill, who is tuned so finely to what he denotes as Othello's 'radical insecurity of placelessness'.[81]

In a brief tailpiece to a paper on jealousy, Joan Rivière highlights the insecurity of Othello which derives from his racial difference in a way that takes us back to the concern with blood and racial purity at the heart of Mediterranean honour codes. Following the line sketched by Jones after Freud, she analyses jealousy as defence, in this case defence against guilt. We should perhaps step back a moment here, and remember that the capacity for guilt is one of the identifying features of the attainment of the depressive position, since it involves a sense of relatedness to the other person, and takes back into the subject some of the feeling of having been hurt or wronged. Othello's guilt, as identified by Rivière, is simply his blackness. She remarks on how his words from V. ii, 'It is the cause, it is the cause, my soul' (V. ii. 1–2)—words which puzzle by their vagueness—gain clarity when we perceive that he goes on almost at once to comment on the whiteness of Desdemona's skin. What Othello does in relation

[81] Neill, 'Changing Places in *Othello*', 126.

to Desdemona is, according to Rivière, to project his feeling of blackness on to her.

Let us try to tease out Rivière's analysis a little further. Her simple statement is the following: 'Does not Othello's blackness . . . sum up in one symbol the whole story of his guilt, doubt, anxiety and his mode of defence against them? Iago the envious is but his alter ego. He cannot endure the evil in himself. He must make Desdemona black instead.'[82] What Rivière argues is that Othello feels bad, and projects that badness on to Desdemona. This seems to be the typical mechanism of the paranoid-schizoid position, although we should note that what she identifies as the projected feeling is probably related, at least in part, to the depressive position. Above all, what is projected, in the light of our comments above on Othello's limited tolerance for ambiguity, is the feeling that things might be one way, and then again, they might be another. Relating this back to the traditional splits made in the honour code between what is man's part and what is woman's (woman being assigned sensuality, transitions, vulnerability), we can see how Desdemona also, within an honour-code understanding of the play, has to contain Othello's disowned sexuality. Shakespeare makes the transfer particularly clear, on the one hand by giving to Desdemona, at least in the early acts, a natural and unencumbered expression of her own sensuality, and, on the other hand, by depicting as counterbalance a repugnance for sensuality which is originally lodged in Iago, but is transferred with such ease to Othello. We might infer from this that ultimately what Othello cannot tolerate is what happens within marriage, that is the vulnerability deriving from man's expression of sexuality with a woman, and closeness to her sexuality, rather than what is an additional complication in the form of marital betrayal.

Othello's attitude is explained in part by his social insecurity. Since he is a man who throughout is portrayed as one who must present himself in order to have his acceptability proven, his stake in remaining honourable is greater than that of other men in the cast. His presentation of himself as strong and honourable is remarkably effective until III. iii, which may make his descent into jealousy the more shocking, but the evidence for his investment in

[82] Joan Rivière, 'Jealousy as a Mechanism of Defence', *International Journal of Psychoanalysis*, 13 (1932), 414–24 (424).

his reputation is there from the start. Although the case of Cassio, who also collapses suddenly on loss of reputation, suggests that the play may present us with a more universal statement on the importance to man of his reputation, Othello provides a signal case of the dishonoured man for reasons that pertain to his background. That is, he has more to lose than other men in the play (white, accepted, of recognized lineage), since, despite the public honours won by soldiering, he starts from such a fragile base. This fragility heightens his inability to 'take in' the natural offer of sensuality in Desdemona, provokes him with such swiftness to jump to the conclusion that having endangered his status by marriage, his feeling of risk about the whole business of marriage and sex is justified, and that his consequent difficulty can only reach some sort of resolution if he ensures without doubt that another person, the innocent Desdemona, and not he himself, functions as scapegoat.

Othello permits us to enter some of the complexities of the workings of the man of honour, tapping the roots of 'honourable' action in concern about place and masculinity. In so far as there is here, to a greater degree than in the Spanish examples discussed earlier, an articulation of the mechanisms set in motion by anxiety about pain, we might consider the play itself, as experienced by the spectator, to offer the route to a depressive position. But one wonders whether the offer made is to the male or to the female spectator, or to both?

Again let us return to the fact that theatre is a public spectacle, offered to a mixed audience. I would argue that the prevailing mode of understanding of that theatre, at least in public terms, is likely to be masculine. That this has obtained to a large degree in criticism also is evidenced by the sort of shifts in critical views on which I have commented both in relation to the Spanish honour plays, and to *Othello*. This last play would seem still to speak to men, to the male spectator, albeit presenting him with a potentially depressive view of what happens in masculine insecurity, masculine jealousy. It breaks those feelings down, casts them bare in a way that might almost seem unbearable for the male spectator, and oddly relieving to those female spectators who might otherwise feel that, along with Desdemona, they have been given all the guilt and responsibility experienced by Othello, and by the men for whom, emblematically and dramatically, he stands.

5
The Adulteress's Husband

TANNER MAKES a telling reference to the perception of Denis de Rougement that Europe and America, to judge by their literature, take an enormous interest in adultery, and to his belief that this represents 'some unappeased hunger for misfortune, unhappiness, and death, which is not simply engendered by the institution of marriage but is involved in passion as such'.[1] While this is acute in pointing to the emotional tone of novels of adultery, which are more given to the sad, dull ache of frustration and social confinement than to the raw agony of other portrayals of the pain of sexual transgression, it passes over what is a crucial differential factor in the novel of adultery, if we are to understand by this form those novels which come from recent rather than earlier centuries. The main feature of this differential is the sudden and dramatic placing of the woman centre-stage and the concentration on her life of inner guilt. Both husband and lover come to be relatively peripheral in this telling of the infidelity drama, when we compare their roles in the adultery novel with the prominent place they have occupied in both the cuckold and the man-of-honour version of the drama.

Human experience inevitably carries strong elements of universality: we are born, we die, we have sexual partners, we have children. But when difficulties arise, they may be more or less exacerbated by social convention of the time, and it is this in part which accounts for the shifts in focus when we survey the telling of the infidelity story as it occurs at different times and in different places. Thus some times and places may put greater emphasis on the stigma of illegitimate or otherwise suspect birth, and in earlier chapters I have noted how illegitimacy appears to have had some implied status of acceptance in twelfth-century England, but also how 'tainted blood' constituted a major social disability in the Spain of the sixteenth and seventeenth centuries.

[1] Tanner, *Adultery in the Novel*, 87, referring to de Rougement, *Love in the Western World* (1940), rev. and augm., trans. M. Belgion (Princeton, NJ, 1983), 3–4.

What the nineteenth century offers in particular, at least in some countries, is the option of not ending the infidelity drama in either ridicule (as in the cuckold story) or death (as in the honour story). The possibility of legal separation, if not of divorce, is on offer for at least some of the characters involved (Anna Karenin, Effi Briest, Edith Dombey), although others such as Emma Bovary find it impossible to contemplate an alternative to death as the ending to their infidelity, and it is clear that Ana Ozores' living death in the claustrophobia of provincial life has little or nothing to recommend it. We learn that heroines of adultery novels may indeed be allowed to survive, but it is questionable whether they find that survival an acceptable option.

Adulteresses' husbands represented in the nineteenth-century novels of adultery discussed in this chapter range through the entire spectrum from cuckold to man of honour, with the majority moving between the two. There are differences of emphasis, so that the husbands of *Dombey and Son* and *Effi Briest* are, in their different ways, related to the man of honour but are both ultimately redeemed from their paranoid state, at least by the author. Víctor, of *La Regenta*, is both failed man of honour and cuckold, but one whose emotions are revealed in their pathetic complexity.

Pozdnyshev, of *The Kreutzer Sonata*, combines the cuckold and the man of honour, by having reacted like the latter in his suspiciousness, his paranoid reaction to sexuality, his extremes of feeling, yet at the same time lacking all sense of social propriety, so that in the recounting of his tale he has the naïvety and lack of social *savoir-faire* of the cuckold, rather than the self-protection of the man of honour.

Novels of adultery are notable not only for the degree to which they articulate the reactions of husbands to infidelity, but also for the way in which they explore in even greater depth issues raised in other texts discussed so far: questions of masculinity, of public and private identity, and of the relationship with emotion. I shall therefore take the texts in which these husbands occur in an order which moves from a close focus on the issue of infidelity in itself towards texts which deal with broader issues: the experiences of emotion and sexuality as problematic in themselves, and the experience of marriage itself as problematic.

First, then, I shall take examples of texts where the husband can most closely be aligned with one or other of the models discussed so far: *Madame Bovary*, *He Knew He Was Right*, *Effi Briest*. Then I shall take *La Regenta* as an example of a text where the treatment of the husband is more complex, where the possession or lack of masculinity is an important feature in the majority of the male characters in the novel, but where the central theme is still the husband's relation to infidelity. *Dombey and Son* and *The Kreutzer Sonata* will then be taken as examples of narratives where infidelity is a text covering powerful subtexts of denial and splitting in the face of emotion and sexuality. Finally *Anna Karenin* provides a text where the complexity of the husband's reaction to infidelity is set in a web of meditation upon marriage and society, and where the problem of what occurs after adultery is explored most fully.

MODELS OF DECEPTION: CHARLES BOVARY, TREVELYAN, INNSTETTEN

Charles Bovary stands out among adulteresses' husbands for his total lack of connection with the man of honour.[2] Indeed, in respect of the models of the deceived husband we have explored so far, and compared with other husbands considered in this chapter, Charles Bovary is characterized in a way that places him unequivocally in the role of cuckold, a portrait to be softened only by his clumsy essays at fatherly love, and by his spontaneous entry into abject grief as the denouement of Emma's adulterous adventures is reached.

Whether in an attempt at parody, or to emphasize more devastatingly his final margination from the action, and from novelistic importance, Flaubert misleads the reader by placing Charles centre-stage in the opening pages, filling in the scenes of his family and his boyhood as one might expect in a *Bildungsroman*.[3] But whereas that genre is concerned with tracing the

[2] References to *Madame Bovary* (1857) will be to the translation by Alan Russell (Harmondsworth, 1950) the roman reference being to the part, the first arabic reference to the chapter, the second to the page number.

[3] This contrasts with the reading given in Enid Starkie, *Flaubert: The Making of the Master* (London, 1967), 314–15, where the reason for the initial highlighting of Charles is given as Flaubert's intention to demonstrate Emma's far-reaching influence upon him.

development to manhood and maturity of its chosen protagonist, Charles's development is pushed to one side. We are not denied details of it, but they are of inverse value, all to demonstrate his qualifications for being regarded as stupid, a man to be ridiculed and, eventually, cast aside. That is, he is placed in the foreground only to be pushed into the background as cuckold.

In her discussion of the nature of the protagonist in nineteenth-century novels, Carla Peterson shows how female protagonists are excluded from the trajectory of the typical male protagonist of the *Bildungsroman*. Thus, in place of a protagonist who grows into effective possession of his maturity, a man who will eventually form the link between past and present by (in most cases) the foundation or continuation of a family dynasty, the female protagonist is relegated to a characterization where maturation is likely to be denied. Peterson notes how, for example, the feminine protagonists of novels of this period are typically marginated, the unloved members of their step-family, relegated to a position outside society. Peterson's particular interest is in what she terms the 'reader-protagonists', that is, those who, bereft of families to provide their sense of identity and direction, turn to reading 'to recapture symbolically their lost unity and original identity'.[4] Their reading, however, inevitably provides an imperfect substitute for a real sense of grounding in life.

Charles Bovary is not, of course, a female protagonist. But he shares with Carla Peterson's female protagonists certain key characteristics. The initial vision of him is as a schoolboy and then a student, and we are shown, via the perceptions of his peers, all ready to mock him, his fumbling, clumsy, incomprehending attempts to go about his studies. Learning is not his world, and yet he is forced on and into it, primarily by his mother. Like the mother of Fermín in *La Regenta*, she has to swallow pride early in life, and attempts to realize her ambitions through the medium of her son. Charles is, however, the victim of parental conflict in his education: although his mother is ambitious, the form of her ambition is advancement through learning, whereas his father draws on more physically stereotyped ideals of masculinity, and 'had in his head a certain manly ideal of boyhood, according to which he tried to fashion his son' (I. 1. 19). Charles reacts badly

[4] Peterson, *The Determined Reader*, 28.

to the Spartan ways imposed by his father, a reaction which ties him in consequence to his mother's apron-strings, and denies him all future chance of independence. In this parental distribution of influence upon Charles we might note an irony in that his mother is urging him to enter that realm (the intellectual) traditionally the domain of man in the cause of social advancement (also, within the Hegelian view, the public sphere proper to man), whereas his father's impulse, although in a masculine framework, could be seen as a return to the body—which could also be viewed as entering feminine territory.

It is, perhaps, possible to over-emphasize the importance of Charles's mother in his formation, and in the manner in which he accomplishes his destiny of cuckold (since destiny it seems to be, from the ill-fated moment when he appears in school with his extraordinary hat, 'one of those pathetic objects that are deeply expressive in their dumb ugliness, like an idiot's face' (I. I. 16)). It is, however, the case that Charles moves from the influence of his mother to fall under the thumb of his first wife, a widow of 45. Significantly, this wife is found for him by his mother, in order to save him from what are seen to be his dissolute ways (frequenting pubs, neglecting his studies). This marriage is a caricature of the overbearing wife and the browbeaten husband, although the deception in this instance is not that Charles is cuckolded by his wife but that he is deceived by her in financial terms, her riches on marriage turning out to be less substantial than believed. (The deception on the physical front is arguably less: there was little to hope from her, and the nature of their physical relationship is tellingly recalled by Charles (I. 5. 47), who early in his marriage to Emma contrasts a new-found happiness with the fourteen months spent with the widow 'whose feet were like blocks of ice in bed'.)

Parody is everywhere in the portrayal of the unfortunate Charles. Condemned by his mother to attend school in unsuitable headgear which will make him a figure of fun, he is then mocked by his creator, through subversion of traditional images associated with masculinity.

The horse as emblem of masculinity is so traditional as to seem a parody in the novels of adultery, even when used with serious intent. Thus the undercurrent of cliché in the association of horse-riding and adultery (seen as forming an equation with satisfactory sexual experience for the wife) in *Effi Briest*, *Anna Karenin*, and, of course, for Emma Bovary. As is the case with Effi, Emma is encouraged to take up riding for her health (an element which carries a subtext of information about the lack of health resulting for the two from the shortcomings of their conjugal relationships). Charles, as archetypal cuckold, is blind to the possibility that his wife might be on the brink of an affair with Rodolphe, and eagerly takes up the suggestion of this lover-to-be that riding might benefit Emma. More than that, he overrides Emma's objections (she at least goes through the motions of considering whether such outings might seem odd in society), and himself contacts Rodolphe to communicate Emma's acceptance, in terms which carry prefigurative allusions to the outcome of the excursions.[5] Charles's first marriage is also not without its subversive allusion to the horse as an emblem of masculinity. In the marriage to Héloise, Charles, as we have noted, is under her control, a fact referred to with bitterness by his father, who complains that his wife has ruined their son 'by hooking him up to an old harridan whose harness was no better than her hide' (I. 2. 32). Thus, at most, Charles is a work-horse, and far from the masculine rider of a steed that displays his masculinity. His destiny is to serve, not to be served. Even in the veterinary sense of 'serving', Charles takes a back seat and lets others take his place, Rodolphe on horseback, Léon in the wild excursion in the horse-drawn carriage. This destiny of service only goes to compound the image drawn of Charles in relation to his medical studies, where he tries to learn, but fails to grasp, and yet carries on trying: 'He performed his daily little task like a millhorse tramping round blindfold, grinding away at he knows not what' (I. I. 22). The image of the virile horse is thus reduced to the image of domestic subjugation, analogous to that of the ox, and related by tradition, as noted in Chapter 2, to the cuckold.

Similarly the activity of smoking (particularly of smoking a cigar) is used for Charles in a parodic exemplification of his sexual

[5] The wording of the original is significant here. Russell renders it as 'Charles wrote to Monsieur Boulanger to say that his wife awaited his convenience, and that they would be most grateful' (170), whereas there is a double meaning in the French: 'Charles écrivit à Monsieur Boulanger que sa femme *était à sa disposition*, et *qu'il comptait sur sa complaisance*' (my emphasis) (*Madame Bovary* (Paris, 1964), 192). The first phrase has a clear ambiguity, the second carries the shade of one, in that 'complaisance', while here included in a set phrase of courtesy, also refers to Charles's complacency, and his virtual destiny as a 'mari complaisant'.

ineptitude. Charles comes home from the meal at the Château with two cigars, and arouses Emma's scorn by trying to smoke them (I. 8. 69). His efforts at smoking can be read as his attempts to take on the grandeurs of the masculine image as, it would appear, he has perceived it at the dinner, despite his social ineptitude there. He coughs, spits, has to rush out for a drink of water: Emma, in exasperation, throws the cigar-case to the back of the cupboard. (Though her gesture is angry and careless, Emma's retention of the case appears to lay emphasis on the social form of sexuality that she desires, whereas Charles's thoughts are directed to the performance of sexuality itself, with the implications for masculinity that this entails.)[6]

Flaubert, unlike Alas, leaves us with the image as a concrete emblem of failure, to be compounded presently as we glimpse Rodolphe (II. 9. 174), cigar in mouth as he attends to a bridle, the seduction of Emma now achieved. Later, there is an element of further self-parody in the use of smoking as an emblem, as Flaubert adds to the description of Rodolphe writing his farewell note to Emma, on the eve of what was to have been their elopement, the detail that he smokes three pipes before he retires to bed (II. 13. 215). This is matched by the graphic reiteration of the connection (in Charles's mind, if nowhere else), between cigar-smoking and masculinity, when the two finally meet by chance after Emma's death. Charles has finally been disabused about the innocence of his wife (as in *Effi Briest*, a letter provides the proof, III. 11. 353), but is mesmerized, rather than fired by jealousy, as he gazes at Rodolphe, who, for him at least, now represents forever the masculinity he has never had: 'Leaning across the table, [Rodolphe] chewed at his cigar as he talked, and Charles, confronted with those features that she had loved, lapsed into a

[6] Emma's retention of the cigar-case is a symbol interpreted by Lucette Czyba as standing in opposition to her wedding-bouquet (I. 9 opens with the former and closes with the latter). The case, in this interpretation, signifies love, and noble, mythic adultery, whereas the bouquet symbolizes the bourgeois union of marriage. See *Mythes et idéologie de la femme dans les romans de Flaubert* (Lyon, 1983), 85. This interpretation of the nature of adultery is consonant with Flaubert's reported views on the subject, in relation to Louise Colet: 'When his passion for her had been at its height, the word "adultery" had seemed to him the most beautiful of human words, vaguely enveloped with an exquisite sweetness, fragrant with a peculiar magic, full of a supreme poetry compounded of voluptuousness and blasphemy' (Francis Steegmuller, *Flaubert and 'Madame Bovary'* (London, 1958), 80).

daydream. It was as though he were looking at something of her. It was a miracle. He would have liked to be that man' (III. 13. 359). The way in which Charles is drawn to Rodolphe is more explicit than the attraction Víctor feels towards Alvaro in *La Regenta*, and for reasons similar to those applying to that novel, gives us final confirmation here of Charles's now dimly conscious desire to be other than he is, a desire which is rendered muted and pathetic by the implied naïvety of its nature. It is not insignificant that the meeting of the two takes place over a table, since Charles's marital history contains Emma's habit of providing him with food rather than with love.[7]

Everything possible is done to deprive Charles of his masculinity. Like Lorca's Don Perlimplín, Charles does not actually manage to propose to Emma himself, and one assumes that someone else proposed on his behalf to his first wife. (While it is also true that Innstetten does not initiate direct discussion of marriage with Effi herself, but rather with her parents, in that case what happens is simply according to an accepted social code of arranged marriage, and devoid of the implications of blundering incompetence that Charles displays.) Despite his lack of initiative in the proposal, Charles's second marriage is viewed by his mother as an act of defiance, an opinion she conveys by her lack of involvement in the second wedding (I. 4. 43). Consonant with its meaning as an act of defiance, this new union seems, if briefly, to bring about a transformation in the bridegroom.[8] Flaubert's account is none the less disparaging: 'Next morning, however, he seemed a different man. He was the one you would have taken for yesterday's virgin. Whereas the bride gave nothing away' (ibid.). And, it has to be added, while Perlimplín really does move into a new mode of being when he loses his virginity, although the new

[7] See Lilian Furst, 'The Role of Food in *Madame Bovary*', *Orbis Litterarum*, 34 (1) (1979), 53–65 (58). There is an excellent analysis of the way in which Emma herself is driven to a desperate and twisted relationship with food in Ion K. Collas, *Madame Bovary: A Psychoanalytical Reading* (Geneva, 1985), 23–55. See also the symbolic role of food in the Ozores marriage: Alison Sinclair, 'The Consuming Passion: Appetite and Hunger in *La Regenta*', *Bulletin of Hispanic Studies*, 59 (3) (July 1992), 245–61. For a fuller discussion of Girard, see the second section of this chapter.

[8] A comparable, but more pathological, example of transformation and maturation is that of Maxi in Galdós's novel *Fortunata y Jacinta*. As with Charles, Maxi's sudden maturing, stimulated by his rebellious decision to marry, is doomed to be short-lived.

state of maturity is simultaneous with his attainment of the state of cuckold, Charles's transformation is to be only a temporary one, and he soon relapses into old ways of submissiveness, blindness, and stupidity.

I have concentrated so far on Charles as a man who is portrayed as lacking in masculinity, rather than as a husband who is deceived. This is because it is the former rather than the latter which is emphasized in the novel. Although the core of the narrative comes to be dominated by Emma by Part I, chapter 2 (that is, after the deceptive trailer for a *Bildungsroman* protagonist in Part I, chapter I), and although, within that narrative, her conjugal dissatisfaction and desire to escape through adultery are relentlessly to the fore, there is relatively little emphasis on the reactions of Charles. The exception is in a series of references which outline him as cuckold: his failure to notice what is going on, examples of his stupidity, his foolish delight in what he believes to be his bliss. Most of this comes conveyed through Emma's perceptions, and as such gives further fuel for her dissatisfaction. What is lacking for the reader is sufficient sense of Charles himself, so that it is difficult to reach the level of concern needed to engage with his problems as a husband who is deceived. This is particularly so since it is with such consistency that, in the guise of the extremely unaware cuckold, he fails to notice what is going on. The result is that we are only able to perceive him in the role of deceived husband when he himself comes to the realization that this is the nature of his fate (III. 11).

The major change wrought in Charles at his wife's death is a conversion from an automaton-like being to one so Romantic in his grief that he might have satisfied even Emma's phantasies. It is, ironically, the logical extension of his earlier devotion to Emma, which rendered him such a boring husband, and a return to the lyricism of his early childhood, when his relationship with the natural world stood at odds with the dry theories of his father. Until that point of conversion, he functions on a type of automatic pilot, at times more faltering than others, but still mechanical. He moves from being the patient but unseeing mill-horse of his youth to the man so unseeing that he neglects to remove the wedding bouquet of his first wife from the house to which he welcomes his second bride (I. 4. 45). His mechanical nature is emphasized at this point, being displayed above all in his sexuality. Thus not long after marriage to Emma we learn that his 'ardours had lapsed into a routine, his embraces kept fixed hours; it was just one more habit' (I. 7. 56–7).

The gap between Charles's Romantic capacities, displayed after Emma's death, and his sexual clumsiness, relates primarily to his lack of social style. It is important to distinguish between his inability to love in a manner acceptable to Emma, because he is clumsy, and any fundamental lack of the capacity to love. He just does not know how to demonstrate it acceptably. He loves, but is not a lover.[9]

Charles lacks the awareness either to be a man of honour, or, in Emma's eyes, even to be a decent husband. His bovine nature (alluded to somewhat obviously in the name his creator gives him) is reflected in physical detail, especially as noted by his wife: 'his thick lips trembling, which lent an added stupidity to his face' (Emma's perception, II. 5. 114), but above all in that failure to realize that he is found wanting by her: 'His unquestioning belief that he made her happy seemed to her a stupid insult' (II. 5. 120). When he does perceive that all is not well with his wife, he falls into the cliché of believing her ill. One can regard as either pathetic or touching his collapse alone into tears in his surgery: the text suggests that it should be the former, by adding the clinching detail that his course of action is to send for his mother (II. 7. 138). In believing his wife ill, Charles is, of course, without malevolence, relegating her to a role designated by many nineteenth-century husbands for their wives (in reality as in fiction), sharing with Víctor the touching belief that illness really is the cause of conjugal distress.[10] (The reader, however, may just escape the ironic mesh laid by Flaubert and see it as the latter.)

Emma has a brief attempt to redeem her husband for a heroic role, in the affair of Hippolyte's club-foot. Charles operates, ill-advisedly and with disastrous results, although a total fatality is avoided. What occurs here is an interesting inversion of a motif connected with the man of honour. Within the honour code, honour is an attribute that can be gained and then possessed by a man, and can be tainted by a woman attached to him. In the

[9] See the description offered by Alain de Lattre, *La Bêtise d'Emma Bovary* (Paris, 1980), 9: 'Un homme qui aime, sans doute. Qui a le poids d'aimer, mais ne sait pas aimer.'

[10] See Ch. 4, n. 62.

supposition that Charles might attain medical heroism by the performance of a new type of operation on Hippolyte, there is an attempt to raise him to the status of hero, and the belief that there might be dual success (both in the operation and in the subsequent elevation of Charles in the estimation of his wife) is such that Emma even comes to note with some surprise that 'his teeth weren't bad at all' (II. 11. 189), a detail in the text which is to the advantage of neither of them. The failure of the attempt to gain heroism (consonant with honour) makes Emma feel tainted, and she feels a version of the ridicule traditionally given to the dishonoured husband: most of all she is astounded at herself, thinking about the man for whom she considers herself to have 'given all': 'for him! for that creature, that man without feeling or understanding, who sat there in perfect placidity, never dreaming for a moment that the ridicule attaching to his name would now sully her as well' (II. 11. 197).[11]

Charles is, however, not of the heroic mould (at least not until Emma's death). He is, above all, domestic, in a manner akin to the domesticity of Víctor, and in this sketching-in of his domesticity we see how the novel depicts him—if less than man of honour—at least as more than a cuckold. By contrast with Charles in his domesticity, Emma is periodically perceived as masculine, at least in her dress and demeanour.[12] The fears entertained by some of the Spanish Golden Age protagonists discussed in Chapter 4 about the potential marriage had for robbing them of some of their masculinity are now reformulated in these nineteenth-century considerations of marital problems. We see Charles's domesticity partly in the pleasure he takes in the early days of his marriage to Emma, and the speed with which he settles into, and settles for, a routine of ordinariness.

In contrast to the representation of the dangers for masculinity

[11] There is a similar reversal of gender-roles in the affair between Emma and Léon in III. 5, where Emma takes over the 'masculine' active role, and Léon complies, again related in a quasi-parody of gender-expectation derived from romantic fiction: 'He was prompted less by vanity than by the sole desire of pleasing her. He never questioned her ideas, he concurred in all her tastes. He had become her mistress rather than she his' (p. 289). Collas, *Madame Bovary* (58, 74–7) discusses the ambition of both Emma and Charles, and advances the view not only that Emma's ambition is compensatory, but that she would like Charles as an auxiliary ego: the two are linked.

[12] Collas, *Madame Bovary*, 61 and 79.

portrayed in honour drama, here domestic is not necessarily equivalent to despicable. While Emma is portrayed throughout *Madame Bovary* as a bad mother (she sends her child out to a wet-nurse, she neglects her on her return, she deals ill and well with her in emotional fits and starts), Charles for his part has some love for the child: he takes pleasure in dreaming of a future for the small Berthe, unaware of the financial chaos that envelops the family (II. 12. 207). In his final grief, Charles's sole external concern is with the well-being of his daughter, and fittingly it is she who finds him when he dies (though Flaubert resists melodrama by introducing farce, as Berthe pushes him in play and he falls to the ground, dead (III. 11. 360)).

Charles's most typical appearance in the novel, when he is not perceived as stupid, blundering, physically unattractive, is as a man weeping. He is aware enough of his surroundings at least to experience grief and to show concern, both attributes of the depressive position. This nakedness of the emotions is what sets him apart from the majority of the other deceived husbands of the cuckold mould we have considered so far.

One interpretation of his tears is that they give yet one more proof that he is a mother's boy, unable to cope, certainly unable to react to his situation with the stoic social front that his society associates with masculinity (and which his father had unsuccessfully attempted to instil in him). A different interpretation, however, relates to the poles of possible masculine models within this novel, or rather within concepts of behaviour entertained by characters in the mode. The most prominent constellation of ideal behaviour-forms is that of the Romantic hero, particularly as perceived by Emma. Such a hero is required to be dashing and masculine, but also sensitive, open to the emotions. The concept of the hero exists more in Emma's head than in any of the men she encounters: hence her alternation between attempts to educate them (whether Léon or Charles) and frustration when they fall short of her ideals.

Charles does not, of course, weep because he thinks this is the proper reaction of the Romantic hero. There is no indication that his tears are ever other than spontaneous—whether in despair or simple grief. It is this which emphasizes his humanity, a humanity which has been all too evident in his inability to be heroic, either in a Romantic heroic mould as desired by Emma, or in the stoic mould as desired by his father, or even in the local-hero mould as Homais attempts to form him.[13]

In the fact that Charles weeps, there is some measure of his acceptance of his fate, and an indication that he does not cut himself off from reaction to it. That one could consider this as the attainment of the depressive position in relation to his wife's infidelity is, however, quite questionable. To argue that would fly in the face of the abundance of evidence as to Charles's general incapacity to understand what goes on around him, or indeed fully to comprehend what happens or has happened to him.

A different way of viewing the attainment of the depressive position in this novel, however, is to consider it as conveyed by the text itself in relation to what is related. A characteristic of novels of adultery is that they do not provide any false catharsis, any illusion that the problem has been solved, dealt with, made to go away. Emma dies, it is true, but she does so by her own hand. In the fact that she commits suicide, rather than being killed by her husband, we can see one major departure from both the cuckold story and the man-of-honour story. Neither does she live on to enjoy her infidelity, nor does her death occur within the context of her husband's restoration of her honour. One connection her death does have with the man-of-honour story, however, is that the events of the narrative are evidently considered, or indeed experienced to be, intolerable, even if the subject who finds them so is the wife rather than the offended husband. Charles lives on, briefly, with the knowledge of his wife's infidelity.

This is a period of intense grief, as opposed to the much longer preceding period of stress and uncertainty, which had been evident even to his senses. Though he is perceived by his wife as imperceptive, and not given credit for much more by his creator, the evidence of his unhappiness is none the less there, if unclearly expressed. In the very unsatisfactoriness of the marriage relationship created in this novel, and its antithesis with the idea of Romantic love as entertained by Emma, there is the action of the author to force the reader, if bluntly, to an appreciation that love

[13] Starkie again (*Flaubert: The Making of the Master*, 159) argues this as an example of Emma's influence from beyond the grave. That Charles should become a Romantic hero unconsciously is, however, much more consonant either with Flaubert's irony, or, conceivably, with his salvaging of Charles as a character able to be spontaneous, if only tragically so.

is not ideal, nor marriages likely to be happy. Flaubert's unrelenting irony, his refusal to be kind to any of his creations, opens up the possibilities of much more complex emotions and reactions than any simple tale of love, honour, or infidelity could do, and by his irony Flaubert forces a reading which cannot admit of illusions. That this can be termed a working-towards a depressive position is possible but may also be debatable, as the contrast with *Anna Karenin* will show.

So much for the cuckold. What of the model of the man of honour? There certainly are other novels of adultery which portray husbands as men of honour, although few are presented in such a way as to stimulate admiration or awe—the sort of reaction which, in a pure form, the man-of-honour model is designed to provoke. Trollope's novel *He Knew He Was Right* (1868–9), for example, is the tale of a husband whose reaction to what he (wrongly) supposes to be his wife's infidelity is extreme, but his wife makes it clear that to her his attitude is unacceptable. Thus his first response is challenged on a primary level by his wife's refusal to acknowledge what he seems to view as his sovereign right to be as suspicious, demanding, and unreasonable as he likes. His reaction, were it to have been enclosed in a play of the Spanish Golden Age, would have seemed in no way unusual. In those works, however, the extraordinary level of reaction to suspicion in no way deters the husband from moving through to a bloody conclusion in which he will wash his honour with blood. The difference with the Trollope account is in the surprise offered both husband and reader by the wife's opposition and—since we are now dealing with nineteenth-century England rather than sixteenth-century Spain—the fact that there is no bloody outcome. Instead there is all the high-handedness of reaction of Trevelyan the husband, with the emphasis so characteristic of Trollope on epistolary dalliance as an activity which must be stamped on. Trevelyan, like any man of honour, is of course convinced that he is right, and remains emphatically, even vociferously, so convinced for the greater part of the novel. The shift evident between the sixteenth and the nineteenth centuries is in the perception of the husband's stance. There is no reticence in Trevelyan's articulation of his position. But it is opposed by his wife and those who support her, and then he is perceived in his activity to be both absurd and base (resorting finally to the dubious ministrations of a gumshoe suggestively named Bozzle in his attempts to secure custody of his son, and to prove the impropriety of his wife's behaviour). Trevelyan's bid for honourable behaviour soon takes on, not just the cloak, but the underlying reality of paranoia, as the stress involved in his position leads to his eventual breakdown, verging on insanity. Brought to this point, he reaches the fate of pitiable victim of his own suspicions, and finally becomes child and patient to his wife's care. After a final if tacit confession to her that he had not, after all, been right, he dies.

A more straightforward example of the man of honour is Innstetten, the husband of Effi Briest, in the novel of that name (1895).[14] In this work, the actual manner of the narrative conveys most powerfully an apparent ideal of the comportment of the man of honour operating in the nineteenth century: it is discreet, and we are kept firmly distanced from most of the feelings of Innstetten, the husband. *La Princesse de Clèves* (1678), which pre-dates *Effi Briest* by a good two centuries, initially appears to offer a precedent in its contained and restrained narrative. Despite its courtliness, its elegance and restraint, however, it has a live emotional tone throughout, a painfully clear level of access to the feelings of the wife, and access finally to the feelings of the husband in that novel, a man who by the sheer level of honesty and undefended emotion he is able both to feel and express, belongs with the men of distinction of Chapter 6 of this book. In *Effi Briest*, the sense of distance remains throughout. We are kept firmly at bay from most of the feelings of Innstetten, the husband, and gain access to those of Effi only in the briefest, most discreet form. The novel echoes by the discretion and non-committal nature of its own narrative the discretion of the actual occurrence of the adultery, so that the reader only receives full information and confirmation of the event at the same time as the husband, the medium of information being the old bundle of love-letters retained by Effi and discovered in the course of a minor domestic emergency.

The discretion or restraint of the novel has given rise to varied

[14] Theodor Fontane, *Effi Briest* (1895), trans. Douglas Parmée (Harmondsworth, 1987). All references will be to this edition, the first arabic reference being to the chapter, the second to the page number.

interpretation. Amongst the more positive is that of Michael Minden, who signals 'tact' as the way of understanding the social subtleties of the novel, while taking account of the underlying anxiety.[15] An interpretation which indicates a yet greater level of anxiety is that based on embarrassment, as proposed by J. M. Ritchie. This reading, however, while sensing an emotional content of considerable unease below the text of social nicety, does not perceive any real conflict within Innstetten himself, and classes his 'passion' in terms of the control he adopts to deal with his uncertainty, that is, his urge 'first and foremost to further his career, and second to play the schoolmaster'.[16]

There is a sense of anaesthetized numbness through the greater part of the novel. An initial scene of the playful domestic bliss of Effi's childhood contains, quite inexplicably (were it not for a still-accepted social convention of the arranged marriage), the settling of the marriage between Effi, a child (it is emphasized) of 17, and Innstetten, a man of 39 who had previously been suitor to Effi's mother. This mismatch of age, and all the possible entanglements of a transferred love-attachment, are indicated but never fully pursued. It is left to us to surmise what lies beneath Frau Briest's ready agreement to the marriage of her daughter to her own former suitor, an agreement that suggests she fosters the match for her own vicarious enjoyment, a misdeed that she will then punish in her rejection of Effi after the adultery.

The marriage is, then, a conventionally arranged one, but with this curious added detail that the husband was formerly suitor to the bride's mother, and was turned down in favour of Briest, the better-established man. Innstetten thus shares with Víctor of *La Regenta* the fate of someone cuckolded *avant la lettre*, with the difference that he has been ousted, oedipally as it were, by a man more advanced in power and maturity, and with a substitution of daughter for mother. This slightly unorthodox detail aside, the emphasis of the whole narrative is on quietly organized social life, in which status and standing are given due attention, but in which

[15] He puts this e.g. as the 'projection of the flight into the social, the recourse to the world of tact'. See '*Effi Briest* and *Die Historische Stunde des Takts*', *Modern Language Review*, 76 (4) (1981), 869–79 (875).

[16] J. M. Ritchie, 'Embarrassment, Ambiguity and Ambivalence in Fontane's *Effi Briest*', in Jorg Thunecke (ed.), *Formen realisticher Erzählkunst* (Nottingham, 1979), 563–9 (569).

the standing of Innstetten, as that of Karenin, is based on the exercise of administrative office, rather than on military exploits (as is frequently typical of earlier models of the man of honour).

We could speculate briefly here that even in the transfer of occupation of the husbands in these novels from the sword to the pen, there is a hint of their retreat from masculinity. There is little visible activity in their professions that might be attached to gender-behaviour norms for masculinity. Charles Bovary alone, within our selection, exercises a practical profession (and does it, as everything, with good nature but no sparks of intelligence). Otherwise, the husbands we have to consider are not, unlike Othello or Spanish honour-play heroes, men of action; they are either retired (Víctor) or are paper-pushing civil servants or officials (Innstetten, Karenin, Pozdnyshev). Only in the case of Karenin will there be a real sense that this is a man of ambition (to be thwarted at the time of his domestic problems). Although Innstetten's career is also traced with some care, there is no real penetration of the world of his work, merely a sense of promotions and advances glimpsed and desired, in a way that leaves us perhaps as uninformed about its meaning and import as is the case for his young wife. And although Innstetten has plenty of status in the external world, through his administrative activity, it is clear that this has no effect on his wife's opinion of him, nothing to mitigate her perception of him as a man who is cold, unresponsive, and who earns from her the significant clichéd remark, 'All you can do is smoke a cigar'—referring to the gesture that makes him the blood brother of the other adulteresses' husbands considered here. Thus the underside of the man of honour—at least for his wife—is that there is emptiness, lack of life.

To return to the attitudes to the arranged marriage, there are presumably implications also as regards the state of mind of the husband, both at the time of marriage, and, later, at the time of his discovery of Effi's infidelity. Why is he content to be the second fiddle, transposed by a generation? The nature of this text, however, is such that the reader is kept as uninformed as Effi herself on the matter of the nature and reactions of Innstetten. Throughout he is only just visible, a man, as it were, of upright novelistic bearing, conveyed to us partly through the eyes of his young wife, and partly through the estimation that others have of his social position.

Beneath the surface of social norms and niceties, there are currents of feeling, excitement, and sensuality. There is an element of titillation within the text itself, and within the narrative conducted by those in the text. There are nuances of something other than the conventional in the way Innstetten is introduced, since Effi announces his arrival to her friends as an old friend of her mother's from her younger days. There is, for Effi, romance attached to this 'love story with a hero and heroine who gave each other up' (1. 17). But her perception of the disappointed lover is determined above all by his social status, by the fact that he is 'Geert von Innstetten and a baron' (1. 19), a man who was pipped at the matrimonial post by Effi's father, who was older, and more advanced in public life. When the proposal is announced to Effi (it is made to her parents, and not to her directly), it is the social and public advantages of the match that are emphasized by her mother. That is, her mother shows considerable distance, indeed an extraordinary denial of what must be her personal knowledge of, and feelings about, the man when she sums up her daughter's position to her: 'It's true that he's older than you, which, all things considered, is an advantage, and he's a man of character and he's well-bred and he has a good situation, and if you don't say no, which I can hardly imagine my clever Effi doing, then by the age of twenty you'll have gone as far as others have at forty' (1. 24). (The succession of clauses linked by 'and' may indicate something of the mother's nervousness and denial of feelings, but this is the only indication.)

It is Effi's mother who will eventually write the note of parental rejection in which the future of the woman who has been discovered adulterous is spelled out. Not for the turn-of-the-century wife the horrors of sixteenth-century revenge, but emotionally violent none the less is the rejection formula: 'you'll be one of the many who have been forced to do without fresh air and sunlight. You'll be living a lonely life and, if you don't want to do that, you'll probably have to move out of your social class. You'll be excluded from the society in which you've been moving up till now. And the saddest thing for us and for you (even for you if we understand you rightly) is that you will be excluded from our house, too' (31. 232).

A distinction which perhaps needs to be made here is that between the requirements of society and the requirements of the man of honour, since by the period of this novel, it seems that the former is what is to be emphasized, although it may take the shape of the latter. Innstetten, when the adultery is discovered (six years after the event), acts like a man of honour, or rather, an 'honourable' man, but there is at least as much emphasis given, if not more, to the general social opprobium to be meted out to the erring wife. In situations where the erring wife is killed, the question of the reaction of society to her behaviour does not arise, except in so far as it is contained in a social reaction of (as a minimum) acceptance of the husband's retaliation or (as a maximum) positive approbation of the husband's retaliation. Where it is possible for the wife not to be killed, but simply divorced or set aside, then the wife as a social entity remains, as an issue not just for the husband but for the society in which they live, and becomes a type of living test-case for the beliefs of that society. Having said this, *Effi Briest* stands out as a novel in which the general social reaction to the adultery is stressed as much as is that of the husband. This reaction forms so strong an element that it can barely be the topic of conversation, still less of discussion. The closing words of the novel, spoken, we may note, 'calmly' by Effi's father, summarize all: 'That is *too* big a subject' (36. 267). A response to the question of whether Effi was too young to have married, it stands equally well as a measure of how far both readers and participants are kept from the events of the novel, with their possible causes and repercussions.

As noted, it is Effi's mother who writes the letter of parental rejection, and it becomes clear, when they are approached by Effi's doctor about the possibility of taking her back, that rejection was an attitude imposed on her father rather than readily adopted by him. This diversity of reaction within the Briest household initially seems surprising: if society condones Innstetten's reaction to the infidelity, would one not expect Effi's father to be more explicitly in favour? One could, of course, argue that Briest is either a passive cuckold-figure (accepted only as a good social catch by his wife, who preferred the then more exciting Innstetten), and that he continues to be passive in the face of his wife's unbending reaction to their daughter, or that he is an individualist who is able to hold a view distinct from those about him. The latter is hard to believe, since it appears Briest does not speak up until others make it easy for him to do so, with the result that it is easy for him to combine the reaction of forgiving generosity with the line of least resistance to his wife.

Frau Briest's reaction is also worth examination. A woman who put society first, in her youth, she has an investment in obliging others to do the same. In addition, there is the possibility that in condemning Effi she is defending her own original decision (to make a socially acceptable marriage), and distancing herself from any feeling of responsibility for what has happened. We might also note that Fontane, despite the questioning of the honour code which will underlie Innstetten's final vacillations, not only opts for 'punishment' for his erring heroine (thus keeping the score tidy on how to deal with marital discord), but also neatly avoids the man's responsibility for it, by placing all the weight of decision and exclusion on Frau Briest. The erring wife/daughter is disposed of by the bad mother (bad as the rejecting mother, and bad as the mother/wife who has played with the fascination of marrying her daughter to the former suitor), and men are excluded from the blame of the executioner—a step which moves the author away from the depressive willingness to accept guilt and responsibility.

In following the reaction of the Briest parents to Innstetten's repudiation of Effi, we are, of course, anticipating the action, and we are avoiding the issue of the reaction of Innstetten himself. The fact is, however, that in the novel itself, the relationship between Effi and her parents seems to be infinitely better drawn, more lively and warm in character, than the relationship between Effi and her husband, which is characterized by fear, tentativeness, tensions. This novel, like *Dombey and Son*, reverts unerringly to parental rather than matrimonial concerns, emphasizing the inevitably close link between the two.

Even to single out Innstetten himself calls for some effort. He is introduced as a powerful man, one who will have a place in the public world—but is given little else as an indication of his character or nature. There is a singular dearth of physical description for all of the characters, and Innstetten, who has been reported by Effi to her friends as 'with a good figure and very manly-looking' (1. 17), is simply described as 'slim, brown-haired, and military in bearing' (2. 24) when he meets Effi after making his proposal to her parents. Other characters seem to have summed him up in firm and simple manner, ranging from Niemeyer's 'He's a man of character, a man of principles!' (4. 39), to Effi's father's more negative and questioning 'with all his good qualities, he's not the sort of man who'd find it easy to make her love him' (5. 42). This view of Innstetten as an unbending man is one which will last until the end of the novel—at least as far as society is concerned, so that the response of the minister's wife when Effi asks her to help her to see her daughter again endorses the earliest views of the man: 'Your husband—forgive me if I refer to him as I used to—is not a man who acts according to moods and whims but according to principles, and he'll find it hard to give them up or even to relax them temporarily' (32. 245).

To a large degree Innstetten is presented through the eyes of others, and then reinterpreted for others, as in the above example. Most prominent of all the interpretations are those which present him as the man of honour, acting according to principle, to what he believes to be right, not giving the impression at any point that he will be swayed by the changing emotions of the moment.

Effi herself, however, has access to more than the social man, and her complaints at the vacuum she encounters are explicit. There is ample evidence that Effi finds Innstetten lacking as a husband, lacking in responsiveness. While this is not expressed with the frustrated anger of Ana Ozores, she is none the less outspoken about his reserve. Returning from paying a call in Kessin she remarks 'You might give me just one kiss. But you don't ever think about that. Throughout the whole long journey, you didn't touch me once, you're as chilly as a snowman' (9. 68). This is followed by that remark which suggests the existence of a nineteenth-century cliché of female dissatisfaction, 'All you can do is smoke a cigar.' For a young woman, Effi reaches a remarkable degree of assertiveness in pinpointing the root, as she sees it, of Innstetten's concern for his status. Thus, when he refuses to sell their house because of her fears of a ghost, she is sparked to respond in no uncertain terms: 'all you can say to me is that you don't feel like making yourself ridiculous in the eyes of the Prince or the town. That's no consolation' (10. 79). In this way she both describes the reaction of the man of honour, and exposes what, for her, is his emptiness: she sees it as a hollow regard for the opinion of others, which has no connection with her need for emotional recognition.

It is worth remembering that Effi has a somewhat stereotyped view of men: she has a concept of the 'manly man' (which may not, for example, square with her experience of her father, the man who holds his peace, and who is not afraid to express affection). Against this she finds the romantic swoonings of Innstetten's cousin a target of criticism. She will not take him seriously, and says as much to her husband. There is, however, the question of whether she simply feeds back to Innstetten an image of the man that he would like to present himself to be, or whether she is indeed giving her own view: 'But he's a namby-pamby. And that's something that women can't bear even when they're still only half grown up, which you always reckoned me to be and perhaps still do, in spite of all the progress I've made. Namby-pambies aren't for us. Men should be men' (21. 167). In Effi's words, there seem to be shades of 'What a man's gotta do' and 'the right stuff' here, the tendency to speak in stereotypes winning the day over real experience. In a less positive, more honest moment she confesses (as her mother reports) that 'Innstetten was always a very fine man. There aren't many men like him, but I couldn't really get close to him, there was something remote about him even when he was affectionate. Yes, most of all then. There were times when I was frightened by it' (24. 197).

Undermining this impression of Innstetten as a remote man is the degree to which we see him as a man with an investment of control of his domestic situation, which he pursues to the extent of controlling or 'educating' Effi by playing on her fear of the ghost of the Chinaman. It is easy to stop, as some critics have done, at the point of Innstetten's control itself.[17] Others, however, have been sensitive to the defensive nature of that control, and have focused on the underlying tensions and denials. Christine Ann Evans, for example, while acutely observing that many prevailing critical readings of Innstetten have in fact followed the view of Innstetten held by Crampas, who in portraying to Effi a view of her husband as a controlling man has a clear vested

[17] See George C. Avery, 'The Chinese Wall: Fontane's Psychograph of Effi Briest', in Karl S. Weimar (ed.), *Views and Reviews of Modern German Literature* (Munich, 1974), 18–38 (21–30). Others have regarded Innstetten's control or education of Effi as a simple sign of nastiness. See e.g. A. Bance, 'The Heroic and the Unheroic in Fontane', in Thunecke (ed.), *Formen realisticher Erzählkunst*, 404–45. Bance criticizes Innstetten for being *in loco parentis*, and is judgemental about his 'trampling upon the susceptibilities of the immature, poetic girl', seeking to '*use* them for his own ends'.

interest in it, sees Innstetten's coldness, exemplified in his refusal to accommodate Effi's fear of the Chinaman, as a denial of the rational itself.[18] A yet more sensitive reading of Innstetten as a man susceptible to the irrational rather than impervious to it is that offered by Erika Swales. In this reading, Innstetten's level of tension and unease can be interpreted as signs of his 'vulnerability to the pressures of an unacknowledged realm of experience'.[19]

A further dimension to Innstetten is that revealed by Effi's reinterpretation of him after the adultery and her repudiation. At this point, she lives a solitary existence in Berlin, with only Roswitha her maid, and, eventually, the dog for company. When Annie, her daughter, is finally allowed to visit, Effi is horrified at what she has turned into—in her eyes a prissy young girl now. She turns on her husband, and her analysis of what he is like under the honourable exterior comes remarkably close to a description of the reversals in the perception of the world that take place in the paranoid-schizoid position: 'I thought he had a noble heart and I've always felt small beside him but now I know it's he who is small. And because he's small, he's cruel. Everything small is cruel' (33. 249).

This is the bitter analysis arrived at by Effi, who only sees the paranoid-schizoid model of her husband—unsurprisingly, since the man-of-honour front is what he presents to the world. It emphasizes the degree to which she appears not to have moved on to maturity in the novel, but has been kept—by her creator as much as by anyone else—firmly in the status of child, who cannot and will not be able to perceive her husband with the insight permitted by an equal footing. Yet another way of interpreting this reaction, which might otherwise seem to condemn Effi to having no more than a diminished insight (which the reader is not obliged to share) into her husband, is to view her as the recipient of Innstetten's projection. Because he feels threatened, insignificant, small, he defends against such feelings. He projects out the feeling of insignificance—with such fierceness in these latter

[18] Christine Ann Evans, 'New Wine in Old Bottles: On Appropriating Male Speech in *Effi Briest*', *Germanic Notes*, 19 (3) (1988), 38–41. For Evans, Crampas's view of Innstetten is 'interested, skewed' (p. 41).

[19] Erika Swales, 'Private Mythologies and Public Unease: On Fontane's *Effi Briest*', *Modern Language Review*, 75 (1980), 114–23 (117).

stages that it is communicated to its main recipient, Effi, counter-transferentially, and as a result she experiences it rather than being able to observe it.[20]

In the few instances where we are allowed to see fractionally into Innstetten via himself, a slightly modified view emerges, and some glimmers, if not of the depressive position in relation to his situation, at least of the realization that an attitude of that type might have been possible. Initially he appears either to have, or to allow himself, only limited self-awareness: the latter seems the more likely, and the more consistent with his position as he later comes to see it, since awareness brings with it the pain of existence as well as the pleasures.

He remains opaque to the reader as well as to Effi (apart from what can be deduced about the defensive nature of his coldness and control) until the novel is well advanced, and it is only after the discovery of Effi's old love-letters from Crampas that any inner view of him is obtained. Until that point, we are restricted either to what has been observable by Effi (which includes her own belief of what the honourable man is like), or to the interpretations of others, or to the briefest externals (his look of quick suspicion when they receive Crampas's letter announcing his departure (20. 159)), or to Effi's perception of what might be a sign of suspicion (Innstetten goes pale when he perceives her immense relief at the news that they are to move definitively to Berlin (21. 168)).

After the move to Berlin a somewhat less suspicious Innstetten seems to emerge, and this transformation is combined with some settling into domestic life. His attention to their daughter Annie is noted (26. 209–10), and it is, of course, Annie's accident which ironically triggers the discovery of Effi's adultery—some six years after the event.

Once he has recognized Crampas's handwriting on the love-letters, Innstetten acts swiftly. We have little information about his state of mind, beyond the immediate 'his head began to spin' (27. 211), an indication of a state of confusion that will lie beneath the

[20] Counter-transference here is used in the Kleinian understanding of non-verbal affective communication which can exist between analyst and patient, and in which the analyst acts as the container for those experiences of the patient which are intolerable. For discussion and further definition see Hinshelwood, *A Dictionary of Kleinian Thought*, 255–62.

surface, despite the decisiveness of his subsequent actions. All the others are able to observe is that he is silent, pale, angry (the observation of the maid, (27. 212)). Unlike Víctor, Innstetten has the capacity to act swiftly, and within the space of a couple of hours from the discovery he has set in motion the arrangements for a duel.

Only in conversation with Wullersdorf, whom he approaches to arrange the duel for him and to be his second, does Innstetten reveal his feelings—surprisingly inconsistent with the façade of the cool man of honour who simply avenges himself swiftly. Erika Swales perceptively notes that the debate with Wullersdorf is essentially one with himself.[21] Here he admits to feeling, but not of the expected type: 'It's just that I'm infinitely unhappy. I'm humiliated, I've been shamefully deceived and yet in spite of that I have no feeling of hatred at all, or even a thirst for vengeance' (27. 214). And, perhaps most surprising of all, he declares that he loves, no, that he *still* loves his wife.

Thus Innstetten disarmingly unpicks what may lie behind the reaction of the man of honour. He is not so led by his feelings that he delays in agony, as Víctor does, but none the less aware that he is reacting automatically, and in the face of how he feels *vis-à-vis* society rather than *vis-à-vis* his wife. There is a degree of novelistic inverisimilitude, perhaps, in Innstetten's self-examination, which traces out the anxieties associated with the paranoid qualities of the man of honour. Control is all, but it can cramp one's capacity for action: 'I'm in an impasse. I've only myself to blame; if you like, I should have been more guarded and shown more self-control, have kept everything to myself and fought it all out in my own mind. But it came so suddenly and violently that I can hardly blame myself for not having been able to control my reactions more successfully' (27. 215). Here there is an interesting turn, since he envisages using more control to prevent himself from going into the immediate man-of-honour position of provoking a duel, a thought which combines some awareness of the paranoid folly of what he has been led into with a failure to realize that the method proposed only serves to compound that type of reaction. The decision to go ahead with the duel thus becomes a failure of that control, an expression of his desperate need to resolve

[21] Swales, 'Private Mythologies', 119.

uncertainty by exactitude.[22] Later, Innstetten is described as pursuing similar thoughts and vacillations after the duel (an event recounted in its barest detail, with scarcely a pastel shade of emotion), this time simply revealing that now he has less conviction about what he has done than previously. At the level of the text, there is again an odd disjunction, in that the functioning of the character is revealed but, as is consistent with the detachment of the man of honour's position, lacks a level of live emotion.[23]

In his ability to mull over what has happened, and what might have been different, there are glimmerings of a depressive position in Innstetten, particularly as he thinks of the dying Crampas. 'When I think of his last look, resigned and yet smiling in his misery, it seemed to be saying: "Innstetten, always standing on principle . . . You might have spared me that and yourself as well." And perhaps he was right. I can hear myself saying something similar.' And Innstetten proceeds to speculate that his action was determined not by feelings of hatred or vengeance, but 'merely to support a fantasy, an abstraction' (29. 222). In all this, he seems to reveal himself as the model deceived husband, that is, one who is undeceived—not about his wife's infidelity, but about his reaction to it. The flaw in all this is his detachment in doing so, and the not inconsiderable irony contained in the way that he fixes on Crampas as the man who 'informs' him about the nature of reaction, since Crampas throughout has been presented as a caricature of a lover, and, as much as Innstetten, was a man who operated on a level of phantasy and play-acting.

22 Ibid. 119. Having viewed the debate as containing for Innstetten a 'quasi-private motivation', she interprets the decision to have the duel as related to his question of identity: 'By fighting the duel and facing the consequences he hopes to wrest some kind of experiential authenticity from his confusion and uncertainty.'

23 The detailing of emotional complexity in relation to the duel belies the simple critical interpretation which lays heavy emphasis on the weight of society—an influence which would render Innstetten bound to fight a duel, and Effi's parents bound to shun her from their house. This is a line of argument pursued by Lilian Furst, '*Madame Bovary* and *Effi Briest*', *Romanistisches Jahrbuch*, 12 (1961), 124–35 (132). See, by contrast, the more subtle social readings of Minden, '*Effi Briest*', and Donald C. Riechel, '*Effi Briest* and the Calendar of Fate', *Germanic Review*, 48 (3) (May 1973), 189–211, who notes the degree to which the 'matter of the duel has become acutely questionable and complicated by the fact that the social order has lost its validity' (p. 196). Minden ('*Effi Briest*') argues persuasively that the interview with Wullersdorf is one in which direct emotion is contained rather than suppressed (that is, a situation which in a Kleinian frame would be seen as depressive). This containment is an 'exercise of tact', a quality the exercise of which he sees as subtle, and not reprehensible.

TRIANGLES OF TRANSITION: *LA REGENTA*

It was Spain that provided us with the literary examples of the man of honour. To be expected, then, perhaps, is some link between the mode of action of the man of honour (and the possible resolution of plot) and the unfolding of the tale of *La Regenta*.[24] The link as we shall see, however, is more in the form of parody and a displaced reaction of the man of honour into a character other than the husband. The original husband begins with features of the cuckold type (while possessing the emphasis on status and social position of the man of honour), and moves swiftly to the model of father. Most significant of all, however, in the figure of the husband, is the degree to which he is portrayed, not only as inadequate, but as patchily aware of his inadequacy, with the result that he alternates between being a figure of fun and being a figure of pathos. Of the husbands discussed in this work, he has perhaps suffered most signally from neglect, either by simple omission or by readings that see him as no more than a necessary pivot in the plot—a far cry from the man of honour, who is notionally at the centre of it.[25]

Much of one's initial impression of Víctor places him, as I have indicated, within the type of cuckold: an older man, shy, sexually inept, passive, quickly seen as ridiculous by almost all around him. He attempts to counterbalance this impression by presenting himself as a man of honour, but this turns out to be a mode that he is able to favour only in literature. What prevents Víctor from being simply a cuckold, or simply a man of honour, is first, that he has some insight at least into his own deficiencies, and second, that we as readers are given too much insight both into his deficiencies and into the degree to which he suffers as a result of them for us to class him neatly as embodying either of the two models.

In this discussion he occupies a transitional place in so far as he moves between the models, and yet the matter is much more complex. He is type-cast by Alas as cuckold in a novel where the

[24] Leopoldo Alas, *La Regenta* (1884–5), trans. by John Rutherford (Harmondsworth, 1984). All references will be to this edn., the first arabic reference being to the chapter, the second to the page number.

[25] See e.g. Moraima de Semprún Donahue, 'La Doble Seducción de *La Regenta*', *Papeles de Son Armadans*, 71 (211) (Dec. 1973), 209–28: 'Don Víctor, el marido legítimo ante la ley, no es más que una conveniencia estructural para la tragedia que se desarrolla dentro de la trama novelesca al morir en un duelo provocado por la infidelidad de su esposa' (p. 210).

whole of social life is organized and mediated through literature.[26] Yet his occupation of the role of man of honour is his own hopeful, aspiring type-casting for himself, a type-casting which proves disastrous. It is underscored by the presence of a variety of triangles in which, characteristically, he is a lesser man seeking to strengthen his masculinity by identification with another man, who is thus perceived as role-model rather than as rival.

This lengthy, almost unwieldy novel, hovering between a naturalistic socio-account of the claustrophobia of life in a northern province of Spain and a tale of (would-be) romance and passion, is the obvious Spanish candidate for a discussion of novels of adultery. This is not to say that adultery is absent from other Spanish novels of the period. Far from it. Galdós's masterpiece *Fortunata y Jacinta* (1886), almost exactly contemporary with *La Regenta*, presents a complex and variegated portrayal of adultery, with an unusual focus on the unhappiness caused to a wife (Jacinta) by her husband's adulterous love for a woman of the *pueblo*, Fortunata. Running in counterpoint to Jacinta's suspicions and distress is a form of the expected adultery tale, but much altered, consisting of the much more pointed and even more poignant portrayal of the suspicions and distress suffered by Maxi, Fortunata's sickly, insane, and ill-fated husband, who solves his distress by a mixture of rationalization, idealization, and a retreat into madness. Adultery is closely approached in *Un viaje de novios* (1881) by Emilia Pardo Bazán. Here the commission of adultery would have more than sufficient justification in the form of the husband's infidelity and poor marital behaviour, but, in a rare moment of social verisimilitude, adultery as a solution to marital distress (rather than as the cause of marital distress) is eschewed by the authoress for her heroine, who returns to her paternal home, leaving both husband and lover behind.

It is *La Regenta*, however, which contains the elements characteristic of the major European examples of the genre: the eponymous heroine, normally alluded to in connection with the name of her husband (thus highlighting simultaneously her

[26] Stephanie Sieburth, *Reading 'La Regenta': Duplicitous Discourse and the Entropy of Structure* (Amsterdam, 1990), particularly good on the role of the *folletín* in the text. See also Benigno Sánchez-Eppler, 'Stakes: The Sexual Vulnerability of the Reader', *Romanic Review*, 78 (1987), 202–17.

novelistic identity and prominence and her lack of independent social identity); the tense but luxurious delineation of the hesitations and desires which finally culminate in an adulterous union; the ending, which consists either of death or, as in this case, effective death in the social neglect or ignominy of the heroine. In so far as it is a novel embedded in the petty, trivial frustrations and mediocrities of provincial life, it is closest to *Madame Bovary*, but focuses even more narrowly than its sister novel on the milieu in which the adulterous affair occurs.

More akin to another tradition, however, one which is allied to anti-clericalism and social criticism, is the way in which the novel toys, somewhat sensationally, with the salacious thrill of proposing a priest as a possible agent of adultery. Thus it stands in relation to Zola's offering of *La Faute de l'Abbé Mouret* (1875), and Eça de Queirós's novel *O crime do Padre Amaro* (1876). The union of married woman and priest kills two moral birds with one stone: it takes up a liberal moral stance of criticism of immorality in the clergy, and at the same time produces a salaciously titillating version of adultery, in that in committing adultery with a priest, the woman commits a type of sacrilege (whether or not she acts as the prime mover in the establishment of the affair).

At a superficial level, *La Regenta* presents a simple model of the adultery novel. Ana Ozores, orphan of both mother (Italian dressmaker, whose profession is later converted by gossip to the more appropriate one of dancer) and father (a woolly-minded liberal, all decent intentions and lack of solid support), has marriage as a career virtually forced upon her. Her aunts, acting as reluctant guardians, are eager to get her off their hands, and propose a match with the vulgar and rich ex-colonial, Don Frutos Redondo. She is saved from this uncertain fate by an alternative proposal from the ex-Regente, Don Víctor Quintanar, the relationship having been initiated and encouraged by Víctor's friend, Frígilis. The novel opens with Ana, some years later, about to change confessor, impelled by the need to talk to someone about her current temptation: that of being seduced by Don Alvaro Mesía. She transfers to a new confessor, Don Fermín, a momentous event, and spends the remainder of the novel vacillating between Alvaro and Fermín, until, in the gap between the final two chapters, she commits adultery with the former. Her husband, reluctantly, finds himself forced into a duel, and receives a fatal wound in the bladder. Ana is rejected by all except Frígilis, and most dramatically by Fermín.

The element of the confessor makes the novel depart from the simple triangle of wife–husband–lover, and provides two alternative triangles—wife–husband–priest, and wife–priest–lover (where the priest adopts the role and behaviour of husband). In addition, there are numerous interlocking triangles at the level of sub-plot. The most crucial of these are those involving Petra, Ana's maid, who tempts Víctor with her attractions, but who also claims the favours of Alvaro as payment for her assistance in the affair between him and Ana, and has as an ultimate goal that of substituting herself for Fermín's maid Teresina, whose duties—it is hinted strongly—go beyond the simply domestic. A further shadow-husband is sketched out briefly in the character of Frígilis, Víctor's friend and shooting-companion, thus forming another triangle. The difference with this triangle is that it can also be interpreted as indicating the unfaithfulness of Víctor to Ana. In the initial triangles, the struggle in the heart of the heroine is not about whether or not to be unfaithful to her husband, although this is part of the plot, but much more about whether she is to be unfaithful to her husband with Alvaro or with Fermín (although infidelity with the latter is an aspect she is unaware of through most of the novel, her belief being that her devotion to the priest is within the context of religious dedication). The later triangles throw up questions about deflected, envied, and vicarious activity.

The novel is clearly triangular, then, but even at the level of the central plot, the husband, Víctor, comes a poor third to other rivals, both for the attentions of the novelist and for those of the reader. The triangle has been examined at length by René Girard in *Deceit, Desire and the Novel*,[27] with more recent discussions of his ideas by Tony Tanner[28] and Eve Kosofsky Sedgwick.[29] The Girard-based perception—itself, as Sedgwick points out, based on the conviction that the Oedipal triangle is one which is repeated in later life—concentrates not on the relationship between lover and beloved (typically male lover and another's wife), but on

[27] *Deceit, Desire and the Novel: Self and Other in Literary Structure*, original French version, *Mensonge romantique et vérité romanesque* (Paris, 1961), trans. Yvonne Freccero (Baltimore, 1965).

[28] *Adultery in the Novel*, 89–91.

[29] *Between Men*, 21–3. See also Ch. 3, n. 38.

the implied relationship between two rivals for the affection of another. The bond between the two rivals is not consequent on the triangle's being formed, but is itself the reason for its formation. That is, as Sedgwick puts it, 'the choice of the beloved is determined in the first place, not by the qualities of the beloved, but by the beloved's already being the choice of the person who has been chosen as a rival'.[30] The *why* of male bonding is, it seems to me, harder to divine than the apparent ease of its observation might suggest. That it may well relate defensively to gender-acquisition at an early stage is, however, to be borne in mind, and the obvious anxiety which surrounds Víctor's personality makes this explanation particularly persuasive. Above all, his characterization suggests a bonding through uncertainty of identity.[31]

As will be evident from earlier chapters in this book, I believe that for the source of gender-formation of the man, and for norms which are to obtain for his behaviour, we can look, not solely to identification with the father (which may be related to fear of his power, and desire to possess a similar power), but to reactions deriving from the relationship with the mother. This relationship is one from which the boy has to struggle to emerge, consequently forming an exaggerated and aggressive form of his masculinity. In this context, the nature of rivalry between two men (Girard and Sedgwick both focus on the triangle which consists of one woman and two men) will take the form not of rivalry for the object, but of rivalry about being the best kind of subject. The rival values the object of the possessor because at some level he envies the potency of the possessor and wants to be like him. The driving force, then, for the man in the triangle will be of desire and/or the need for identification.

A difference between my approach, then, and that deriving from Girard, is in my emphasis on the primary reaction, of man to

[30] *Between Men*, 21.

[31] See in connection with this the observation of Joel Fineman based on Kleinian theory about the importance of pre-Oedipal experience (in the context of a discussion of Shakespeare): 'In contrast to Freud, then, alienation from the object of desire is the preliminary condition both for male self-consciousness and for masculine desire . . . for the male at least . . . there is a psychological need to build a distance between himself and his desire, lest he lapse into the psychotic discovery of No Difference between self and object, between his self-regard and his imagination of his mother, between his identity and the context of his identity' ('Fratricide and Cuckoldry', 103). See also Ch. 1, n. 22.

woman, which will then form the base of secondary reactions, both to men and to women: thus women are feared and socially cloistered (not for their safety, but to keep the world of the man intact and protected), and thus also other men are either feared, because they might breach that safety-boundary, or desired, because they show themselves to be in a position of superior potency in their handling of their masculine gender-situation.[32]

While I do not think the 'between men' interpretation is the most useful for most of the novels considered in this chapter, there are distinct signs in *La Regenta* that it is a model that could be applied. First there is the close friendship between Víctor and Alvaro Mesía, Ana's would-be lover. Alvaro is admired, liked, cajoled by Víctor into closer contact with his domestic situation, enjoined by Víctor to participate in the plan of getting Ana to have a wider social life. Secondly there is Fermín as the shadow-husband to Víctor and shadow-lover to Alvaro.

A visual realization of what underlies the relationship between Alvaro and Víctor, that is, a concern about virility, is presented by the clichéd contrast between the two in chapter 16, when Alvaro's rather dashing appearance on horseback has relieved the tedium of a grey day for Ana, and Víctor is delighted to find him talking to his wife. The imagery of the horse, here as elsewhere, is less than subtle, indicating Alvaro's superiority to Víctor in the virility stakes. Víctor's lengthy speech on morality in art, delivered to Alvaro as he waits on an ever more impatient and spirited horse, not only places Víctor in ridicule because of his lack of sense of the appropriate, but points the way to the pattern of the future. Alvaro will have to spend many hours in Víctor's company as the price (as he sees it) of getting closer to his goal. The motif of the horse recurs later in the novel, in chapter 27, when Fermín, going to see Ana at El Vivero, sees Alvaro and his friends on dashing white thoroughbred horses, to which the hired nag pulling his carriage is a sad contrast (27. 614). *La Regenta* is unlike other novels of adultery in that there is no motif of the adulteress

[32] Consistent with this type of reading is the observation made by M. Nimetz, '*Eros* and *Ecclesia* in Clarín's Vetusta', *Modern Language Notes*, 86 (2) (1971), 242–53, that *La Regenta* contains various elements of sexual neutralization, both of women and of men. That is, fear surrounds the whole notion of gender, throughout the novel, in relation to both sexes, forming a text which both avoids, and is insistent upon, sexuality and gender-difference.

herself on horseback, unlike the striking image of Anna Karenin when visited by Dolly in the country, or, as in *Madame Bovary* and *Effi Briest*, where outings on horseback not only prefigure sexual excitement, but also provide the opportunity for the adultery to occur.

If there is an envy of possession, it is not Alvaro's envy of Víctor's possession of Ana, but rather Víctor's envy of Alvaro's possession of the attribute of virility. Indeed, in Neoplatonic terms, it seems that Alvaro has the primary possession of Ana, before there is even the beginning of a courtship by Víctor. The possession—in spirit and intention only—had been confirmed by an exchange of glances (5. 114) as Alvaro departed for Madrid, vowing that Ana would be one of his first conquests on his return. There is no evidence that Víctor is aware of this (he is like the typical cuckold in that one of his prime features is his general lack of perception), although he must be aware that when he presents himself as a fully-fledged suitor for the hand of Ana, his suit will be heard only because a rival but unsuitable claim for her in marriage has been made by Don Frutos Redondo. Although this technically makes him a sort of cuckold *avant la lettre*, in that he has been making cautious suit to Ana before Don Frutos's proposal comes, via the aunts, in terms of Ana's affections, the attachment to Alvaro, unperceived by him, and which pre-dates his oblique and gentlemanly courtship of her, is one which will always relegate him to the role of second string.

That Víctor perceives Alvaro as the support to his own questionable virility is displayed not only in his encouragement of the relationship with Ana (Alvaro will be able to arouse Ana out of her apathy and low spirits, where Víctor has failed to do so), but, more disastrously and painfully (in the perception of the reader), in the extent to which he uses Alvaro as a resident agony-aunt for consultation on his wavering attempts at extra-marital dalliance. Here Víctor is neither cuckold nor man of honour, but uncomfortably crossing boundaries of silence and decorum, as he creates a triangle of confidentiality between himself, Alvaro, and Ana. He is not totally separate from his feelings of inadequacy, nor is he aware of the ridiculous figure that he cuts. He remains with the emotion of insufficiency, neither defended against it as the man of honour might be by action, nor enjoying the cuckold's lack of awareness. At the level of the plot which overtly and obviously concerns us, there is the strand—belonging to the Romantic pot-boiler—of the husband who encourages the friend to have ever closer contact with his wife, because of his admiration for the friend, so that at a superficial level we watch with bated breath as more and more opportunities for the adultery desired by Alvaro present themselves. But below this level, and much more troubling, there is the unfolding of the tale of Víctor's inadequacy—his bungling, his hesitation, and his ineptitude in dealing with the consequences of his dalliance in the form of the threat of blackmail (as he perceives it) by Petra, the maid, who, in classic fashion, he has tried to grope when the occasion has presented itself. Without saying so explicitly, he has some level of admiration for the virility of Alvaro. One assumes that even Víctor hears, as others do, the tales of Alvaro's exploits, recounted at the Casino, even if he may not have much sense of what it is that brings Alvaro his success with women. Nor does he seem to perceive that Alvaro desires his wife—unless it is in an unconscious recognition which for Víctor will carry a validation of his own virility, in that Alvaro desires the woman Víctor 'possesses' (that possession—though legal only, ironically—denoting a public image of superior potency, even if the private reality is quite other). Admiration for virility is also expressed, naïvely, in Víctor's interest in the actor Perales. He was 'in love with' Perales (16. 374), who plays Don Juan in the performance of Zorrilla's *Don Juan Tenorio*, the play that (in a manner so quaintly a set-piece of the adultery novel) they all attend. So naïve is his admiration that he tries to get Ana to share it, and it is clear that the actor represents a desirable norm of virility for him: 'He is a handsome fellow, is he not, my child? And such artistic movements of the arms and legs! People say that it is artificial, that men do not really walk in that way. But men should! And no doubt we Spaniards did walk and gesticulate in that way in the Golden Age, when we were masters of the world' (16. 374).[33]

At what for Víctor is one of the lowest points of the novel, chapter 26, when Ana fulfils her vow to walk barefoot as a penitent in the Easter procession, an occasion where the whole town turns out to ogle the white flesh appearing beneath the folds

[33] For full discussion of the theatre in this novel see Roberto G. Sánchez, 'The Theater in Clarín's *La Regenta*', *Hispanic Review*, 37 (1969), 491–509.

of a specially designed and luxurious penitential robe of purple, the two men, Víctor and Alvaro, watch from an upper storey. Alvaro acts, literally, as front man, standing defiantly at the balcony to watch the whole scene, while Víctor, overcome now with shame and horror at what his wife is doing, remains in the shadows (26. 592–3). Víctor is moved not to anger but to tears as he lives through the awareness of his wife's public humiliation (which is worse than any of them, particularly she, had anticipated, and which signals her submission to the power of Fermín as priest). Responding to Alvaro's words of consolation, he swears to Alvaro that he would rather see his wife in the arms of a lover: 'find me a lover for her, seduce her for me, anything rather than seeing her in the arms of fanaticism' (26. 597). Alvaro here is made to be the witness in public of what happens. This contrasts with the private and painful witnessing Víctor finally has to engage in of the evidence of his wife's adultery, at a point where no one can act as his stand-in, least of all Alvaro, who is the evidence of infidelity he observes.

La Regenta reveals itself as a type of transitional work in the treatment of the deceived husband in the degree to which we are involved not so much in the dynamics of what the husband will do on the discovery of the adultery (as we shall see, this novel has a sad and rather desperate treatment of that aspect of the denouement), but rather in the underlying relationship between husband and wife, the mismatch in emotional and sexual terms which leads—inevitably, as it seems—to the outcome of adultery. Where it falls short of being a depressive text is in the limitation placed on the awareness of those involved of what they are doing or feeling, even though it may be apparent, uncomfortably so, for others. This is particularly so of Víctor, who all too often is exposed to others, but not with the flamboyance of a flasher—no power exerted here—but rather with the shame of the man who is found wanting. Thus not only does he have concern about his lack of masculinity, but this concern is repeatedly made evident to others, whether by their perception or, at times, by his stumbling confession.

We have seen that Víctor has some awareness of his own incapacity, in that he seeks out the advice and support of others, although he does so in order to find out how to deal with Petra rather than how to please his wife. The reader is enlightened to a striking degree as to Ana's awareness of her husband's incapacity, and her own reaction to it. Like Emma Bovary, she is fully aware of the level of her frustration with her husband. But while Ana shares some of Emma's literary Romanticism, and hence shares with her an impossibly idealized sense of the desired lover, she also periodically manages to come to the fore more acutely as a woman who is angry in her disappointment. Others may view Víctor as the public man, as well-meaning, even of some social stature, so that the description given of him to Ana's aunts by Frígilis, acting in the capacity of go-between, as 'A good, honest, brave Aragonese gentleman—a fine huntsman, most honourable, and very fond of the theatre' (5. 116) is not inaccurate. Ana, however, while being able at times to see the Víctor presented to the public, provides the means for undermining the private person underlying that public view. For her, Víctor is the man incapable even of smoking his cigars to the full, a shortcoming which she equates with being unable to enjoy a woman to the full (16. 351). He is a man who prefers to go shooting partridges rather than engage in conjugal love (10. 206). But on reflection, it is the goodness, the irreproachability of Víctor that most galls her. Had she married the vulgar Don Frutos Redondo, then she could have contemplated infidelity and its outcome: Don Frutos lying in a pool of blood, killed by Alvaro in a duel. Ana later repeats this fantasy, but with Víctor as corpse (16. 379). In her angry and resentful musings in chapter 10, Ana becomes trapped, literally, in a snare used by Víctor and Frígilis, a snare which only traps and does not kill the animal. The humanity indicated by the nature of the snare (the intention is only to dissuade the foxes it traps) seems to Ana to be yet one more sign of Víctor's inadequacy, a perception that throws up her own idealizing and alternative image of man as capable of violent and bloody acts, not one who is indecisive about whether to do anything or not with the animal he snares (the uncertainty of fate being reflected precisely in the uncertainty of what Ana feels is her marital fate). The type of impatience she reveals here may be as much an expression of personal frustration as of her anger that he does not match up to some rather exaggerated social norm of the masculine. This norm would be violent, not gentle, would consume, not taste, and would be dominating (contrasting with the gentle, domestic image so frequently associated with Víctor at moments of crisis).

Ana's recollections of her honeymoon (10. 210) show an awareness, before the event, of what she might have enjoyed but did not. There are no half-measures in her feelings about this time, which are unequivocal in their implied criticism of Víctor: 'And she remembered, half in shame half in anger, that her honeymoon had meant no more than futile arousal, a false alarm for sensuality, a cruel practical joke' (10. 210). Ana's fury in relation to Víctor as exemplified here is striking. It tends to surface only in moments of isolation, when she finds herself trapped alone in her marriage, rather than trapped into a contact she rejects in her marriage, and is a more modern expression of one of the underlying principles of the cuckold story, that is, that women will want sexual satisfaction, and that failure to secure it may have its consequences.

The suggestions of impotence contained in chapter 10 and elsewhere are to receive confirmation in Víctor's confessions to Alvaro about his difficulties in affairs. There are early indications of Víctor's hesitant desire to stray, conveyed by the scornful recollection of Petra: 'Don Víctor was an old man with a weakness, perhaps, for easy love, but with her he had never ventured beyond the occasional insistent sticky stare and a few complimentary remarks made in roundabout terms which did not compromise him' (9. 184). This is presumably part of the peccadillo (a considerable one) he keeps back when, at Ana's insistence, he goes to confess with Fermín (21. 492), and which he expands on, almost to the limits of Alvaro's tolerance, in the closing lines of chapter 28 (pp. 645–6). Víctor's fault, in his own eyes, is that he lacks the courage for the final move. His awareness of himself remains partial, relating to indecision only with Petra, not with Ana. At the close of the chapter, Alvaro, arguably egged on by this account of a negative example, finds his moment to make love to Ana, and vicariously acts again for Víctor, but this time not as witness to public shame, but as principal in the drama of marital deception.

It is possible, as we have seen, to apply the 'between men' model to this novel, seeing Víctor as the man who is drawn to the rival who will supplant him, drawn because of his admiration for the other's possession, not of his wife, but of his own virility. Víctor has other props, the most important of which is Frígilis, his shooting-companion but, more significantly, the man who in the first instance introduces him to Ana. The career of go-between is in many cultures one reserved for women. In Spain in particular, the occupation of *alcahueta* is a female one. Frígilis, in apparently occupying this role, is thus engaging not in cross-dressing (an activity apparently imposed upon Fermín by his priestly function), but in 'cross-behaving'. He appears to have a total absence of his own sexual life, preferring, we assume, to have it by proxy, by arranging the sexual lives of others, an activity mundanely also expressed in the form of arranging the grafting of plants. There is evidence of Frígilis's knowledge of others, and hence power over them (such as his knowledge of a previous murky duel of Alvaro, referred to in chapter 30 (pp. 698–9)) as he tries to avert disaster for all parties after the adultery has been discovered. He comes the closest ever to his attainment of Ana in the aftermath of the adultery, when he takes to sleeping in the lower floor of her house, to protect her, and to relieve her solitude by a distant presence. His anger (30. 704) at Alvaro's treatment of Ana is in tenor like that of an outraged husband, as he scorns Alvaro for 'cowardly' behaviour, but he has, of course, not been exposed to the full experience of being a husband.

Ana has eventually to choose between two men: Alvaro and Fermín, the two alternatives to her husband. Indeed, at one point she thinks of turning to her husband as a refuge (25. 566), although this is a last resort. In turning to her husband she would be turning not to virility but to domesticity. That is, there is no change in the nature of Víctor for her, or in her perception of it. If he has been able to see himself as less than capable, it is this in its turn which makes him the possible refuge for her. Víctor, while initially seen as a good match because of his position in society, and while going through the motions of being the man of honour (hence his passion for Golden Age theatre, which extends to reading aloud his favourite passages in his solitary bedchamber, at the other end of the house from where Ana sleeps) is a man most clearly drawn to a role that is domestic, rather than to one which is sexually dynamic or involves the exercise of authority. Hence he acts as a perfect nursemaid for Ana in her periodic nervous crises, offering comfort and broth[34] (though failing to see the degree to which his own shortcomings have contributed to those crises). For Ana also, the retreat to the role of the angel in the house, sharing

[34] Broth is the sign for Lévi-Strauss of the desire to establish or restore domestic ties. See Alison Sinclair, 'The Consuming Passion: Appetite and Hunger in *La Regenta*', 253 and n. 12.

simple domestic pleasures with her husband, provides a more restful alternative to the two extremes of the adulterous (but satisfied) wife, and the mystic *beata* who views Fermín, at the height of their relationship, as a spiritual brother (21. 476).

Domesticity is, however, also a refuge for Víctor, and his peace in it contrasts with his otherwise characteristic indecision. He can play the 'angel in the house' more easily than the lover. The stereotyped masculine roles available to him throw him into confusion about whether to be the actor or the spectator, the husband or the lover, and ultimately whether to engage in a duel or to give in to feeling.[35] His view of proper social behaviour is derived from the stage: he is enamoured of the honour code as it appears in the theatre. Both this, and his former ambition to be an actor, point to the degree to which he has deflected his attention away from real life to fiction, because, presumably, he finds it more tolerable that way, and living according to fiction is a means of imposing order. No information is supplied about why he has not married earlier than he does, only that he is into his forties. Rather like Lorca's Don Perlimplín, he marries late, encouraged into it by others. Once within the marriage, he is puzzled and more than a little discomfited by Ana's excesses, and although he goes through the motions of showing concern for her, there is also the side of him which would rather not be troubled by her emotional states and storms. Víctor evidently finds it difficult to maintain any role. Simple avoidance is one option, and like many a nineteenth-century husband, he spends time away from his wife, but the difference here is that it is quite clear that he does so because he feels more comfortable that way. Thus he is happy to come to the arrangement by which they sleep apart (an easy way of avoiding some of his sexual problems), and additionally 'betrays' Ana

[35] Noel de Valis, *The Decadent Vision in Leopoldo Alas* (Baton Rouge, La., and London, 1981), 88, observes how difficult, even impossible, it is for Víctor to be human, rather than engage in play-acting. Knowledge, however, is not enough in this situation: 'But Don Víctor, though he now knows he has been play-acting, is not strong enough either to withstand the pressures of external reality (society's contempt for the cuckold) or to deny the inner vacuity which he senses within himself. He assumes the role of the outraged, betrayed husband, goes through the motions of a duel, and is killed for his pains.' Jo Labanyi, 'City, Country and Adultery in *La Regenta*', *Bulletin of Hispanic Studies*, 43 (1986), 53–66, puts Víctor's indecision on to the conceptual level of being unable to distinguish between country and city in a persuasive article in which these two areas imply codes of behaviour and reaction crucial to the fiction of adultery (p. 58).

by leaving for his hunting-trips at a clandestinely early hour. He develops a series of external interests, linked to hunting and ornithology, demonstrating his desire (or perhaps more accurately, his willingness) to engage in the activities of catching, collecting, and naming as an alternative to relating to people.[36] There is more than a little irony and authorial stress on the nature of Víctor and his functioning as a mechanism in the way that in chapter 10 Ana is caught, on her way to find him in the night, by a trap that had been deemed out of use because of a mechanical fault).[37] There is also poetic justice, one could argue, in the way that Víctor himself is finally deceived about the hour at which he should rise to go hunting, a deception which provides his undeceiving about his wife's infidelity with Alvaro.

An alternative to Víctor as embodiment of the man of honour is Fermín the priest. Fermín largely carries the expected reactions of the man of honour, and is much closer than Víctor to acting on them. He is also, however, much closer than Víctor to realizing the persona of the lover. That is, he embodies both the imagined masculinity of the lover, whose virility is unbounded by marriage, and that of the man who can act decisively to protect or avenge honour. If Ana thinks of Fermín as brother, this is contrary to the majority of the indications given elsewhere in the text about the way he, at least, views the relationship, and indeed contrary to the conceptions of Alas, although Fermín bears many features of an uncertain gender-possession, from the elegant skirts of his clerical garb to the strained and intimate relation with his mother. It is, significantly, Fermín who dominates the opening pages, just as he dominates the spiritual life of the town, and it is with his repudiation of Ana (publicly as an adulteress, but privately as a woman who betrayed him in love) that the novel closes. He exudes an air of power and authority, though inwardly has a sense of unused potential. His elegant priest's dress is admired in the cathedral by Bismarck and Celedonio, their interest displaying a perverse envy, but privately (II. 232) he looks at his well-maintained torso and laments 'the other self he has lost'.

Fermín's style of masculinity is defensive and with clearer roots in a difficult early relationship with woman (his mother) than is

[36] See Labanyi, 'City, Country and Adultery', 59.

[37] See the full discussion by Sieburth on this, *Reading 'La Regenta'*, 79–80.

indicated for Víctor. On the face of it, his role as priest keeps his masculinity safe from matrimonial betrayal, but it affords no real expression of that masculinity. Fermín manages to blind himself for a long time to the degree of his involvement with Ana. On hearing of Ana's presence at the casino dance, however, with the detail that she had fainted in Alvaro's arms, he reveals a reaction of outrage at betrayal not only characteristic of the man of honour, but, more revealingly, signalling the roots of that forceful response: 'his mother had never betrayed him' (25. 558). His pain at the news is described as deep, cold, and beyond consolation, with the possible exception (25. 558) of his mother as provider of solace. In chapter 28, before Ana's adultery has occurred, Fermín suffers *celos* (jealousy) (28. 640) on hearing of Ana's recuperative stay at El Vivero with her husband. His full reaction as jealous 'husband' occurs, however, in chapter 29, when Petra goes to tell him about Ana's affair with Alvaro. He is doubly angered—by his condition as priest, which casts him as a eunuch in this situation, and by his belief that Ana is his legitimate wife, who has now been unfaithful to him (29. 662). He is overcome by the news that she has deceived him, dishonoured him, 'like any other woman'.[38]

While in man-of-honour mode, Fermín goes through sea-changes. When faced with the reality of what he is himself (as priest he has no place in the denouement of this adultery drama) he is uncertain, and cast back into his own tumultuous emotions. Later (29. 662) he vacillates between the certainty that springs from his conviction that he is indeed the 'true' husband, and therefore can act in revenge (in this case to kill Alvaro), and the realistic perception that, as Petra realizes, given the social truths of the situation, he can do no such thing (29. 658). The cool, decisive aspect of the man of honour then takes over as he recognizes Petra as the agent of his revenge—the instrument to set in play a further instrument, Don Víctor.

To focus on the parallelling of Víctor and Fermín as alternative husbands we need to concentrate on the point where, if they were men of honour, they would be impelled to action. The turmoil

[38] The Rutherford translation here, 'His wife, Ana—for she was his wife, his real wife' (30. 662) in referring to Ana by her first name rather than that of her husband, misses the reminder given in the original of whose wife Ana actually is: 'Su mujer, la Regenta, que era su mujer, su legítima mujer' (*La Regenta*, ed. Gonzalo Sobejano (2 vols.; Madrid, 1981), i. 464).

caused Fermín by his discovery of Ana's 'infidelity' to him (an infidelity to him, not Víctor is how he construes it) lasts until the closing pages of the novel. He is fuelled by his outrage to go to Víctor, aware that the only way in which he, Fermín, can gain revenge, is through the agency of another (29. 664). Here he appears not even to notice his relegation to the role of one who has to have an agent: 'he sensed a new man inside himself: the man who kills for vengeance, the criminal, the man blinded by passion' (29. 664), and is also as yet unaware that Víctor will fail to react as the perfect Golden Age husband, and be that agent for him. Here Alas conducts a symphony of frustration on the part of Fermín, and unexpected suffering and vacillation on the part of Víctor (unexpected, that is, for Víctor himself—no one else is left surprised, except at the painstaking detailing of that suffering). Before the discovery of Ana's adultery, Víctor has suffered already, his sense of shame and public humiliation reaching their culmination in the terrible Easter procession where Ana walks barefoot, although this is a moment where he is able to bring in Alvaro as the surrogate husband to bear the public shame for him. Although we are not told in detail of what happens immediately afterwards, it seems clear that he is not held to ridicule, nor does he take any type of revenge on the man (Fermín) who has brought about his ridicule. We are simply shown an amazing period of recovery, a brief Indian summer in their marriage, where Ana recuperates in his company at El Vivero. What has happened here, of course, is that Víctor, or Alas, or the two combined, have taken refuge in the medical model of the errant woman: she causes shame and uproar, therefore she must be ill.[39] In Ana's case there is the possibility that we have an example both of the degree to which women took refuge in hysterical symptoms in order to express their dis-ease within society, and also of the degree to which women were classified as hysterical because they presented unacceptable excesses or expressions of feeling.

When forced by Fermín to see his wife's infidelity, Víctor is unable to act as the man of honour, able neither to kill Ana as she

[39] De Valis, *The Decadent Vision*, 93–105, and Jo Labanyi, 'Mysticism and Hysteria in *La Regenta*: The Problem of Female Identity', in L. P. Condé and S. M. Hart (eds.), *Feminist Readings on Spanish and Latin-American Literature* (Lampeter, 1991), 37–46, have argued for Ana to be seen as a classical form of hysteric.

sleeps, nor, initially, to challenge Alvaro. The degree of his hesitation, mulled over in almost the same loving detail as Ana's feelings in the period just before she commits adultery, is such as to present him simply as he is, rather than allowing him to be cast into any straightforward mode of reaction. Notably absent from Víctor's response to the revelation of his wife's adultery is any feeling of anger. He goes through the motions (29. 666) of behaving as the man of honour, but almost immediately is overcome by his own fatigue, his sense of age, his realization that infidelity may occur in life, not just in literature, and that the reactions proposed in literature, seem, somehow, not to come readily as responses to it. He has no feeling of jealousy or shame (29. 668), but rather a sense that he has been deceived and betrayed, and it is revealed to him that he had had more affection for Ana than he had been aware. In the exposure of Víctor to the reader the novel moves closer to the depressive text, just as Víctor, if momentarily, moves through a phase of living with the reality of emotional distress, rather than acting out or acting on a solution that would relieve him of the necessity to feel that distress.

By contrast, Fermín's final feelings are kept hidden from the reader. His reaction is to use the defence of the man of honour, a defence which goes to the extent of excluding the reader. Alas explores the feelings of the man who is a failure but who tried, but leaves well alone the frustrated anger of the man who can get no relief, not even that of participating in a duel.

A crucial element of Fermín's story, on which I have barely touched so far, is the depth of his attachment to his mother—one of the most powerful accounts of family discomfort to be found in Spanish literature. Fermín is a man used by his mother to fulfil her social ambitions: she sees entry into the priesthood as the way to rise in the world, and since she cannot attain this for herself, she ensures that her son does so. This of course has its consequences for him, delineated so clearly by Alas in the opening chapters of the novel, in which Fermín appears both masculine and feminine, the strong masculine torso encased within the elegant flowing skirts of the priestly garb, and in the closing pages, where it is apparent that his priest's role is the factor which prevents him from acting as a man of honour.[40] The intensity of Fermín's rela-

[40] For a full discussion, see Nimetz, '*Eros* and *Ecclesia*', 246–9.

tionship with his mother is evidenced by the way it is principally expressed as a need for separation—a separation that, in Stoller's terms, is a desperate attempt to differentiate. Thus his living-quarters are severely separate from those of his mother. Thus also the tension about whether he returns for meals, and whether he informs her if he will not. Hence the tension of chapter 15, in which she reproaches him for having left her alone at a mealtime. While these exchanges may incline us to think that he has been turned into a passive mother's boy, the reality is far more tense, more productive of the passionate need to escape. At the same time, however, there is the lurking belief that, in emotional terms at least, the love of his mother is the one emotional security on which he can rely (25. 558).

It is this awareness, coupled with Víctor's realization of how much he has loved his wife, which makes a novelistic alliance of the two men, independent of their plot-driven association as rivals for the same woman. Indeed, one could speculate about whether Ana, presented as a virginal ideal to the two of them (neither takes the practical view of her as a physical woman which Alvaro has), seems to meet some sort of phantasy about a woman who will be safe because distant, or kept harmless because ill, and yet will realize all their ideal desires about the perfect woman.

Ana's end is that she is spared punishment/recrimination by her husband, is rejected by the would-be lover and pseudo- or proto-husband, and finally exposed to lasting discomfort by her creator, and consequently discomfort in the experience of her reader. Víctor does not even see her as responsible for her 'crime' (30. 693). Once again responsibility is shifted to Fermín, who cannot, even at the end, act fully as the man of honour. In his final spurning of Ana (30. 714–15), which causes her to faint in the cathedral, he makes the only combination possible between priest and man of honour, and uses (if inappropriately) the power of the Church—to judge and reject, rather than to forgive and accept, since acceptance would entail an intolerable closeness to the pain of his own rejection by Ana. He makes a 'paso de asesino' (killer's step) towards her when she has approached the confessional. The raising of his arm as if to strike her has been seen by Nimetz as a 'womanly expression of wrath',[41] and confirms the inability of

[41] Ibid. 248.

any of the men in this novel to carry an action or a role through to its conclusion. The end is not in an action that resolves cathartically, but in one which does not resolve, because it is not completed. Ana, significantly, having been spurned (she cannot be released from either life or the novel) is left with her standing in relation to the surrogate husband unresolved, and a feeling of nausea—finally carrying the bad feeling of the whole of the novel. The nausea is the sign that experience in the novel was both too much and too little for the maintenance of life.[42]

DENIAL AND SPLITTING: *DOMBEY AND SON* AND *THE KREUTZER SONATA*

Among the eccentricities of English literature is its lack of an 'adultery novel' to correspond with others discussed in this chapter, that is, a lack of novels in which the question that is central to the working of the plot and the characterization of the female protagonist is that of whether a married woman will commit adultery, and what, in the event, will be the consequences of her action. On the other hand, a number of novels containing adultery provide sharp and perceptive explorations of the emotional backcloth to it. A case in point is *Dombey and Son: Wholesale, Retail, and for Exportation* (1846–7).[43] This novel combines an example of the degree to which adultery in the English novel is incidental, peripheral, a consequence of a set of circumstances, rather than a cause of them, and a curiously acute perception of the dynamics which may underlie the malfunctioning of a marriage. That relationships are askew in this text is conveyed by the title: it is not, apparently, a novel about man and woman, but about man and trade, and about a man and the concept he has of himself based

[42] The simple interpretation of the nausea is that Ana has 'taken in' too much of Vetusta. If, however, we apply an interpretation that has been made of Emma Bovary, the nausea paradoxically indicates deprivation and consequent frustration. Ion Collas remarks on Emma's 'spasmes' and extreme form of loss of appetite as 'the immediate effect of a sudden and intolerable withdrawal of love . . . Nausea is here . . . the expression of that particular kind of moral suffering that is brought about by being frustrated in one's love feelings' (Ion K. Collas, *Madame Bovary*, 40).

[43] The edition used is Charles Dickens, *Dombey and Son* (1846–7), ed. P. Fairclough (Harmondsworth, 1970). References to this edition will be given in the text, the first arabic figure denoting the chapter, the second figure the page number.

on his money and the social standing which derives from its possession and manipulation. The only human relation alluded to is the extension Dombey hopes for of himself, an extension into his son, which takes the form of an investment expressed in human terms but bounded by the mechanical and unbending approaches used in trade. Dombey, or rather, Mr Dombey, as he is referred to throughout the novel, is only dimly capable of grasping his infant son as a person, and of viewing the relationship which is formed, then lost (when the child dies), as other than one which is to do with his own aggrandizement, not with the child in his individual right. The novel has received some excellent analysis in recent years, highlighting in particular the intrafamilial tensions contained in it.[44]

The adultery that eventually occurs in the novel is between Mr Dombey's second wife, Edith, and Mr Carker, the man Dombey had tried to use as the means to humiliate and control her. The elopement of the couple occurs well on in the novel, in chapter 47 of a sixty-two-chapter book. The elopement of Mrs Dombey is, however, far from the major tragedy it might initially appear, or that it would characteristically constitute were it in another novel of adultery more precisely focused on the marital relationship. The reason for this lies partly in the treatment of the subject, which itself constitutes a form of literary adultery: that is, the central relationships of the novel are filial rather than marital, and it is filial relationships which are destroyed and then partially restored.

The text is full of failures of perception. Mr Dombey's view of himself is that he is all bound up with his son, and the text initially reiterates this view. Den Hartog, in commenting on the way that Paul, Dombey's son, is the means of revealing Dombey's anxieties and repressions in relation to masculinity, indicates the turbulent undercurrent of the text, in that Paul 'would seem to offer us an oblique understanding of the buried life in his father that it is the nature of Dombey's own suppressed character to obscure for us'.[45] The first Mrs Dombey, who dies giving birth to

[44] See esp. Dirk den Hartog, *Dickens and Romantic Psychology: The Self in Time in Nineteenth-Century Literature* (Basingstoke, 1987); Lynda Zwinger, 'The Fear of the Father: Dombey and Daughter', *Nineteenth-Century Fiction*, 39 (4), (Mar. 1985), 420–40; Nina Auerbach, 'Dickens and Dombey: A Daughter After All', *Dickens Studies Annual*, 5 (1976), 95–114; Mary Montaut, 'The Second Mrs Dombey', *Dickens Quarterly*, 4 (3) (Sept. 1987), 141–53.

[45] Hartog, *Dickens and Romantic Psychology*, 45.

young Paul, is merely the means for Mr Dombey to acquire the son he desires: her death is reduced to the level of mere regrettable incident, a loss of possession, which Dickens alludes to with cutting detachment: 'To record of Mr. Dombey, that he was not in his way affected by this intelligence [of his wife's imminent death], would be to do him an injustice. He was not a man of whom it could properly be said that he was ever startled or shocked, but he certainly had a sense within him, that if his wife should sicken and decay, he would be very sorry, and that he would find a something gone from among his plate and furniture, and other household possessions, which was well worth the having, and could not be lost without sincere regret.' (I. 54). The implied indirect speech, or indirect thought, which emphasizes the careful, defensive position-taking of Dombey in response to emotional upheaval, is one which will be strongly echoed by Karenin in his first response to his wife's infidelity, and which arguably also indicates the (masculine) author's cautiousness in relation to his (masculine) subject.[46]

There is a similar failure to perceive the nature of his young son, and his status as individual. Paul Dombey is there to prolong paternal ambition, and must be shaped and prepared for his destiny. Thus the perception of his frailty is followed by a 'strengthening' regime (significantly undertaken away from the parental home), and then by a regime of intellectual cramming. None of this is notably divergent from social custom of the time, but what is significant is the degree to which Paul is treated as an object throughout, if ultimately a frail object to be strengthened. In particular, there is an emphasis on his nature as a frail *masculine* object to be strengthened, the extreme nature of Mr Dombey's approach to upbringing being in itself indicative both of his own type of masculinity and of its source in anxiety and insecurity.[47]

[46] The moving between the narrator's text of reported speech/thought and a narrator's text which stands outside the character and yet is somehow contaminated by continuity, is an example of what is termed by Bakhtin as doubly voiced or doubly oriented discourse. For discussion of this, see David Lodge, *After Bakhtin* (London and New York, 1990), chs. 5 and 6.

[47] For discussion of the general dynamic concerning upbringing, see Julian Moynahan, 'Dealings with the Firm of Dombey and Son: Firmness versus Wetness', in John Gross and Gabriel Pearson (eds.), *Dickens in the Twentieth Century* (London, 1962), 121–32. Dombey's style of masculinity has been categorized as 'inveterate phallicism' (Auerbach, 'Dickens and Dombey', 99). Den Hartog argues that Dombey fits the pattern of Reich's category of 'phallic-

The text, however, while recording Mr Dombey's excessive, blinkered and peculiarly insensitive obsession with his son, has other emphases which are pressed upon the reader, so that what the reader is encouraged into is a type of infidelity to the stated primary tale of Mr Dombey and his son. The alternative tale is that of Mr Dombey and his daughter, mediated by his second wife, Edith. Indeed, the subtext of the novel proclaims that it is actually about Florence, the daughter born to the first Dombey marriage six years before the birth of Paul. Against all the odds, Florence loves her chilly, distant father. Here it is as though Dickens, with the idealism he entertains for both childhood and motherhood, combines the two, in that Florence is the perfect child, unembittered by her history of utter paternal rejection, and the perfect mother, acting with maternal solicitude to both father and brother, and achieving a full and final maternal flowering in the last emotional redemption of her father, and her direct (and this time appropriate) experience of mothering her own two children. Another, more general, way of viewing Florence would be as a perfect example of the feminine, or—more to the point, given the splits, antagonisms, and fear expressed in the novel—an example of the perfect feminine (as perceived, but barely admitted by Mr Dombey).[48]

The text by which the reader is seduced, openly and yet collusively through the awakening of empathy for the daughter as victim, is then that of Florence and her father, rather than the text characteristic of adultery novels in which the reader is seduced by

narcissistic', and notes (pp. 42–3) that 'strengthening' is effectively a weaning-away from the feminine. In the case of Dombey, the investment in the exercise of weaning, and the difficulty of carrying it through, is what leads to his overly aggressive manner. Reich's definition of the 'phallic-narcissistic' as summarized by den Hartog is that it is 'whilst seeming very masculine and being therefore often sought after by women . . . in fact contemptuous of them and often sadistic, since he unconsciously thinks of the phallus not as a source, but as an instrument of revenge against an initially disappointing mother' (p. 39).

[48] See Auerbach, 'Dickens and Dombey', who argues that Dombey and Florence are 'memorable less for their individual psychologies than for their magnitude as embodiments of masculinity and femininity as these were conventionally perceived', and relates the conceptualization of gender to ideals shown in contemporary conduct-manuals (p. 97). The rift between masculine and feminine is absolute: they are 'male and female principles who can neither evade nor understand each other, whose tragedy and whose force come from their mutual exclusiveness' (p. 97), the severance and the enforced contiguity being a mechanism explained by Klein's concept of splitting and projective identification.

the illicit affair of the wife and lover. In *Dombey and Son* the attachment is open and direct from daughter to father (made discreet only by her awareness that she must not impinge too directly on him, since to do so is to arouse irritation and anger). The fascination that the daughter has for the father is, however, more complex in its roots, and less favourable, initially, to Mr Dombey, than Florence's guileless filial passion is to her. That is, Dickens is less reticent about presenting the ideal form of love than the resentful, envious form of emotional reaction characteristic of Mr Dombey.

While overtly he ignores her, Mr Dombey entertains a fascination with his daughter, rarely acknowledged either by him or by his creator, and which is central to the discussions so far about the splits between men and women that may be imposed either by individual fears or by collective ones expressed in sharp divisions between the sexes in society. We are told time and again of Florence's observation of her father, an observation characterized by pity, longing, and love. Much less frequently, we are told of the father's observation of Florence, or more specifically, of Florence's capacity to engage in loving relationships. In this latter set of observations, Dickens traces for us Mr Dombey's awareness of a crucial lack in himself: the lack of capacity for emotion.

If we relate this both to the theories of Klein and to the mechanisms which we saw operating in honour literature, and in honour-code societies, we can see the relationship between Mr Dombey and his daughter as one which spells out in all its human disaster the division by which emotion and subjectivity are deemed to belong to women, and all that is intellectual, rational, and non-emotional is deemed to be properly the possession of men. Mr Dombey demonstrates unequivocally the envy which may be at the root of such disparagement. The chief emotion to which we see him succumb, apart from the haughty pride he displays to all his household, but most particularly to his second wife, Edith, is one of longing for the emotional capacity of his daughter, and the loving relationships to which it gives her access. Florence's emotional capacity has made it possible for her to have a level of union with her mother completely denied to him. Thus when he observes Florence with Paul, he is minded first of her link with his wife, and then of her link with her brother: 'The last time he had seen his slighted child, there had been that in the sad embrace between her and her dying mother, which was at once a revelation and a reproach to him. Let him be absorbed as he would in the Son on whom he built such high hopes, he could not forget that closing scene. He could not forget that he had had no part in it' (3. 83). His incapacity is confirmed by his observation of the present moment: '[he could not forget] That, at the bottom of its clear depths of tenderness and truth, lay those two figures clasped in each other's arms, while he stood on the bank above them, looking down a mere spectator—not a sharer with them—quite shut out' (3. 83).[49]

Mr Dombey does not remain at the level of observation and longing for participation: Dickens immediately traces for us the mechanics of a split which leads him to his hostile relation to his daughter. A possessor of unknown capacities (from which he has arguably separated himself at some previous point), she is now viewed with suspicion, since he feels her to be aware of his incapacity: 'Unable to exclude these things from his remembrance, or to keep his mind free from such imperfect shapes of the meaning with which they were fraught, as were able to make themselves visible to him through the mist of his pride, his previous feeling of indifference towards little Florence changed into an uneasiness of an extraordinary kind. He almost felt as if she watched and distrusted him. As if she held the clue to something *secret in his breast*, of the nature of which he was hardly informed himself. As if she had an innate knowledge of one jarring and discordant string within him, and her very breath could sound it' (3. 83–4—emphasis mine). The violence of the feeling here indicates the possible reason for Dombey's rejection even of the standard and 'safe' role of 'little mother' for his daughter.[50]

These brief revelatory moments are significant in highlighting Mr Dombey's secret fears and feelings of envy—the former charac-

[49] While Dickens keeps adult sexuality firmly off-stage here, it has been reinstated by critics. Den Hartog focuses on a hidden reciprocity of feeling in Florence's phantasies about a death-bed reunion with her father in ch. 24: 'Florence here is fantasizing herself as a kind of death-bed flirt, tempting her father on to an agonising surrender of his pride, and then flitting off into immortality, almost as if in ingenious revenge' (p. 67). He concludes that Dickens is unaware of the absurdity of what she is thinking. An alternative view is to see Dickens as taking on the anxieties of his male protagonist, sketching out a consolation in the hidden phantasies of the elusive female object of desire that Florence represents.

[50] See Zwinger, *Dickens and Romantic Psychology*.

teristic of the paranoid-schizoid position, the latter showing an insufficient capacity to make the initial splitting which makes it possible for the infant to retain a sense of the good object as simply that, as a result of which the desire for the good object is inextricably tangled with the need to spoil and denigrate it. The paranoia is made particularly evident when Florence attempts to console her father, his reaction being one which strikes even her with fear. He has achieved a total distancing from her, but it is one motivated by his own inability to tolerate what she represents:

> If anything had frightened her, it was the face he turned upon her. The glowing love within the breast of his young daughter froze before it, and she stood and looked at him as if stricken into stone.
>
> There was not one touch of tenderness or pity in it. There was not one gleam of interest, parental recognition, or relenting in it. There was a change in it, but not of that kind. The old indifference and cold constraint had given place to something: what, she never thought and did not dare to think, and yet she felt it in its force and knew it well without a name: that as it looked upon her, seemed to cast a shadow on her head. (18. 328)

That is, Florence is not just potent in that she possesses qualities that Mr Dombey envies, but is viewed by him as antagonist. Auerbach explains this through Florence's function of 'exposing him rather than completing him by her unlikeness'.[51]

More frequently, however, we perceive Dombey stifling his emotion (though that there should be emotion to stifle heralds Dickens's ultimately redemptive intentions towards his character).[52] Thus the perception of the dying child Paul that perhaps his father might have cried (14. 276), with his observation of sudden, unaccustomed feeling in his father who sits by his bed. This raises for him the question 'was this his father?', with the response in action, 'But the face so altered to his thinking, thrilled while he gazed, as if it were in pain; and before he could reach out both his hands to take it between them, and draw it towards him, the figure turned away quickly from the little bed, and went out at the door' (16. 294).

[51] Auerbach, 'Dickens and Dombey', 100.

[52] See Arlene Jackson, 'Reward, Punishment and the Conclusion of *Dombey and Son*', *Dickens Studies Annual*, 7 (1978), 103–28. A contrary view of Dombey—that is, that he is not redeemed—is advanced by Ross H. Dabney, *Love and Property in the Novels of Dickens* (London, 1967), 65.

It may seem curious that Mr Dombey's marital relations have so far figured little in this discussion. This is, to a large degree, their status in the text itself, in which the first marriage is brought to an untimely end by death in the opening pages, and in which the second marriage is brought about as an event without rhyme or reason, in the bartering of money and beauty which are bitterly portrayed as being at the heart of (some) bourgeois marriages. It has even been suggested by Mary Montaut that Edith's role in the novel is merely functional in relation to Florence, allowing the latter to remain the passive (and therefore acceptable) woman, while Edith takes responsibility for major happenings. It is ironic that, as Montaut observes, Florence receives the blow from Dombey which is intended for Edith, a blow which sends her into freedom—so that Edith is used not only as scapegoat, but also as redemptrix.[53] The only live emotional exchanges associated with the second marriage are between Edith and Florence, a fact of which Mr Dombey is fiercely jealous—so that a construction we may put on the course of the marriage is that, at least as Mr Dombey perceives it, Edith is unfaithful to him with Florence. By showing the sexual passion of the ousted husband at this level of awareness, Dickens shows exceptional insight into the complexity of transferential emotions that may be contained in a marriage. Not for him, in this text, a simple discussion of sexual jealousy, in which the husband finds himself ousted by a younger, more desirable lover, or in which he finds that his wife is fickle, unfaithful, unworthy of the trust he has placed in her. The case of Mr Dombey explores something which is much more grave: the emotional incapacity of the husband, and his anguish at the contemplation of others whose emotional capacity is greater. In this he provides the forerunner of that other chilly husband of English literature, Soames of Galsworthy's *Forsyte Saga*.

From the outset, Mr Dombey's second marriage is presented as a matter of calculation—not on the part of the future husband, but on the part of the future mother-in-law.[54] The marriage is intended to make good an earlier error, in that Edith was previously

[53] Montaut, 'The Second Mrs Dombey', 141.

[54] Dickens, like Galsworthy in the early novels of the *Forsyte Saga*, places the blame for plotting on women, reiterating the misogynistic commonplaces of women as wily go-betweens, women as predatory and after men for their money.

married to a man who would eventually inherit considerable wealth (which she as his wife, and ultimately widow, would have come to enjoy): fate interferes with this plan to acquire wealth by causing the death of the first husband before he reaches the age of inheritance. It is made clear that all the calculation belongs to Edith's mother, and not to Edith herself, who before and after her marriage to Mr Dombey is mainly motivated by anger and bitterness at the way in which she has been made an object for trading in the marriage market. Thus in chapter 27 she berates her mother for the upbringing she has received, which makes her an apt companion for the trade-orientated Dombey: 'You know he has bought me . . . Or that he will, tomorrow. He has considered of his bargain; he has shown it to his friend; he is even rather proud of it; he thinks that it will suit him, and may be had sufficiently cheap; and he will buy tomorrow. God, that I have lived for this, and that I feel it!' (27. 472). The only feeling that is stronger than this is Edith's awareness that she is already known to the full, in emotional terms, by another man, before whom she has 'even less of self-respect or confidence' than before herself: a reference to Mr Carker, with whom she eventually elopes, but not before he has been made the instrument of her marital humiliation at the bidding of Mr Dombey.

In making Edith the object produced by her mother, and consequently 'bought' by Mr Dombey, Dickens is able to tread a path between indicating the dangerousness of women (as exemplified by the false and grasping Mrs Skewton) and their innocence (as exemplified by that side of her daughter which responds to the innocent and virtuous Florence).[55] Thus a split between attributes is operated at the level of the text itself, as though the conflict of intention within characters were too complex to tolerate—although there is an attempt to portray and contain conflict in the character of Edith herself, who displays a warm, tender side to Florence, and bitterness and haughtiness both to Dombey and, eventually, to Mr Carker, in the tempestuous (and for a Victorian woman, highly assertive) declarations of chapter 54. It is perhaps only in these last accusations to Carker, in which she also takes

[55] It should be noted, however, that Florence has been denigrated in traditional criticism. See Zwinger, *Dickens and Romantic Psychology*, 432.

responsibility for her own status and shame (54. 856–60) that Edith achieves the status of integrated character, acting out of a sense of the depressive position of her history and her present.

The author's ambivalence in relation to his subject is indicated to some degree by this apparent attribution of what we could term the attainment of the depressive position by the very character who has been obliged to carry the burden of guilt in the novel. At the same time, as we have observed earlier, there is a strong feeling of collusiveness between author and male protagonist elsewhere in the text, in which the author participates in the splits and projections of his character.

The collusion between author and male protagonist is yet more prominent, and has a more identifiable foundation, in Tolstoy's novella *The Kreutzer Sonata*. The novella has been described as 'A story which is about a woman who is disappointed in her marriage and abandoned by her lover' (Radio 3, 13.9.90). That this is emphatically not the way the story reads will emerge from an examination of how the text itself functions, and particularly from focusing on the fact that we are told all we know by the husband, so that the account is likely to be as accurate as a divorcee's account of the honeymoon.

As is the case with Mr Dombey, Pozdnyshev, the narrator-protagonist of *The Kreutzer Sonata* displays, both through his narrative and the actions related in that narrative, something obsessional and paranoid at a basic and primitive level. The fact that the oddities in Pozdnyshev's attitude to women and to marriage are those of Tolstoy himself at this period in no way invalidates the assessment that this is a story about a man torn superficially by his wife's suspected infidelity, but more profoundly by his inability to come to terms with the sensuality and potential eroticism of women. So strong are the feelings related to this, and so pervasive the obsessive attitude, that the apparent text of adultery is virtually eclipsed by the subtext of the wretched husband who not only suffers in courtship and marriage, but who is then compelled by the continuing obsession he feels to tell all and sundry (in this case a complete stranger (male) in a railway carriage) about his sexual misfortunes.

A short work which comes more than a decade after the complex and masterly *Anna Karenin* (1874–6), and which predates the detached and chilly *Effi Briest* of Fontane, *The Kreutzer Sonata*[56] provides an extremely uncomfortable account of adultery, and is distinguished by the fact that, like *Manon Lescaut*, it is narrated from the point of view of the injured husband. In the case of that novel, it can be argued, as Naomi Segal has done, that the account is analogous to a smutty joke, in that it is intended for the hearing of a man, and is related by a man so that woman is excluded, as the third party, and thus the original target of bad feeling is tamed by being made the object of a joke which will be told between two men.[57]

The Kreutzer Sonata is a story told on a train, between two strangers, one the narrator, who we gather is a man, but principally by dint of the way that others in the train treat him, rather than by direct information. The other stranger is the deceived husband, Pozdnyshev. The setting itself goes against the grain of certain elements of the man-of-honour story, and indeed of the cuckold story, since here is a man who is not only aware of what happened to him, but is telling it in public, and, what is more, to a perfect stranger.[58] The representation of the self to another is a recurrent motif in other husbands discussed, notably those who fall within the man-of-honour mould. Husbands of Spanish honour plays are given to self-representation and self-justification in the face of others, and Othello is the man who wins Desdemona by 'representing' himself to her in stories of his adventures, and who in his dying moments articulates in advance the speech that he anticipates others will, or should, make over his dead body.

[56] The edition used is *The Kreutzer Sonata and Other Stories*, trans. David McDuff (Harmondsworth, 1985). References are given in the text, the first arabic figure referring to the chapter, the second arabic figure to the page number.

[57] Naomi Segal, *The Unintended Reader*, pp. xi–xii. See also Peter Ulf Møller, *Postlude to 'The Kreutzer Sonata': Tolstoy and the Debate on Sexual Morality in Russian Literature in the 1890s*, trans. from Danish by John Kendal (Leiden, 1988), 13, who rightly assigns this work as an example of 'male confessional literature', pointing out that the masculine gender of both intended reader and listening narrator is obvious.

[58] The importance of the train, and the disagreeable 'moral' atmosphere of the railroad in Tolstoy's eyes is signalled in Elisabeth Stenbock-Fermor, *The Architecture of 'Anna Karenina'* (Lisse, 1975), 68. The telling of a tale to a stranger is rightly emphasized by Angus Calder, 'Man, Woman and Male Woman: Tolstoy's *Anna* and After', in id., *Russia Discovered: Nineteenth-Century Fiction from Pushkin to Chekhov* (London, 1976), 234. Calder's judgement, however, that this text shows that Tolstoy 'could still struggle to a sufficient distance from his own more absurd and anti-human views to write first-rate fiction again' is surprising given the extreme and deeply split nature of the text.

Pozdnyshev seems to take the question of self-representation further, to a remarkably uncomfortable point. As noted, in his recounting of what happened, he is clearly engaging in an obsessive exposure of his misfortunes. In this openness, which is shocking not so much for the content of what he has to say about his wife's infidelity, but for what it reveals about his own role in the matter, he displays the disarming unawareness of the cuckold. He is also of the cuckold type in the extreme uncertainty and suspicion he has shown in relation to his wife throughout their marriage, and in the detail of how he accomplishes his final revenge: he removes his boots and creeps up on his stockinged feet to surprise his wife and her 'lover' (chapter 27).

The music by Beethoven which gives the story its title provides us with clarification of the events described. On the surface, it is a case of a woman who, having borne her husband five children, becomes involved with a man with whom she plays music. The activity of playing violin and piano duos is one which makes the husband extremely jealous and which, in his eyes, is translated into an extra-marital affair. It is finding his wife and her companion alone at their house, when he returns unexpectedly early from a journey, that spurs him into killing her in a fit of jealousy. The 'lover', meanwhile, manages to make a quick escape, in a style that smacks of music-hall farce (as do the stockinged feet): he ducks under the piano and is off (27. 112).

The lover, however, is something of a blind in the tale, since the other corner of the adulterous triangle is the music itself, or rather the capacity to indulge in music. If, as in *La Regenta*, we pursue Girard's idea that the prime dynamic in an adulterous triangle is not between one man who desires the woman possessed by another, but between the two men involved, we can see that there is a pattern by which the husband appears to be fascinated by the capacity of the lover to engage with his wife in a more exciting way than he himself is able to do. This is expressed in the form of the music which the wife and lover play together.

Pozdnyshev may have certain surface characteristics of the cuckold, but he also presents a classic example of the paranoid-schizoid position, displaying all the features of that position as expressed in the honour code. Apparently the mouthpiece for what had come to be Tolstoy's extreme views on marriage, he has nothing but disgust for sexuality and sensuality, and is clearly repelled by everything that is associated with it, either in himself or in his wife.[59] He disowns whatever feelings of sexual attraction he has, lodges them in his wife (and eventually in the lover, whom he covertly envies), so that they then become the more terrifying and repugnant for him.

One of Pozdnyshev's first statements reveals his distrust of women, and a sharp distinction drawn by him between man's possible fidelity and woman's almost certain infidelity (2. 34). A further generalization occurs at the start of his account of himself. Before his marriage he lived 'a life of debauchery' (3. 37), a fact which for him is a generalized one. That is, 'debauchery' is both a norm for him and a norm which automatically carries connotations of excess and resultant guilt. The words which punctuate his account of his youthful initiation into sexuality are all loaded ones: 'filth', 'torment', 'fornicator', standing in opposition to notions of 'purity', 'lost innocence'. Pozdnyshev's split view of sexuality is that of the honour code, but pushed almost to the level of parody. He sees young girls as associated with purity, and himself, in consequence, with impurity, so that he refers to his own experience of sex in pejorative language. A shift in his perceptions then takes place, and he realizes that these young girls, in the process of having sexual experience (whether inside or outside marriage) become involved with that activity (the sexual act in which he plays a part) which he had classified as being disgusting and unspeakable. As a consequence, such young girls (or, in this case, his wife), come to be the containers for his own rejected sexuality. Thus he comes not just to be attracted by his wife, but simultaneously disgusted by her, and disgusted by his attraction to her. In a telling phrase which reveals the type of split he is making, he refers to himself at 30 as 'wallowing in the slime of

[59] In Tolstoy's 'Postface to *The Kreutzer Sonata*', printed in the edition used, 267–82, he summarizes the points he was making in the story, namely, that he contests the idea that sexual intercourse is an activity indispensable to health, that he believes that abstinence from sexual activity is possible, that carnal love associated with marriage is not 'a sublime, poetic condition' but 'a condition of animality that is degrading to human beings', that procreation has come to be believed an obstacle to love relations, and that this belief is injurious and wrong, and that the education of children should be such as to restrain rather than to inflame their sensuality. This set of points he then follows with his description of what he believes should be the nature of Christian marriage, a virtual non-possibility.

debauchery, and at the same time looking for girls who might be pure enough to be worthy of me' (5. 42).

Pozdnyshev is not entirely without the ability to see that it is not possible to make a split so that either men have all the impurity and women the purity or vice versa, and recognizes that there are illusions about what goes on which are created by society. Thus he sees some sort of process by which young girls might be pure, but are bound to be contaminated by their contact with marriage, and furthermore that men are 'base', however much they may speak about 'lofty emotions' (6. 45).

So Pozdnyshev trundles obsessively and horrifyingly through his views on sex and marriage, full of hate both for himself and for women, and eventually and especially for the woman to whom he gets married. But there is more to it than this. He perceives women as dominating men, as having all the rights and privileges, even though, he concedes, 'woman has been brought to the lowest degree of subjection' (9. 49). Pozdnyshev takes a back-to-front view of the relation between the sexes, and of what is there in the first place, and what is brought into being as a reaction. His analysis runs as follows: 'the woman is deprived of the rights possessed by the man. And, in order to compensate for this, she acts on the man's sensuality, forces him into subjection by means of sensuality, so that he's only formally the one who chooses—in actual fact it's she who does the choosing. And once she has mastered this technique, she abuses it and acquires a terrible power over men' (9. 49). Pozdnyshev could be said to have a reasonable grip of the mechanics involved, but the alternative way of making his analysis is to begin with man's fear of woman's association with sensuality and emotion, and to work from there to the rejection of such qualities. In this context the deprivation of rights of the woman, referred to by Pozdnyshev, is something which arises from the activities and fears concerned with sexuality, and is an attempt on the part of the man to find a remedy for those fears.

Pozdnyshev comes to the conclusion that 'the sex instinct, no matter how it's dressed up, is an evil' (11. 56), and it is small wonder in this light that he finds his honeymoon a dismal disaster. It is clear that he has approached it in an inappropriate state of idealism, and cannot face the ordinariness of life. The quarrels he refers to from this period themselves indicate the sorts of splits and acts of disowning that result from the paranoid-schizoid position and its failure to accommodate.

For Pozdnyshev, however, women within marriage represent a danger that needs to be contained. For some time, a form of containment is provided by the fact that his wife is occupied with bearing children and feeding them. This activity is one which, as he puts it, 'saved me from the tortures of jealousy' (15. 67). The containment is, however, precariously maintained, so that with the years, hostility increases in the marriage, and both parties try to distract themselves with further, extraneous activity. Eventually Pozdnyshev's wife is advised to have no more children, and given the instruction in contraception to attain this end—something which her husband finds as revolting as his initial debauchery. For him, the consequences are dire: 'The last excuse for our pigsty existence—children—had been removed, and our life together became even more repulsive' (18. 77). The subsequent improvement in his wife's health is presented as a threat, and Pozdnyshev uses the familiar equine image to suggest it: 'She was like an impatient, well-fed horse that has had its bridle taken off, the same as ninety-nine per cent of our women. I could sense this, and it scared me' (18. 78).

On to this scene comes the potential lover, but, as Pozdnyshev makes it clear to his interlocutor, there is little importance in the identity of the man himself: if he had not come along, someone else would have (19. 81). His view is extreme: 'all husbands who live as I lived must either live in debauchery, get divorced, or kill themselves or their wives, as I did' (ibid.). What Pozdnyshev does here, besides seeing his situation in terms of either/or (still, that is, in retrospect, unlike Innstetten, who has some glimmering of insight) is to justify himself by the use of generalization: this is the way it is, it must be, for everyone. The paranoid-schizoid position, while placing in operation severe splitting and projection, is also one in which there is not the possibility for other constructions of the world to exist.

True to the Girard hypothesis, there is an almost immediate and strong bond between husband and lover, although again, as in the case of Víctor and Alvaro, the attraction is apparently held by the lover for the husband rather than vice versa. Pozdnyshev is particularly attracted by Trukhachevsky's playing, and that this is a metaphor for sexual capacity is further emphasized by the fact that it appears that he himself had previously played a great deal. There is clearly a special investment in the relationship from Pozdnyshev's point of view: 'I found a special significance in each word, each expression either of us uttered' (21. 86). Pozdnyshev goes on to introduce the man to his wife, preparing his own downfall.

The Kleinian concept of projective identification can be used to understand the relationship between Pozdnyshev and the man to whom he is drawn.[60] Trukhachevsky possesses qualities that Pozdnyshev desires—the ability to play music, to be sensual, to relate spontaneously to his wife—and these are qualities which Pozdnyshev simultaneously desires and denigrates in an ever worsening process of projective identification.

As the relationship, desired and detested, sought and avoided, progresses—not only between wife and lover, but between husband and either the lover's power to love (play music) or the love existing and expressed between wife and lover—it can only worsen, although Pozdnyshev both retains the capacity actually to appreciate his musicianship (21. 87) and to observe that there is something uncannily close in the way he himself relates to the lover.

The outcome is not to be avoided, and the progress towards it is marked by increasing suspicion and paranoia, overlaid with what appears to be Pozdnyshev's conviction that there is something inappropriate, almost undignified, about the fact that the expression of sensual excitement between his wife and the man he is convinced is her lover is Beethoven's sonata: a fine piece of music that sits oddly with what he perceives as the triviality of salon life (23. 97).

As Pozdnyshev moves towards his fateful act, and indeed as, in his narrative, he moves towards the recounting of it, it is clear that he is above all aware of the uncontrollable feeling which dominates him. He imagines the two together: 'I was consumed with rage, indignation and a kind of strange, drunken enjoyment of my own hurt pride as I contemplated these pictures, and I couldn't tear myself away from them' (25. 103). Although the act he finally commits, stabbing his wife to death, is one which fits the model of the man of honour, here we have the distinction that he

[60] See the explanatory note in Ch. 4 in the section on *Othello*.

makes explicit the combination of rage and enjoyment, exultation, even self-indulgence in it. The killing of his wife is recounted in detail—not here the detachment associated with the killing of Crampas, where all that is remembered is a look, rather than the physical sensations associated with the killing. It is only later that he resumes the outlines of the man of honour, when he is asked to go in and see her, and 'realizes' that this is now the appropriate action, the one that he would deem to be in accordance with what is proper: 'I . . . knew that I must go in and see her, that when a husband had murdered his wife, as I had done, the correct thing was for him to go in and see her' (27. 116). That he is in a dream state, where he has to take refuge in rules and orderliness, is underlined not only by his reiteration to himself that '"If that's the correct thing to do, then I must go in", I told myself' (ibid.), but also by the fact that he carefully thinks of putting slippers on, so that he will at least not be in his stockinged feet.[61]

When Pozdnyshev has reached the end of his tale, he ceases conversation with the narrator. His obsessive nature, revealed in everything he has said, is revealed also in the way he has been compelled to retell events, in exhaustive detail. For a man who has laid such emphasis on containment, he has shown his lack of such a capacity, and at the same time, the need for a container in one who can listen to what he has to say, and can tolerate it, thus providing the tolerance of the depressive position from the outside, since it is not available in his inner world.

At the same time, the text itself, or perhaps more properly Tolstoy as author, seems to have lost the capacity to contain the woman who has caused such psychological disruption in the narrating husband. For Judith Armstrong, the disappearance of the female figure conceived as guilty constitutes relegation rather than redemption, a relegation which occurs simultaneously with the laying of guilt upon the male protagonist.[62] Conceivably, the

[61] This forms an example of what Donald Davie refers to as Tolstoy's technique of 'making strange'. He further comments that this is a way of 'dis-civilizing' the act of murder, and points out the curiosity that while most readers would agree that murder is uncivilized, there is something worthy of comment in that in chs. 5 to 9 Tolstoy similarly 'dis-civilizes' courtship, adding that 'few readers, perhaps, would agree that this institution is uncivilized and requires to be so presented' (Donald Davie, 'Tolstoy, Lermontov and Others', in id. (ed.), *Russian Literature and Modern English Fiction* (Chicago, 1965), 164–99 (193)).

[62] Judith Armstrong, *The Unsaid 'Anna Karenina'* (London, 1988), 125. One

protagonist husband is thus elevated to hero, nobly carrying all the novelistic blame, and no longer obliged to share the novelistic stage with the woman who bears his projected feelings.

FAMILY CONTAINMENT IN *ANNA KARENIN*

The notion that there might be some trans-European development in the genre of the novel of adultery in the nineteenth century is quickly dispelled by an examination of dates, and is evident from the lack of chronological sequence of this discussion of the novel. There is no easy progression from a novel which is simple in form and focus to one which, like *Anna Karenin*, is complex and all-encompassing.[63] As I shall argue, *Anna Karenin*, viewed in the Kleinian terms we have used so far, is the best example, as an actual text, of the attainment of the depressive position in relation to the infidelity of woman, even though it is debatable whether such a position is actually achieved by any of the husbands in the novel. Critics have recognized that above all it is a novel not about wives or lovers or husbands or adultery, but about the state and nature of marriage itself.[64] As such it moves us on from the early primitive dyadic dynamics most closely linked to splitting and projection, to a text where the complex constellation of the analogous fates of different families, and concern for children, come to occupy a greater role than in other texts discussed so far.

What one could view as the developmental status of *Anna Karenin* is, however, linked to how it functions as a complete text, and is not based on the nature of the deceived husband alone, although Karenin himself is one of the most complex husbands to

has the impression here that the desire to make a political point has blurred the interpretation in the summary of Tolstoy's novelistic progression: 'In later works [Tolstoy] still gnaws at the problem of sexuality, but no longer is the woman the centre of interest . . . Thus, paradoxically, the later stories absolve the female of guilt, which is laid in each case upon the male protagonist; but they do her an immeasurably greater disservice than is done to Anna Karenin, because in them the female is relegated once more to the position of object.'

[63] Leo Tolstoy, *Anna Karenin* (1874–6). The edition used is the translation by Rosemary Edmonds (Harmondsworth, 1954, repr. 1968). All page references will be to this edition, and given in the text. The roman figure indicates the part, first arabic figure the chapter, and second arabic figure the page number.

[64] See e.g. A. F. Boyd, 'An Anatomy of Marriage: Leo Tolstoy and *Anna Karenin*', in id., *Aspects of the Russian Novel* (London, 1972), 90.

be considered. Despite this complexity, one cannot argue that there is, as it were, a developmental chain that leads from *Madame Bovary* to *Anna Karenin*. Charles Bovary, as we saw earlier, is a character given the essential traits of the cuckold, and is, among the husbands, remarkable for his total lack of characteristics pertaining to the man of honour. If we were to concentrate on that fact alone, and take note of the date of publication of *Madame Bovary*—a good two decades before that of *Anna Karenin*—then we should indeed argue for development. But as we saw in relation to the text as a whole, *Madame Bovary* contains a number of features which can be related to the depressive position, not least its capacity to confront us with the hurt and deceived husband. *Effi Briest*, when seen in terms of the text's capacity to contain the problem of the deceived husband, is much less 'developed' than either *Madame Bovary*, *Anna Karenin*, or *La Regenta*, all of which pre-date it. In so far as the novel of adultery is one in which one might consider that the issue to be 'contained' is as much the question of the deceived husband as of the erring wife, then it shows little real ability to contain either, although it does allow for elements of departure from the man-of-honour position in the husband, and for elements of complexity in the text (created mainly by understatement and omission).

There are two ways in which I should like to approach *Anna Karenin*: first by examining Karenin himself in terms of the models proposed so far, and secondly by seeing how the dynamics of the text itself work in relation to that portrayal.

As with all the other novels considered in this section, *Anna Karenin* takes as its focus the predicament of the adulterous woman. But as this title, in common with the majority of the others, indicates, the adulterous wife has a status and identity indissolubly linked to those of her husband. Indeed it is that link which makes her activity adultery rather than fornication.

Karenin's first entry into the novel is as violent a presentation as it could be, through the exasperated perception of his wife, and with no small sense of the ridiculous. As she catches sight of him at the station, her detachment and repulsion are combined in her thought of 'Good heavens, why are his ears like that?' (I. 30. 119). In a manner akin to the extraordinary hat of Charles Bovary, Karenin's protruding ears testify to the sense of the physically ridiculous and unattractive that he constitutes for Anna, and of which she and the reader are kept fully conscious. As Anna proceeds to note, 'the cartilages of his ears pressing up against the brim of his round hat', sketch out the brief outline of the cuckold to come. Thus the physical feature that could be no more than a signal of the comic is communicated under the aegis of its meaning as an indicator of Anna's sexual aversion to her husband. To a greater degree than with any of the other husbands, we have an impression of Karenin as physically unattractive, ungainly, and ultimately repulsive. Charles Bovary is seen characteristically as stupid, his fat lips and thickening waistline being part of that image, but at least he has momentary elevation into the category of the barely acceptable for his wife (acceptable in terms of physical attraction, that is) at the start of the heroic episode of Hippolyte's club-foot, when Emma notices that his teeth are 'not bad'. Karenin is, however, always unattractive for Anna. There is no alleviation of the fact that, in company with Víctor and Innstetten, he is a good twenty years older than his wife, fitting him to the model of cuckold. Furthermore, as the novel progresses, he is shown as subject to stress and ill-health, a man neither in the prime of life, nor any longer on the upward path of political ambition. While it is remarked that Innstetten has good bearing, Karenin is characterized by the oddities of his extremities, his ears, his hands, which are soft and white, his flat feet, his pince-nez, and, above all, his voice, habitually high in pitch, its shrillness an indication of his inner tension.[65] Placed against the norms of masculine attractiveness as embodied in Vronsky (all muscle, and his baldness barely incipient, a man with energy and physical skills), or even against Oblonsky, who charms as much as he exasperates, Karenin fails badly. He is above all chilly, weary, and—a phrase often used—lifeless. A cold fish, from start to finish. Anna's reaction of 'a disagreeable sensation' (in response to her seeing his protruberant ears) is one which remains with the reader throughout.

Karenin does his utmost to comport himself like a man of honour, perceiving readily that there is a distinction to be made between what he sees as the dignity of behaviour required by such a position, and the reaction of paranoid jealousy which charac-

[65] Armstrong, *The Unsaid 'Anna Karenina'*, 80, reminds us that on the evidence of *War and Peace*, 'men with small white hands are suspect'.

terizes some of the extreme paradigm husbands of that type. Before the event, at least, his attitude is that marital ruffles are to be avoided by those who know how to, and when Anna reports an approach made to her earlier on by one of his subordinates, his answer is that 'every woman in society was exposed to that sort of thing, but that he had complete confidence in her tact and could never permit himself to demean himself and her by being jealous' (I. 33. 124). In a careful picking-through the reaction of Karenin to his wife engaging in conversation with Vronsky, Tolstoy suggests, through the very pace of the description, this husband's desire to make all follow the rules of logic, but also to be saved from the impropriety of excess reaction. Thus we learn that he 'had seen nothing peculiar or improper in his wife sitting at a separate table and talking animatedly with Vronsky; but he noticed that the rest of the party considered it peculiar and improper and for that reason it seemed to him, too, to be improper' (II. 8. 158). There is here, of course, what could be interpreted as the ultimate weakness of the man of honour, in that he does not create his own standards of behaviour but follows those established by society. Karenin will later show more mettle and more individuality in his attempts to depart from those set norms. Again, in the tracing of Karenin's attitude to jealousy there is an element of defence against what he perceives to be an undignified position. Tolstoy follows the same line of painstaking tracing of thought that indicates the ponderousness, the lack of spontaneity in Karenin's reaction: 'He was not jealous. Jealousy, in his opinion, was an insult to one's wife, and a man should have confidence in his wife. Why he ought to have confidence—in other words, a full and firm conviction that his young wife would always love him—he never stopped to ask himself. But he had had no experience of distrust, because he had confidence in her and told himself that it was right to have it. Now, however, though his conviction had not broken down that jealousy was a shameful feeling and that one ought to have confidence, he felt face to face with something illogical and irrational, and he did not know what to do' (ibid.). At the start of this quotation we have Karenin's desire to be above the common run of husband, 'more honourable than thou', or at least more dignified. In the belief that the husband ought to be above jealousy there is an implied value-system which holds that the husband is such, and believes—or, more than that, knows—that his power over his wife is such, that it is beyond challenge. That is, the husband who does not react to an infidelity may not do so because he is unaware of what is happening (the cuckold) or because his security about his position is such that it cannot be threatened (the position to which Karenin aspires). Karenin is, however, shown to be a man confronted early on with the discrepancy between the code of behaviour he would like to adopt and the sudden rush of the illogical which faces him. If we tie this to the mechanism involved in splitting and projection, we can see how the initial splitting-off from unwelcome feeling (he declares himself above jealousy) then means that the feeling when it comes is the less tolerable. Although I have argued that Karenin's cold response to Anna's infidelity is essentially one of defence, the defence is none the less a convincing one, and emphasizes the degree to which Karenin manages to live according to the social persona he has adopted. That he is even able, as illustrated above, to stand back and analyse whether or not he should feel jealousy reminds us of the coldness of that persona, and of his overwhelming desire not to lose face in society. This contrasts with the liveliness of response from Anna to the possibility of Vronsky neglecting her, but most spectacularly it contrasts with the waves of extremities of jealousy suffered by Levin in relation to Kitty, with additional force deriving from the fact that the Kitty–Levin marriage is presented as either normative or idealized in comparison with the Karenin marriage.

Karenin's initial reaction to his wife's adulterous love for Vronsky is, as perceived, defensive, defending against that emotion—jealousy—which has itself been classed as defensive against other feelings of loss and anxiety.[66] He endeavours first to place himself above it, then to deal with it through a bureaucratically ordered series of actions and reactions intended to safeguard his own honour and that of his family. The reduction to cuckold is, however, rapid. Initially presented as physically ridiculous (his ears protruding from under his round hat) he is then likened with painful exactitude to one of the sources of the cuckold's horns: the ox. In chapter 8 of part II he has done all possible, he has been quiet, he has been dignified, he has tried to

[66] See the references to the work of Jones, Coen, and Rivière in the discussion on *Othello*.

talk to his wife, but he is at a loss. His very nervousness of matters emotional makes him, here as elsewhere, overly pompous, the defensive nature of the attitude showing in its forcedness. In trying to deal with this emotional matter without touching his own emotions he draws a blank, and—normally a powerful man, at least in public affairs—is left helpless: 'Like an ox with head bent, he waited submissively for the axe which he felt raised above him' (II. 10. 164).

Nervousness in the presence of emotion, and the inability to contain or even to witness it, is a characteristic of Karenin which appears as a *leitmotif* through the text. It does not surface clearly in the text until there is an incident which makes the state of the Karenin marriage public and unmistakable, that is in part II, chapter 28, at the steeplechase, when Vronsky is eventually thrown, although it is then presented as a characteristic which Karenin has had and has been aware of for some time. Anna is unable to keep her feelings private, and Karenin somehow has to work out how to manage in this difficult situation. Even before the accident, tension is high, and we are told of Karenin's strategy for coping with his tensions. He is extremely talkative, and this grates upon Anna, who does not perceive, as is conveyed sympathetically by the narrative, that this was 'merely the expression of his inner distress and uneasiness' (II. 28. 226). Again, in the image used now to clarify Karenin's stratagem, we see a shift to sympathy, in that the ox who had borne impending doom is now converted to a more live being: 'As a child that has been hurt skips about, making his muscles move to drown the pain, so Karenin needed mental activity to drown the thoughts of his wife' (II. 28. 226).

The shift here in the narrative is to reveal a more sentient being, one not associated by tradition with the convention of the cuckold. It also points the way to what will be Tolstoy's careful delineation of Karenin's reaction to emotion as something which explains his stiffness, his aloofness, all those characteristics which make him difficult for others to deal with. In part III, chapter 13, this sympathetic attitude is spelled out yet more clearly, again from a viewpoint which suggests intimate access to Karenin (a feature not always made explicit in relation to the husbands of adultery novels). That is, Tolstoy himself seems now to show compassion and softening in his depiction of this still ungainly husband: 'None but those who knew Karenin most intimately was aware that, while on the surface the coldest and most rational of men, he had one weakness quite inconsistent with the general trend of his character. Karenin could not with equanimity see or hear a child or woman crying. The sight of tears upset him and made him lose all power of reflection' (III. 13. 300). His defensive reaction to emotion, experienced as intolerable, is provoked by the fear of that emotion being aroused in himself: thus, seeing Anna in tears, Karenin is both angry and 'aware at the same time of a rush of that emotional turmoil always produced in him by tears', a reaction that makes him wary of any expression of feeling, since it puts him on a knife-edge between control and lack of control. What we have here, then, in relation to Karenin, and in contradistinction to other, less sympathetic, portrayals of husbands, is the careful tracing of the mechanics of his reaction, so that it may be understood by the reader, even if it can have no material effect on his conjugal relations. Our observation of the complex and defensive emotional mechanisms which lead him to attitudes that appear to be haughty or contemptuous affords us a greater approximation to Karenin's state.[67]

In placing the emphasis within the portrayal of Karenin upon the tolerance or otherwise of emotion, the text brings us close to a more primitive level of reaction than that sketched out in Víctor's thoughts about his inadequate virility in *La Regenta*. The primitive level of the pain involved is further indicated in the nature of Karenin's relief when his wife's adulterous love has been talked of between the two of them: it is akin to the relief of a man who has had an aching tooth extracted. That Karenin's reaction is one general to him is highlighted on the occasion of Anna's giving birth to Vronsky's child. With her life in danger, Vronsky is understandably distraught. Karenin's emotion, surprisingly, is bound to Vronsky's distress, and not to anger in relation to Vronsky or to the event of which his distress is the material sign: thus, seeing Vronsky's tears, he is caught up in general transferential reaction, rather than a specific one, and 'became aware of a rush of that nervous emotion that the sight of suffering in others always aroused in him' (IV. 17. 437). Later, in a situation

[67] This reading runs counter to that of Elizabeth Gunn, in *A Daring Coiffeur: Reflections on 'War and Peace' and 'Anna Karenina'* (London, 1971), referred to below, p. 247.

much more directly affecting Karenin's sense of himself, that is, when his wife has left to live with Vronsky, we have further detailing of the tensions caused in him by negative emotions, most particularly, he feels unhappiness to be a dangerous possession, which will cause further stress when others perceive it in him. Initially what is intolerable here is the feeling of contempt which he believes others are showing, and will continue to show in relation to him. He sees the cause for their hate not as something within himself, that is, not 'something fundamentally wrong in himself' (v. 19. 534), but 'because he was disgracefully and odiously unhappy'. In this transfer of reaction, he disowns his distress, experienced in his inner world, or at least sees it as the cause for the hate for him by others in the outside world.

Karenin's difficulties with emotional reaction are not exclusive to him, but are also, it would appear, part of Tolstoy's view of what is properly masculine, as opposed to what is properly feminine. Thus Levin, who throughout embodies the ideal alternative to both the stiff coldness of Karenin and the immoral lovability of Oblonsky, is also in difficulties in the processing of emotions, but has a greater tolerance for them than Karenin enjoys, and has the 'gift' of spontaneous and deeply felt jealous reactions.

Some husbands whose reaction to adultery is in the man-of-honour mode, operating on a split between feeling and a 'rational', would-be dignified front to present to the world, are kept distant from the reader—so that our experience of them remains alien, apart from access to their reactions to emotion. In the case of Karenin, however, there is repeated access to the fact that what goes on in him is a mechanism of defensive control. He is cold, plodding, officious, bureaucratic. Simply to be given this information would ensure a reaction of discarding him as a character who is potentially of functional importance only in the adultery drama (that is, will he or will he not take reprisals against the lovers, or permit an enabling divorce?). Instead the text makes it impossible to dismiss him, by investigating his reactions in detail, and by not restricting the focus to functional importance alone. This consideration at times takes the form of a painstaking reiteration of the different layers and stages of Karenin's attempts to control his reactions. Thus in the early stages of suspicion about his wife, Karenin keeps a tight rein on himself: 'He did not want to think at all about his wife's conduct and feelings, and actually succeeded in not thinking about them ... he did not allow himself to think about it, and he did not think about it ... but all the same ... he knew beyond all doubt that he was a wronged husband, and he was profoundly unhappy about it' (II. 26. 220). That there is tension there is, as it were, to his credit: he is not the cold fish he appears to be, an impression given more glamorous form in the image used by the doctor to Karenin's secretary: that of a violin string strained to its utmost, so that the pressure of a finger is enough to snap it (II. 26. 222). This is an image that brings him unexpectedly close to the portrayal of strain in Anna, who, on the train journey back to her husband after the visit to Moscow in part I, when she has met Vronsky, feels 'her nerves being stretched more and more tightly, like strings round pegs' (I. 29. 116), an image which she reiterates to Oblonsky as she makes him her confidant in part IV, chapter 21. The passage of the image of a strained string from the narrator's view of Anna to a view of Karenin by another character and back to Anna's own articulation of her state, envelops Karenin in the exposition of Anna's drama, albeit at the subtle level of reference only.[68] When, at the races, Karenin does see the irrefutable evidence of his wife's involvement with Vronsky, that tension is itself conveyed in the taut sentence-structure: he is 'striving not to read what was so plainly written on it [Anna's face], and against his own will with horror read on it what he did not want to know' (II. 28. 228). This delineation of tension is there to be banked away in our impressions of Karenin, to undercut later examples of him acting in cold, imperious fashion, uttering stilted sentences in a shrill voice, and to counter-balance the later view of his son, who comes to feel that 'his father always talked to him ... as if he were addressing some imaginary boy out of a book' (V. 27. 553).

A characteristic all too frequently present in the cuckold and the man of honour is a relative lack of complexity deriving from the simplicity of the literary vision of the type. In their different ways, novels of adultery depart from this simplicity of presentation, so that in *Madame Bovary* there is a shift from ridiculous cuckold to pathetic, well-meaning man, finally caught up in the acting-out of Romantic grief, while in *La Regenta* the husband's role is reduced to that of cypher, both by wife and novelist, with the exception of

[68] See also Stenbock-Fermor, *The Architecture of 'Anna Karenina'*, 72.

Víctor's naïve exposing of his uncertain virility. A factor in both the cuckold story and that of the man of honour is a set of clear norms about the features of masculinity: the dramas will revolve around these norms, even if the preoccupation with them, as I have argued, comes not as a primary reaction of competitiveness between men, but as a secondary reaction of competitiveness in the face of a primary reaction of fear towards the feminine. Within the novels of adultery, the question 'What is a man?' is to a large extent played down, or filtered either into the concentration upon honourable or gentlemanly behaviour or, more privately, into concern about the effective (or not so effective) management of private love-affairs. When the husbands of adultery novels fail, whether in the eyes of their wives or in those of society, it is more likely to be through their blundering manner rather than by falling short of ideals of masculinity.

The concept of 'What it is proper for a man to do' is, however, not entirely absent, and in the case of Karenin surfaces progressively through the text, being relatively absent in the early stages, and becoming more prominent as his social position comes under greater scrutiny. The issue of what should constitute the proper behaviour of a husband in reaction to infidelity is concentrated around the issue of whether a duel should take place between Karenin and Vronsky. Neither party envisages it as a solution, but both can see it as a possible catalytic factor. For Karenin the killing of Vronsky would still leave him with the problem of his wife, and he realistically faces the possibility that it might turn out badly for him, and takes some comfort in the probability that his friends would not allow him to participate anyway (III. 13. 302). For Vronsky, meanwhile, a possible duel is an event which would bring change, if not a solution, to his relationship with Anna, an anticipation that points to the discrepancy between their views, and to his much more heightened awareness, when compared with hers, of social censure (III. 22. 338–9). The two men wrestle separately with what a duel might mean, while popular opinion on the matter is to be relayed (compassionately, as it were, in relation to another adultery) in the news that Pryatchnikov has killed Kvitsky in a duel, on account of his wife, and this is deemed to be acting 'like a man' (IV. 12. 417).

Karenin does, in part V, chapter 21, confess that he feels 'unmanned' when his wife has finally left him, after all the attempts to offer forgiveness (v. 21. 326). It is in normal social intercourse, however, that he feels this, not in any direct confrontation with his rival. It is the minutiae of everyday life, such as the paying of Anna's millinery bills, that daunt him—much as they would in the event of a bereavement. His sense of loss of manliness is therefore presented in a text which details with exactitude and some degree of compassion the fumbling incertitude of a man who has finally lost what he had—his wife.

I would like presently to discuss Karenin in terms of loss, but before that to draw attention to those aspects of him which fit with neither the cuckold nor the man of honour, and which one could view as presentations of aspects of his feminine side, rather than of the striving for masculine recognition or the avoidance of masculine dishonour which mark the reactions of the honour system. Alternatively, these aspects of Karenin, within a domestic, caring role which he shares with other husbands of this genre, could be explained as exemplifications of the capacity for concern and desire for reparation which for Klein were prime characteristics of the depressive position.[69] In common with most of the husbands we have discussed so far, Karenin shows a capacity for parenthood which, because of the social conventions of the nineteenth century, we might understand more in terms of motherhood than of fatherhood. Charles Bovary shows love and concern for his daughter, cares for her, finally fixes his dreams upon her; Innstetten in the period spent in Berlin, before the discovery of Effi's love-letters, is increasingly fond of his daughter; Víctor has no children, but acts as a nurturing, nursing, caring figure for Ana Ozores. Karenin initially shows himself as the distant, organizing father (a rather warmer version of Dombey), who disposes material conditions for the upbringing of his son, and takes an interest (if an authoritarian one) in his education. The apparent lack of an emotional bond is, as we saw earlier, noted by Seriozha his son, and although the explanation is arguably that it is a defensive withdrawal from an emotional relationship, rather than an absence of feeling, it is none the less representative of the stilted and cold demeanour characteristic of Karenin through most of the narrative. It is, however, Karenin who, in part IV, chapter 19, in

[69] See Ch. 1, and Ch. 1, n. 11; also Melanie Klein, 'Love, Guilt and Reparation' (1937), in ead., *Love, Guilt and Reparation*, 306–43.

the chaos that ensues when Anna has become ill with puerperal fever after the birth of Vronsky's child, makes sure that the child is cared for, even though she is not his. This capacity to, as it were, make the cuckold's position an honourable one (need it be a disgrace to care for the child of another man?) stands in contrast with Vronsky's melodramatic despair, expressed in his attempt to kill himself. That is, Karenin demonstrates the possibility here that both cuckold and man of honour, in their different ways, are able to show concern for the family which will develop, while the principals in the adultery drama remain bound, if temporarily, in their own situation alone. And it is not merely a concern of domestic administration that draws Karenin to care for the child that is not his, but an urge that seems unconscious, explained only perhaps by the state in which it leaves him: 'sometimes he would sit gazing for half an hour at a stretch at the downy, wrinkled, tomato-coloured little face of the sleeping baby, watching the frowning forehead and the chubby little hands with their curled-up fingers, rubbing the tiny eyes and nose with the backs of its fists. At such moments especially Karenin felt quite calm and at peace with himself, and saw nothing abnormal in his position, nothing that need be changed' (IV. 19. 445). That this state is elusive, and only reached with difficulty, rather than being one easily attained, is explored at greater length elsewhere in the novel.

That Karenin may have feminine aspects is suggested, as we have seen, by some of his physical attributes, which depart from masculine norms: his soft, white hands, his high-pitched voice—both suggestive of diminished masculinity where ideals are of the muscled activity of the alternative man, Vronsky. They are also features which grate on, or exasperate, Anna. The 'feminine' feature of Karenin which causes most difficulty in the novel, however, is his attempt to depart from the norm of the man of honour who is only offended and forgives nothing, while not enjoying the excuse of the cuckold that he does not know what is going on. Although an initial discomfiture is caused to both Anna and Vronsky by Karenin's determination not to make a public fuss about their relationship, much harder to bear is his gesture of forgiveness at the birth of their child. This is seen in terms of his making a connection with the emotional side of himself against which he has been erecting such firm defences: 'By his sick wife's bedside he had given way for the first time in his life to that feeling of sympathetic compassion which the suffering of others produced in him, and which he had hitherto been ashamed of, as of a pernicious weakness' (IV. 19. 444). His feeling of forgiveness for his wife which comes in a wave with his compassion for her, with the attitude of total co-operation expressed in the letter he shows to Oblonsky, (IV. 22. 455) expresses a generosity which—as Oblonsky, with his intuitive grasp of the situation, puts it—crushes her. The underlying suggestion here seems to be that there is an urge, a requirement, in the adultery situation of these novels, that husbands be not understanding, for to act in this way causes greater confusion and shame. That is, if we place Karenin's move towards forgiveness and understanding in the context of Tanner's idea about the concern of the novel of adultery with transgression, then we find in the motion of the novel, from the very parties who are the participants in the transgression, a desire for containment and firmness, which will stand in opposition to the transgression. Without such a boundary, the margination and loss of identity of the lovers become complete, since they run the risk of not even retaining their identity as outsiders.

The nature of the depressive position is one of acceptance that there can be negative experience, loss and pain, and the ability to tolerate such things. The toleration is possible partly because of the knowledge that other, more positive types of experience may exist at other times. More crucially, however, the depressive position is one in which strength can be derived from knowing that it is possible to tolerate the experience that one actually has, with all its conflicts and negative aspects. In Chapter 3 I suggested that in so far as the model of the cuckold is linked to the process of ageing and consequent impotence (and hence to the inevitability of death as the outcome for us all), the use of the cuckold as a literary type was a way of placing that awareness of our limitations safely—because of the comic element—within the context of our general awareness: laughing at the cuckold is a way of not failing to perceive that we are all subject to ageing and death. A different form of the depressive position in this context of adultery, and arguably a truer one, is to accept that such disasters occur, and to find it possible to tolerate their occurrence without recourse to the palliative of laughter. This, I would argue, is the essential step forward made by the novels of adultery when compared with the cuckold version of the tale of infidelity.

Within the central narrative of *Anna Karenin*, much of the time is taken by Karenin avoiding the depressive position, his splitting-off from what is happening being the subject of repeated comment within the text. Tolstoy as author stands and judges him for it: 'He, who was so intelligent and shrewd where official affairs were concerned, did not realize the insanity of such an attitude [of detachment] to his wife. He did not realize it because it was too dreadful to him to face the true situation, and he shut down and locked and sealed that compartment of his soul which contained his feelings for his family—that is, for his wife and son' (II. 26. 219).

The possibility that Karenin represents a disowned projection of Tolstoy himself has not gone unnoticed. The view that Tolstoy himself cannot stand what Karenin is or represents and therefore treats him with singular harshness is advanced by Gunn.[70] But while Gunn argues that Karenin is a disowned projection, the text of the novel itself seems to reveal more understanding of Karenin than is consistent with such a view. Gunn partially concedes this,[71] but holds in general to a reading of 'unfair treatment' of Karenin. In connection with Tolstoy's attitude to Karenin, it is worth noting that Karenin's character was originally that of a 'gentle, easily put out, weak and almost unworldly figure, with a kind smile and kind blue eyes'.[72]

Implied in the concentration on Karenin's inability to accommodate what is happening in his marriage is an alternative view: that there can be acceptance rather than defence. Karenin aspires briefly to accommodation at the start of part IV, when we learn that he hoped 'this passion like everything else in the world would pass, that people would forget about it, and his name would remain unsullied' (IV. 1. 378). This state of hope is, however, bound to a longing for anaesthesia, some distance from acceptance of what happens. It is, however, in part IV, as we have seen, that Karenin makes his massive attempt at forgiveness, and causes a turn of events in the plot which confuses all around him. Certainly

70 Gunn, *A Daring Coiffeur*, 122–7.

71 Ibid. 125, 131.

72 See H. Gifford, 'Further Notes on *Anna Karenina*', in Davie (ed.), *Russian Literature and Modern English Fiction*, 160–63 (161). That the novel contains projections of Tolstoy's own feelings is also suggested by Judith Armstrong, *The Unsaid 'Anna Karenina'*, here indicating that Pozdnyshev and Oblonsky represent parts of Tolstoy (p. 68), and that Anna is a projection of Tolstoy's sexual passion and his aspiration towards death (p. 136).

it puzzles, shames, and humiliates Vronsky (the humiliation suggesting that the act of forgiveness may itself be a subtle wielding of power). Vronsky's view of Karenin—called by Anna when she believes that she is dying—shows how, in his eyes, the husband has escaped from the traditional mould: 'The deceived husband—who had figured till now as a pitiful object, an incidental and somewhat ludicrous obstacle to his happiness—had suddenly been summoned by her herself, elevated to an awe-inspiring pinnacle, and on the pinnacle that husband had shown himself not vindictive, not false, not ludicrous, but kind, straightforward, and dignified' (IV. 18. 440–41). That Karenin is viewed in this way from the outside does not, of course, mean that this is the way he will be henceforward, even if the momentary peace contemplating the infant daughter who is not his suggests such a hopeful future. Furthermore, Vronsky, in his puzzlement, perceives no conflict in the husband he has ousted.

At a later stage, in part V, chapter 21, when Karenin has to face the definitive loss of his wife, we see much more clearly the conflicts and uncertainties he is now obliged to confront, the period of forgiveness of part IV appearing in retrospect as a chimera. In a chapter following on the narrative of the death of Levin's brother, and the announcement of Kitty's pregnancy (two poles of death and life, the wretched and the ideal), Karenin is left with his loss, and unable to defend himself against it. Foremost is the problem of his accommodation to what has happened, expressed paradoxically in terms of a failure to accommodate, while the recognition of that failure is itself an accommodation to the reality: 'The most painful part of it was his inability to connect and reconcile the past with what was now. It was not the past when he had lived happily with his wife that troubled him. The transition from that past to a knowledge of his wife's infidelity he had lived through miserably already: it had been a difficult time, but a comprehensible one. Had his wife left him then, after informing him of her unfaithfulness, he would have been wounded, unhappy, but he would not have felt himself in such a hopeless, unintelligible impasse. He could not now at all reconcile his recent act of forgiveness, his emotion, his love for his sick wife and for the other man's child with the present position—that is, with the fact that, as if in return for all this, he now found himself alone, put to shame, a laughing-stock, unwanted and despised by all'

(v. 21. 533). Here all the elements of Karenin's existence are summarized, including loss of wife, reputation, and his attempts to escape from the conventions surrounding a man in his position.[73]

Tolstoy makes no final resolution. His adulterous heroine dies, in desperation, like Emma Bovary. She is not left to face a fate of margination like Ana Ozores or Effi Briest; but her experience of such treatment (as much as any romantic disappointment) leads to her suicide. The two male principals in the drama continue in their different ways.

The novel as a whole, however, has a sense of completion, even if on examination it is a shade contrived. The opening words of the text announce that it will be about marriage and not adultery, and it is this which forms the containing membrane, which enables us to contemplate the otherwise intolerable conflicts, losses, and disappointments consequent on the story of adultery.[74] 'All happy families are alike but an unhappy family is unhappy after its own fashion', the text announces (I. I. 13). A persuasive comment, if unreliable. While the text unweaves the domestic affairs of Anna and Karenin, it simultaneously constructs the domestic affairs of Levin and Kitty Shcherbatsky. This latter match forms the ideal within the novel, a pole of counterbalance to run against and alongside the story of adultery. Both stories unfold haltingly, with vacillations and hesitations, and to these twists and turns are added the twists and turns in the view of marriage which results from their intertwining in the narrative. Thus moments of separation in the Karenin household are followed by moments leading to joining in the Levin relationship, and the departure of the newly married couple is followed by the travels abroad of Anna and Vronsky (v. 6–7). Relief is provided at difficult moments, so that the anguish and tension of the Karenin couple after Vronsky's fall in the steeple-chase is followed by the lighter matter of Kitty's stay in the German watering-place (II. 29–30).[75] A different type of counterpoint is provided by the marriage of Oblonsky and Dolly,

[73] See Judith Armstrong, *The Novel of Adultery* (London, 1976), 106, on the possibility that such revelation of emotion for the husband may include realization of uncomfortable truths.

[74] Elizabeth Gunn in particular, *A Daring Coiffeur*, 93–5, argues the case of the novel as concerning acceptance, self-awareness, and responsibility.

[75] See also the comparison of Anna and Kitty, Levin and Vronsky, in Calder, 'Man, Woman and Male Woman', 224. The most detailed discussion of the structure of the novel is in Stenbock-Fermor, *The Architecture of 'Anna Karenina'*.

the subject of the initial comment about unhappy marriages. Here it is the story of an unfaithful husband, not an unfaithful wife, and we are witness to both Dolly's distress and Oblonsky's puzzled discomfiture. Oblonsky is the man who exasperates, but who also disarms, by his kindliness, his ability to smooth social situations, his willingness to act as a diplomat in matrimonial difficulties. He is also shown as possessed of a certain level of realism, from an early moment, and it is his view that 'it was impossible to put right or patch up their relationship because it was impossible to make her attractive and lovable again or to turn himself into an old man incapable of love' (1. 3. 21). There is an engaging suggestion in this that Oblonsky represents a reasonable, even a healthy, acceptance of things as they are: a mode of mind that is likely to make for survival. And we may note that Oblonsky tries, in his way, to keep his own marriage afloat, as well as acting as matrimonial mediator in the unhappy Karenin marriage. The possible worth of Oblonsky despite his faults has not escaped comment, but it is not clear what it is that he appeals to. It may be the reader's underlying urge to see a representation, and indeed a restoration, of harmony, as argued by Armstrong.[76] Alternatively, the persuasion of the reader that Oblonsky is not only to be indulged but also to be forgiven and to be seen as a positive force for good, may be based on the Hegelian perception of the right of men (as opposed to the lack of right of women) to particularity of desire.[77]

The narrative division between the stories of different marriages represents, however, a split in Kleinian terms, so that the Karenin marriage is doomed, the Levin marriage one of growth and development, and the Oblonsky ménage one of simple human survival.[78] What is of particular interest is the degree to which, in the Levin marriage, presented as an ideal, Tolstoy draws lines of division of attributes strongly reminiscent of the divisions operative in the honour code (just as later, in *The Kreutzer Sonata*, he will affirm those divisions yet more stridently). The division in the Levin

[76] 'For the reader, the urge to see the marriage saved, despite some challenging reasons against it . . . is powerful . . . The text . . . works, in other words, for the maintenance of the *status quo*, for the return to things as they were' (Armstrong, *The Novel of Adultery*, 52).

[77] For the concept of particularity of desire as the prerogative of man according to Hegel, see the discussion in Lloyd, *The Man of Reason*, 80.

marriage is a classic one: man as a creature of the intellect and reason, and for that reason blundering in matters emotional; woman as a creature of the intuitions and emotions. Man is puzzled and hurt when confronted by pain and death; woman is able to tolerate it. Thus while Levin tries to keep his wife separate from his dying and dissolute brother, Kitty steps in and handles Nikolai's transition through death with simplicity and deftness. These splits in the attributes are made most articulate in part V, chapter 18, at the time of Nikolai's death, but are also evident in Levin's experience of jealousy. Through Levin is revealed the exceptional danger for the man of close association with his wife, since it brings inevitable emotional pain. A feeling of indissolubility within the marriage thus ensures that any rupture is virtually intolerable. Thus at their first quarrel, 'he clearly understood what he had not understood when he led her out of the church after the wedding: that he was not simply close to her, but that he could not tell where he ended and she began. He realized this from the agonizing sensation of division which he felt at that instant. He was hurt for a moment but immediately knew he could not be offended with her because she was himself. For a second he felt like a man who, suddenly receiving a violent blow from behind, turns round angrily to find and be revenged on his assailant, and discovers that he has accidentally struck himself, that there is no one to be angry with and he must endure and try to still the pain' (V. 14. 508). Levin is the character who suffers, who experiences jealousy, who has the fierce, divisive man-of-honour reaction to his wife, and who yet manages to retain an awareness of what happens, and is able to remain in touch with his emotional turmoil. Oblonsky's thoughts early on in the novel had sketched what now seems to be almost a parody of acceptance, with his musing of 'And the worst of it is that I am to blame and yet I am not to blame. That is the whole tragedy' (I. 1. 14).[79] Levin's final

[78] See Armstrong, *The Novel of Adultery*, 30–31, on the split between the attitudes of Levin and Oblonsky, as something which may be 'only an artistic solution'.

[79] Gunn's elegiac gloss on this, *A Daring Coiffeur*, 94, is powerful and appealing, yet indicates an attitude of more sobriety and self-knowledge than is really evidenced by characters of the novel, with the possible intended exception of Levin: 'When we are adult there is no-one else to blame. We are both to blame and not to blame. We are what we have unconsciously, unthinkingly become. Not only are we not in control—we are no longer, as youth assumes, allowed the illusion of being so.'

thoughts, on which the novel closes, could stand as exemplum of the depressive position:

> I shall still lose my temper with Ivan the coachman, I shall still embark on useless discussions and express my opinions inopportunely; there will still be the same wall between the sanctuary of my inmost soul and other people, even my wife; I shall probably go on scolding her in my anxiety and repenting of it afterwards; I shall still be as unable to understand with my reason why I pray, and I shall still go on praying—but my life now, my whole life, independently of anything that can happen to me, every minute of it is no longer meaningless as it was before, but has a positive meaning of goodness with which I have the power to invest it. (VIII. 19. 853)

What Levin, or Tolstoy, have recourse to, and which is not part of the depressive position, is the miracle of faith. This aside, however, Levin expresses the ideal one might move towards. It is characteristic of the novel that this possibility of maturity and growth is contained within it, but noteworthy that Tolstoy continues to maintain a split within his own novelistic attitude, in that this acceptance is placed finally within the marriage that does not come under threat, while the one which has suffered rupture through adultery cannot be mended.

6
Men of Distinction

LEONTES: Come, and lead me
To these sorrows.
(*The Winter's Tale*, III. iii. 240–1)

IN HIS discussion of *The Winter's Tale*, Wilbur Sanders dwells on the unusual fact that Leontes, wrongly suspecting his wife of adultery, and receiving the news that she has died as a result of his wrath, opts to draw close to his grief, and face it in all its intensity.[1] In this chapter, I would like to concentrate on those images of exceptional husbands, men of distinction, who, in the awareness of the fact that they have been deceived, are portrayed as able to react to the fact in a way unbounded by the two models that have served as the basis for the discussions in previous chapters. In a sense, I am aware that I am pursuing a chimera, in perhaps the idealized belief that it may be possible to locate the ultimate depressive position in relation to the deceived husband. Such an ultimate position would have two dimensions: the capacity of the deceived husband as character to confront his grief, and the capacity of the literary text to contain and articulate that experience. The depressive position *vis-à-vis* woman's infidelity was sketched if not in relation to the cuckold, at least in the social fact and implications of the literature of cuckoldry. In its turn, it was replaced by the depressive position as exemplified in the novels of adultery, where the greater approximation to a facing of the husband's pain in the text contrasted with the comic escape-route of dismissal characterizing the literature of cuckoldry. The husbands of the novels of adultery, however, still bear the traces of the two models, while revealing other potential formations in the interstices between the models. The novels themselves, by shifting the characterization of the husband between the two models, by introducing other possible formations (the husband as

[1] Wilbur Sanders, *The Winter's Tale*, Harvester New Critical Introductions to Shakespeare (Brighton, 1987), ch. 3.

domesticated, the husband as one who cannot confront emotion in itself, let alone in response to betrayal), and by using the counterpoint of other experiences and other narratives that either reiterate or contrast with the central experience of betrayal and marital failure, offer a reading that is itself closer to the accommodation and inclusiveness of the depressive position.

What, however, of texts that are the exception to the patterns of portrayal discussed in the preceding chapters? There is a temptation to argue that all representations of the deceived husband will, one way or another, in some mixture or other, conform to the two models of the cuckold and the man of honour, albeit in the very mixed forms offered in the novels of adultery. Certainly, even in works which we could class as exceptions, the configurations of the two models can still frequently be recognized. But some exceptions do remain, whether in the characterization of individual men, who in other senses remain within the framework of one of the two models, or in the possible responses to adultery that different works sketch out, or in the total manner of confronting the problem of how to represent the husband's experience of his wife's adultery.

First some examples that relate most closely, at least in the first instance, to the cuckold model. In Chapter 3, we saw how the cuckold, even for Boccaccio, need not necessarily be the figure of complete ridicule that society expects him to be. Alberto, though old, retains dignity through his awareness of his possible ridicule. The salvation of the cuckold from his ridicule is also shown in a striking way in Cervantes' two versions of the tale of the jealous Extremaduran: the novella of 1613, *The Jealous Extremaduran* (El Celoso extremeño); and the theatrical version of the same story, *The Jealous Old Man* (El Viejo Celoso), an *entremés*, or interlude, of 1615.[2] In both the story and the theatrical interlude,

[2] The novella itself exists in two versions, the one usually cited, from the collection of 1613, and an earlier one, known as the Porrás version, dating from about 1600. Some of the main differences between the two, and their import, particularly in moral and theological terms, are discussed by Paul Lewis-Smith, 'The Two Versions of *El Celoso extremeño*: On the Questions of Authorship and Intent', *Neophilologus*, 76 (1992) 559–68. The broad lines of the portrayal of the husband, discussed here on the basis of the 1613 text, are essentially the same in the earlier version, though less convincingly put forward. The Porrás version of the novella can be found in Cervantes, *Novelas ejemplares*, ed. J. B. Avalle-Arce (2 vols.; Madrid, 1982), i. 223–63. For an English version of the novella see Cervantes, *Exemplary Stories*, trans. C. A. Jones (Harmondsworth, 1972), and for

a man of 48 (Filipo de Carrizales in the story, Cañizares in the interlude), prosperous by his own efforts, decides that the time has come to have a rest, and that marriage and the production of an heir are what is now appropriate. He is an extremely jealous man, and marries a young girl. All the prerequisites for the cuckold story are there, and in the theatrical version, the husband remains firmly within the model of the cuckold. In the interlude, the traditional lines of the cuckold story are adhered to throughout. The husband is elderly, and his young wife shows all the commitment to a young woman's need of a young man shown by Chaucer's May and Alisoun. In the manner of the theatrical farce, the lover is introduced into the house by a trick, much to the pleasure of the wife, and his exit is similarly effected. The wife is guilty but—in marital terms and in the quest of her own pleasure—triumphant. The husband, anxious and overzealous from the start, remains unaware of betrayal yet still goes whining his general complaints against the world. In the novella form, however, a number of surprising features are included.

Although a trick is used to introduce the lover into the house, there is much less emphasis than in the interlude on the lines of knockabout farce, and a greater emphasis on mood and emotions. The imagined response of the husband to the infidelity of his wife is couched in terms that remove all blame from her: the young man was cunning, the duenna was false, the wife was an ignorant girl persuaded by others. On being confronted with the apparent reality of his wife's infidelity (she is lying with the young man, though has resisted his advances), Filipo has a striking range of emotional reactions: his heart stops, he is angry, but then overcome with grief. He resolves to take revenge, but when going quietly back to her room he is again overcome with grief and faints. While this might echo the cuckold's alleged weakness, it is also the revelation of the inner, suffering man. The human side then comes conclusively to the fore: Filipo sends for the girl's parents, kisses her, does not blame her, and begs her to marry the young man after he, the husband, is dead. The reaction to all this magnanimity is that his wife, despite all the problems of the early part of the marriage, wants him to live on. At his death she enters a convent.

the *entremés* of *The Jealous Extremaduran*, see the dual-language text, *The Interludes of Cervantes*, trans. S. Griswold Morley (Princeton, NJ, 1948).

The strong delineation of the model to be ridiculed at the start of the story makes more effective the unpicking of the attributes and expected reactions of that model. A much more modern use of this technique comes again from Spain, in Lorca's short play *The Love of Don Perlimplín and Belisa in the Garden* (El Amor de don Perlimplín con Belisa en su jardín) (1933),[3] where the models of both cuckold and the man of honour are, as it were, firmly tried on for size, and their conventions then exploited and subverted to suggest the reality of the suffering and vulnerable human being underneath.

Don Perlimplín is a play which shows how the conventions of theatre can be exploited so that human experience is not simply tamed and contained, but is hinted at as existing in its raw and barely tolerable state within the safety of the literary container. It opens with pure lines of traditional farce as an arranged marriage for Perlimplín, an old, bookish bachelor who has remained nervous of marriage all his life (in his youth he heard of a shoemaker whose wife had strangled him) is set up. The main agents for this are his maid Marcolfa and the grotesque mother of Belisa, the bride. Farce continues as Belisa is apparently unfaithful to him with five men on the wedding night. In his naïve questions about the reason for five silken ladders and five hats, Perlimplín is the archetypal unaware cuckold. But the resemblance does not last long. He has, in his own way, been transformed by the wedding night, is for the first time aware of beauty and the pain of desire. That is, even at this early point, where he is still characterized as cuckold, the fact that there is a man inside the model comes to the fore, a man for whom there will be an emotional crisis quite other than that of sexual betrayal by his wife with other men. What Perlimplín has to face is the immeasurable chasm between his desire, now awakened, and his wife's body, which he cannot (whatever that means—and we are never told in precise terms) enjoy. Alongside this experience of a trauma of feeling which cannot be forgotten, the problem of being a deceived husband is, for Perlimplín, barely relevant.

For the social context in which he is placed, his wife's infidelity

[3] Federico García Lorca, *El Amor de don Perlimplín con Belisa en su jardín* (1933) in *Obras completas*, ed. A. de Hoyo (2 vols.; Madrid, 1980), ii. 321–60. The play is translated by Gwynne Edwards as *The Love of Don Perlimplín and Belisa in the Garden*, in *Lorca Plays: Two* (London, 1990), 41–64.

is, of course, highly relevant, a fact which agitates Perlimplín's servant Marcolfa, concerned, like a good Spaniard, for her master's honour, his public reputation. Perlimplín, however, refuses to enter into the mode of the man of honour, even though it is laid upon him. There is no hint of jealousy, paranoia, or desire for revenge. From Act II onwards he behaves with a firmness and decision hitherto unglimpsed, treating Belisa in the mode of a kindly, all-seeing, and understanding father, discussing extra-marital dalliance with her as though it were a matter in which he had a positive concern for her welfare and happiness. Yet at the same time as he acts in a manner completely contrary to that either of the cuckold or of the man of honour (he is fully aware of her infidelity, and yet is apparently neither jealous nor vengeful in reaction to it), he employs one of the characteristic modes of response of the husband of honour plays in that he lays a plot to surprise his wife with her lover. That it is a plot in which he plays the part of the lover, and goes out to kill himself, gives a stylishness to the action which almost cloaks the tragedy of the man who has acted in so lucid and decisive a manner.

Almost, but not quite. Belisa, contemplating the body of her husband, who has in fact deceived her (he has invented a lover in a red cloak who sent her letters of sensuous intensity), is bemused. Never, she says, had she thought he was so complicated. But the incomprehension of this fluffy siren (fully in the tradition of the whore, not of the madonna) is not shared by the spectators. They have witnessed Perlimplín's emergence into the world of experience in the course of the play, an experience which bites deep, and which gives to his life a meaning it had not previously had. The primacy and irreplaceability of the experience of love and desire, new for Perlimplín, are, however, tinged with the anguish of what is never to be attained—full sexual enjoyment of his wife. The action he takes, cast though it be in the man-of-honour mould, has nothing to do with the defence of his reputation, and is solely bound up with his need for release from his pain. Yet it is also an action performed with the intention that his wife too should be educated into the depths of feeling he now knows of, depths which are due to the knowledge that what is desired can never be attained. That the education is lost on her (she turns from pondering on the complicated nature of Perlimplín to wondering where the elusive young man in the red cape has got to) is an irony presented to the spectator, though mercifully not to her dead husband. Thus the depressive confrontation of the various dimensions of pain comes through the literary experience in a reiteration of the husband's own final experience, but is given the extra bitter edge—for the spectator—of the ironic knowledge of final failure.

Perlimplín departs from norms of honour not only in not killing his wife, but in the act of committing suicide, a suicide undertaken in a different spirit from that of Othello. In so doing, he directs all the aggression provoked by Belisa's infidelity on to himself alone.

The fact that aggression may be an inevitable component of the situation resulting from a wife's adultery appears to be suggested by two further plays where the husband adopts an unconventional response. In this case, the presence of aggression is the more surprising since the husband's reaction appears to be one of forgiveness.

Don Perlimplín contains elements of both the cuckold and the man of honour, but in it both conventions are played with and subverted. By contrast, an Italian example leaves behind all suggestions of the comic, and faces less humorously the implications of the honour code for modern society. *The Mask and the Face* (La Maschera ed il volto) (1916) by Luigi Chiarelli takes place, as Lorca's play does, in a society where the norms of the honour/shame culture have obtained for centuries. But whereas *Don Perlimplín* is Hispanic but not situated in a precise chronology (the eighteenth century is suggested, but the conventions move the play between the extremes of the sixteenth century in reworkings of the *commedia dell'arte* and the honour drama), Chiarelli's work is firmly situated in a modern Italy in which there is a glaring contrast between social practice and the nightmarish, fantastic possibility that some husbands might still, within the honour mode, commit murder in response to infidelity. The subtitle, 'A Grotesque Comedy in Three Acts', signals the black and uncertain humour of a play in which a man attempts to skirt a social code no longer supported by its social context—a humour which is belied by the apparent seriousness of the denouement.

The brittle and immoral society which is the background to the action has more than a little in common with the Marjorie Ferrar 'set' attacked for its skittish disregard for morality in the lawsuit brought by Fleur, the daughter of Soames Forsyte in *The Silver*

Spoon.[4] Chiarelli's play opens with gay but distinctly unpleasant banter about affairs, which appear to be conducted left, right, and centre by the majority of the characters. The exception to them all is Paolo, a husband who firmly declares that erring wives should be killed by their husbands and that he, in such a circumstance, would do so. A different type of exception is represented by Cirillo, who appears to exercise a total tolerance of his wife's extra-marital wanderings. Cirillo's wife rehearses all the expected arguments about the lack of masculinity that she perceives in her husband because of this, and hints that the type of man she needs would, in a sense, be one who would live up to the expectations of our initial quotation from Easthope, a man such as the intolerant Paolo: 'A man in love with me, ardent and cruel, who would have held me as a slave, subdued me with caresses and fear. A man who would have placed in my life a background of voluptuousness and tragedy.'[5]

Inevitably, what happens is that Paolo discovers that his wife Savina is having an affair. After an initial move to attack her he backs off. What is going on, and what Chiarelli apparently wishes to convey, is all in the stage directions: 'he at once relaxes his grip and backs away from her with an instinctive gesture of horror at what he was about to do . . . Paolo has clearly the conviction that he cannot commit this crime' (I. 263). Chiarelli is thus outspoken about his attitude at least to the proposed action, and this lack of subtlety in approach makes the play a rather superficial and intellectual exploration of possible action, despite a melodramatic level of expressed feeling in the closing moments. The plot too is contrived. Paolo has all believe that he has killed his wife, and then is tried for murder. Ten months later he is acquitted, and at this moment his wife reappears—a fact he tries unsuccessfully to hide. Before the disclosure of her living state, Paolo is shown as uncomfortable in the face of congratulations on his acquittal, and unwilling to participate in the celebrations laid on for him. A final scene brings the husband and wife together in implausible romantic euphoria.

[4] John Galsworthy, *The Silver Spoon* (1926), middle novel of the second Forsyte trilogy.

[5] Luigi Chiarelli, *La Maschera ed il volto* (The Mask and the Face), trans. Noel de Vic Beamish, in *International Modern Plays*, ed. Anthony Dent (London, 1950), 256. All references will be to this edition and given in the text, roman figures denoting the act, and arabic the page reference.

A difficulty with the play is its desire to make a point, and the uncomfortable fit between initial cynicism and ultimate elevation of feeling. Theoretically it goes through all the right motions, but a combination of the superficiality of the social scene depicted with such force in the first act, and the melodramatic extremes finally reached, lead to a reaction in the spectator which is closer to disbelief or perplexity than emotion. This is despite the clear articulation by Paolo of his feelings on discovering the adultery. Unlike probably the great majority of husbands so far discussed, he actually articulates (albeit in Act III, when all the dust has settled, at least between himself and his wife) the full force of his feeling for his wife. The feeling he expresses, however, is that aroused by their reconciliation, rather than that (suggested only by the stage directions) provoked by the discovery of her infidelity. But his feelings in Act III appear to be some reiteration, some action-replay of what might have been a genuine desire to kill her, that is, one dictated not by social conventions about what men of honour should do but by what this man as an individual felt like doing. This is the more powerful coming from the very character who had declared himself at the start (I. 248) as one who believed in the rightness of killing errant wives. Paolo's declaration points to a reaction that seems primitive and not social (perhaps revealing him as the 'brute' manly man that Elisa appears to have desired). As such he represents the phantasy of the primitive, violent, and natural he-man, desirable not for his manners but for his animal energy: 'When I felt your trembling body responding to my passion! . . . I was filled with a madness to destroy! . . . I felt all the most primitive instincts, hatred, cruelty, all that was bestial and vile, rising within me. I wanted to tear you to pieces, crush and annihilate something in you for ever, for ever! . . . It was the beast leaping to recover what had been wrested from him by a childish trick, and who felt his talons caught in a veil woven in mystery!' (III. 295). Thus, having appeared at the outset as a man set into the chilly defensive reaction of coldness that one associates with Karenin, Paolo reveals a feeling underside that contrasts with Karenin's almost total avoidance of contact with emotion.

The difficulty with Chiarelli's exploration of infidelity here is that there is a desire to retain, or indeed to affirm, the values of a civilized society while declaring that civilization does not inevitably bring the desired goal of vitality of response. There is too much of an agenda here connected with the state of modern man (degenerate, or better, potentially, than ever) to allow for a fully worked confrontation with the grief of the deceived husband. There is the need, it seems, to declare that society has got beyond the rigorous reactions of honour/shame cultures, but has not suffered a real loss in vitality (though the tinny superficiality of the opening act suggests this may be a real danger).

The degree to which Chiarelli's work is locked into an argument about proper social responses, and consequently loses a measure of force in its representation of a human dilemma, becomes the more evident if we compare Paolo with a much earlier, English, example of a forgiving husband (again drawn from the theatre): Frankford of *A Woman Killed with Kindness* (1607) by Thomas Heywood.[6]

A first reading of this may suggest that it has difficulties in common with *The Mask and the Face*, and which derive from the briefly sketched theatrical form used—a form which does not have the witty stylization and allusive reference to other modes shown in *Don Perlimplín*. However, it does share with *Don Perlimplín* that ability to suggest and evoke sobriety and intensity of feeling in a way that is ultimately more effective than the anguished and somewhat melodramatic expressions of the latter section of *The Mask and the Face*.

Frankford's feelings about the married state are given some prominence in the early scenes, so that one gains the impression of a man satisfied with the move made and in what will later seem to be a state of illusory bliss. That he has a concept of what being married entails is revealed at the very start, in that he does not participate in the dancing at the wedding feast. This refusal is the statement of a man who senses he has come to a more sober position in society, but may also be related to the sense that emerges from some of the honour plays in Spain that marriage somehow diminishes man. Thus he sends his wife to dance with her brother:

> Aye, you may caper, you are light and free.
> Marriage hath yoked my heels, pray then pardon me. (1. 10–11)

[6] Thomas Heywood, *A Woman Killed with Kindness* (1607), ed. Brian Scobie, The New Mermaids, gen. ed. Brian Gibbons (London, 1985). All references will be to this edition and given in the text. The play is divided into scenes not acts: first arabic references are to scenes, and second arabic references to line numbers.

The implication is that he is no longer able to participate in frivolity, but there is an alternative reading which somehow suggests that as a married man he is unable to participate in the active, spontaneous life of the unattached, in sexuality. The abundance of dance-references with sexual connotations in the first scene suggests a strong link between dancing and sex, and therefore points to a way in which the husband, by his participation in the virtuous and stable activity of marriage, may be separated from the freedom of sexual activity.[7]

That there is a gap between the calm affections proper to marriage—or at least those present in the initial stages of the Frankford marriage—and the passions of love, is pointed out by David Cook, who lays at Frankford's door the accusation of lack of awareness.[8] This may well be the difference between *buen amor* and *loco amor* as distinguished in the Middle Ages. There is, however, no hint that Frankford's content in his marriage is a complacent one: to take this view we would have to regard him as a character who undergoes an unrealistic change revealing depths of feeling quite impossible when faced with the infidelity of his wife. It is the reality of his content that makes him offer the hospitality he does to Wendoll, having no suspicion that an adulterous passion will result because of the complete degree of his certainty about his wife. Thus he lacks the paranoia of the man of honour (who might otherwise be deemed to share the feeling of well-being deriving from a secure place in society), and is in no way given the attributes of ridicule or silliness that would place him in the cuckold mould.

The sterling qualities of Frankford are, at least initially, shared by his wife—and indeed by the lover, Wendoll. In the early stages before the adulterous love is declared, the play in fact operates a split between vice and virtue. Within the structure itself there is a further split, between the triangle of the main plot, and

[7] The social activity of dancing, with all the sexual *double entendres*, is replaced in Scene 8 by that of cards. This second social activity requires a more definite action of opting in to the influence of chance, and may underscore the role of fate in determining that the adultery of Anne should come about. Cards also carry connotations of submission to a fate which may itself be fatal, and thus have darker resonances than the activity of dancing which, in this play at least, is related only to sexuality, and not, for example, to the Dance of Death.

[8] David Cook, '*A Woman Killed with Kindness*: An Unshakespearian Tragedy', *English Studies*, 45 (1964), 353–72.

the unsavoury sub-plot involving the exploitation of Susan Mountford and her brother by Sir Francis Acton. The sub-plot in fact serves to provide a contrastive example of behaviour, since Susan is treated with less than kindness, unlike Anne, who receives apparently exemplary kindness from her husband. Francis Acton, for example, plotting to seduce Susan, plans to 'bribe the fool|To shame herself by lewd dishonest lust' (7. 81–2). We could regard the split between the two plots simply as an example of artistic balance,[9] or as forced by the need to separate grief, love, and aggression. That there are complexities in the relationship between these feelings is displayed in Acton's own sentiments towards Susan, in Frankford's reaction to his wife's affair, but also in the manner in which the affair begins. Scene 6, in which Wendoll declares his love for Anne, is overlaid with feelings of honour for Frankford, a submissive style of courtly love from Wendoll to Anne, and Anne's reproaches, genuine, and based on concern for the honour of herself and her husband. Towards the end of the scene, however, things become confused, on the one hand by the fact that Anne is moved by Wendoll 'to passion and to pity' (6. 139), and on the other by Wendoll moving swiftly from professions of regard for honour to professions of his concern to guard secrecy in the adultery he plans.

This sudden sequence involving change in attitude to morality is followed by an illustration of the way in which some, at least, of these changes come about. Acton is apparently overtaken by feelings of love, and this leads him to his decision to defend against them by conquering them. He would like to be 'master of|My perfect senses and directest wits' (7. 106–7), queries why he should be 'in this violent humour|Of passion and of love' (7. 108–9), and decides, defensively, to deal with the feeling by removal, that is, he will conquer her (that is, treat her as an object), and thus 'Purchase my soul free and immortal rest' (7. 113).

In contrast with Acton, Frankford is notable for a first reaction to his wife's adultery which emphasizes feelings rather than, or at least as much as, concern for honour—that is, he does not detach himself from personal disaster. This is evident both in his reaction

[9] This balance is argued by Michel Grivelet, *Thomas Heywood et le drame domestique elizabéthain* (Paris, 1957) 199–210.

when told about the affair by his servant, and then in his feelings when he sees his wife at cards. His feeling of betrayal is uppermost (8. 82–3): 'Man, woman, what thing mortal may we trust, | When friends and bosom wives prove so unjust?' When he sees his wife at cards, the personal hurt, rather than the hurt to honour, comes to the fore, and, after a series of unpleasant asides and comments that reveal his angry jealousy, he moves to the feeling of loss and abandon:

> [*Aside*] Thou robb'st me of my soul, of her chaste love;
> In thy false dealing, thou has robbed my heart.
> Booty you play; I like a loser stand,
> Having no heart, or here, or in my hand.
>
> (8. 186–90)

Frankford does not move into instant confrontation but, like any Golden Age Spanish husband, lays his plot for the discovery of his wife's guilt. Thus far he shows the cool of detachment. A different source of restraint appears to surface at the moment of that plot's denouement: Frankford considers that the sanctity of his wedding chamber has been profaned but, by the same religious spirit that observes this in horror, is moved not to kill the two lovers. He does not reject what has happened in the shocked tones adopted by Othello to express the physical disgust provoked by sex. Thus he does not kill them (though wishing to do so), out of concern that their souls should not be damned.

Frankford's solution is, in a sense, like that of Paolo in Chiarelli's play, and indeed of Briest. He decides to put his wife away. This action has tended to be regarded as a virtuous response, and indeed the whole play is viewed as having a homiletic nature, displaying the rightness of action which is informed by Christian virtue.[10] Although he tells his wife that he will not martyr her, or give her a bad name (as 'strumpet'), Frankford none the less seems to have aggressive intent, since he will 'with usage | Of more humility torment thy soul, | And kill thee, even with kindness' (13. 155–7).

The aggression contained within this decision has, it appears, no impact upon bystanders, who, with the inclusion of Anne herself, are struck by what they see as the virtue and honour of Frankford's

[10] H. H. Adams, *English Domestic or Homiletic Tragedy, 1575–1642* (New York, 1943), 144–59, for example.

action. It is, however, interesting that Anne decides that she will, in her seclusion, starve herself to death, thus regaining control over her own fate and at the same time relieving him of the guilt of actually killing her—which fits in conveniently with a plot and a whole work designed to promote the virtue of the husband.[11] (In so acting she sets the model for accommodating adulterous wives of later works who, like Emma Bovary, Anna Karenin, or Effi Briest, either obligingly dispose of themselves or conveniently fade away.) Frankford's distress when he learns that she is dying suggests that he may not have intended to kill her, particularly since he goes as far as to express the wish to die with her (p. 89). In her dying moments he also restores her to her position of honoured wife, and the play ends with his declaration that she was killed by his kindness.

What are we to make of this puzzling work? Is Frankford really a convoluted character who manages to achieve vengeance while conserving the reputation of purely virtuous husband, who cannot be condemned since he has not killed his wife as he might have done? That is, is he an extremely subtle form of the man of honour who manages to cover up paranoid immediate social concern for honour, and still retain a glowing social reputation based upon his Christian virtue? Cuckold he is not, for he is neither unaware nor indecisive. Nor can he be dismissed either as unfeeling or as unable to accommodate feeling. But there is an unsettling result from his clear intention to kill with kindness, even though one could construe that intention as being purely a verbal formula and not a statement of intent. In addition, although feeling is retained in his reaction to events, it is closely linked to Christian virtue, and Frankford is protected by a framework of virtue and action that contain his emotion. This contrasts with the failed attempt of Karenin to borrow a mode of Christian virtue and forgiveness in a situation in which he feels offended as public man, and too overcome by difficulty in relation to emotion to pursue his course of forgiveness.

At various points during the writing of this book it has been suggested to me that the subject of the deceived husband might

[11] In her action of killing herself by starvation Anne could be construed as making the same bid for control as is observed in anorexics. See references in Ch. 5, n. 7 for discussion of this.

become somehow irrelevant once one moved firmly into the twentieth century, in which—at least in Europe—marriage mores have been modified, even if marriage has not gone out of existence. Social pressures on the husband to take action, or even social views that mock the deceived husband, may have altered with time, but the underlying pressures in the situation of the deceived husband do not seem to disappear—the fear of betrayal, loss of a possession, the realization of failing powers and the approach of death. The logic of changed mores and expectations with regard to marriage may indeed focus more sharply than ever on the personal meaning of loss that is undergone by the deceived husband, without the distracting smokescreen of concern for public reputation that cloaked such personal reactions in earlier forms of portrayal of this type.

Perlimplín had provided one example of the cutting-through of conventions regarding marriage and adultery so that the focus is on the personal, and on the barely tolerable. Two novels by Julian Barnes from the 1980s provide contrasting yet related approaches. *Before She Met Me* (1982) shows a husband operating at the paranoiac extreme of the man of honour, and has an unusual conclusion (oddly related to that of Perlimplín), in that he obliges his wife to be the witness to his suicide.[12] In this novel, the husband's preoccupation with his wife's infidelities is kept relentlessly, obsessively in the foreground of the narrative. It is emphasized the more by the fact that his concern is not with any current infidelity, but with a type of infidelity *ante facto*—that is, with those lovers she had in her past. The boundlessness of the husband's suspicion and suffering dominate the novel to a level characteristic of the man of honour, but—a feature of the exaggerated form—with a note of comedy and ridicule that are associated elsewhere with the cuckold figure, and not with the supposed dignity of the man of honour.

In contrast with *Before She Met Me*, *Flaubert's Parrot* of 1984[13] is the most reticent and tangential of adultery texts, and indeed the reader could be forgiven for believing that adultery has

[12] For a full discussion of this novel, see Mark Millington and Alison Sinclair, 'The Honourable Cuckold: Models of Masculine Defence', *Comparative Literature Studies*, 29 (1) (1992), 1–19.

[13] Julian Barnes, *Flaubert's Parrot* (London, 1984). Page references will be to this edition and given within the text.

little or nothing to do with it, so discreet is its presence. Yet it *is* present, insidiously, with the tender pain of a barely healed wound. It is distinct in tone and approach from all other texts so far discussed.

The title of *Flaubert's Parrot* alerts us to at least three terms of reference for the novel. The reference to Flaubert provides an almost instant association to his character Emma Bovary, and to the novel which bears her name. The parrot, however, refers us to 'A Simple Heart' (Un coeur simple) of the *Trois contes* of 1877, published a good two decades after *Madame Bovary*. Here the dominating theme is of fidelity and devotion—a fidelity rendered the more feasible for the protagonist, Félicité, given that the object of her affections is unable to give her the unwelcome reward of betrayal. The parrot itself, however, contrary to Félicité's perceptions in 'A Simple Heart', can give no love: it is dead, stuffed, and unresponsive. The title reminds us, furthermore, that it is Flaubert's parrot, not Félicité's parrot. Barnes thus adds a dimension of dialogue between the 'real' and the supposed, between art and truth—ironizing the ideal that the real might exist, but not negating our desire to attain it, or, alternatively, to realize or evade that desire through art or imagination. This idea of the real, or the authentic, is sketched in the search of the narrator for the *real*, that is, the original, parrot, a search which leads to a series of look-alikes. The object of desire who will be eternally faithful emerges as elusive, inauthentic. It is as much a chimera as is the Romantic love desired and sought, but never attained, by Emma Bovary.

Flaubert's Parrot is a sophisticated, allusive text, but also a text of deception, since it contains, beneath the sophisticated surface, the complementary underside of the dull pain of betrayal and loss. The surface text of the novel purports to be a type of notebook reconstruction or account of an investigation into the life and works of Flaubert. Deeply embedded and almost hidden within this convention-challenging text is the anguish of the narrator, who will only after some time reveal himself as deceived. It is only gradually that the brief details of his family life emerge—the fact that he is now sixty, that his wife is no longer living, and that something—exactly what, the reader is not immediately told—marred his memory of his wife.

So convincing is its ingenuous, off-the-cuff, journalistic ease, so quirky and matter of fact its tone, that one could be forgiven for failing to notice initially that this is a novel with a narrator, rather than a whimsical revelation of the working account of a biographer's mind. Even when we perceive that narrator to be the fictional Geoffrey Braithwaite, the undertones of private suffering are well hidden beneath the diversionary and apparently primary task of reclaiming or recreating Flaubert the man. Clear if brief information that what we have on our hands is a narrator not an author does, however, come relatively early, in a reference that hints, through a trail of punctuation, that under the narrative there may lie a marital drama: 'But I was a doctor, married with children. You can only do one thing well: Flaubert knew that. Being a doctor was what I did well. My wife . . . died' (13). It will not be until the thirteenth of fifteen chapters that full detail of this drama will emerge.

The text is reticent about personal details affecting the narrator, but at the same time provides hints, clues, suppressed temptations to offer digression and allusion. At the level of both surface and subtext, the narrative's direct, conversational tone implies a reader, or a listener, but in contrast with other texts (*The Kreutzer Sonata*, for example), there is no clear sense of a tale being told to a masculine reader who might provide a type of masculine peer-validation. Initially it is emphasis and choice of detail in relation to Flaubert that will signal the underlying narrative, although the awareness of the significance of choice of detail cannot emerge until the personal drama is presented, retrospectively explaining the narrator's inner life through the way that he has externalized it. In the early chapters, the reader's attention is focused upon the narrator's excavation of Flaubert's life, with all the awareness that a narrative point of view will completely determine the nature of a biographical narrative. This is a point nicely made in the two versions of Flaubert's life, the first buoyant, positive, full of public reputation and achievement, the second dominated (significantly) by death, loss, illness (23–31). A third version, composed of quotations from Flaubert in the course of his life, provides the detailed, non-coherent, but intensely human counterpoint to the exaggerated extremities of the preceding two versions (32–7). The points about biography, autobiography, and narrative presentation gain additional poignancy when we apply them—or if we apply them (for we are not expressly invited to do so)—to the guarded and hesitant narrative made in the course of the text by the narrator about his marital misfortunes.

In the surface text we become aware of an interest in fidelity, in the devotion that endures everything, including death. True to his ironic master, Flaubert, Braithwaite the narrator considers, fascinated, the devotion of Félicité to others whom she serves (16). They all die or depart, save Loulou the parrot, which she is able to have stuffed. The suspicion that only true security may come from animals is reinforced by the section on dogs in chapter 4, where Flaubert's journal records an instance of how he and Du Camp were brought to safety in Greece by a village dog. In Braithwaite's exploration (18) of the possible links between Félicité, Loulou, and Flaubert (Félicité the one who feels love, Loulou the object of love, Flaubert the combination of the two) there is a veiled further exploration, namely of the notion that Flaubert externalized his own experience of loss and betrayal by the writing of his story, just as Braithwaite in turn externalizes his own parallel experience in his writing of Flaubert's story. The illusion that somewhere there might exist true fidelity is signalled in the account of Gertrude Collier's devotion to Flaubert (70–71). True to his master, Flaubert, Braithwaite follows this with an example of betrayal—this time by detailing how Gertrude's explorer son-in-law, Stanley, finding himself in difficulties in Africa, finally discarded all reading-matter save the Bible and Shakespeare, the last book to go being Flaubert's *Salammbô*. Devotion has betrayal as its inevitable sequel.

Other examples of betrayal in the diversionary surface text are as veiled as the one just referred to of Stanley's ultimate casting-off of his affection for Flaubert's writing. Thus Braithwaite's anger at Enid Starkie's 'betrayal' of Flaubert in her carelessness towards his text: 'It would be interesting to compare the time spent by Flaubert making sure that his heroine had the rare and difficult eyes of a tragic adulteress with the time spent by Dr Starkie in carelessly selling him short' (80).

Braithwaite's level of rage ('Now do you understand why I hate critics? I could try and describe to you the expression in my eyes at this moment; but they are far too discoloured by rage' (81)) seems far-fetched—until, that is, we decode the concern, and read it as the expression of the man who has suffered the infidelity of his wife.

What this text does in relation to the portrayal of the deceived husband discussed thus far is to bring a new and subtle variation to the subject, where the delineations of reaction explained by Kleinian theory are less immediately evident, but none the less capable of providing the basis of understanding. The central paradox of *Flaubert's Parrot* is that the issues of infidelity, its import and its impact, are heavily coded in the text, so that they are in the first instance defused and rendered more tolerable. But once the veils of coding are revealed fully in chapter 13 (a significant choice of number, one is tempted to speculate), the surprise is that Braithwaite, while being fully aware of his wife's infidelities, and alive to his own reactions to them, none the less seems to have reached a level of acceptance of them which goes beyond any of the other depressive and quasi-depressive examples considered up to this point. The puzzle is that the coding of the story so that it sits well below the surface narrative suggests that the underlying material is too hot, too painful to handle, and yet when the inner story is revealed—that is, in Braithwaite's own account of what happened—it appears to be an experience already handled, already now, in full knowledge of loss and betrayal, tolerated.

The encoding of the narrator's personal story suggests a defensive measure adopted in the face of difficulty. Instead of a situation of splitting and projection, however, we have a type of splitting that, like the communications of the schizophrenic, results in a displaced narrative, so that the one who is perceived to suffer loss, betrayal, and the general vicissitudes of human existence is not Braithwaite but the object of his literary and creative exploration, Flaubert. That is, Braithwaite, the deceived husband (as it eventually emerges), neither remains unaware of his state nor suspects it with the paranoia of the man of honour. He makes no attempts to deny it—other than in his hesitation and reticence about introducing himself into the narrative. What he does is to talk about it—under the guise of a text about those things that we might know, or might not know, about Flaubert.

In the emphasis on the uncertainty of knowledge, there is a clear bridging-point between the screen-narrative relating to Flaubert and the encoded narrative in which the narrator's knowledge of his marital situation and his reaction to it will clearly be an issue. The bare bones of the encoded narrative are spare, even sparse. More than that, by the time they emerge through the narrative they appear to be almost unremarkable, and yet by their nature seem potentially more dramatic than remarkable. Emphasized in this area of the text, as in the area dealing with literary excavations related to Flaubert, is the belief that truth and reality are what you make of them.

The same applies to Braithwaite, who, true to the image of the cuckold, is a man in his sixties. He is a doctor and his wife—he tells us—is dead. That there might be more to his story is hinted relatively early, in chapter 6, 'Emma Bovary's Eyes'. Here he suddenly emerges from and through the text with his writer's humanity: 'Look, writers aren't *perfect*, I want to cry; any more than husbands and wives are perfect. The only unfailing rule is, if they seem so, they can't be. I never thought my wife was perfect. I loved her, but I never deceived myself. I remember . . . But I'll keep that for another time' (76). In the following chapter he ventures further, first signalling the vulnerability of the armed man (and thus hinting both at his own man's vulnerability, but also at the short-cut to an awareness of death that the cuckold's story contains): '"If I make an appearance one day, it will be in full armour," had been his boast; but even in full armour the armpit and the groin are never completely protected' (83). That he quotes initially from Flaubert here is a sign of his tentative approach to the touchy subject of his own vulnerability and could be classed a defensive move; but that he glosses on Flaubert's words in his own persona as narrator, stressing the mortal and the sexual threats that cannot be protected against, reveals a depressive willingness to face a vulnerability that might be his just as much as it belongs to Flaubert. The ability to face at least the transitory nature of some states surfaces in his comment on the cross-channel ferries: 'I like these out-of-season crossings. When you're young, you prefer the vulgar months, the fullness of the seasons. As you grow older you learn to like the in-between times, the months that can't make up their minds. Perhaps it's a way of admitting that things can't ever bear the same certainty again. Or perhaps it's just a way of admitting a preference for empty ferries' (83).

If we were to consider that there might be a level of coding of difficult subject-matter in the names given to chapters, then we would here observe that a transitional stage of the narrative itself is being passed through. The preceding chapter, 'Emma Bovary's Eyes', was all about betrayal, albeit the betrayal of a created character by a critic. It was also a chapter in which, for the most part, the subject of the narrator's own suffering from marital deception was kept at a distance. All of this we could regard as a splitting-off from unwelcome information, with dislocation of it into another arena so as to render it safe. The title of this chapter, 'Cross Channel', overtly signals the subject-matter of cross-channel ferries, but also alludes to the narrator's venture into more risky territory, at least in regard to what he is about to relay to the reader. Thus the congruence also with the narrator's preference, stated in the next chapter, for transitional states. The move into the unknown—whether it be the unknown of the lover or the unknown of whether or not the lover will be faithful, or the unknown of the move first into maturity and then into ageing and death—all these are states which the narrator has been able to face, and faces again in the retelling of his life through the narrative. It is also in this chapter that the narrator reveals his hand, that is, he reveals that the retelling of the life and circumstances of Flaubert is not unrelated to his own story. He is still mysterious at this point about the contents of the personal stories (of the fictional 'real' situation, as it were), yet clear about the mechanism of displaced narrative focus: 'Three stories contend within me. One about Flaubert, one about Ellen, one about myself. My own is the simplest of the three—it hardly amounts to more than a convincing proof of my existence—and yet I find it the hardest to begin. My wife's is more complicated, and more urgent; yet I resist that too . . . Ellen's is a true story; perhaps it is even the reason why I am telling you Flaubert's story instead' (85). There is, admittedly, some level of splitting and distancing even here, in that he separates Ellen's story from his own, as though he were not affected by her life and its events, but the narrative honesty of the admission of diversionary tactics stand in counterbalance to this partial disowning of what actually must have concerned him.

Braithwaite is able to face some things quite squarely. He is prepared to call a spade a spade, to call 'mad' mad and 'adultery' adultery (91). On the other hand, by his own admission, he is not keen to provide a welter of information for the reader. This is partly a move of self-preservation. If the narrator remains relatively unknown to the reader, then the reader is left simply not in a position to judge the narrator's actions with regard to his wife's death. Braithwaite presents his reticence about his part in his wife's death within a discussion of information as such, and simply as a question of choice: 'Either I have to give you so much information about myself that you are forced to admit that I could no more have killed my wife than Flaubert committed suicide; or else I merely say, that's all, that's enough' (97). What Braithwaite as narrator does for himself as character is to avoid the fate of either cuckold or man of honour. This he does by moving himself out of the public arena—the place where the cuckold is ridiculed, and where the man of honour must fight for his reputation.

In some ways Braithwaite could be seen to be defending himself by coming clean, by appearing to be extremely open. He appears to be able to confront knowledge, and to talk about it, while simultaneously being guarded about it. Having been cautious about 'wanting to know the worst' (that is, about the infidelity or not of a spouse), and signalling its possible perverse nature, he admits briefly and frankly that 'I loved Ellen, and I wanted to know the worst' (126). He even follows this up with an observation that appears to come from a level of depressive-position acceptance: 'But here's the difference. With a lover, a wife, when you find the worst—be it infidelity or lack of love, madness or the suicidal spark—you are almost relieved. Life is as I thought it was; shall we now celebrate this disappointment?' (127). What is going on here is an internal dialogue within Braithwaite about whether or not to tell the truth (to the reader)—to go public—and whether or not this may take the form of art. But it is also a dialogue which challenges the reader to decide what he or she wants or requires of art—so that we too are involved in the consequences and dynamics of the revelation of the truth: 'Do you want art to be a healer? Send for the AMBULANCE GEORGE SAND. Do you want art to tell the truth? Send for the AMBULANCE FLAUBERT: though don't be surprised, when it arrives, if it runs over your leg' (136).

It emerges that Ellen had had affairs, and eventually committed suicide—or rather attempted to do so. She was left in a state where she was technically alive, but not more. It was left to Braithwaite to switch off the machine that kept her alive. In this modern version of events, two contradictory traditions are observed: the husband kills the erring wife, and (the alternative ending of the novel of adultery that absolves the husband of murderous guilt) the wife commits suicide. Because it is observed at a distance of time and person (none of the close observation of

Emma Bovary in her death-throes here), we are separated as readers from the event of Ellen's death. This very separation is, however, what permits us the approximation to Braithwaite's state as husband. He has, it should be said, gone through the motions of the jealous husband before this point—or rather, to be more accurate, in his account of himself he has spoken of his jealous reactions *before* reaching that sense of numbness in relation to her death. He relates simply: 'At first I was hurt; at first I minded, I thought less of myself' (163), and this standard reaction of the jealous, man-of-honour husband is provoked and preceded by first the bawdy joke which likens Betty Corrinder to the Eiffel Tower ('Not everyone's been up the Eiffel Tower'—a joke in the cuckold tradition) and Braithwaite's recall of the 'uncomplicated advice' of Dumas *fils*: 'Kill her'.

This particular account of a deceived husband alters the focus of attention from the outrage of the man who has lost reputation, or a possession, and centres instead on a man who grapples with the thickets and problems of ordinary life. Possession is clearly an issue that is touched on, and which we have an account of Braithwaite avoiding in Chapter 3, 'Finders Keepers', as he and another man become rivals for the copy of a volume by Turgenev. There are the overtones of sexual desire and sexual challenge insinuated into this anecdote, in the hand-on-hand gesture of the two men reaching for the same book. A neat illustration of the Girardian triangle, it might seem, but in fact a send-up of it. This is bibliophile lust (Barnes's term) rather than sexual lust, and their desire clearly for the object, and not for one another. The response is initially that of the duel of honour, 'Step outside and let's discuss it', but the outcome an inconclusive one of chat over tea.

This is another example of 'safe' possession, like that of Félicité and her parrot (safe because dead), the coded form allowing the betrayal to be recounted in greater detail. Similarly we have the coded information about betrayal relayed through the account of Louise Colet, betrayed by Flaubert, who points out the ineluctable facing of risk that love brings. Love for a woman is, as expressed by Louise, something quite different: 'I was different, you see. Prostitutes were uncomplicated; *grisettes* could be paid off too; men were different—friendship, however deep, had its known limits. But love? And losing yourself? And some partnership, some equality? he didn't dare risk it. I was the only woman to whom he was sufficiently drawn; and he chose, out of fear, to humiliate me' (141). Here the account of betrayal is passed through two angles to deflect attention from Braithwaite himself. He works on Flaubert for distraction, but does not take the obvious route of detailing the betrayal of the man with whom, on so many levels, he identifies, preferring instead to look at the woman who was betrayed by him.

But more significant than the above, which is picked out to show the congruence with other accounts of deceived husbands, is the fact that chapter 13 also reveals the story of a grappling with loss, death, and human isolation, but telling less of Ellen's infidelity than of her death. This might have been expected in the light of my comments in Chapter 3 about the connotations of death that can be held by the cuckold story, and at the same time provides a novel gloss on the way that the man of honour might be involved in his wife's death. It is as though the incidence of both infidelity and death as explored in previous examples is now defused of its original (or is it merely surface?) set of sexual connotations, and is seen now in the context of our mortal existence. Braithwaite's story—of himself and Ellen—dwells on her death and his sense of loss, and the fact of infidelity is, as it were, merely incidental, if inextricably attached to the circumstances which led to her death.

First, then, loss, and the facing of death. Only later will this be set in any context of the rest of Ellen's life and Braithwaite's view of it. It is Braithwaite's reaction to her death that is highlighted, and the reflection of the numbness, the not-knowingness that death plunges us into: 'I loved her; we were unhappy; I miss her. She didn't love me; we were unhappy; I miss her' (161). Then the reaction to her adultery emerges—but as a reaction alone, with no *anecdote* of what the adultery was about, no sense of the other. Braithwaite remains throughout focused on his wife alone, as though this were all that mattered. That is, he appears to remain within the primary dyadic relationship, and within the suffering and acceptance involved in such a relationship at various levels, without moving (one is tempted to add 'unnecessarily') into the jealous mode of the post-Oedipal relationship. Suddenly Oedipal jealousy and its developmental forbear, the Oedipus complex, is made to seem the more primitive, the less developed. By concentrating on his wife alone, Braithwaite excludes his concern with the other man or men as though to shift attention in that direction were diversionary, a sign of immaturity and non-growth (running counter to the idea that Oedipal-rooted activity is somehow the activity of maturity).

What this account highlights is the degree to which we could regard jealousy not as the *later* stage in development from the first dyadic relationship, but as an infantile stage in which people or characters have somehow got stuck, and which is thus a stage of impeded development. Characters such as Braithwaite are therefore arguably involved still in the depths of a primary dyadic relationship because this is the challenge of maturity—a challenge by the side of which all the 'between men' aspects of reactions to infidelity pale as being potentially life-saving red herrings designed to allow the deceived husband not to face the reality of what is happening to him: the betrayal within the dyadic relationship.

In the case of Braithwaite and Ellen, the betrayal is, it appears, multiple—the details without importance. At least they are counted as without importance for the narrative (though this may be a defensive feint employed by the narrator to avoid acquainting the reader with his drama—a possibility that is merely hinted at in the comments about art's being one sort of ambulance or another).

What emerges is the idea that infidelity may be the most extreme sign of human isolation, the negation of any union that might replace the first union before boundaries of mother and infant were established. Ellen's adultery is classed by her husband as part of her secret life, part of her despair, the main pathos of which is that these were areas inaccessible to him. That is, the infidelity is placed in the context of the unreachability of one human being by another. There is some ordinariness about it that Braithwaite classes as her 'mood', which came upon her at about fifty, and had also existed before the children. He protests that this is not a moral tale (and implies that it is about simple humanity): 'For God's sake, her life is not a moral tale. No one's is. All I'm saying is that both her secret life and her despair lay in the same inner chamber of her heart, inaccessible to me. I could touch the one no more than the other' (166). Ellen's despair is mirrored by that of her husband. They remind us that it is not together but separately that we face grief, loss, and the separation of death.

7
Conclusion: Love and Death

In the Western literary tradition, love and death appear regularly in conjunction with one another, death posited as the extreme, or perhaps the only possible expression, of true love, love the only human experience we have that appears sufficient to stand in counterpoise to our inevitable and ever approaching mortality. In the early part of this book I argued that the representation of cuckoldry in literature provides an artistic containment for our anxieties about physical waning, which will lead inexorably towards death. Here comedy sweetens the pill, as does distance, relieving the reader of the pain of identification with a male character whose fate he would presumably rather not share. Honour literature moves to a different point on the scale, dealing with human emotional vulnerability by defence, by the splitting-off and projecting-out of unwanted weakness, including the susceptibility to love and passion. The artistic distancing within honour literature expresses the splits of the honour code. This then leads to a secondary form of splitting between the spectator and the work, in that what we are invited to engage with is a code, a set of values, and that itself rests on the mechanism of disowning what is felt to be uncomfortable.

Some of the texts of Chapters 5 and 6 have brought us closest, in terms of a Kleinian reading, to the depressive position, in the degree to which they both represent and provoke a process of accommodation of painful and unwelcome knowledge. They have a further, crucial relationship with the depressive position because of the fundamental link it has with the experience of bereavement, a link which illustrates the degree to which experiences of love and death will continue to evoke one another, and provides the reason for their mutual stimulation, and re-stimulation.

It is no coincidence that the representation of the deceived husband as a man bereaved should occur so forcefully and so poignantly in some of the texts discussed. Throughout I have argued the relation between the feelings that follow on from the infidelity of a loved one, and the early emotional experiences of the small infant, different in their colouring and eventual import for the two sexes. In so far as infidelity may at its extremity be experienced if not as total loss, at least as the partial loss of an original good object (the faithful spouse), we can see the analogy between the fate of bereavement and the fate of the spouse deceived, and, in turn, the relation of both bereavement and the suffering of infidelity to the earliest losses incurred in life. For Klein, the mourning that follows bereavement is closely, indeed inextricably, linked with the earliest losses suffered by the child—the loss of the good mother, of the presence of the warmth and nourishment of the breast. In Klein's delineation of the depressive position, it is evident that even at the early infant stage, the breast which is lost already stands for a whole world, and its loss produces fears, suspicions, and a sense of remorse—presumably for what is phantasized as a wrong that has been done and for which the state of deprivation is a consequence and a retribution: 'The object which is being mourned is the mother's breast and all that the breast and the milk have come to stand for in the infant's mind: namely, love, goodness and security. All these are felt by the baby to be lost, and lost as a result of his own uncontrollable greedy and destructive phantasies and impulses against his mother's breasts.'[1]

Within this framework of terrible loss we can place the experience of Charles Bovary, of Karenin, and of Braithwaite, the narrator of *Flaubert's Parrot*. In all three of these novels (as so frequently in adultery novels—so frequently as to seem virtually inevitable in the telling of woman's infidelity) there is an actual bereavement, at least in the end. It is as though the literary representation of the fate of the deceived husband is obliged to provide a material demonstration of the extent and enormity of his loss. Yet as we saw, the sense that Karenin was bereaved occurred at the moment when he accepted Anna's departure as final, and the saddened acceptance of distance by Braithwaite anticipates by a noticeable margin the final physical loss of his wife.

For Klein, a fundamental feature of the infant's reactions in the

[1] Melanie Klein, 'Mourning and its Relation to Manic-Depressive States' (1940), in ead., *Love, Guilt and Reparation*, 344–69 (345).

depressive position, as noted in the quotation above, was the awakening of a sense of concern, and indeed of guilt or remorse for what was feared to have been the result of angry or destructive feelings towards the mother. Remorse, however, has been less evident in the discussions of the preceding pages—with the exception perhaps of Braithwaite's muted assessment of his marriage. This significant omission may indicate yet one more degree in which the depressive position regarding the wife's infidelity is only partially reached by the husbands of fiction and their (masculine) creators. Deceived husbands of literature may be accused of responsibility for their fate by the robust mode of the cuckold story, and they may brood in the novel of adultery, but literature in general appears to draw back from the disturbing consideration that their loss may be of their own making. This is perhaps just as well in so far as guilt in relation to loss will often be illusory. This is so in the loss of the mother (it is, of course, only the infant's phantasy that he is the cause of his loss). In another case, the loss of our own vitality, the loss is not illusory (there is nothing to be done), and in that loss of our own vitality, even if we might be partially responsible, there is nothing to be done. We could even take comfort in the perception that, for most people, while death is inevitable, it need not be construed as a personal castigation. On the other hand, the lack of remorse in the literary deceived husband may be an act of massive literary denial on the part of the patriarchal society that produces him. The other feature of the depressive position, however, the capacity for concern, as a reparative action in the face of acknowledged loss (and acknowledgement of possible responsibility) is clearly expressed in those deceived husbands who stand out for their sense of bereavement.

Other considerations of love and death spell out different messages. The denouement of *Memento Mori* (1959) by Muriel Spark suggests that in the face of death the infidelity of a spouse is of diminished import: there are weightier things to think about. The irony is in the close association between our feelings on betrayal, and those evinced by death as noted above. For Klein, we might note, loss and mourning in later life are sharpened in their impact by dint of being reawakenings of earlier trauma—and are not just related to death in so far as the loss of a beloved or an idealized beloved object is experienced as bereavement, but also in so far as the loss itself leaves the bereaved/deceived one in a state so terrible as to seem death-threatening. With that unerring ability to articulate the painful, she comments, in an essay of 1963, that 'throughout life the fear of death plays a part in loneliness'.[2] This is because with what is felt to be the death of the mother, the external mother, the infant also—for the moment—loses his image of the internal good mother, and is thus cast back into the frightening preceding stage of paranoid fragmentation where the feeling of threat to his own existence is paramount.

The equation between love and death is turned yet another way round in Klein's claim that the 'love' of Don Juan, most classic of lovers, is itself a defence (or indeed, one might say, an act of defiance) against the death of the loved one. Thus she asserts that the typical Don Juan 'is haunted by the dread of the death of loved people', and in his endless philanderings is proving to himself that 'his *one* greatly loved object (originally his mother, whose death he dreaded because he felt his love for her to be greedy and destructive), is not after all indispensable since he can always find another woman to whom he has passionate but shallow feelings'.[3] The link between Don Juan's feverish acts of dalliance (a repetition compulsion if ever there was one) and the concern of this book may seem elusive, except in so far as Don Juan represents a literary tradition of no small importance, and thus literature itself could be argued to flesh out the conviction that lies beneath his acts: it is a defiant rebuttal of emotional engagement with the other sex, and placed alongside the fate of man brought to sorrow by the treachery of women it confirms to all (the author and the masculine reader—if not the feminine one) that there is no really worthy object to be bothered about, so there is nothing really to be feared.

Melanie Klein's last paper, 'On the Sense of Loneliness' (1963, published posthumously) highlights in premonitory manner the essential solitude of the human condition, a solitude of which we get the earliest intimation in the first sense of separation from the mother. In Klein the sense of solitude is always tinged with desolation, unlike the concept of the 'lyrical I' of Winnicott, who described solitude in the presence of an implied other person, and in which

[2] 'On the Sense of Loneliness' (1964), in ead., *Envy and Gratitude*, 300–13 (304).

[3] Klein, 'Love, Guilt and Reparation', 306–43 (323).

the reassurance of the mother's presence is not felt to be lost.[4] In this last paper of Klein, and elsewhere in her work where she speaks of the urge to creativity and reproduction as reactions against our inexorable progress towards death, the sense of loneliness, and its most extreme form, death, is set alongside that thing that is first lost—the early sense of union with the mother experienced by the child, and in which is implied 'a close contact between the unconscious of the mother and of the child . . . the foundation for the most complete experience of being understood and . . . essentially linked with the preverbal stage'.[5] In the wake of this seamless shared (unconscious) experience, any later relation with another will contain 'an unsatisfied longing for an understanding without words' (ibid.). Union is impossible, separation inevitable, the first loss one which can only be repeated in later years. In this stark perception of the human condition little comfort is offered. At most we can, as in the depressive condition, accommodate ourselves to our fate. As such the deceived husband facing his loss, his bereavement, can become an icon for experience not just generalized but universal, and his extraordinary prominence in the literature of patriarchal society easier to grasp by dint of the strongly gendered terms in which it is clothed. Clothing, after all, need not be seen as disguise but, in later years, as a compassionate covering for our deficiencies.

[4] Donald Winnicott, 'The Capacity to be Alone' (1958), in id., *The Maturational Processes and the Facilitating Environment: Studies in the Theory of Emotional Development* (1965, repr. London, 1985), 29–36, in which he argues that initially the mother holds the child in play, and later the ego is able to 'hold' the self in solitude.

[5] 'On the Sense of Loneliness' (1963), 301.

Bibliography

GENERAL BIBLIOGRAPHY AND BACKGROUND WORKS

ARMSTRONG, J., *The Novel of Adultery* (London, 1976).

BAKHTIN, M., *Rabelais and his World* (1965), trans. H. Iswolsky (Cambridge (Mass.) and London, 1968).

BARKER, F., HULME, P., IVERSEN, M., and LOXLEY, D. (eds.), *The Politics of Theory* (Proceedings of the Essex Conference on the Sociology of Literature, July 1982), (Univ. of Essex, 1983).

BIANCHEDI, E. T. DE, SCALOZUB DE BOSCHAN, L., CORTIÑAS, P. DE, and PICCOLO, ELSA G. DE, 'Theories on Anxiety in Freud and Melanie Klein: Their Metapsychological Status', *International Journal of Psychoanalysis*, 69 (1988), 359–67.

BION, W., *Experiences in Groups* (London, 1961).

BLACK, M., *The Literature of Fidelity* (London, 1975).

BLOCH, R. H., 'Tristan, the Myth of the State and the Language of the Self', *Yale French Studies*, 51 (1974), 61–81.

—— *Medieval French Literature and Law* (Berkeley, Calif., 1977).

—— *Etymologies and Genealogies: A Literary Anthropology of the French Middle Ages* (Chicago and London, 1983).

BOULAY, J. DU, *Portrait of a Greek Mountain Village* (Oxford, 1974).

BOURDIEU, P., 'The Sentiment of Honour in Kabyle Society', trans. Philip Sherrard, in J. G. Peristiany (ed.), *Honour and Shame: The Values of Mediterranean Society* (London, 1965), 193–241.

—— 'The Berber House' (1971), in M. Douglas (ed.), *Rules and Meanings* (Harmondsworth, 1973), 98–110.

BOWIE, M., 'Jacques Lacan', in J. Sturrock (ed.), *Structuralism and Since* (Oxford, 1979), 116–53.

BRANDES, S., *Metaphors of Masculinity: Sex and Status in Andalusian Folklore* (Philadelphia, 1980).

CAILLOIS, R., *Les Jeux et les hommes* (1958), trans. M. Barash, as *Man, Play, and Games* (London, 1962).

CAMPBELL, J. K., *Honour, Family and Patronage: A Study of Institutions and Moral Values in a Greek Mountain Community* (Oxford, 1964).

CAPELLANUS, A., *The Art of Courtly Love*, trans. J. J. Parry (New York, 1969).

CARO BAROJA, J., 'Honour and Shame: A Historical Account of Several Conflicts', trans. from Spanish by R. Johnson, in J. G. Peristiany (ed.), *Honour and Shame: The Values of Mediterranean Society* (London, 1965), 81–137.

CASTRO, A., *De la edad conflictiva* (2nd edn.; Madrid, 1961).

CIRLOT, J. E., *A Dictionary of Symbols*, trans. from Spanish by J. Sage (2nd edn.; London, 1962).

COCCHIARA, G., *Il Mondo alla rovescia* (Turin, 1963).

COEN, S. J., 'Pathological Jealousy', *International Journal of Psychoanalysis*, 68 (1987), 99–108.

COHEN, E. S., 'Honor and Gender in the Streets of Early Modern Rome', *Journal of Interdisciplinary History*, 22 (4) (Spring 1992), 597–625.

CORBETT, P., *The Roman Law of Marriage* (Oxford, 1930).

COWARD, R., *Patriarchal Precedents: Sexuality and Social Relations* (London, 1983).

DAVIS, N. Z., 'The Reasons of Misrule: Youth Groups and Charivaris in 16th-century France', *Past and Present*, 50 (1971), 41–75.

—— *Les Cultures du peuple* (originally *Society and Culture in Early Modern France* (1965), trans. into French by M.-N. Bourguet (Paris, 1979).

DONALDSON, I., *The World Upside Down* (Oxford, 1970).

DOUGLAS, M. (ed.), *Rules and Meanings* (Harmondsworth, 1973).

—— 'Jokes', in ead., *Implicit Meanings: Essays in Anthropology* (London and Boston, 1975), 90–114.

EASTHOPE, A., *What a Man's Gotta Do* (London, 1986).

EICHENBAUM, L., and ORBACH, S., *Understanding Women* (Harmondsworth, 1985).

FREUD, S., *The Standard Edition of the Complete Psychological Works of Sigmund Freud*, ed. S. E. Strachey (24 vols.; London, 1981).

—— 'Some Neurotic Mechanisms in Jealousy, Paranoia and Homosexuality' (1922), *SE* xviii. 223–32.

—— 'Anxiety and Instinctual Life', *New Introductory Lectures in Psychoanalysis* (1933), *SE* xxii. 81–111.

—— 'The Dissection of the Psychical Personality', *New Introductory Lectures in Psychoanalysis* (1933), *SE* xxii. 57–80.

FROMM, E., *The Forgotten Language: An Introduction to the Understanding of Dreams, Fairy Tales and Myths* (London, 1952).

GALLOP, J., *Feminism and Psychoanalysis: The Daughter's Seduction* (London and Basingstoke, 1982).

GIRARD, R., *Deceit, Desire and the Novel: Self and Other in Literary Structure* (original French version, *Mensonge romantique et vérité romanesque*, Paris, 1961), trans. Yvonne Freccero (Baltimore, 1965).

GIVEN-WILSON, C., and CURTEIS, A., *The Royal Bastards of Medieval England* (London, 1984).

GOODY, J., 'A Comparative Approach to Incest and Adultery', *Comparative Studies in Kinship* (London, 1969).

GRANT, H., 'El Mundo al revés', in D. M. Atkinson and A. H. Clarke (eds.), *Hispanic Studies in Honour of Joseph Manson* (Oxford, 1972).

GRANT, H., 'The World Upside-Down', in R. O. Jones (ed.), *Studies in Spanish Literature of the Golden Age Presented to Edward M. Wilson* (London, 1973).

—— 'Images et gravures du monde à l'envers dans leurs relations avec la pensée et la littérature espagnoles', in J. Lafond and A. Redondo (eds.), *L'Image du monde renversé et ses représentations littéraires et para-littéraires de la fin du XVe siècle au milieu du XVIIe. Colloque international, Tours, 17–19 nov. 1977* (Paris, 1979).

HART, S. M., 'Some Examples of the *Topos* of the World Upside-Down in Modern Hispanic Literature and Art', *Revista Canadiense de Estudios Hispánicos*, 12 (3) (Spring 1988), 459–72.

HINSHELWOOD, R. D., *A Dictionary of Kleinian Thought* (London, 1991).

HORNEY, K., 'The Flight from Womanhood', in J. Baker Miller (ed.), *Psychoanalysis of Women* (Harmondsworth, 1974).

JAQUES, E., 'Death and the Mid-Life Crisis', *International Journal of Psychoanalysis*, 46 (1965), 502–14.

JAMES, C., 'W. R. Bion's Contribution to the Field of Psychotherapy: An Appreciation', in L. Wolberg and M. Aronson (eds.), *Group and Family Therapy* (New York, 1981).

—— 'Bion's "Containing" and Winnicott's "Holding" in the Context of the Group Matrix', *International Journal of Group Psychotherapy*, 34 (2) (Apr. 1984), 201–13.

JONES, E., 'Jealousy' (1929), in id., *Papers on Psychoanalysis* (5th edn.; London, 1948), 325–40.

KELLER, E. F., *Reflections on Gender and Science* (New Haven, Conn., and London, 1985).

KIERKEGAARD, S., *Two Ages: The Age of Revolution and the Present Age: A Literary Review* (1846), ed. and trans. H. V. Hong and E. H. Hong (Princeton, NJ, 1978).

KLEIN, M., *Envy and Gratitude and Other Works 1946–1963* (London, 1988), introduction by H. Segal, includes: 'Notes on Some Schizoid Mechanisms' (1946), 1–24; and 'A Study of Envy and Gratitude' (1957), 176–235.

—— *Love, Guilt and Reparation and Other Works 1921–1942* (London, 1988), introduction by H. Segal, includes: 'Early Stages of the Oedipus Conflict' (1928), 186–98; 'Love, Guilt and Reparation' (1937), 306–43; and 'The Oedipus Complex in the Light of Early Anxieties' (1945), 370–419.

KNIGHT, C., 'Lévi-Strauss and the Dragon: *Mythologiques* Reconsidered in the Light of an Australian Aboriginal Myth', *Man* (NS), 18 (1) (Mar. 1983), 21–50.

LEMPRIÈRE, J., *Classical Dictionary of Proper Names Mentioned in Ancient Authors Writ Large* (1788) (3rd edn.; London, 1984).

LLOYD, G., *The Man of Reason: 'Male' and 'Female' in Western Philosophy* (London, 1984).
LODGE, D., *After Bakhtin* (London and New York, 1990).
MACDOWELL, D. M., *The Law in Classical Athens* (London, 1978).
MAKARIUS, L., 'Ritual Clowns and Symbolical Behaviour', *Diogenes*, 69 (1) (1970), 44–73.
MITCHELL, J., *Psychoanalysis and Feminism* (Harmondsworth, 1974).
—— and ROSE, J., *Feminine Sexuality* (London, 1982).
NEUSCHEL, K. B., *Word of Honor: Interpreting Noble Culture in Sixteenth-Century France* (Ithaca, NY, and London, 1989).
NICOLL, A., *Masks, Mimes and Miracles* (London, 1931).
PERISTIANY, J. G. (ed.), *Honour and Shame: The Values of Mediterranean Society* (London, 1965).
PETERSON, C. L., *The Determined Reader: Gender and Culture in the Novel from Napoleon to Victoria* (New Jersey, 1986).
PITT-RIVERS, J., 'Honour and Social Status', in J. G. Peristiany (ed.), *Honour and Shame: The Values of Mediterranean Society* (London, 1965), 21–77.
PLECK, J. H., *The Myth of Masculinity* (Cambridge, Mass., 1981).
PORTER, R., *A Social History of Madness* (1987, repr. London, 1989).
RADFORD, E., and RADFORD, M. A., *Encyclopedia of Superstitions* (1948), ed. and rev. C. Hole (3rd impr. London, 1961).
RENOIR, A., 'The Inept Lover and the Reluctant Mistress: Remarks on Sexual Inefficiency in Medieval Literature', in E. Vasta and Z. P. Thundy (eds.), *Chaucerian Problems and Perspectives: Essays Presented to Paul E. Beichner* (London, 1979), 180–206.
REYNAUD, E., *Holy Virility: The Social Construction of Masculinity*, trans. R. Schwarz (London, 1983).
RIVIÈRE, J., 'Jealousy as a Mechanism of Defence', *International Journal of Psychoanalysis*, 13 (1932), 414–24.
ROPER, L., 'Will and Honor: Sex, Words and Power in Augsburg Criminal Trials', *Radical History Review*, 43 (1989), 45–71.
ROUGEMENT, D. DE, *Love in the Western World* (1940), rev. and augm., trans. M. Belgion (Princeton, NJ, 1983).
RUSTIN, M., 'Kleinian Psychoanalysis and the Theory of Culture', in F. Barker *et al.* (eds.), *The Politics of Theory* (Proceedings of the Essex Conference on the Sociology of Literature, July 1982) (Univ. of Essex, 1983), 57–70.
SÁNCHEZ PÉREZ, F., *La Liturgia del espacio* (Madrid, 1990).
SAND, M., *The History of the Harlequinade* (London, 1915).
SEARLES, H., 'Schizophrenic Communication' (1961), in id., *Collected Papers on Schizophrenia and Related Subjects* (1965, repr. London, 1986), 381–428.
SEDGWICK, E. KOSOFSKY, *Between Men* (Columbia, SC, 1985).

SEGAL, H., 'Notes on Symbol Formation', *International Journal of Psychoanalysis*, 38 (1957), 391–7, republ. in *The Work of Hanna Segal* (New York, 1981), 49–64.

—— *Introduction to the Work of Melanie Klein* (London, 1986).

SEGAL, N., *The Unintended Reader: Feminism and 'Manon Lescaut'* (Cambridge, 1986).

—— *Narcissus and Echo* (Manchester, 1988).

SEYMOUR, G., 'A Reply to Michael Rustin: Kleinian Psychoanalysis and the Theory of Culture', in F. Barker *et al.* (eds.), *The Politics of Theory* (Proceedings of the Essex Conference on the Sociology of Literature, July 1982) (Univ. of Essex, 1983), 71–8.

SHOWALTER, E., *The Female Malady* (London, 1987).

SMITH, P., 'Perfect Murderers', *New Statesman*, 7 July 1989, 14–16.

SNOW, E. A., 'Sexual Anxiety and the Male Order of Things in *Othello*', *English Literary Renaissance*, 10 (1980), 384–412.

SONTAG, S., *Illness as Metaphor* (1977, repr. Harmondsworth, 1983).

SPIELMAN, P. M., 'Envy and Jealousy: An Attempt at Clarification', *Psychoanalytical Quarterly*, 40 (1971), 59–82.

STOLLER, R., *Presentations of Gender* (London and New Haven, Conn., 1985).

TANNER, T., *Adultery in the Novel* (Baltimore, 1979).

UNAMUNO, M. DE, *En torno al casticismo*, *Obras completas*, ed. M. García Blanco (9 vols.; Madrid, 1966), i. 818–22.

WEISSER, M. R., *The Peasants of the Montes: The Roots of Rural Rebellion in Spain* (Chicago and London, 1976).

ZEID, A. A. M., 'Honour and Shame Among the Bedouins of Egypt', in J. G. Peristiany (ed.), *Honour and Shame: The Values of Mediterranean Society* (London, 1965), 245–59.

LITERARY TEXTS

ALAS, L. (CLARÍN), *La Regenta* (1884–5), trans. J. Rutherford (Harmondsworth, 1984).

BARNES, J., *Before She Met Me* (London, 1982).

—— *Flaubert's Parrot* (London, 1984).

BOCCACCIO, G., *Il Decameron* (The Decameron) (1350), trans. G. J. McWilliam (Harmondsworth, 1972).

CALDERÓN DE LA BARCA, P., *A secreto agravio, secreta venganza* (Secret Revenge for a Secret Fault) (1635), in id., *Obras completas*, ed. A. Valbuena Briones (3 vols.; Madrid, 1966, repr. 1969), i.

—— *El Médico de su honra* (The Physician of His Honour), in id., *Obras completas*, ed. A. Valbuena Briones (3 vols.; Madrid, 1966, repr.

1969), i, trans. Gwynne Edwards as *The Surgeon of Honour* in *Calderón Plays: One* (London, 1991).

CERVANTES, M. de, *El celoso extremeño* (The Jealous Extremaduran) in *Novelas ejemplares* (Exemplary Stories) (1613), ed. J. B. Avalle-Arce (2 vols.; Madrid, 1982), trans. C. A. Jones (Harmondsworth, 1972).

—— *El viejo celoso* (The Jealous Extremaduran) in *Entremeses* (The Interludes of Cervantes) (1615), trans. S. Griswold Morley (Princeton, NJ, 1948).

CHAUCER, G., *The Canterbury Tales* (1387–), *The Riverside Chaucer*, ed. Larry D. Benson (Oxford, 1987).

CHIARELLI, L., *La Maschera ed il volto* (The Mask and the Face) (1916), trans. N. de V. Beamish, in *International Modern Plays*, ed. A. Dent (London, 1950).

DAVIES, R., *The Lyre of Orpheus* (Harmondsworth, 1989).

DICKENS, C., *Dombey and Son* (1846–7), ed. P. Fairclough (Harmondsworth, 1970).

FALKBERGET, J., *Den Fjerde Natlevakt* (The Fourth Night Watch) (1923), trans. R. G. Popperwell (Madison, Wis., and London, 1968).

FLAUBERT, G., *Madame Bovary* (1857), trans. A. Russell (Harmondsworth, 1950).

FONTANE, T., *Effi Briest* (1895), trans. D. Parmée (Harmondsworth, 1987).

GALSWORTHY, J., *The Silver Spoon* (1926), middle novel of the second Forsyte trilogy.

GARCÍA LORCA, F., *El Amor de don Perlimplín con Belisa en su jardín* (The Love of Don Perlimplín with Belisa in the Garden) (1933), *Obras completas*, ed. A. de Hoyo (2 vols.; Madrid, 1980), ii. 321–60, trans. Gwynne Edwards, *Lorca Plays: Two* (London, 1990), 41–64.

HEYWOOD, T., *A Woman Killed with Kindness* (1607), ed. B. Scobie, The New Mermaids, gen. ed. B. Gibbons (London, 1985).

LAFAYETTE, MME DE, *La Princesse de Clèves* (1678), trans. N. Mitford (1962, rev. edn. Harmondsworth, 1978).

SHAKESPEARE, W., *Othello*, in *William Shakespeare: The Complete Works*, ed. Stanley Wells (Oxford, 1986).

—— *The Winter's Tale*, in *William Shakespeare: The Complete Works*, ed. Stanley Wells (Oxford, 1986).

TOLSTOY, L., *Anna Karenin* (1874–6), trans. R. Edmonds (Harmondsworth, 1954, repr. 1968).

—— *The Kreutzer Sonata and Other Stories*, trans. D. McDuff (Harmondsworth, 1985).

TROLLOPE, A., *He Knew He Was Right* (1868–9) (Oxford, 1986).

VEGA, LOPE DE, *El Castigo sin venganza* (Punishment Without Revenge) (1635), ed. C. A. Jones (Oxford, 1966).

VEGA, LOPE DE, *Los Comendadores de Córdoba* (The Knights Commander of Córdoba) (1596), edn. of Real Academia Española: *Biblioteca de Autores Españoles*, xxiv (Madrid, 1968).

LITERARY TEXTS: SECONDARY WORKS

ADAMS, H. H., *English Domestic or Homiletic Tragedy, 1575–1642* (New York, 1943).

ARMSTRONG, J., *The Unsaid 'Anna Karenina'* (London, 1988).

AUERBACH, N., 'Dickens and Dombey: A Daughter After All', *Dickens Studies Annual*, 5 (1976), 95–114.

AVERY, G. C., 'The Chinese Wall: Fontane's Psychograph of Effi Briest', in K. S. Weimar (ed.), *Views and Reviews of Modern German Literature* (Munich, 1974), 18–38.

BANCE, A., 'The Heroic and the Unheroic in Fontane', in J. Thunecke (ed.), *Formen realisticher Erzählkunst* (Nottingham, 1979), 404–5.

BARBER, C., *The Theme of Honour's Tongue: A Study of Social Attitudes in the English Drama from Shakespeare to Dryden*, Gothenburg Studies in English 58 (Gothenburg, 1985).

BOOTHMAN, J., '"Who hath no wyf, he is no cokewold": A Study of John and January in Chaucer's Miller's and Merchant's Tales', *Thoth*, 4 (1963), 3–14.

BOWERS, F., *Elizabethan Revenge Tragedy, 1587–1642* (Princeton, NJ, 1940).

BOYD, A. F., 'An Anatomy of Marriage: Leo Tolstoy and *Anna Karenin*', in id., *Aspects of the Russian Novel* (London, 1972), 87–108.

BRADLEY, A. C., *Shakespearian Tragedy* (London, 1905).

BREWER, D. S., 'The Fabliaux', in B. Rowland (ed.), *Companion to Chaucer Studies* (Toronto, 1968).

—— *Chaucer and His World* (London, 1978).

—— *Symbolic Stories* (Woodbridge, 1980).

BRYSON, F. R., *The Point of Honor in Sixteenth-century Italy: An Aspect of the Life of the Gentleman* (New York, 1935).

CALDER, A., 'Man, Woman and Male Woman: Tolstoy's *Anna* and After', in id., *Russia Discovered: Nineteenth-Century Fiction from Pushkin to Chekhov* (London, 1976), 211–36.

CASA, F., 'Honor and the Wife-Killers of Calderón', *Bulletin of the Comediantes*, 29 (1) (1977), 6–23.

Coleridge's Criticism of Shakespeare, sel. and ed. R. A. Foakes (London, 1989).

COLLAS, I. K., *Madame Bovary: A Psychoanalytical Reading* (Geneva, 1985).

COOK, D., '*A Woman Killed with Kindness*: An Unshakespearian Tragedy', *English Studies*, 45 (1964), 353–72.

COOKE, T. D., *The Old French and Chaucerian Fabliaux: A Study of their Comic Climax* (Columbia and London, 1978).

COUNCIL, N., *When Honour's at the Stake* (London, 1973).

CRUICKSHANK, D. W., '"Pongo mi mano en sangre bañada a la puerta": Adultery in *El Médico de su honra*', in R. O. Jones (ed.), *Studies in Spanish Literature of the Golden Age Presented to E. M. Wilson* (London, 1973), 45–62.

—— Introduction to *El Médico de su honra* (Madrid, 1986).

CRUZ, A. J., '*Homo ex machina*? Male Bonding in Calderón's *A secreto agravio, secreta venganza*', *Forum for Modern Language Studies*, 25 (2) (Apr. 1989), 151–66.

CZYBA, L., *Mythes et idéologie de la femme dans les romans de Flaubert* (Lyon, 1983).

DABNEY, R. H., *Love and Property in the Novels of Dickens* (London, 1967).

DAVIE, D., 'Tolstoy, Lermontov and Others', in id. (ed.), *Russian Literature and Modern English Fiction* (Chicago, 1965), 164–99.

ELLIS, K., 'Ambiguity and Point of View in Some Novelistic Representations of Jealousy', *Modern Language Notes*, 80 (1971), 891–909.

EVANS, C. A., 'New Wine in Old Bottles: On Appropriating Male Speech in *Effi Briest*', *Germanic Notes*, 19 (3) (1988), 38–41.

FERRANTE, J. M., 'The Frame Characters in the *Decameron*: A Progression of Virtues', *Romance Philology*, 19 (1965), 212–26.

FINEMAN, J., 'Fratricide and Cuckoldry: Shakespeare's Doubles', in M. M. Schwarz and C. Kahn (eds.), *Representing Shakespeare* (Baltimore and London, 1980, repr. in paperback 1982), 70–109.

FURST, L., '*Madame Bovary* and *Effi Briest*', *Romanistisches Jahrbuch*, 12 (1961), 124–35.

—— 'The Role of Food in *Madame Bovary*', *Orbis Litterarum*, 34 (1) (1979), 53–65.

GAINES, J. F., *Social Structures in Molière's Theatre* (Columbus, Oh., 1984).

GIFFORD, H., 'Further Notes on *Anna Karenina*', in D. Davie (ed.), *Russian Literature and Modern English Fiction* (Chicago, 1965), 160–63.

GREENE, T., 'Forms of Accommodation in the *Decameron*', *Italica*, 45 (1968), 297–313.

GRIVELET, M., *Thomas Heywood et le drame domestique élisabéthain* (Paris, 1975).

GUNN, E., *A Daring Coiffeur: Reflections on 'War and Peace' and 'Anna*

Karenina' (London, 1971).

HARTOG, D. DEN, *Dickens and Romantic Psychology: The Self in Time in Nineteenth-Century Literature* (Basingstoke, 1987).

JACKSON, A., 'Reward, Punishment and the Conclusion of *Dombey and Son*', *Dickens Studies Annual*, 7 (1978), 103–28.

JONES, C. A., 'Spanish Honour as Historical Phenomenon, Convention and Artistic Motive', *Hispanic Review*, 33 (1965), 32–9.

JONES, G. F., *Honor in German Literature* (Chapel Hill, 1959).

KAHN, C., *Man's Estate: Masculine Identity in Shakespeare* (Berkeley, Calif., 1981).

KNIGHT, G. W., 'The Othello Music', in id., *The Wheel of Fire* (London, 1930), 107–31.

KOVEL, J., '*Othello*', in M. Solomon (ed.), *Myth, Creativity, Psychoanalysis: Essays in Honor of Harry Slochower* (Detroit, 1978), 113–19.

LABANYI, J., 'City, Country and Adultery in *La Regenta*', *Bulletin of Hispanic Studies*, 43 (1986), 53–66.

—— 'Mysticism and Hysteria in *La Regenta*: The Problem of Female Identity', in L. P. Condé and S. M. Hart (eds.), *Feminist Readings on Spanish and Latin-American literature* (Lampeter, 1991), 37–46.

LARSON, D., *The Honor Plays of Lope de Vega* (Cambridge, Mass., 1977).

LATTRE, A. DE, *La Bêtise d'Emma Bovary* (Paris, 1980).

LEAVIS, F. R., 'The Criticism of Shakespeare's Late Plays', in id., *The Common Pursuit* (London, 1958), 173–81.

MCCRARY, W., 'The Theatricality of Male Orientation in the *Comedia*', in R. Fiore, E. W. Hesse, J. E. Keller, and J. A. Madrigal (eds.), *Studies in Honor of William C. McCrary* (Lincoln, Nebr., 1986), 27–33.

MCKENDRICK, M. C., *Woman and Society in the Spanish Drama of the Golden Age: A Study of the 'mujer varonil'* (Cambridge, 1974).

—— 'Celebration or Subversion: *Los Comendadores de Córdoba* Reconsidered', *Bulletin of Hispanic Studies*, 41 (1984), 352–60.

—— 'Honour/Vengeance in the Spanish *Comedia*: A Case of Mimetic Transference?', *Modern Language Review*, 79 (1984), 313–35.

MANN, J., *Chaucer and Medieval Estates Satire: The Literature of Social Classes and the General Prologue of the Canterbury Tales* (Cambridge, 1973).

—— *Geoffrey Chaucer* (London, 1991).

MAZZOTTA, G., *The World at Play in Boccaccio's 'Decameron'* (Princeton, NJ, 1986).

MILLINGTON, M., and SINCLAIR, A., 'The Honourable Cuckold: Models of Masculine Defence', *Comparative Literature Studies*, 29 (1) (1992), 1–19.

MINDEN, M., '*Effi Briest* and *Die Historische Stunde des Takts*', *Modern Language Review*, 76 (4) (1981), 869–79.

MØLLER, P. U., *Postlude to 'The Kreutzer Sonata': Tolstoy and the Debate on Sexual Morality in Russian Literature in the 1890s*, trans. from Danish by John Kendal (Leiden, 1988).

MONTAUT, M., 'The Second Mrs Dombey', *Dickens Quarterly*, 4 (3) (Sept. 1987), 141–53.

MOYNAHAN, J., 'Dealings with the Firm of Dombey and Son: Firmness versus Wetness', in J. Gross and G. Pearson (eds.), *Dickens in the Twentieth Century* (London, 1962), 121–32.

MUSCATINE, C., *Chaucer and the French Tradition* (6th impr., Berkeley (Calif.), 1969).

NEILL, M., 'Changing Places in *Othello*', *Shakespeare Survey*, 37 (1984), 115–31.

NIMETZ, M., '*Eros* and *Ecclesia* in Clarín's Vetusta', *Modern Language Notes*, 86 (2) (1971), 242–53.

NYKROG, P., *Les Fabliaux* (Copenhagen, 1957, repr. Geneva, 1973).

PARTEN, A. C., 'Cuckoldry in Shakespeare' (Ph.D. thesis, Yale, 1983).

PATERSON, A. K. G., 'The Alchemical Marriage in Calderón's *El Médico de su honra*', *Romanistisches Jahrbuch*, 30 (1979), 263–82.

—— 'Calderón's *A secreto agravio, secreta venganza*: A Theatre of the Passions', *Modern Language Review*, 79 (1984), 589–608.

PODOL, P., 'Non-conventional Treatment of the Honour Theme in the Theater of the Golden Age', *Revista de Estudios Hispánicos*, 7 (1973), 449–63.

POTTER, J. H., *Five Frames for the Decameron: Communication and Social Systems in the Cornice* (Princeton, NJ, 1982).

PRING-MILL, R. D. F., Introduction to *Lope de Vega (Five Plays)*, trans. Jill Booty (New York, 1961).

RIECHEL, D. C., '*Effi Briest* and the Calendar of Fate', *Germanic Review*, 48 (3) (May 1973), 189–211.

RITCHIE, J. M., 'Embarrassment, Ambiguity and Ambivalence in Fontane's *Effi Briest*', in J. Thunecke (ed.), *Formen realisticher Erzählkunst* (Nottingham, 1979), 563–9.

SÁNCHEZ, R., 'The Theater in Clarín's *La Regenta*', *Hispanic Review*, 37 (1969), 491–509.

SÁNCHEZ-EPPLER, B., 'Stakes: The Sexual Vulnerability of the Reader', *Romanic Review*, 78 (1987), 202–17.

SANDERS, W., *The Winter's Tale*, Harvester New Critical Introductions to Shakespeare (Brighton, 1987).

SCHWARZ, M. M., and KAHN, C. (eds.), *Representing Shakespeare* (Baltimore and London, 1980), 70–109.

SEMPRÚN DONAHUE, M. DE, 'La Doble Seducción de *La Regenta*', *Papeles de Son Armadans*, 71 (211) (1973), 209–28.

SIEBURTH, S., *Reading 'La Regenta': Duplicitous Discourse and the Entropy of Structure* (Amsterdam, 1990).

SINCLAIR, A., 'Avant-garde Theatre and the Return to Dionysos', in P. Collier and J. Davies (eds.), *Modernism and the European Unconscious* (Cambridge, 1990), 246–64.

—— 'The Consuming Passion: Appetite and Hunger in *La Regenta*', *Bulletin of Hispanic Studies*, 59 (3) (July 1992), 245–61.

SPEARING, A. C., 'Chaucerian Authority and Inheritance', in P. Boitani and A. Torti (eds.), *Literature in 14th-century England* (The J. A. W. Bennett Memorial Lectures; Perugia, 1981–2) (Cambridge, 1983).

SPEIRS, L., '*Anna Karenina*: A Study in Structure', *Neophilologus*, 50 (1966).

STARKIE, E., *Flaubert: The Making of the Master* (London, 1967).

STEEGMULLER, F., *Flaubert and 'Madame Bovary'* (London, 1958).

STENBOCK-FERMOR, E., *The Architecture of 'Anna Karenina'* (Lisse, 1975).

SWALES, E., 'Private Mythologies and Public Unease: On Fontane's *Effi Briest*', *Modern Language Review*, 75 (1980), 114–23.

VALIS, N. DE, *The Decadent Vision in Leopoldo Alas* (Baton Rouge, La., and London, 1981).

WADSWORTH, P. A., *Molière and the Italian Theatrical Tradition* (York, SC, 1977).

WANGH, M., '*Othello*: The Tragedy of Iago', *Psychoanalytical Quarterly*, 19 (1950), 202–12.

WARDROPPER, B. W., 'Poetry and Drama in Calderón's *El Médico de su honra*', *Romanic Review*, 49 (1958), 3–11.

WATSON, C. B., *Shakespeare and the Renaissance Concept of Honour* (Princeton, NJ, 1960).

WILSON, E. M., 'Family Honour in the Plays of Shakespeare's Predecessors and Contemporaries', in id., *Essays and Studies* (London, 1953).

—— '*Othello*, a Tragedy of Honour', *The Listener*, 5 June 1952, 926–7, collected in id., *Spanish and English Literature of the 16th and 17th Centuries: Studies in Discretion, Illusion and Mutability* (Cambridge, 1980).

ZUCKERMAN-INGBER, A., *El Bien más alto: A Reconsideration of Lope de Vega's Honor Plays* (Univ. of Florida Monographs (Humanities) 56 (Gainesville, Fla., 1984).

ZWINGER, L., 'The Fear of the Father: Dombey and Daughter', *Nineteenth-Century Fiction*, 39 (4) (Mar. 1985), 420–40.

Index

accommodation 28, 51, 52, 54, 65, 79, 95, 109, 118, 131, 132, 195, 231, 247–8, 254, 265, 281
Adams, H. H. 264
administration, *see* husband: profession of
adulterer, *see* lover
adulteress:
husband of 16, 24, 28, 32
see also Alas: Víctor Ozores; Dickens: Dombey; Flaubert: Bovary; Fontane: Innstetten; Heywood: Frankford; Tolstoy: Karenin, Pozdnyshev; Trollope: Trevelyan; wife: guilty
adulterous triangle, *see* triangles
adultery 18
criminalization of 47
etymology of 46–8
laws about 20–2
see also novel of adultery
age 26, 133, 188, 190, 215
positively viewed 91–2
age-appropriate activity 79
age-bar for lovers 71–2, 90
disregarded 72, 90
ageing 65, 72–3, 75, 76–9, 110, 111, 155, 157–8, 246, 272
acceptance of 110
January symbolizes 76–7, 78–9
and sexuality 90
and women 90
Agilulf, King, *see* Boccaccio
Agilulf's groom, *see* Boccaccio
Alas, L. 199–217
Fermín 201–2, 204, 207, 210–11, 212–17; mother of 176, 212–13, 215–16
Frígilis 202, 208, 209–10
Mesía, Alvaro 201, 204–7
Ozores, Ana 174, 193, 201–2, 205–12, 214–15, 216–17
Ozores, Víctor 174, 199–200, 201, 202–3, 204–9, 211–12, 213–15, 217, 236, 240, 242–3, 244
La Regenta 174, 199–217
see also horns: on cock; cuckold; duel; honour; husband; lover; novel of adultery; wife
Alberto, *see* age; Boccaccio
Alisoun, *see* Chaucer
Alvaro Mesía, *see* Alas
amor, buen, see *buen amor*
amor, loco, see *loco amor*
Andalusia:
honour code in 86
masculinity in 41
angel in the house 210, 211
anorexia of wife 265
see also food
anthropology 19, 20, 22–3
see also du Boulay; Bourdieu; Brandes; Campbell; Caro Baroja; Douglas; Makarius; Peristiany; Pitt-Rivers; Zeid
anticlericalism 201
anxiety 3, 23, 110, 111, 113, 116, 120, 125, 126, 134, 140, 144, 150, 152, 155, 171, 172, 188, 203, 218, 219, 222, 238
see also Freud
Armstrong, J. 233–4, 236, 247, 249, 250, 251
Athens, classical, *see* law
audience, reaction of 123–4, 130, 134, 172
Auerbach, N. 218, 219, 220, 223
author 126, 134, 135, 144, 174, 185, 192, 219, 223, 226, 233–4, 247
authority 4, 5, 14, 17, 18, 27, 64, 73, 81, 100, 104, 106, 116, 122, 134, 157, 158, 210, 212
Avery, G. C. 194
awareness 7, 24, 37, 51, 65, 66, 79, 82, 98, 99, 102, 111, 112, 121, 148, 149, 155, 184, 196, 197, 199, 205, 207, 208, 209, 214, 216, 221, 222, 224, 225, 227, 232, 239, 253, 254, 256, 257, 265, 270, 271
of father 9, 10
of gender difference 9
lack of 37, 38, 69, 71, 87, 99, 135, 181, 182, 184, 202, 205, 207, 214, 215, 228, 238, 240, 243, 246, 249, 251, 255, 256, 262
of mother 9

surfeit of 99

Bakhtin, M. 60, 219
Bance, A. 194
Barber, C. 43, 101
Barnes, J. 266–76
Before She Met Me 266
Braithwaite 267–8, 269, 270–6
Ellen 268, 270, 272, 273–4, 275
Félicité 267
Flaubert 267, 268, 269, 270, 271, 272, 273, 274; 'A Simple Heart' 267
Flaubert's Parrot 266–76
bastards, *see* illegitimacy
Beatriz, *see* Vega, Lope de
Bedouins 107, 114
Belisa, *see* García Lorca
Berbers 114
bereavement 277, 278, 279, 281
see also loss
Bergson, H. 55
betrayal 11, 15, 16, 49, 57, 65, 71, 79, 80, 121, 153–4, 155, 158, 165, 168–70, 171, 211, 212, 213, 215, 243, 254, 255, 256, 264, 266, 267, 269, 270, 271, 274, 275, 276, 279
between men 11, 84–5, 112, 152, 165, 166, 202–10, 274, 276
Girard, R. 202, 228, 231
Kahn, C. 86, 113
Sedgwick, E. K. 83, 202–3
bildungsroman 24, 175–6
Bion, W. 2, 5–6, 8
blackness:
of Othello 170–1
Bloch, R. H. 20, 21, 22, 85
blood, *see* inheritance; purity
blood-letting to murder 121
Boccaccio 35, 37, 50, 52, 53, 80–96, 97, 99, 110
Agilulf 83–5; wife of 83–4
Agilulf's groom 83–4
Alberto 91–2, 94, 95, 254
betrayal 80
Chinzica, Ricciardo de 87, 91; wife of 87
class in 66–7
The Decameron 80–96
Dioneo 92; sensuality of 94–5; as shaman 95–6
Filomena 94
frame of *Decameron* 80–1, 92–5
Masetto of Lamporrecchio 89
Paganino 89
Pampinea 83, 92
plague 92–4
Puccio 91
Spinelloccio 85–7; wife of 85–7
Zeppa 85–7; wife of 85–7
see also age; ageing; cuckold; death; fabliaux; husband; lover; wife
bonding:
male 51–2, 152, 166, 202–7, 209–10
with reader 51–2, 202–3
see also collusion
Boothman, J. 79
du Boulay, J. 115, 117
boundaries 22, 34, 46, 54, 57, 63, 101, 107, 122, 204, 205, 215, 246, 276
Bourdieu, p. 22–3, 45
Bovary, Charles, *see* Flaubert
Bovary, Emma, *see* Flaubert
Bowers, F. 127
Bowie, M. 4
Bowlby, J. 8
Boyd, A. F. 234
Bozzle, *see* Trollope
Bradley, A. 163
Braithwaite, *see* Barnes
Brandes, S. 41, 86
Brewer, D. 26, 66, 76, 78
Briest, *see* Fontane
Bryson, F. R. 43, 127, 128
buen amor 262
bull 39, 40

Caillois, R. 60
Calder, A. 227, 249
Calderón de la Barca 120–1, 131, 142–55, 158–61
Gutierre 159, 160–1
Juan 143, 151–2, 153, 154
Leonor 146, 147, 148, 149, 150, 151, 153, 154, 155
Lope, Don 142–53, 154
Luis 148, 153–5
The Mayor of Zalamea 155
Mencía 160
The Physician of his Honour 121, 155, 158–61
Secret Revenge for a Secret Fault 120–1, 142–55
Campbell, J. K. 117
Capellanus, A. 71–2, 90

Carker, *see* Dickens
carnival 58–61, 96
  and change 61, 82
Caro Baroja, J. 45, 106, 108, 111, 118
Carrizales, *see* Cervantes
Casa, F. 141, 152
Casandra, *see* Vega, Lope de
castration:
  in etymology of cuckold 39–41
  fear of 10–12, 15, 158
Castro, A. 44, 111
Cervantes, M. de 254
  Carrizales 254
  cuckolds in 127, 131
  The Jealous Extremaduran 127, 254
  The Jealous Old Man 127, 254
Chaucer 1, 19, 37, 50, 53, 68, 72–3, 74, 75, 81, 99, 110
  Absalon 68–9, 71
  Alisoun 68–70
  Canterbury Tales 65–80; structure of 66–7
  class in 66
  Damian 70, 75, 78, 79
  January 72, 73–5, 81, 99
  John 67–8, 70–1
  and marriage 66
  May 75, 76–7, 79
  Merchant 72
  Merchant's Tale 70, 71–9
  Miller's Tale 50, 66–71
  Reeve 78
  Troilus and Criseyde 73
  see also cuckold; death; fabliaux; husband; lover; symbols; wife
Chiarelli:
  The Mask and the Face 258–61
  Paolo 259, 260, 261
  Savina 259
Chinzica, Ricciardo de, *see* Boccaccio
  wife of, *see* Boccaccio
  Christ 89, 90
Church, Catholic 110
  see also Alas: Fermín; anticlericalism
cigars, *see* masculinity: symbols of
Cirlot, J. 40
class 45, 66, 68, 106, 110, 190
  see also Boccaccio; Chaucer
clowns 63
  ritual 64
cock, *see* horns: on cock
collusion:
  between author and male protagonist 192, 226
  between author and male reader 227
  in *The Kreutzer Sonata* 52
  of male reader 52, 72
  not offered 286
  of spectator of drama 135, 136
  of wife 86
comedy, *see* theatre
commedia dell'arte, *see* theatre
container:
  containment 52, 53, 54–8, 62, 64, 71, 74, 80, 82, 93, 109–10, 113, 114, 125, 141, 152, 156, 168, 171, 191, 196, 198, 226, 229, 231, 233, 235, 239, 246, 249, 253, 256, 265, 267, 277
  Desdemona for Othello 171
  Iago for Othello 166
  joke as 54–7
  Juan for Lope 152
  lack of 156
  listener as 233
  and marriage 54, 156
control 197
  accommodation and 95
  defensive control in Karenin 241
  jokes and 55–6
  of women 58, 115–20
Cook, D. 262
Corbett, P. 21
core-gender theory, *see* gender; Stoller
Council, N. 161, 162
counter-transference 120, 123–4, 196
Coward, R. 10
Crampas, *see* Fontane
O crime do Padre Amaro, *see* Queirós
Cruickshank, D. 160
Cruz, A. 152
cuckold 1, 2, 15, 16, 18, 24, 25, 28, 29, 31, 32, 35, 37, 38, 46, 50–65, 66, 68, 69, 70, 71, 74, 76, 77, 79, 80, 81, 82, 83, 84, 86, 87, 88, 90, 92, 95, 96, 97, 98, 99, 100, 101, 109, 112, 126, 127, 128, 131, 132, 135, 151, 155, 157, 166, 169, 173–8, 181, 183, 184, 185, 188, 191, 199, 205, 209, 211, 227, 228, 235, 238, 239, 242, 244, 245, 246, 252, 253, 254–5, 256, 257, 258, 262, 266, 271, 273, 274, 275, 279
  avant la lettre: Briest 188; Pozdnyshev 228; Víctor 205
  blind 76

cuckold (*cont.*):
  in Boccaccio 35, 37, 80–96
  in Chaucer 35, 37, 65–80
  cuckold husbands, *see* Alas: Víctor Ozores; Boccaccio: Puccio, Spinelloccio, Zeppa; Cervantes: Carrizales; Chaucer: January, John, Merchant; García Lorca: Perlimplín; Tolstoy: Karenin
  etymology of term 20, 32–40, 105; in English 34–7; in German 33, 34; in Italy 39–40; in Old French 33, 34; in Provençal 33; in Spain 38–9
  gullible 67, 70, 99, 135
  ignored 67–71
  as joking statement 56–7
  lack of rights of 71
  lover as 68–9
  not fate of husband 83–5
  outside patriarchal order 61
  reproached by wife as 88
  splitting and denial in 50, 65, 67
  symbolic function of 59
  and transgression 64
  see also cock; deceived husband; horns; husband; laughter
cuckoldry 15, 32, 34, 36, 37, 45, 46, 47, 51, 52, 53, 54, 56, 62, 64, 65, 67, 68, 71, 72, 73, 82, 84, 86, 95, 96, 109, 111, 112, 113, 127, 152
  and depressive position 50–65, 75, 95–6, 110, 252
  literature of 16, 18, 28, 100, 101, 253
  and marriage 36, 54
  and transgression 64–5
  see also Boccaccio; carnival; Cervantes; Chaucer; depressive position; fabliaux; Molière; theatre
cuernos, *see* horns
Curteis, A. 22
Czyba, L. 179

Dabney, R. A. 223
Davie, D. 233
Davies, R. 84
Davis, N. Z. 41, 60, 61, 62, 77
death 25, 29, 52, 65, 66, 71, 73, 79, 109, 110, 111, 112, 121, 122, 129, 148, 153, 157, 158, 159, 160, 173, 174, 179, 181, 182, 185, 201, 219, 222, 224, 225, 246, 247, 248, 251, 255, 264, 265, 266, 268, 269, 271, 272, 275–6, 277–81
  see also women
The Decameron, *see* Boccaccio
deceived husband 1, 6, 15, 16, 17, 18, 19, 20, 24, 28, 31, 33, 35, 36, 38, 39, 40, 46, 49, 51, 62, 83, 175, 177, 181, 184, 198, 207, 212, 227, 234, 253, 256, 261, 266, 267, 269, 270, 274, 275, 276
  neglect of 16
  positive presentation of 18
  temporal orientation of 100, 112
defences:
  against death 280
  in Gutierre 159
defensive control:
  against emotion 240
  in Briest 194–5
  in Karenin 237–8, 239, 241–2
denial 50, 60, 62, 65, 67, 71, 72, 74, 75, 76, 78, 104, 112, 117, 119, 123, 125, 150, 167, 168, 175, 190, 194, 195
  in *Dombey and Son* 217–26
  and emotion 175; in drama 123–4
  in Jones 14
  in *The Kreutzer Sonata* 226–34
  in Othello 167
  of sensuality 112
depressive position 34, 39, 50, 51, 52, 53, 54, 56, 58, 60, 62, 63, 64, 65, 71, 74, 75, 76, 79, 80, 95, 109, 110, 111, 118, 140, 148, 152, 168, 170, 171, 172, 184, 185, 186, 192, 196, 198, 233, 246, 253, 254, 258, 270, 271, 273
  and author 192
  and Braithwaite 270, 271, 272
  and carnival 60, 108–9
  in *Dombey and Son* 226
  of female reader 52
  and historical context 109–11
  and Innstetten 196, 198
  and Karenin 246–7
  in *The Kreutzer Sonata* 233
  and Levin 251–2
  literary texts of 28, 29, 34, 185, 207, 215, 234–5, 246, 252, 253, 258
  of male reader 52
  and maturity 53
  Othello 170, 172
  and reader 74, 76, 78–9
  and stability 53

and transgression 63–5
and Víctor 215
see also cuckoldry; Klein; novel of adultery
Desdemona, *see* Shakespeare
desire:
object of 222, 267
in Perlimplín 256
Dickens, C.:
Carker 218, 225
Dombey and Son 28, 48, 174, 217–26
Dombey, Edith 174, 218, 220, 221, 224–6
Dombey, Florence 220–3, 224, 225
Dombey, Mr 174, 218–26
Dombey, Paul 218, 219–20, 223
Skewton, Mrs 224, 225
dignity 26
Dioneo, *see* Boccaccio
displacement 149, 151, 153–4, 164, 267–72, 274, 275
distance, comic 15, 46, 56, 74–5
divorce 174
Dombey, Edith, *see* Dickens
Dombey, Florence, *see* Dickens
Dombey, Mr, *see* Dickens
Dombey, Paul, *see* Dickens
Don Juan 156–7, 280
Douglas, M. 55–6
duel:
of Innstetten 197–8
of Víctor 215
of Vronsky 243
dyadic relations 13, 170, 275–6
dynamics 234

Easthope, A. 1, 8–9, 259
Effi Briest, *see* Fontane
Eichenbaum, L. 13
Eliot, T. S. 163
Ellen, *see* Barnes
emotion:
in *Before She Met Me* 266
in Bovary 184–5
in Braithwaite 268, 269, 273–4, 275–6
in Carrizales 255
denied by Don Juan 280
envy of, in Dombey 221
fear of: in Dombey 175; in Karenin 239–42, 244, 248; in Pozdnyshev 175
in Frankford 263–4, 265
in Innstetten 197–8
lack of, in Dombey 221
in Leontes 253
in Levin 251–2
in Paolo 260
in Perlimplín 256–8
in Víctor 205, 207, 215
envy:
in cuckold 50
in Dombey 221–3
penis envy 4
of possession 205
see also Klein
epic literature, husband in 38
etymology:
of adultery 46–8
of cuckoldry 32–8
of honour 42–6
of infidelity 31
Evans, C. A. 195
external world 3, 6, 7, 43, 44, 46, 51, 93, 94, 102, 109, 122–3, 124 138, 189, 196

fabliaux 15, 18, 65, 66, 76, 110
failure 23–7, 51, 52, 56, 57, 63, 71, 75, 100, 101, 126, 179, 183, 197, 209, 215, 236, 243, 248, 254, 258
Fairbairn, D. 2
Falkberget, J. 48
family:
drama 26
filial relations in 156, 157–8, 164, 218, 220–3, 224
fragmentation in 21
horizontal/vertical 21
tensions in 217–18
father:
authority of 4
in gender formation 4, 10–11
kills daughter 21
requires son to kill stepmother 121
Víctor as 199
father-figure:
lack of strong 26–7, 78
Perlimplín as 257
Víctor as 199
see also parents
La Faute de l'Abbé Mouret, *see* Zola
Federico, *see* Vega, Lope de
feminine 58, 93, 114, 116, 118, 119, 120, 123, 146, 147, 215, 220, 241,

feminine (*cont.*):
243, 244, 245
Florence as 220
Karenin as 245
risks of 58
and sensuality 57
world of 45
femininity:
infant's sense of 12
of mother 5
rejection of by boy 13
feminist criticism 27
see also Coward; Eichenbaum; Horney; Keller; Mitchell; Orbach
Fermín, *see* Alas
mother of, *see* Alas
Ferrante, J. M. 94
Ferrara, Duke of, *see* Vega, Lope de
fidelity:
concern for 31
expectation of 30
in *Flaubert's Parrot* 267, 269
Filomena, *see* Boccaccio
Fineman, J. 13, 203
Flaubert, G. 175–86
Bovary, Charles 175, 176–7, 179–80, 181–2, 184, 189, 235, 236
Bovary, Emma 178, 179, 180, 181, 182–3, 184, 185, 267
Léon 178
Madame Bovary 175–86
Rodolphe 179–80
see also cuckold; hero; masculinity; novel of adultery
Flaubert's Parrot, *see* Barnes, J.
Fontane, T. 187–98
Briest, Effi 174, 188, 189, 190–6; father of 188, 190, 191–2; mother of 188, 190, 191, 192
Chinaman 194–5
Crampas 194, 196, 198
Effi Briest 174, 187–98; distance in 187–8; honour in 192, 195, 197–8
Innstetten 180, 187, 188–90, 191, 192–8, 231, 236
norms of masculinity in 192–4
Oedipal ousting in 188–9
society in 190–1
see also duel; honour: man of; husband; lover; masculinity: symbols of; novel of adultery; wife
food 180, 210
see also anorexia
fool 63–4
forgiveness:
of Frankford 261, 265
of Karenin 244–7
Fortunata and Jacinta, *see* Pérez Galdós
The Fourth Night Watch, *see* Falkberget
France 20, 32, 62
Frankford, *see* Heywood
Frankford, Anne, *see* Heywood
Freud, S. 3, 4, 6, 8, 10, 11, 12, 55, 62, 168, 170, 203
anxiety 3
'Anxiety and Instinctual Life' 3, 62
'The Dissection of the Psychical Personality' 3
ego 3
gender theory 9–13
on jealousy 14, 168
on jokes 55
and Klein 3–4, 8–10
and object relations 3
Oedipus complex 10–11
'Some Neurotic Mechanisms in Jealousy, Paranoia and Homosexuality' 168
Fromm, E. 26
frustration;
toleration of by infant 8
Furst, L. 180, 198.

Gaines, J. F. 127
Galdós, *see* Pérez Galdós
Gallop, J. 5
Galsworthy, J. 224, 258–9
Soames 224
games 60
of honour 23
García Lorca 180, 211, 256–8, 266
El amor de don Perlimplín 256–8
Belisa 256–7
Perlimplín 180, 211, 256–8, 266
gender 51, 73, 114, 115, 116, 118, 134, 142, 189, 204, 212, 220, 227
acquisition 115, 117
in audiences 123, 172
core-gender theory 12
difference 10–15, 23; in honour code 102–9; in honour drama 134
difference, lack of 204
differentiation 107, 216
feminine, rejected 13, 116

formation 4, 11, 202, 203; Freud on 10–11; Stoller on 2, 11–13, 15, 116, 216
gender roles reversed 183
identity, girl's problem with 13
and place 22, 23, 115
uncertainty 209–10, 212, 215–17
see also feminine; femininity; honour; marriage; masculinity; splitting; woman
genre, literary:
and deceived husband 17, 18
and novel of adultery 29
see also cuckoldry; depressive position: literary texts of; novel of adultery
Gifford, H. 247
Girard, R., see *between men*
Given Wilson, C. 22
goat, *see* symbols
Golden Age Drama, *see* theatre: Spanish, wife-murder plays
good object, *see* object
Goody, J. 22
gratitude 7
see also Klein
Greece:
Greek mime, *see* theatre
Sarakatsani 117
village life 117
widows 117
Greene, T. 94
grief 29, 62, 148, 175, 181, 184, 185, 242, 253, 255, 261, 263, 276
Grivelet, M. 263
group psychology 5–6
guilt:
in infant, capacity for 7
in *Othello* 170–1
Gunn, E. 240, 247, 249, 251
Guntrip, H. 2
Gutierre, *see* Calderón

Hartog, D. den 218, 219–20, 222
Hegel 57, 177
particularity of desire 250
hero, Romantic:
avenger as 140
Charles Bovary 181, 184–5
heroism 17
Heywood, T.:
Frankford 261, 262, 263–5
Frankford, Anne 263, 264–5
Wendoll 262, 263
A Woman Killed with Kindness 261
Hinshelwood, R. 196
history 1–2, 19, 20, 29, 173, 186
homosexuality 8, 14, 166, 168
honour 32, 35, 42–5, 46, 47, 54, 57, 69, 83, 84, 85, 87, 88, 89, 100, 101, 102, 103, 104, 105, 106, 107, 108, 109, 111, 112, 114, 116, 118, 120, 121, 122, 127, 128, 130, 131, 133, 136, 137, 138, 141, 142, 143, 144, 147, 149, 150, 151, 152, 153, 154, 155, 158, 159, 160, 162, 163, 164, 166, 167, 172, 182, 185, 186, 212, 238, 257, 258, 263, 264, 265
code 15, 38, 101, 103, 106, 107, 111, 113, 118, 119, 122, 124, 125, 126, 128, 130, 131, 134, 136, 138, 139, 141, 142, 143, 144, 145, 147, 148, 149, 150, 151, 152, 153, 154, 155, 161, 162, 164, 169, 170, 171, 182, 192, 211, 221, 228, 244, 250, 258, 261; in *Anna Karenin* 250–1; in Bedouins 107, 114; in Berbers 114; in Greece 114–15; identity in 100; inverted 182–3; in Italy 129, 158; in Kabyle 114; in *The Kreutzer Sonata* 229; masculine ethos in 119; in patriarchal society 15, 102; and psychoanalytic theory 108–20; relationships in 101; split in 106, 113; theory of 101
drama 15, 17, 28, 44, 52, 60, 72, 89, 95, 109, 110, 111, 112, 113, 114, 118, 120, 122–4, 125, 126, 128, 129, 130, 131, 132, 133, 141, 142, 143, 157, 161, 184; complexity of dynamic in 122–6, 137–42; criticism of 129–33, 137–42; emotion in 125, 143–7; king in 120, 121, 134, 136; as phantasy 123; projection in 126, 144; splitting in 134, 149–50, 154–5, 158; splitting in interpretation of 125, 130, 138; *see also* Calderón, Chiarelli, García Lorca, Vega, Lope de, Shakespeare: *Othello*, theatre
etymology of 42–5, 112–16
games of 23
h'aram 45, 114
h'urma 45, 114

honour (*cont.*):
inherent 43–4
'ird 45, 107, 114
loss of 85, 101, 102–3, 105, 119, 121, 122, 127, 128, 161, 164, 169, 172, 244
man of 2, 16, 17, 18, 24, 25, 29, 32, 52, 67, 98, 99, 100, 101, 119, 122, 124, 125, 126, 128, 131, 135, 137, 139, 143, 145, 149, 152, 153, 163, 166, 169, 172, 173, 174, 175, 182, 183, 185, 186–7, 189, 191, 193, 195, 197, 199, 200, 205, 210, 212, 213, 214, 215, 216, 227, 232, 235, 236, 241, 242, 244, 245, 251, 254, 256, 257, 258, 260, 262, 265, 266, 270, 273, 274, 275; and action 99, 124–5, 142, 257; detachment of 124–5; fathers as, *see* Fontane: Briest; husbands as: Agilulf 83–5, Dombey 174, 218–26, Duke of Ferrara 155–8, Frankford 262, 263–5, Gutierre 159–60, Innstetten 174, 192–4, 195–8, John 67, Karenin 236–8, Othello 161–4, 166, 169–72, Perlimplín 257–8, Pozdnyshev 174, 228–31, 232, Puccio 91, Soames 224, Trevelyan 186–7, Veinticuatro 133–40, Víctor 174, 199, 205; paranoia of 186–7; *see also* Tolstoy: Pozdnyshev, Vega, Lope de: Veinticuatro; and recognition 134
see also jealousy; revenge; splitting; wife: killing of
nif 45
as reputation 43
and shame 102–4, 106, 114, 115, 116
sharaf 45, 107, 114
of woman 44–5, 87, 104
to be won 102
Horney, K. 11, 116
horns:
on Christ 89
on cock 41
in etymology of cuckold 38–42
in Japan 41
of moon 41
origin of symbol 39–42
suggested: on Bovary 177; on Karenin 235–6
horses, symbolic of:
adultery 177, 204–5
masculinity 177–8, 204
sensuality 231
house, symbolic of the female 23
house-scorning 115
husband 30, 31, 32, 33, 34, 35, 37, 38, 39, 41, 42, 45, 48, 49, 50, 51, 52, 61, 63, 66, 67, 68, 69, 70, 71, 73, 74, 75, 76, 77, 78, 81, 82, 83, 84, 85, 87, 88, 89, 90, 91, 96, 97, 98, 100, 105, 107, 116, 120, 121, 122, 124, 126, 127, 131, 132, 133, 134, 135, 137, 138, 141, 142, 143, 147, 148, 151, 153, 155, 157, 159, 161, 164, 165, 166, 167, 172, 174, 175, 177, 181, 182, 183, 185, 199, 200, 201, 202, 204, 206, 207, 208, 210, 211, 213, 214, 216, 217, 224, 225, 227, 228, 231, 233, 234, 235, 236, 237, 239, 240, 241, 242, 244, 246, 248, 249, 250, 253, 254, 255, 257, 258, 259, 260, 262, 263, 264, 265, 266, 271, 273, 274, 276
of adulteress, *see* Alas: Víctor Ozores; Dickens: Dombey; Flaubert: Bovary; Fontane: Innstetten; Heywood: Frankford; Tolstoy: Pozdnyshev; Trollope: Trevelyan; wife: guilty
aged, *see* Alas: Víctor Ozores; Boccaccio: Ricciardo de Chinzica; Chaucer: January, John; Fontane: Innstetten; García Lorca: Perlimplín
as baby 70
bereaved 277; *see also* Barnes: Braithwaite; Flaubert: Charles Bovary; loss; Tolstoy: Karenin
and children 37
deceived, *see* Alas: Fermín, Víctor Ozores; Barnes: Braithwaite; Boccaccio: Agilulf, Ricciardo de Chinzica, Spinelloccio, Zeppa; Calderón: Gutierre, Lope; Cervantes: Carrizales; Chaucer: January, John; Chiarelli: Paolo; Dickens: Dombey; Fontane: Innstetten; Galsworthy: Soames; García Lorca: Perlimplín; Tolstoy: Karenin, Pozdnyshev; Trollope: Trevelyan; Vega, Lope de: Duke of

Ferrara, Veinticuatro
denial by 67
domesticated 183, 184, 208, 210–11
as father 199, 257
feminine 236, 245
guilt of 47–8
illness of 200
inadequate 178–80, 189, 193, 208–9
inefficient 97
ingenuity in 83–4, 85
intelligent 84
jealous 88
and lover 179–80, 198, 202–7, 231–2; see also *between men*; lover
lover has status of 68–71, 143, 151–2, 153, 209, 210, 213–14, 216–27
material status of 32
as nursemaid 210
paranoid 88–9
presented positively 18
profession of 189
status of 19, 189
wealth of 91
see also *between men*; cuckold; denial; emotion; honour: man of; marriage; masculinity
hysteria 214

Iago, *see* Shakespeare
identification 51, 52, 71, 75, 124, 129, 138, 139, 143, 200, 203
identity 52, 98, 100, 110, 111, 116, 119, 145, 148, 174, 176, 198, 201, 203, 235, 246, 275
see also collusion
illegitimacy 31, 156, 173
English law on 22
positive view of bastards 61
illness:
of Ana Ozores 210, 211, 214
of Emma Bovary 178, 182
of honour 121, 155, 158–61
of Maxi 200
individuation 62
inefficiency, sexual 97
inequality between sexes 31
infant:
and anger 6
concern of 7
and external world 6–7
femininity, sense of 12
frustration, capacity to tolerate 8
guilt 7
and memory 112
see also Klein; Winnicott
infidelity 278
absence from text 37
Boccaccio's view of 53–4
celebration of 53
concept of 30
of women 16, 30, 83
inheritance 22, 31, 32, 36, 72, 107, 225
of family name 105
of purity of blood 105–6
Innstetten, *see* Fontane
isolation 276
Italy 32, 39–40, 129

Jackson, A. 223
James, C. 8, 56, 110
January, *see* Chaucer
Janus 77
Japan 41
Jaques, E. 29
The Jealous Extremaduran, *see* Cervantes
The Jealous Old Man, *see* Cervantes
jealousy 14, 32, 42, 67, 88, 90, 115, 121, 124, 129, 135, 142, 153, 154, 155, 159, 161, 162, 163, 165, 166, 167, 168–71, 179, 213, 215, 224, 228, 231, 236, 237, 238, 241, 251, 254, 255, 257, 264, 274, 275, 276
in Braithwaite 274
in Dombey 224
in Fermín 213
in Frankford 264
horns of 42
Jones on 14
in Karenin 237–8
in Levin 251
Rivière on 170–1
John, *see* Chaucer
joker 57
jokes:
and control 96
in smut 51
Johnson, Dr 35–7
Jones, C. A. 130
Jones, E. 14, 169, 170
Jones, G. F. 127
Juan, *see* Calderón

Juan, Don, *see* Don Juan
Jung, C. G. 62

Kabyle, *see* honour: code
Kahn, C. 13
see also *between men*
Karenin, *see* Tolstoy
Karenin, Anna, *see* Tolstoy
Keller, E. Fox 12, 116
Kierkegaard, S. 26
king, *see* honour: drama
Kitty, *see* Tolstoy
Klein, M. 2, 3, 4, 5–9, 10, 12, 13, 14, 16, 27, 29, 49, 50, 51, 59, 108, 110, 115, 120, 167, 169, 198, 203, 220, 221, 232, 234, 244, 270
  concern, sense of 5
  and deceived husband 28, 29
  depressive position 7–8, 9, 16, 27–9, 246, 277, 278–9
  envy 5, 8
  and Freud 3–4, 8–10, 13
  gratitude 7, 8
  guilt 7
  and honour 108
  infant, world of 6, 7
  and Lacan 4
  loneliness 280–1
  loss 278–81
  'Love, Guilt and Reparation' 244, 280
  mother 5, 278–81; importance of 12; and infant 6
  mourning 278–80
  'Mourning and its Relation to Manic-Depressive States' 278
  'Notes on Some Schizoid Mechanisms' 8
  Oedipal triangle 15, 49
  Oedipus complex 9–10
  paranoia 280
  paranoid-schizoid position 6–8, 16, 28, 29
  phantasy, defined 7
  pre-Oedipal stage 3, 9
  projection 5, 60
  projective identification 5, 167–8, 220, 232
  splitting 5, 50, 220
  'A Study of Envy and Gratitude' 8
  symbol-formation 58
  theory 27; and carnival 59–60; and literature 50; and reader 51
  see also containment; counter-transference; denial; depressive position; infant; loss; mother; paranoid–schizoid; projection; projective identification; splitting
Knight, G. Wilson 161
Kovel, J. 163, 168
The Kreutzer Sonata, *see* Tolstoy

Labanyi, J. 211, 212, 214
Lacan 4
land:
  and adultery 21
  and marriage 22
language of infidelity 30–49
Larson, D. 98, 129, 131–3, 137–8
Lattre, A. de 182
laughter 55
  at deceived husband 17
law:
  of classical Athens 21
  and honour code in Spain 128
  of imperial Rome 21
  inequality in 19
  natural 98
  reliance of husband on 48
  and sexual behaviour 20–1
  and society 20
Lazarillo de Tormes 127
Leavis, F. R. 161
left hand, sacred of 114
Leonor, *see* Calderón
Leontes, *see* Shakespeare
Levin, *see* Tolstoy
lineage, *see* inheritance; purity
Lloyd, G. 57, 250
loco amor 146, 262
Lope, Don, *see* Calderón
Lorca, *see* García Lorca
loss 86, 133, 138, 155, 160, 238, 244, 246, 248, 249, 264, 266, 267, 268, 270, 275, 276, 278–81
  in *Flaubert's Parrot* 267, 268, 270, 275–6
  in Frankford 264
  and jealousy 168–71
  in Karenin 238–9, 244, 248–9
  of status 58
lover 32, 34, 41, 46, 48, 50, 66, 67, 68, 69, 70, 83, 84, 85, 86, 88, 89, 90, 97, 98, 112, 120, 121, 129, 132, 136, 142, 148, 151, 153, 155, 157, 173, 178, 182, 190, 198, 200, 202,

204, 207, 208, 211, 212, 216, 221, 224, 226, 228, 229, 231, 232, 234, 255, 257, 262, 272, 273
admired by husband 204–6
and husband 90
see also Alas: Alvaro Mesía, Fermín; Boccaccio: Agilulf's groom, Masetto, Paganino, Spinelloccio; Calderón: Luis; Chaucer: Absalon, Damian; Dickens: Carker; Flaubert: Léon, Rodolphe; Fontane: Crampas; Heywood: Wendoll; Tolstoy: Trukhachevsky, Vronsky; Vega, Lope de: Federico
Luis, *see* Calderón

McCarthy, D. 33
McCrary, W. 148
McDowell, D. M. 21
McKendrick, M. 54, 104, 111, 118, 128, 129, 139, 140, 142
Madame Bovary, *see* Flaubert
Makarius, L. 64
man:
and emotion 28
old 50
rights of 14, 22
Mann, J. 66, 73, 76
Marc 85
margination 67–71, 76, 84, 87, 163
marriage 19, 30, 31, 34, 35, 36, 38, 40, 42, 47, 48, 52, 53, 54, 61, 62, 63, 64, 66, 68, 72, 73, 74, 79, 81, 82, 87, 97, 98, 100, 110, 119, 120, 121, 122, 128, 135, 140, 142, 143, 145, 146, 147, 148, 149, 150, 151, 152, 153, 154, 155, 156, 157, 160, 164, 165, 168, 171, 172, 174, 175, 177, 178, 179, 180, 182, 183, 186, 188, 189, 190, 201, 205, 209, 211, 212, 214, 217, 220, 224, 225, 226, 228, 229, 230, 231, 234, 238, 239, 247, 249, 252, 255, 256, 262, 266
and adultery 48
in *Anna Karenin* 175, 234, 238, 247, 249–52
and Bedouins 107
in *Canterbury Tales* 66, 72, 73, 74
and cuckoldry 36, 47, 52
domestic obligation in 142, 147–8
inequality in 22, 87
and land 22
in *Madame Bovary* 177
in *Othello* 164, 171–2
in patriarchy 82
and power dynamic 147, 156
praised by Veinticuatro 135, 140
in restoration of honour 120, 121
in *Secret Revenge for a Secret Fault* 142, 145–9, 153, 154–5
as threat to masculinity 142, 146–8, 150, 261–2
transforms 180–1
views of Tolstoy on, *see* Tolstoy
views of wife on 148–9
in *A Woman Killed with Kindness* 261–2
see also honour: code; illegitimacy; inheritance; law; widow; wife
masculine figures, lack of strong 26
masculinity 1, 12, 13, 15, 35, 41, 51, 52, 56, 58, 61, 71, 73, 116, 119, 120, 123, 124, 133, 134, 138, 140, 142, 144, 145, 146, 148, 149, 150, 154, 156, 172, 174, 175, 176, 177–81, 183, 184, 189, 200, 203, 204, 208, 211, 212, 215, 218, 219, 220, 236, 241, 243, 244, 245
in Andalusia 41
anxiety about 16, 31, 133–4, 156, 218–19
attainment of 12
defensive 212–13
desirability of the masculine 165
failure of 16
lack of 175–81, 207, 259
loss of 32, 41, 212, 243–4
and the military 142, 145, 147–8
norms of 56, 192, 193–4, 206, 243, 260
proof of 19
symbols of: cigars 178–80, 189, 193, 208; horses 133, 177–8, 181, 204–5
threatened, *see* marriage
uncertainty of 215–17
of wife 183
Masetto of Lamporrecchio, *see* Boccaccio
maturity, *see* depressive position; individuation
Maxi, *see* Pérez Galdós
May, *see* Chaucer; symbols
Mazzota, G. 94
medical model of adultery, *see* illness

Mediterranean:
  see honour: and shame
Mencía, *see* Calderón
Mesía, Alvaro, *see* Alas
mid-life crisis 29
Millington, M. 266
mime and *commedia dell'arte*, *see* theatre
Minden, M. 188, 198
misrule:
  Abbots of 62–3, 108
  carnival 59, 61
Mitchell, J. 9, 11
Molière 18, 110, 127
Montaut, M. 218, 224
mother 5, 55, 56, 58, 106, 110, 116, 118, 158, 220, 221, 222, 225, 256, 276
  bad 184, 192
  betrayal by 16
  boy and 14
  of Charles 176, 177, 180, 182, 184
  of Effi 188, 190, 191
  of Fermín 176, 212–13, 215–16
  -figure 26
  good 278
  and lineage 45
  loss of 278
  power of 10
  separation from 12–13
  see also parents
Moynahan, J. 219
Muscatine, C. 66, 68, 76
music:
  symbol of sensual capacity 231–2
  violin as symbol of tension 242

nausea:
  in *La Regenta* 217
  in *Madame Bovary* 217
  see also food
Neill, M. 163, 164, 166, 170
nif, *see* honour: nif
Nimetz, M. 204, 215, 216
Norse literature 28, 32
novel of adultery 26, 173, 200–1, 217
  and depressive position 246, 253–4, 278, 279
Nykrog, P. 66

object:
  good 223
  see also desire; woman
object relations theory 2, 4
  see also Bion; containment; counter-transference; denial; depressive position; Fairbairn; Guntrip; Hinshelwood; James; Klein; Oedipus; paranoid-schizoid; phantasy; projection; projective identification; Rustin, splitting; transference; Winnicott
Oblonsky, *see* Tolstoy
Oedipus:
  Oedipal crisis 13; and jealousy 168–9, 275–6
  Oedipal ousting 188–9
  Oedipal situation 70
  Oedipal threat 157–8
  Oedipal triangles 15, 49, 70, 202; in novel 188–9
  Oedipus complex 4, 9–11, 13–15, 275
  Oedipus myth 26
  Oedipus plays 27
  post-Oedipal relationship 275–6
  pre-Oedipal stage 9, 168, 203
omnipotence 8
Orbach, S. 13
order:
  and change 111
  and disorder (Dioneo) 94–5
  disrupted by plague 93–4
  natural 80–1, 82, 83, 87
  patriarchal 80–1, 89
orderliness 233
  in Karenin 238
outsider figures 62–5, 163, 165, 169
  lovers as 246
ox:
  Karenin as 238–9
  as symbol 40, 178
Ozores, Ana, *see* Alas
Ozores, Víctor, *see* Alas

Paganino, *see* Boccaccio
Pampinea, *see* Boccaccio
Pantaloon 157
  see also theatre: *commedia dell'arte*
paranoia 99, 118, 125, 133, 155, 168, 174, 187, 197, 223, 226, 232, 236, 257, 262, 265, 266, 270
  see also Tolstoy: Pozdnyshev; Trollope: Trevelyan; Vega, Lope de: Veinticuatro
paranoid-schizoid position 45, 49, 50,

58, 108, 109, 111, 112, 113, 120, 168, 171, 195, 223, 228, 231
and cuckold 50
in Dombey 222–3
and honour 45, 108–20
in Innstetten 195
and literature 28
in Pozdnyshev 228–31
see also Klein
Pardo Bazán, E.:
Un viaje de novios 200
parents 10, 49, 70, 105, 176–7, 188–92, 198, 201, 244–5, 255
Parten, A. 86
paternity:
deduced 5
see also etymology: of cuckoldry; illegitimacy; inheritance
Paterson, A. K. J. 130, 144, 152
patriarchal code 89, 90, 100
patriarchal law 5
patriarchal society 4, 6, 17, 30, 281
and cuckoldry 50–1, 56
and failure 24, 27
family in 16, 18
and fidelity 81, 82
and Freud 10
honour in 102
text of 51
and transgression 58–65
and vitality 98
penis:
envy 4
lack of 11
see also castration
Pérez Galdós, B.:
Fortunata and Jacinta 180, 200
Maxi 200
Peristiany, J. G. 45, 101
Perlimplín, *see* García Lorca
Peterson, C. 25, 176
phallic-narcissistic type 220
phantasy 7, 65, 68, 69, 72, 74, 76, 123, 181, 198, 222, 260, 278, 279
The Physician of his Honour, *see* Calderón
Pitt-Rivers, J. 68–9, 102, 103, 104, 105, 106, 114, 152
plague 110
see also Boccaccio: frame of *Decameron*
Pleck, J. 152
Podol, P. 131
Porter, R. 159
possession, sense of 205, 274
anxiety about 16
in boys 14–15
in man 21
see also rights; wife
potency 11, 19, 31, 35, 39, 41, 48, 63, 65, 71, 77, 78, 90, 110, 116, 133, 152, 156, 157, 203, 206
loss of 15, 16, 25, 54, 77, 78, 111, 246
Potter, J. H. 94
Pozdnyshev, *see* Tolstoy
La Princesse de Clèves 18, 187
Pring-Mill, R. 44
private life, domain of woman 17, 57
boundary with public 57
projection 108, 109, 114, 117, 118, 119, 120, 123, 124, 126, 130, 138, 139, 144, 145, 149, 151, 155, 171, 195, 226, 231, 234, 238, 247, 270
in honour code 109
in honour drama 126
in Innstetten 195
in Jones 14
in man of honour 28
in Othello 167–8, 170–2
see also Klein
projective identification 120
in *Dombey and Son* 220
in *The Kreutzer Sonata* 232
in *Othello* 167–8
see also Klein
property of husband 36
see also inheritance
Provence 32
psychoanalytic theory 19, 22, 144
see also Bion; Freud; Jung; Klein; object relations; Winnicott
public concern 30, 57, 58
public life 17, 177
games of honour in 23
see also gender: and place; honour
Puccio, *see* Boccaccio
Punishment without Revenge, *see* Vega, Lope de
purity:
of blood 45, 105, 136, 143, 164, 170–2, 173
loss of 229–31
of woman 106
see also illegitimacy; inheritance

Queirós, Eça de:
  O crime do Padre Amaro 200

race 164, 169, 170
  purity of, *see* purity
reaction-formation 28, 50, 72, 140, 147
reader 50–3, 57, 65, 67, 68, 69, 70, 71, 72, 74, 75, 76, 80, 85, 130, 144, 163, 175, 176, 181, 182, 185, 186, 187, 189, 191, 195, 196, 220, 227, 236, 240, 241, 250, 266, 267, 268, 272, 273, 274, 276
  and cuckold 72, 75
  female 51–2, 85
  and husband 71–8
  male 24, 51, 227
  seduction of 68, 220–1
Reeve, *see* Chaucer
La Regenta, *see* Alas
repetition compulsion 156–7, 280
reputation 19, 25, 31, 36, 43, 100, 103, 150, 163, 172, 257, 266, 273
  loss of 35–6
  see also honour
revenge 85, 87, 100, 107, 122, 124, 129, 141, 213, 265
  husband praised for 120
  of Othello 162
  vicarious 214
Riechel, D. C. 198
right-hand, sacred of 114
rights 82
  of boys 14
  loss of 98
  of men 14, 22, 81
  in natural order 81
  of women 22
Ritchie, J. M. 188
ritual 58
Rivière, J. 171
Rodolphe, *see* Flaubert
romance 18
Romantic hero, *see* hero, Romantic
Romantic love 185
Roper, L. 45
Rougement, D. de 173
Rubys, C. de 60
rule-breaker, *see* outsider figures; transgression
Rustin, M. 9

sacred, of right and left hand, *see* left hand; right hand
Sánchez, R. G. 206
Sánchez Pérez 23, 115
Sánchez-Eppler, B. 200
Sanders, W. 253
Sarakatsani, *see* Greece
scapegoat:
  Desdemona as 172
  Edith as 224
  Iago as 166
schizophrenia 123, 151, 270
Schwartz, M. M. 13
Searles, H. 123, 151
Sedgwick, E. K., see *between men*
seduction, law on in Athens 21
Segal, H. 4, 7, 8, 58, 167
Segal, N. 4–5, 51, 166, 227
self, representation of 227, 228, 268–9
Semprún Donahue, M. de 199
sensuality 13, 94, 95, 105, 112, 116, 117, 118, 119, 134, 136, 147, 165, 171, 172, 190, 209, 226, 228, 229, 230, 232
  see also woman
separation, task of 12–13
sexuality 54, 58, 71, 72, 77, 98, 104, 108, 117, 119, 171, 174, 175, 179, 181, 204, 222, 228–31, 234, 262
Seymour, G. 9
Shakespeare:
  Desdemona 161, 162, 163, 164–5, 169, 170–1, 172
  fools in 63
  Iago 162, 163, 164, 165–8, 169
  Lear 61
  Leontes 253
  Macbeth 26
  Merry Wives of Windsor 36
  Othello 26, 46, 162–72
  Othello 111, 161–72; criticism of 161–4
  The Winter's Tale 253
shaman 63
  see also Boccaccio: Dioneo; outsider figures; transgression
shame 43, 44, 45, 49, 102, 104, 105, 106, 114, 115, 116, 165, 207, 209, 214, 215, 226, 237, 246, 248, 263

see also honour
sheep, symbolic of men 41
Showalter, E. 159
Sieburth, S. 200, 212
Sinclair, A. 62, 180, 210, 266
Skewton, Mrs, *see* Dickens
Smith, P. 142
smoking, *see* masculinity: symbols of
smut:
applied to cuckoldry 52
defined 51
in *The Kreutzer Sonata* 227
in *Manon Lescant* 227
in *Othello* 166
Snow, E. 163, 167
Soames, *see* Galsworthy
society, patriarchal, *see* patriarchal society
Sontag, S. 159
Soufas, T. S. 144
Spain 32
drama in 54, 118–19; *see also* theatre
purity of blood in 105–6, 118
social change in 108, 111
Spark, M.:
Memento Mori 279
Spinelloccio, *see* Boccaccio
splitting 106, 108, 109, 112, 113, 114, 117, 118, 120, 123, 124, 130, 134, 138, 139, 140, 145, 147, 149, 154, 161, 171, 175, 220, 221, 222, 223, 225, 226, 227, 229, 230, 231, 234, 238, 241, 247, 250, 251, 252, 262, 270, 271, 272
in *Anna Karenin* 249–52
in audience of honour drama 130
in cuckold 50, 60; *see also* denial
between Dombey and Florence 220, 222
in *Dombey and Son* 175, 225
effect of on others 123
in *Flaubert's Parrot* 270, 272
in honour code 109, 112, 134
in honour drama 134
in infant 6
in Jones 14
in man of honour 28
in Pozdnyshev 175
between sexes 221
in *A Woman Killed With Kindness* 262–3
see also denial; Klein
Starkie, E. 175, 185, 269, 271
Stenbock-Fermor, E. 227, 242, 249
Stoller, R. 2, 11–13, 15, 116
suicide 129, 185, 265, 283
see also wife: suicide of
Swales, E. 195, 197, 198
symbol formation, *see* Klein
symbols 22, 58
cards 262
cigars 178–80, 189, 193, 208
dancing 261–2
flood 71
goat 39, 41
horses 133, 177–8, 181, 204–5
house 23
January and May 76–7, 79
Joseph 70
music 228, 231–2, 242
ox 40, 238–9
see also cuckold: etymology of; horns

Tanner, T. 26, 36, 48, 52–3, 173, 202
terror, in infant 6
theatre:
comedy 28
commedia dell'arte 37, 53, 157, 258
English 110, 127
French 18, 110, 127
Greek mime 53, 157
Italian 258
Spanish 24, 54, 89, 99, 110, 111, 125, 206, 210, 258
wife-murder plays 120–61; synopses of 120–1
see also Calderón; Chiarelli; García Lorca; Heywood; honour: drama; Molière; Shakespeare; Vega, Lope de
threat:
of cuckoldry 53
in honour literature 110
to man 119
Tolstoy, L.:
Anna Karenin 28, 175, 234–52
as author 233–4
and Karenin 219, 241
Karenin 48, 234–49, 260
Karenin, Anna 174, 235–7, 238, 239, 240, 241–2, 244, 245–6

Kitty 238, 249, 250–1
The Kreutzer Sonata 52, 174, 226–34
Levin 238, 241, 248, 249, 250–2
Oblonsky 236, 241, 242, 246, 249–50, 251
Pozdnyshev 226, 228–34; wife of 231–3
Trukhachevsky 228, 231, 232
views on marriage of 226, 228, 229
view of the masculine of 241
Vronsky 236, 237, 238, 240–1, 242, 243, 245, 248, 249
transference:
and cuckoldry 54
and honour drama 54
in Karenin 240
transferential emotions 224
see also counter-transference
transgression:
in cuckoldry 53, 63–4
in illegitimacy 61
and law 20
by shamans 63, 89, 95
by wife 122
triangles:
adulterous 2, 16, 97, 98, 202, 228, 262–3
cuckold in 98
with cuckold lover 68–9
in fabliau 66
multiple 202
Oedipal, *see* Oedipus
sexual, lack of clarity in 34
trickster 64
Trollope, A.:
Bozzle 187
He Knew He Was Right 48, 186–7
Trevelyan 186–7
Trukhachevsky, *see* Tolstoy

Unamuno 119

Valis, N. de 211, 214
Vega, Lope de 120–1, 131–3
Beatriz 133–6
Casandra 156, 157, 158
Federico 156, 158
Ferrara, Duque de 155–7
honour in theatre of 44
The Knights Commander of Córdoba 120, 131, 133–41, 142, 147
Punishment without Revenge 121, 155–8
Veinticuatro 133–40
Un Viaje de novios, *see* Pardo Bazán
Víctor Ozores, *see* Alas
Virgin Mary 77
virility:
concern with 204
proof of 19
Vronsky, *see* Tolstoy

Wangh, M. 163, 168
Wardropper, B. 160
Watson, C. B. 160
Weisser, M. R. 111
Wendoll, *see* Heywood
widow 92, 117, 177, 225
wife 30, 31, 32, 34, 35, 36, 37, 38, 39, 41, 46, 48, 50, 59, 61, 63, 67, 69, 73, 74, 81, 82, 84, 86, 87, 88, 89, 90, 91, 95, 97, 98, 99, 100, 101, 105, 106, 112, 119, 120, 121, 122, 123, 127, 132, 136, 137, 141, 142, 143, 146, 148, 149, 150, 151, 152, 153, 156, 158, 160, 162, 168, 177, 180, 186, 187, 189, 190, 197, 198, 200, 202, 204, 206, 207, 209, 211, 212, 213, 214, 215, 216, 218, 219, 220, 221, 224, 226, 228, 229, 231, 232, 235, 236, 237, 238, 239, 240, 241, 242, 243, 244, 245, 247, 248, 250, 251, 253, 254, 255, 256, 257, 258, 259, 260, 261, 262, 263, 265, 266, 268, 271, 272, 275, 278
of cuckold 97
death of 179, 181, 182, 183, 185, 272
disregarded 84, 87, 163, 233
dissatisfaction of 87, 178–80, 189, 193, 208–9
guilty 17, 18, 47, 51, 122, 129, 133, 135, 138, 139, 140, 179, 191, 192, 233, 255, 262, 264, 269, 273
with horns 42
illness of 178, 182
innocence of 120, 129
killing of 21, 120, 121, 123, 128, 129, 141, 142, 153, 233, 268, 273; by lover 121
lack of perception in 84
as masculine 183

opposition of 186
as possession 81, 86
satisfaction of 35, 81
set aside 129, 190, 191, 192, 212, 216–17, 264, 265
suicide of 129, 185, 265, 273–4
as transgressor 122
young 67, 68, 74, 156–7
see also Alas: Ana Ozores; Barnes: Ellen; Boccaccio: Agilulf, w. of, Chinzica, w. of, Spinelloccio, w. of, Zeppa, w. of, Calderón: Leonor, Mencía; Chaucer: Alisoun, May; Dickens: Edith Dombey; Flaubert: Emma Bovary; Fontane: Effi Briest; Heywood: Ann Frankford; Tolstoy: Anna Karenin, Kitty, Pozdnyshev, w. of; Vega, Lope de: Beatriz, Casandra
wife-murder plays, *see* theatre
Wilson, E. M. 44, 101, 129, 153, 161
Winnicott, D. 8, 13, 49, 110, 281
and play 55–6
see also containment
woman 51, 57, 63, 65, 68, 70, 71, 72, 73, 74, 78, 80, 81, 82, 84, 85, 86, 87, 88, 90, 92, 93, 97, 102, 103, 104, 105, 106, 107, 109, 111, 113, 114, 115, 116, 117, 118, 119, 120, 121, 124, 126, 127, 129, 134, 135, 136, 140, 141, 142, 145, 148, 150, 152, 153, 156, 159, 164, 168, 169, 170, 171, 173, 182, 200, 201, 203, 204, 206, 208, 209, 212, 213, 214, 216, 234, 235, 236, 240, 250, 251, 253, 255, 274
in Bedouins 114
and the body 177
as dangerous 225
and death 77, 93
fear of 27, 65
in Greek society 114–15
idealized 216
as innocent 225
in Kabyle 114
marginalized by society 90
as mothers 5, 281
as objects 52, 225
and sensuality 13, 57, 105, 116–17, 134, 136, 164–5, 171–2, 226, 228–31
as unruly 58, 61, 230
see also honour: code, loss of, and shame; mother; widow; wife
World Upside Down 59, 93

youth 26
May as symbol of 77
triumph of 79

Zeid, A. M. 45, 107
Zeppa, *see* Boccaccio
Zola, E.:
La Faute de l'Abbé Mouret 201
Zuckerman-Ingber, A. 138–9
Zwinger, L. 218, 222, 225

The manufacturer's authorised representative in the EU for product
safety is Oxford University Press España S.A. of El Parque Empresarial
San Fernando de Henares, Avenida de Castilla, 2 - 28830 Madrid
(www.oup.es/en or product.safety@oup.com). OUP España S.A. also acts
as importer into Spain of products made by the manufacturer.
Printed and bound by CPI Group (UK) Ltd, Croydon, CR0 4YY
14/09/2026
02216290-0002